W9-AEV-316

OLD ENGLISH STUDIES IN HONOUR OF JOHN C. POPE

EDITED BY ROBERT B. BURLIN
AND EDWARD B. IRVING, JR

Old English Studies in Honour of John C. Pope

UNIVERSITY OF TORONTO PRESS

© University of Toronto Press 1974
Toronto and Buffalo
Printed in Canada
ISBN 0-8020-2132-8
LC 73-91566

Contents

Preface

In 1971 John Collins Pope retired from teaching as Lampson Professor of English at Yale University, the institution with which he had been associated throughout his academic career. His reputation was established in 1942 with the publication of *The Rhythm of Beowulf*, a work which ensured his immortality in the Old English field. His recent edition of Ælfric confirmed, by its unmatchable thoroughness and precision, his scholarly eminence, and his contribution to the Oxford History of English Literature is awaited, not only because it will fill a long-standing need, but because it is certain to be, like all of his work, a model of its kind.

Those of us who were his students and colleagues at Yale knew him in other capacities as well — as a subtle interpreter of Spenser, a wise and humane Director of Graduate Studies, a teacher gifted with fine wit, humility, and patience, a man careless only of his own time and health in his attention to the problems of students and friends. Those who worked closely with him learned by example, and unforgettably, the virtues, and the frustrations as well, of an unflinching scholarly honesty. Excelling in the skills of the traditional philologist, John Pope also brought to the study of Old English literature a critical faculty of uncommon sensitivity and vigour, as his writings testify; long before it was dreamed of in most classrooms, he unhesitatingly proceeded on the assumption that Old English poetry was first and foremost poetry. To any one who has had the privilege of knowing John Pope this volume of essays offers a tribute which needs no justification.

ROBERT B. BURLIN
EDWARD B. IRVING, JR

OLD ENGLISH STUDIES IN HONOUR OF JOHN C. POPE

ACKNOWLEDGEMENTS

The editors wish to express their appreciation to the contributors for their enthusiasm, promptness, and courtesy. We are especially grateful to Marnee Irving for acting as constant courier between Bryn Mawr and Swarthmore, and to Denton Fox for giving freely of his time and skill in generous assistance to the editors. To the Centre for Medieval Studies of the University of Toronto and its director, John Leyerle, we are deeply indebted for the typesetting of this volume; to Susan Jupp, for overseeing its production; and to Elaine Quanz, for her services as compositor

Production of this volume was made possible by the generous assistance of the Centre for Medieval Studies, University of Toronto.

THEODORE M. ANDERSSON

The discovery of darkness
in northern literature

In 1674 Thomas Rymer adapted the Renaissance practice of comparing
set pieces by discussing various treatments of night in ancient and
modern authors. 'Amongst the common places, ...' writes Rymer,
'none has been more generally, and more happily handled, and in
none have the Noblest wits both *ancient* and *modern* more contended
with each other for victory, than in the *description of the night.*'[1] He
goes on to cite Apollonius of Rhodes, Virgil, Ariosto, Tasso, Marino,
Chapelain, Le Moyne, and, finally, having, as he says, exposed our
English to the like impartial censure, he awards the palm to Dryden.[2]
Rymer's comparison is intriguing not least of all because there is so
little to compare — all his descriptions pertain to the stillness and
soporific properties of night. This is no coincidence, but a fair reflection of the part assigned to night in the classical tradition; one indus-
trious American scholar assembled half a hundred descriptions of the
night from various classical and medieval writers, all of which bear out
the point.[3] For these writers nighttime means the suspension of action
and a lull in the sequence of events. As Homer says (*Iliad* II.386-7):
'Let there be no respite, not the slightest, / Except when oncoming
night parts the warriors' fury.' Or more succinctly (*Iliad* VII.282):
'It is well to heed the dictates of night.' Later custodians of the epic
tradition took Homer's directive to heart and henceforward the nightly
respite is observed with few exceptions. Indicative is the procedure
used by the editors responsible for our Homeric book divisions; one
of the natural breaks of which they availed themselves is nightfall and

the intermission which it provides. The dark hours are then left fallow and the action recommences only when rosy-fingered Dawn leaves the couch of Tithonus and appears the next morning. Those activities which are relegated to the night are the even-handed feast, councils of war, dreams, or, at most, long accounts of tribulation at the courts of Phaeacian Alcinous or Carthaginian Dido. The only night action proper in the tales of Homer is the raid of Odysseus and Diomedes on the Thracian camp, an exception which becomes the source of a separate series of imitations in Virgil, Statius, Ariosto, and, ultimately, Byron.[4] But even this tradition betrays a curious unfamiliarity with darkness. There is no adaptation to the peculiarities of night, no apparent awareness of changes in colour, sound, or perspective, no impairment of vision, and very little attempt to create a special night-time atmosphere. Everything happens exactly as if it were day. Virgil is far more imaginative in his depiction of the nocturnal assault on Troy, but the shadowy images of *Aeneid* II are unique in ancient literature.

The Middle Ages were slow to alter this pattern. As long as the classical epic dominates, night remains unexploited. This is true down through the Carolingian period and changes only when Ovidian erotic models begin to displace the Virgilian epic model in the twelfth century. At this juncture, Ovid and the vernacular love lyric, however these two are related and intertwined, co-operate in adding an entirely new scene to the narrative repertory — the lover's tryst. The dawn song, *Tristan*, and Chrétien's romances are the key texts and together they establish nighttime as the special preserve of lovers, a tradition which in turn goes through various permutations, both imitative and parodistic, before merging with the classical stream once more in the Renaissance epic (e.g., *Orlando Furioso* V.xlviii-li or *The Faerie Queene* I.iv.44). But vernacular romance, having reserved the night hours for the convenience of lovers, succeeded in retrieving only a very limited function for darkness; great deeds and the unfolding of plot remain the prerogatives of day.

Rymer wrote at a time when the Northern revival was just underway, some twenty years after the appearance of Junius's edition of the Cædmonian poems (1655), a dozen years after the recovery of the *Poetic Edda* (1662), but ten years before Árni Magnússon, the great benefactor of Icelandic studies, arrived in Copenhagen (1684), and fifteen years before Hickes's *Institutiones grammaticae anglo-saxonicae et moeso-gothicae* (1689).[5] The resources of Northern literature were therefore not available to enrich Rymer's comparison. But for us, after the modern popularization of Germanic prose and poetry, it is easy and tempting to add a few pages on the old theme: descriptions of the night.

Germanic literature has from the very outset a predilection for night as a time not of respite but of action. Passages from *Beowulf* will suggest themselves and the *Fight at Finnsburg* begins as the moon shines fitfully from behind the scudding clouds. The encounter between Cynewulf and Cyneheard in the *Anglo-Saxon Chronicle* (ad ann. 755), for which one has generally assumed some special literary background,[6] also takes place at night. In Paul the Deacon's story of Rosemund and Alboin, which is almost certainly the epitome of a Langobardic heroic lay, the death of Alboin seems to be both plotted and compassed at night.[7]

A literary preoccupation with nighttime action is equally aboriginal in Scandinavia. Rolf kraki was attacked and slain at night as we learn from Saxo Grammaticus' description (II.vii.2):

When therefore the others were sunk in deep sleep, the Swedes, whose eagerness to prosecute their crime cancelled the normal use of the quiet hours, began furtively to slip from their beds. The locked store of weapons was opened forthwith and each man armed himself in silence. Then they sought out the royal chambers and, having penetrated to the inmost recesses, they drew their swords against the sleeping men. Some of them awakened and, affected as much by the dullness of sleep as by the horror of sudden destruction, they resisted valiantly although unable to distinguish whether they were set upon by friend or foe, since this was made uncertain by the confusion of night.[8]

Turning to Eddic poetry, Wayland Smith is surprised and captured by a night patrol described in *Vǫlundarkviða* 6:

The men marched at night,   their mail well soldered,
Their shields shone   in the shorn moon.[9]

The pattern holds true in skaldic poetry, in the earliest example of which Bragi Boddason assigns the attack of Hamðir and Sǫrli on Ermanaric to the night hours.[10] Ermanaric awakens 'við illan draum' ('from' or 'to a bad dream'), a phrase which suggests the almost ghostly nature of the attack, perceived by the victim in a state of suspension between sleeping and waking. This is the first indication in Germanic literature of a realization that night alters perceptions and that darkness has special properties of fear, suddenness, limited awareness, and limited opportunities to react.

A specifically Scandinavian penchant for nighttime exploits is documented by the Norse variant of Sigurd's death. The southern or German version, as attested by *Brot af Sigurðarkviðu*, the *Nibelungenlied*, *Þiðreks saga*, and the express testimony of *Frá dauða Sigurðar*, seems always to have entailed the killing of Siegfried in broad daylight during a hunt. The Norse variant, as reflected by *Sigurðarkviða in skamma*, presumably *Sigurðarkviða in meiri*, and by extension *Vǫlsunga saga*, tells us that Sigurd was attacked in his bed as he slept. The special Norse literary instinct in operation here apparently dictated that Sigurd should succumb to his assassin at night, just as Bragi's Ermanaric, Paul the Deacon's Alboin, and Saxo's Rolf kraki had done.

The persistence of this instinct is confirmed by imitations of Sigurd's fate in the sagas. In *Gísla saga* Gísli carries out his mission of vengeance against Þorgrímr in a night scene closely modelled on *Sigurðarkviða in skamma*, and *Droplaugarsona saga* in turn imitates *Gísla saga* in describing the murder of Helgi Ásbjarnarson.[11] This latter scene devises a particularly ingenious use of darkness, which has not been sufficiently appreciated.

Saga readers will recall how the avenger, Grímr Droplaugarson, reconnoitres his enemy's house, removes his shoes and outer clothing, then steals silently into the hall in which his victim and a large number of guests are asleep. He makes his way to Helgi's bed closet and dispatches him with a sword thrust, but, before he can make good his escape, Helgi's dying shouts arouse the household. Everyone tumbles out of bed and mills around ineffectually in the darkness. The man who, oddly enough, succeeds almost immediately in apprehending the culprit is the blind farmhand Arnoddr. Fortunately for Grímr, he has the presence of mind to rebuke Arnoddr on the pretext that he himself was about to seize the murderer. Arnoddr hesitates, passes his hands over his captive, and, observing that he is without shoes and in linen clothes, assumes that he is indeed one of the sleeping guests and releases him.

Why should it be the blind man who seizes Grímr? The answer is that the author of our saga understands that the elimination of one faculty sharpens the others. Because Arnoddr is blind, he is keener, and since darkness is his natural element, he is better able to interpret the apparently random motion in the darkened hall. There is something about the murderer's more decisive movements, or his breathing, or his tenseness which communicates itself to the blind man. But Arnoddr's selective perceptions are also his weakness, and since he is entirely dependent on a tactile sense, he is fooled by Grímr's clothing and lets him go.

Such ingenious manipulation of darkness is unparalleled in modern fiction until the advent of the murder mystery, but it is far from unparalleled in the sagas. I mention only a few examples.

In *Egils saga* the first cause of the falling out between Egill and Erik Bloodaxe is the slaying of Erik's steward Bárðr.[12] Egill leaves a prolonged drinking bout supporting a sodden companion with the apt name Ǫlvir and accompanied by Bárðr, who continues to ply them with drink. As they step out of the hall, Egill uses the dimness of the entryway to run his sword through Bárðr; the stabbed man collapses gushing blood while Ǫlvir, momentarily robbed of Egill's support, collapses next to him spewing out the evening's consumption. Both lie there in the semi-darkness, each in his own peculiar state of insensibility. Those in the hall are unable, because of the distance and the darkness, to distinguish between these superficially similar states or, presumably, between the fluids which emanate from the two prostrate figures and combine in a spectacle reminiscent of the confluence of blood and beer in Bragi's picture of Ermanaric's demise. Only when Erik orders light to be brought is the murder revealed, but by this time Egill has escaped into the pitch darkness outside. Again, there is in this passage a special appreciation of the properties of darkness or semi-darkness — the large outlines of the fallen bodies are visible, but the details are not. The reactions of the onlookers are therefore curtailed by their limited vision.

A much more elaborate visual deception is contrived in *Óláfs saga helga*.[13] It entails both neutralizing blindness and capitalizing on darkness. King Olaf has captured and blinded the rebellious petty king Hrœrekr, whom he keeps at his court under close guard and constant surveillance. But Hrœrekr's ingenuity is equal to the challenge. He avails himself of the heavy sleep following a hard evening of drinking to make his way out to the latrine with his two ever-present guards. While the three of them are thus unsuspectingly occupied, some of Hrœrekr's men, according to a prearranged plan, counterfeit a noisy quarrel outside the latrine and Hrœrekr directs his guards to quell the disturbance. They are promptly cut down as they descend the steps from the latrine and Hrœrekr is led away to safety by his followers. A little later, King Olaf's faithful skald, Sighvatr Þórðarson, gets out of bed to make the same trip into the courtyard. He slips on the bloodied latrine steps, mistakes the nature of the wetness, and makes a mild joke about King Olaf's liberality in providing drink. But when he returns to the lighted hall, the colour of the fluid with which he is smeared betrays its real nature and there is an immediate realization of what has happened.

This episode is constructed on the awareness that a seeing man can be as helpless as a blind man in the darkness and that visual evidence can be interpreted only with the aid of light. King Hrœrekr owes his success to his exact evaluation of the restricted options provided by darkness.

Darkness in the sagas can also be used to convey psychological effects, mystery, or its opposite, a special transparency.

There is, for example, a rather complicated case of multiple transparencies brought out by darkness in *Gísla saga*. [14] A certain Vésteinn is abroad on a moonlit evening and passes by the farm of Þorgrímr, his sworn but undeclared enemy as a result of some amorous entanglements. A friendly member of Þorgrímr's household, Geirmundr, warns Vésteinn to be cautious, but before he moves on, he is observed and identified by the maidservant Rannveig. She reports to Þorgrímr accordingly. However, Geirmundr, who is eager to protect Vésteinn, contests the identification, claims to have seen indistinctly, and expresses the opinion that the man was a farmhand belonging to Ǫnundr of Meðaldal. The scene is intricate. Geirmundr is lying, but the darkness makes his lie plausible. Þorgrímr must accept the plausibility if not the statement. His response must therefore be based on what he knows about his witnesses and not on what they may or may not have seen. Rannveig, like so many maidservants in the sagas, is a troublemaker since she must know of Þorgrímr's hostility toward Vésteinn and would not tell tales unless she intended mischief. Þorgrímr can scarcely have any illusions on this score. Geirmundr, on the other hand, sympathizes with Vésteinn and Þorgrímr must be aware of this too. Given two bad witnesses, he has therefore no choice but to send for additional information and Geirmundr has at least gained time. (Þorgrímr cannot set out in pursuit just on a chance. If his quarry turned out to be Ǫnundr's farmhand after all, he would not only have become ridiculous, but would also have revealed his secret intentions to one and all.)

Part of the dense psychological texture in the sagas is accounted for by the constant awareness that, as in any confined society, everyone knows about everyone else, even though the knowledge goes unstated. It is the paradoxical role of darkness in this episode to make transparent for a moment just how much the characters do know about each other's sympathies, antipathies, intentions, and, of course, their scandalous involvements.

A simpler transparency may be found in *Laxdœla saga*.[15] Þórðr has divorced his wife Auðr in order to marry Guðrún and the spurned wife takes her revenge by invading Þórðr's bed closet at night and inflicting a serious wound. Þórðr is unable to retaliate and Auðr escapes unidentified, but when he is asked who did it, he voices the supposition that it was Auðr. That his attacker should have been a woman is an odd supposition indeed, but what we are listening to is not so much an educated guess as Þórðr's conscience: he knows what he has done and what he deserves and when the proposal is made to ride after the culprit, he forbids it because he has gotten precisely what he deserves. As in *Gísla saga*, visual confirmation is beside the point and darkness makes the inner workings all the more vivid.

Above all, the saga writers understood the association of darkness and fear. Not only the modern murder mystery, but also the modern ghost story was anticipated in Iceland.

In *Heiðarvíga saga*[16] Snorri goði is charged with transporting the corpse of the slain malefactor Víga-Styrr and halts the cortège to spend the night at the house of a farmer with two young daughters. During the night the two girls are seized with an irrepressible curiosity to get a glimpse of such a notorious fellow. One urges and the other dissuades, but their inquisitiveness gets the better of them and they tiptoe off to peek at the corpse, which is dimly illumined by the eerie glow of dying coals. As they approach, Styrr suddenly rises up in his shroud and recites a stanza. The older girl, who is closer, instantly loses her wits, is restrained by four men, and dies the following day. This is ghost and mummy story all in one and in the best tradition; it makes use of darkness as any modern representative of that popular genre would.

A more familiar and elaborate ghost story is Grettir's encounter with Glámr at Þórhallsstaðir. Even the earlier and less fully developed version in *Beowulf* (702-836) is full of lurid effects. Grendel steals through the dark night as a 'shadow-stalker' and emerges from the moors under a covering of mist and with the dire intention of snatching the sleeping Danes off to the shades. When he has wrenched the door from its hinges, he advances menacingly along the hall with eyes burning like fire, fastens on Handscio, drains him vampire-like, and gulps him down dragon-like before meeting his match in the (for the moment at least) invincible Beowulf.

The uncanny similarities shared by this scene and the one at Þórhallsstaðir in *Grettis saga* are well known.[17] On the whole, Glámr's approach is less effectively described than Grendel's, but the actual wrestling match with Grettir is conveyed with a unique combination of supernatural dimension and realistic detail, embracing such matters as the wrestling holds used by the antagonists and an inventory of the wreckage done in the house. Grettir is not even temporarily invincible and is slowly dragged willy-nilly toward the door. He finally realizes that he has lost the struggle and, in a last-ditch effort to gain the upper hand, he reverses his weight and tumbles his adversary backward over the doorsill. As Glámr lies supine, the full moon passes from behind the clouds and illumines his eyes. Grettir is paralysed by the sight and unable to draw his sword as Glámr intones, no doubt in a suitably hollow voice, that this vision will pursue him the rest of his days and bring about his death. The prophecy is fulfilled in due course because Grettir succumbs to the fear of loneliness engendered at this moment and becomes dependent on an unreliable companion. The latter part of *Grettis saga,* like the latter part of *Gísla saga,* is shrouded in a preternatural sense of darkness.

In comparison to Scandinavian literature, the German cultivation of darkness is very meagre. The only substantial evidence of an indigenous tradition comes from the hybrid heroic romance known as the *Nibelungenlied*; everything else is even later and more diluted or disguised in Latin (*Waltharius*) or Norse (*Þiðreks saga*). The first part of the *Nibelungenlied* is pictured in the full light of courtly romance and the second part uses night scenery in a way which turns out to be secondary and divorced from previous tradition. As nearly as we can tell from a comparison with *Þiðreks saga*, there were two night scenes in the epic source of the second part, but both these scenes (Hagen's interview with the mermaids and his interview with Eckewart) were transferred to the daylight hours by the *Nibelungenlied* poet. On the other hand, the later poet added two new night scenes of his own, the battle with the Bavarians in Adventure 26 and the night watch in Adventure 30. Only the first of these scenes may be credited with anything like the use of nighttime effects. Hagen is in command of the rear guard during a night ride and is brought to a halt by the pursuing Bavarians (st. 1602):

> They came to a standstill,   as needs they must.
> They saw in the darkness   the flash of bright shields.
> Then Hagen no longer   wished to be still:
> 'Who pursues us on our way?'   The answer fell to Gelpfrat.[18]

The darkness here is borrowed from Hagen's previous interview with the mermaids as it was described in the epic source, and if we look at the appropriate passage in *Þiðreks saga,* we discover why the Bavarian shields are visible: 'Högni takes all his weapons and proceeds down the river and there is bright moonlight so that he can see his way.'[19] By putting two and two together, we can therefore deduce that the Bavarian shields shine in the moonlight, just as the shields of Niðuðr's men shine in *Vǫlundarkviða* (above p. 3), but the *Nibelungenlied* poet shows in the ensuing fighting that he has no ability to visualize night action. For all the lighting indications he gives us, the battle might as well have been fought at high noon. Thus, the *Nibelungenlied* serves only to exemplify how the Germanic art of night depiction was lost in the transition from epic to romance.

These illustrations suffice to suggest that one of the specific contributions of Germanic literature was a more fully elaborated use of darkness. But why, we may ask, was this particular contribution left to Germanic narrative and not pre-empted long before? In the eighteenth century the answer would have been easy enough. We would simply have pointed out that at certain seasons Northerners have a more prolonged and more intense experience of darkness so that it was quite natural for them to make a more profound study of it. Today we are less given to climatological explanations and I will speculate in a different vein.

As a general proposition, we may say that the study of darkness in Western narrative has developed in three traditions, the tradition of criminal literature, the tradition of erotic literature, and the tradition of military literature beginning with the final action at Troy. Since there is no evidence in our Germanic texts to support the idea that the Teutons were either great thieves or great lovers, I will proceed along the military avenue and suggest that they derived their special sense of darkness from a long familiarity with nighttime campaigning, a practice which set them apart from the classical world.

As a rule, the classical peoples avoided nighttime engagements if at all possible. It is in fact remarkable how little ancient history was made at night. Herodotus reports exactly one night battle, as he calls it, which turns out not to have been a night battle at all, but the result of an eclipse, for which the astronomers have provided the date 28 May 585 BC. The combatants on this particular occasion, the Medes and the Lydians, were so startled by the unfamiliar element that they immediately separated and made peace (I.74). Thucydides reports a certain number of nighttime actions, usually in conjunction with siege operations, some with a disturbing resemblance to the Greek stratagem at Troy, but he declares that there was only one major night encounter in the whole Peloponnesian War. Judging from the description, the occasion was characterized by incredible confusion and was a source of some frustration to our conscientious war correspondent. As he says (VII.44.1): 'But in a night battle, and this was the only one which took place between great armies in this war, how could anyone know anything clearly?' Xenophon's *Anabasis* likewise reports one nighttime attack on the retreating Greeks (VII.4.14) by the Thynians, a people with a special reputation for night fighting (VII.2.22). But this was not the way of the Greeks or, for that matter, of the Persians, who, Xenophon tells us (III.4.34-5), camped at some distance from the Greeks for fear of a night attack. The explanation which Xenophon offers is that they were apprehensive about the problem of arming, unhobbling their horses, and mounting all at the same time and all in the clamorous confusion of the night.

Fear of night encounters is also the note most commonly sounded by Roman historians. Livy reports some cases of night fighting from the history of early Rome, also frequently connected with siege stratagems (though less elaborate than the Trojan Horse), but it is clear that such encounters were not courted or desired and were apt to be a counsel of desperation. We read such cautionary notes as the following: 'Therefore the enemy despaired of any success in a regular battle and attacked the consul's camp at night, entrusting their fortunes to a very dubious outcome.' Or: 'Marcus Fabius was assigned the cavalry and ordered not to move before dawn because a cavalry detachment is difficult to control in the clamorous confusion of the night.' Or: 'Then at sunset, when not much of the day was left, they thought [the Gauls] would attack them before nightfall; then they thought the plan had been put off until night in order to inspire them with greater fear.' Or: 'For the rest, night inspiring equal fear on both sides restrained them from joining battle until dawn.' Or: 'Fabius heard the noise, but kept his men within the fortifications because he thought it was a trap and shrank in any event from a battle at night.'[20]

The same fear of night fighting is recorded in the first Roman encounter with the Germanic peoples. Plutarch tells us that after an initial but inconclusive victory over the Cimbrians, Marius' troops spent the night listening anxiously to the lamentations of the enemy: 'The plain was filled with a fearful wailing and the Romans with fear; even Marius himself was seized by terror as he anticipated some disordered and confused night battle' ('Life of Marius' XX.3). It is clear from such passages that night fighting ran counter to Roman orderliness.

When Roman legions did become involved in night actions, it was usually because of the enemy's initiative. Sallust's account of the war against Jugurtha includes four nighttime attacks launched against the Romans by the Numidians (*Bellum Jugurthinum*, chaps 21, 38, 54, 97), the last one, Sallust tells us explicitly, because the cover of darkness was advantageous to the Numidians and a handicap for the Romans. Caesar's Gallic campaigns record a couple of nighttime sorties (II.33 and VII.24), but only one regular night engagement (VII.81), and this one initiated by the Gauls.

The picture is not very different in Tacitus. The *Annals* describe one nighttime engagement against the Germans (I.51) and two against the Thracians (IV.48-51). In the *Histories* there is a night battle between the legions of Vitellius and Vespasian because of a chance encounter in the dark (III.22-3) and two regular engagements against the Germans during the uprising of Civilis (IV.29 and V.22). In one of these engagements Tacitus notes that the Germans deliberately chose a dark and cloudy night to cover their advance. In the other engagement there is an interesting contrast in the attitudes of the combatants. Whereas the Germans fight with 'reckless fury' and no apparent concern about the darkness, the Romans are described as being 'aware of the perils' and more cautious. These passages, along with those mentioned earlier, suggest that, even if it is nowhere stated explicitly, the Romans must have regarded night fighting as an aspect of guerilla warfare peculiar to their barbarian neighbours. That the Germanic tribes made no such distinctions is indicated not only by the passages already cited, but also by a note on the Harii in Tacitus' *Germania* 43. We are told that this tribe chose black nights for battle and struck terror into their enemies by capitalizing on fear and darkness like an army of ghosts. If it is permissible to generalize on the basis of such indications, it would appear that night fighting was already institutional among the Germanic peoples in the first century.

But whether or not night warfare was a firm tradition at this early period, it certainly emerges as such when the vikings appear on the historical horizon. The chronicles make it clear that the vikings had a certain preference for early morning or night attacks. Bordeaux fell to a night raid in 848, Chartres in 858, Noyon in 859, St Omer in 861, and Meaux in 862.[21] The *Anglo-Saxon Chronicle* reports nighttime operations by the vikings in 865, 875, 894, 917, and 920. And so the pattern remains when the first more or less contemporary vernacular sources begin to flow. Let it suffice to point out that *Sverris saga* records no fewer than sixteen night encounters with never a note of fear or reluctance such as we find in the classical histories.[22]

What happens when Germanic practice and classical discourse meet? The passage already quoted from Saxo Grammaticus (p. 3) provides the answer. The situation is Germanic, but when Saxo speaks of 'cancelling the normal use of the quiet hours' and of fighting 'made uncertain by the confusion of night.' he is echoing the phraseology of his classical models.

The thought which emerges from this comparison (and I need scarcely dwell on the fragility of such speculations) is that the Germanic aptitude for depicting night action may owe something to a familiarity with darkness fostered by a long tradition of night fighting, perhaps among the Germanic peoples generally, and certainly among the North Germanic peoples. The classical peoples, with no such tradition, tended to exclude the night from their epics, but Northern literature had no such impediment and included night on an equal footing with day in its narrative range.

NOTES

1 Curt A. Zimansky, ed., *The Critical Works of Thomas Rymer* (New Haven 1956), 10
2 Zimansky, 15
3 Arthur Stanley Pease, ed., *Publi Vergili Maronis Aeneidos Liber Quartus* (Cambridge, Mass. 1935), 434-6. See also Lore Paust, 'Die Nacht in der griechischen Dichtung' (Diss. Tübingen 1946 [not available to me]) and Heidemarie Rey, *Die Bedeutung der Nacht in der epischen Erzählung der Aeneis* (Diss. Hamburg 1965 [Hamburg 1967]).
4 *Aeneid* IX.224-449; *Thebaid* X.156-448; *Orlando Furioso* XVIII.clxiv-xix.16; Byron, 'The Episode of Nisus and Euryalus' in *Hours of Idleness*
5 C. F. Tucker Brooke, 'The Renascence of Germanic Studies in England, 1559-1689,' *PMLA* 29 (1914) 150: 'Hickes estimates that from the time when the dissolution

of the monasteries rendered the old manuscripts generally accessible till the year 1689, not more than two foreigners (Vossius the Elder and J. Laet of Antwerp) and about twenty Englishmen had acquired any real mastery of the Anglo-Saxon.' See also Eleanor N. Adams, *Old English Scholarship in England from 1566-1800*, Yale Studies in English 55 (New Haven 1917) and René Wellek, *The Rise of English Literary History* (1941; rpt New York 1966), 117-26. I have outlined the Norse revival in Scandinavia in *The Problem of Icelandic Saga Origins: A Historical Survey*, Yale Germanic Studies 1 (New Haven 1964), 1-21. A lively essay on the Germanic revival in Germany down to the present is Klaus von See, *Deutsche Germanen-Ideologie vom Humanismus bis zur Gegenwart* (Frankfurt a. M. 1970).

6 See for example Francis P. Magoun, 'Cynewulf, Cyneheard, and Osric,' *Anglia* 57 (1933) 361-2.

7 See Paul the Deacon, *History of the Langobards*, trans. William Dudley Foulke (Philadelphia 1907), 81-3, and Ludwig Schmidt, *Die Ostgermanen* (1941; rpt München 1969), 594-5.

8 *Saxonis Gesta Danorum*, primum a C. Knabe & P. Herrmann recensita, recognoverunt et ediderunt J. Olrik & H. Raeder, tomus I textum continens (Hauniae 1931), 52

9 *Edda: Die Lieder des Codex Regius nebst verwandten Denkmälern*, hg. von Gustav Neckel (3te umgearb. Auflage von Hans Kuhn; Heidelberg 1962), 118

10 Finnur Jónsson, ed., *Den norsk-islandske skjaldedigtning*, IB (København 1908), 1

11 *Gísla saga Súrssonar*, ed. Björn K. Þórólfsson in *Íslenzk fornrit* 6: *Vestfirðinga sǫgur* (Reykjavík 1943), 52-4, and *Droplaugarsona saga*, ed. Jón Jóhannesson in *Íslenzk fornrit* 11: *Austfirðinga sǫgur* (Reykjavík 1950), 168-71. I have argued for this sequence in 'Some Ambiguities in *Gísla saga*: A Balance Sheet,' *Bibliography of Old Norse-Icelandic Studies* (1968) 28-39.

12 *Egils saga skalla-grímssonar*, ed. Sigurður Nordal in *Íslenzk fornrit* 2 (Reykjavík 1933), 110-11

13 Snorri Sturluson, *Heimskringla*, ed. Bjarni Aðalbjarnarson in *Íslenzk fornrit* 27 (Reykjavík 1945), 121-2

14 *Gísla saga*, 39-42

15 *Laxdœla saga*, ed. Einar Ól. Sveinsson in *Íslenzk fornrit* 5 (Reykjavík 1934), 97-8

16 *Heiðarvíga saga*, ed. Sigurður Nordal and Guðni Jónsson in *Íslenzk fornrit* 3: *Borgfirðinga sǫgur* (Reykjavík 1938), 233-4

17 *Grettis saga Ásmundarsonar*, ed. Guðni Jónsson in *Íslenzk fornrit* 7 (Reykjavík 1936), 118-23

18 *Das Nibelungenlied*, nach der Ausgabe von Karl Bartsch, hg. von Helmut de Boor, (19te Auflage, Wiesbaden 1967), 254

19 Henrik Bertelsen, ed., *Þiðriks saga af Bern* 2 (København 1908-11), 285

20 The passages are from *Ab urbe condita* IV.27 (bis), V.39, XXII.17, and XXII.18.

21 Walther Vogel, *Die Normannen und das fränkische Reich bis zur Gründung der Normandie (799-911)* (Heidelberg 1906), 122, 162, 170, 180, 186

22 *Sverris saga*, ed. Guðni Jónsson in *Íslendingasagnaútgáfan: Konunga sögur* 2 ([Reykjavík] 1957), 42, 45, 48-9, 59-60, 91-3, 125, 135-6, 196, 198-9, 223-4, 238, 251, 255, 257, 273, 278 (chaps 21, 24, 26, 31, 49, 64, 72, 105, 106, 120, 130, 137, 140, 142, 148, 150)

F. ANNE PAYNE

Three aspects of Wyrd in *Beowulf*

'Wyrd,' like 'God,' is a word out of the language of our pagan past and
names one of the forces determining man's destiny in the universe. An
assessment of the meaning of 'Wyrd' causes us more trouble than 'God,'
in part because 'Wyrd' has not survived as an abstract noun in modern
English, in part because the experience it describes cannot be conveniently contained by personification as 'God' can. The modern English deri-
vatives, however, provide what seems to be the image basic to the concept. The adjective 'weird' and the noun slang term 'weirdo' describe
an event or person whose attributes are suddenly discovered to be outside the bounds of normal expectation and arouse an experience that an
observer contemplates with uncomprehending but compelling uneasiness.
This combination of attraction and awe in the face of an event in a
space whose dimensions are undefined and uncontrollable hovers about
the meaning of Old English Wyrd. As an abstract noun of course Wyrd
represents the agent behind this experience which is unmediated by
any hint of the possible beneficence or latent paternalistic concern
associated with 'God.' While there can scarcely be said to be complete
agreement about the way of capturing that experience beyond the pale
for purposes of analysis, I hope that other writers who contemplate this
subject will permit me to begin with the following general remarks.[1]
    Wyrd is the force that eventually destroys the lives of the violators
of unknowable universal order in the world of *Beowulf*. It is the agent
in the most terrible experience of the day of death. It is the opponent
of man in the strange area of the most intense perception and conscious-

ness. Though it may hold off for a while, the individual in the end makes an error in choice and releases forces whose consequences at the moment of crisis he controls no longer and Wyrd is victorious. Wyrd affects only those with the strength and energy to enter that space where order is at first contingent on their choices. When they fail as they inevitably do because they are human, Wyrd's dreadful power compensates for their inadequacies. While it is completely accurate to say in epic and tragedy in general that the hero seeks his fate, it is totally erroneous to say he seeks his Wyrd. Wyrd is alien to the individual; it is the force which balances his errors, punishes him, at best tolerates him. Wyrd is always the Other.[2]

In this essay, I shall examine three aspects of the subject: the basic similarities between the *Beowulf* poet's and King Alfred's use of 'Wyrd' in his version of Boethius' *Consolation of Philosophy*, the relation of Wyrd to Beowulf's three battles with the monsters, and finally the nature of the error that eventually triggers Wyrd's retaliative force against the kings of the poem.

The relation of man, Wyrd, and God which is represented in *Beowulf* finds its philosophical clarification in Alfred's use of the term in his adaptation of the *Consolation of Philosophy*. Alfred's metaphor for the absolute relation of the three makes Wyrd a great wheel on which men are caught, the worst toward the outer rim, the best near the axle, which is God: 'swelce sio eax sie þæt hehste god þe we nemnað God' (129.23-4); 'swa bioð þa midmestan men onmiddan þam spacan, and þa betran near þære nafe, and þa mætran near ðæm felgum' (130.1-3).[3] The wheel of Wyrd joins all men in a common brotherhood, where the worst men depend on the average and the average on the best, and all depend for their existence on God (130.5 ff). Men's freedom to escape from the whirling of Wyrd consists only in their being able to move nearer the nave, but no man crosses to the axle, to the complete understanding of God. 'Swa doð ða selestan men; swa hi hiora lufe near Gode lætað, and swiðor þas eorðlicon þing forsioð, swa hi beoð orsorgran, and læs reccað hu sio wyrd wandrige, oððe hwæt hio brenge.' (130.15-18)

There are several conclusions that can be drawn from this metaphor. Because the wheel of Wyrd binds all men together, the acts of one man can engage consequences that involve others besides himself. Wyrd surrounds men at all times, as they live their lives according to their lights, whether they are conscious of it or not. They succeed in finding God, in avoiding in some measure the whirling of the wheel as the universe moves relentlessly onward, only to the degree that they lift themselves from their stationary position and move inward toward the axle on the spoke allotted to them. This they accomplish when they set their minds and acts on the highest things they know; however, because they are confined to some specific part of the wheel, what they try to do has no inevitable relation to the whole pattern of Wyrd. When they make the leap of the imagination to find a new and better destiny for themselves and others, they may fail to sense the real possibilities that are open to them and bring the crushing weight of Wyrd against them.

When we turn to the rest of the Old English text and abstract the major paradigm set up by Alfred through his alterations of the Latin *Consolation,* it is clear that the attribute men possess which brings the encounter with Wyrd is freedom. His premises are as follows. Men are free: 'Þæt wære uncynlicre, gif God næfde on eallum his rice nane frige gesceaft under his anwalde. Forðæm he gesceop twa gesceadwisa gesceafta freo, englas and men.' (142.6-9) But men lack omniscience: 'Forðon þe we witon swiðe lytel ðæs þe ær us wæs buton be gemynde and be geæscum, and get læsse þæs ðe æfter us bið.' (148.8-10) Freedom is thus a mixed blessing because God decrees the one way: '[God] sealde swiðe fæste gife and swiðe fæste æ mid ðære gife ælcum men oð his ende; ðæt is se freodom ðæt se mon mot don þæt he wile, and þæt is sio æ þæt he gilt ælcum be his gewyrhtum ægðer ge on þisse worulde ge on þære toweardan swa good swa yfel, swæðer he deð.' (142.11-15)

Angels, the other free beings in the universe, have an advantage over men. Unless they fall,[4] they are prevented from making inaccurate choices by their possession of absolute knowledge: 'Englas habbað rihte domas and goodne willan, and eall þæt hi wilniað hi begitað swiðe eaðe, forðæmþe hi nanes wos ne wilniað.' (140.28-30) And later: 'Þeah we fela smean, we habbað litellne gearowitan buton tweon; ac þam englum nis nan tweo nanes þæra þinga þe hi witon.' (146.21-3) Because men lack such knowledge, they must be content with knowing that their freedom is proportionate to the nobility of their aims: 'ða men habbað simle freodom þy maran þe hi heora mod near godcundum ðingum lætað, and habbað þæs þy læssan friodom þe hi hiora modes willan near þisse weoruldare lætað. Nabbað hi nænne freodom þonne hi heora agnum willum hi selfe unðeawum underðiodað; ac sona swa hi hiora mod onwendað from gode, swa weorðað hi ablende mid unwisdome.' (140.31-141.6) This passage parallels the wheel of Wyrd passage quoted above; deliberate evil brings here the confusion of unwisdom, there the dislocation of Wyrd's whirling; the deliberate search for God brings there the greatest happiness, here the greatest freedom.

Man, in his right to choose, to dislocate the texture of things because he lacks omniscience, performs acts which require the direct attention of God. This attention Alfred calls Wyrd, the work that God does every day: 'Ac þæt þæt we wyrd hataŏ, þæt biŏ Godes weorc þæt he ælce dæg wyrcŏ, ægþer ge þæs ŏe we gesioŏ ge þæs þe us ungesewenlic biŏ.' (128. 18-20) Since, in the same passage, Alfred makes it clear that all other events in the universe are set by natural law from the beginning of time, the work of God can be drawn forth only by those beings free to disrupt the perfect patterns of things. Wyrd is the balance that keeps the free choices of men from sending the universe astray. The universe must operate in terms of an order of its own and if men's choices threaten it, deliberately evil or merely humanly inadequate, Wyrd comes against them.

As God's work, Wyrd has no imaginable form, cannot have been personified as a deity. It is rather a chameleon force which manifests itself in many ways. Alfred, in describing the differing ways in which God employs it, writes: 'Ða wyrd he þonne wyrcŏ oŏŏe þurh ŏa goodan englas oŏŏe þurh monna sawla, oŏŏe þurh oŏerra gesceafta lif, oŏŏe þurh heofones tungl, oŏŏe þara scuccena mislice lotwrencas; hwilum þurh an ŏara, hwilum þurh eall ŏa.' (129.3-7) Wyrd is not a pagan opponent of the Christian God, except from that narrow conception of Christianity which imagines God as sitting in total oblivion to his responsibilities for the terrible, ambiguous consequences of being human; Wyrd is merely God's other face.

The broad outlines of the definition of Wyrd which may be deduced from the wheel simile and Alfred's theory of freedom find their counterparts in *Beowulf*. Wyrd's function here too is the severely limited one, an order unto men alone. Its separation from the order of nature is evident in two passages, the Breca episode (569-70) and the mere (1570-2).[5] In both, a description of sunlight is juxtaposed to the passage describing the mood of Wyrd, and represents the moment when Beowulf's courage has put him back in touch with universal order, hence an escape from the compulsion of Wyrd which would put him there, whether he would or no. In one passage, where the cycles and seasons of nature are mentioned in relation to their ruler, it is God whom the poet mentions (1607).

What gives man creative freedom in *Beowulf* as in the OE *Consolation* is his commitment to the highest order he can imagine, an order beyond the narrow dictates of the code by which lesser men live. While the code would bind Beowulf to fighting monsters who attack his own hall or the hall of his king, it makes no stipulations about freeing the halls of foreign kings from such attacks, nor about facing a dragon whose catastrophic energies destroy not only his hall but also the cities of his kingdom. The dedication that the poet represents in *Beowulf* is the equivalent of Alfred's dedication to wisdom, the only means by which men engage fully the space, the imaginative possibilities open to them, even though Wyrd waits there for their false moves. The poet links this high flight of the human will toward life at its fullest with the search for God.

In the heathen temple passage, we have man's negation of his freedom. The poet bitterly attacks the Danes for worshipping Death, the 'gastbona,' for forgetting the divine names which guide the highest goals of human effort: law (God as Measurer and Judge), fellowship (God as Lord), glory (God as Helm of the heavens, Wielder of glory).

> Metod hie ne cuþon,
> dæda Demend,   ne wiston hie Drihten God,
> ne hie huru heofena Helm   herian ne cuþon,
> wuldres Waldend.   (180-3)[6]

In Hrothgar's words to Beowulf we have the affirmation of the search for divine certainty.

> Bebeorh þe ðone bealonið,   Beowulf leofa,
> secg betsta,   ond þe þæt selre geceos,
> ece rædas;   oferhyda ne gym,
> mæra cempa!   (1758-61)

The exercise of choice in what the individual grasps to be the absolute milieu of wisdom or heroism is his greatest happiness and greatest freedom. It is his untouched, if only momentary, reward for dedicating his life to facing the incomprehensible forces, laws, darkness, the manifestations of Wyrd that ultimately defeat him.

The poem is concerned with the knowledge that even when heroes choose an action and perform it, when they boast and then carry out the act defined, they enter, as they move from the word to the deed, the unformed but carefully watched-over space available to them, the space where Wyrd waits. As their commitments become more complex, their choices become less accurate and they become aware of Wyrd, become aware that they are violating an order whose forms they do not grasp. 'Siððan hit fullfremed bið, þonne hatað we hit wyrd' (128.13-14), Alfred says at one point (see also 129.1-2); the awareness of Wyrd means the deed is already committed. Some of men's choices fit in with the scheme of things, as in Beowulf's decision to fight Grendel; in some their actions manage not to interfere with deep-seated intermeshing of ancient patterns (the 'geosceaft grimme,' 1234), as in Beowulf's battle with Grendel's mother. But in some, as in Beowulf's decision to fight the dragon, preceding choices have already loaded the dice against the act.

When all pretences that man espouses are swept away, even his heroic commitment becomes insufficient to tell him how to choose accurately enough to escape and Wyrd takes him into death. When Alfred calls Wyrd at one point 'þæs þe we ne wenað' (132.22), he emphasizes its mysterious, uncanny ability to exert itself unannounced in that space where man is desperately attempting to take everything into consideration, the position of Beowulf in the dragon fight. Wyrd is the dark side of God, the opponent in reality, the total terrible experience of the encounter beyond the comfortable, well-known games of civilization. It touches what man in his freedom touches. It is man's contact with divinity, shaped in response to his precise acts and thoughts and therefore the most exhilarating and the most terrible experience he ever confronts. While Alfred will say that this experience is the result of God's desire to keep the universe on its course, the *Beowulf* poet does not deal in philosophy. Instead of an answer, he conveys to us the tragic vision of the victory and death of Beowulf.

As we encounter Wyrd in the poem, it is the force that hovers at the outer edge of man's imaginative space. As he is less able to handle the challenge before him, the limiting weight of Wyrd shrinks in upon him. In various ways in *Beowulf,* the poet envisions four stages in man's relation to the space available to him: 1/ the stage in which he feels no obstacle against him; 2/ the stage in which he in a sense sets up an obstacle and freely engages with his actions the materials of the world around him; 3/ the stage of stalemate, in which forces outside himself make his acts threaten only frustrated failure; 4/ the stage of total confinement, the death of mind or body. The eleven instances of Wyrd in the poem reflect these stages of relation to space.[7] Most of the examples of the word refer as one would expect to the time of crisis and death: six to that moment when man or monster does not know how to control the narrowing space around him and the power of Wyrd is darkly engaged in manipulating the flow of events; three to Wyrd as the power that takes man into death, the total confinement and utter loss of the awareness of space.

Beowulf's three battles with the monsters represent his progression from total freedom in the face of Wyrd to his eventual total confinement. At the outer edge of things, where Wyrd does not seem to impinge upon human activities, where Olympian projections of human energy which accord with universal order make success certain, Beowulf can dismiss it with superficial pessimism. 'Gæð a wyrd swa hio scel' (455), he says to Hrothgar as he luxuriates uncomprehendingly the while in the thought of being eaten and the necessity for preserving his splendid but in that event, of course, empty body armour for Hygelac.

His subsequent fight with Grendel exemplifies the human relation to Wyrd where the human choice of an act, as far as man is concerned, has no counterweight thrown against it. The poet's references in this fight place it outside Beowulf's conscious knowledge. Wyrd is set against Grendel to stop him from eating men; it is he therefore who feels its presence, not Beowulf, who is only God's agent. The poet tells us: 'Ne wæs þæt wyrd þa gen, / þæt he ma moste   manna cynnes / ðicgean ofer þa niht.' (734-6) Later he tells us, as Hrothgar pays wergeld for Hond-scioh, that Grendel would have eaten more men 'nefne him witig God   wyrd forstode / ond ðæs mannes mod.' (1056-7) In these instances, there are plans in force that have nothing to do with the conscious will of the hero. Having himself no taint of the Danish retainers' failure that brings this monster, Beowulf in this battle is merely an ideal actor in a universal mystery play. His choice to fight Grendel perfectly fits the occasion and as a result there is no hint in Beowulf's consciousness of the cost of the act.

Beowulf's experience here stands in sharp contrast to Hrothgar's retainers' earlier; for them, Wyrd meant only death. It might be mentioned in passing that although Wyrd is often connected with physical death it does not describe the fact that men are by condition of their creation mortal. Wyrd is connected only with the death of individuals who think their choices give them the option of staying alive, in particular of course when they take on the stance of fighting warrior; that is, when they attempt but fail at the heroic projection of their energies. Hrothgar says of his thanes who boasted that they would stay in the hall and fight Grendel: 'hie wyrd forsweop / on Grendles gryre.' (477-8) In them, we have an instance of the thwarted heroic act, the projection of the imagination, where the act chosen does not match the order of the space in which they wish to carry it out. The retainers, good and bad alike, through their boasting and willingness to stay in the hall, would seem to be heroic, but their heroics are no more effective than those of Milton's fallen angels. For they are caught in a net of disorder created by Hrothgar that only Beowulf, God's champion, can cut.

The second stage of Wyrd describes man's awareness of its presence when he challenges his space with heroic action. Here, after a period of trial successfully passed through, it is thought of as an exciting comrade. 'Wyrd oft nereð / unfægne eorl, þonne his ellen deah' (572-3), Beowulf says of his struggle in the sea which ended in his triumph against Breca. The fight with Grendel's mother also exemplifies this relation to Wyrd. The poet warns us as the Geats and the Danes feast just before her appearance that the result of another violation of rightful behaviour is suddenly to be in evidence: 'Þær wæs symbla cyst, / druncon win weras.   Wyrd ne cuþon, / geosceaft grimme.' (1232-4) Grendel's death and the feast have lulled them to the false security of blissful ignorance which is about to be destroyed. The joy of the hall is a temporary blindness which has no charm for controlling Wyrd's omnipresent power.

But it is the Danes who have set up the errors that draw the power of Wyrd against them; for Beowulf in this battle, Wyrd is the distant adversary. Though the poet does not use the word again in this episode, he describes two moods associated with the experience of Wyrd: its power to numb the mind and its power to exhilarate it. Beowulf is called 'werigmod' (1543), when Hrunting fails and he lies helpless, except for his protecting armour, under the knife of Grendel's mother. The poet does not describe the terrible effort of will and imagination by which he is able to break the dark power of the mother that has encircled him. He merely says: 'witig Drihten, / rodera Rædend   hit on ryht gesced / yðelice,   syþðan he eft astod.' (1554-6) The comma after 'yðelice' is assuredly the correct punctuation. The God of men's propensity for fighting one another, like Athena watching Odysseus' preliminary efforts to fight the suitors without aid, lends strength and help to those who can endure overwhelming odds and still fight on. With Beowulf's successful use of the giant's sword, he rejoices: 'secg weorce gefeh.' (1569) The poet, by his description of the light as brilliant as the sun which suddenly floods the cave, mirrors Beowulf's joy in the blood on the sword and the toppling of the monster's head. The intense elation is caused by the moment in which Wyrd seems to acquiesce in man's

courage and is silent. As Beowulf says to Hygelac, in describing this encounter: 'næs ic fæge þa gyt.' (2141)

In the first two battles, our eyes are on Beowulf's complete successes.
Wyrd seriously affects only the minor characters mentioned in the episodes or is too far distant from the hero to cause us concern. In the
third fight, the mood changes, for it is Beowulf himself who is caught
in the toils of Wyrd and struggles to escape. God is not the opponent of
the dragon as he was of Grendel, nor does Wyrd confine its attention to
another's error as it did in the fight with Grendel's mother. Beowulf
must fight in the clutches of his own error. As he sits on the headland
brooding over the meaning of the battle, the poet tells us:

> Him wæs geomor sefa,
> wæfre ond wælfus, wyrd ungemete neah,
> se ðone gomelan gretan sceolde,
> secean sawle hord, sundur gedælan
> lif wið lice. (2419-23)

The formality of the word 'gretan' suggests perhaps a certain respect
for the man in the poem whose struggle to master the space around him
held out longest. But its search for the soul's treasure, its separation of
life and body suggest a relentless and insidious power to penetrate and
destroy all that Beowulf represents.

Later in the first of the three segments of the dragon fight itself, the
poet tells us:

> ðær he þy fyrste forman dogore
> wealdan moste, swa him wyrd ne gescraf
> hreð æt hilde. (2573-5)

The nature of Beowulf's violation puts him in the narrow place where
no universal forces reflect and magnify his energies. He is completely
alone. He is not able to project in this episode an adequate understanding against the challenge, so as to put himself immediately back in touch
with what he should have done; he is too close to his error. He is for the
same reason not able to adjust freely to the unexpected disclosure of
the dragon's presence; he has too little imaginative space both for preparation and for the fight itself.

The narrowing in of the universal forces with which Beowulf con-
tends is indicated in the lessening of the time he has to consider the

threat of the monster, and in the diminution of the imaginative power of the words which give him the clues he has about the monster's intent. He had learned of Grendel through the songs that had been formulated in the twelve years of the Danes' terror and brought across the sea. While he learns of Grendel's mother as unexpectedly as he learns of the dragon, Hrothgar and the Danes have known of her, and Hrothgar's memorable recreation of the mood of the monsters and their habitat gives Beowulf the imaginative space necessary to formulate his actions. But no one has known of the dragon. No poem or story informs Beowulf of it, only two pieces of reportage: the hall is burned; a thane stole a cup.

Because the space for imaginative preparation in the dragon fight is so sharply confined, Beowulf's boast lacks the encompassing dimensions of those in the first two battles. The complexity of the problem has increased to nearly unfathomable proportions and he is unable to imagine what he will actually face when he enters the monster's territory. Consequently he is less able to avoid Wyrd.

Before the fight with Grendel, Beowulf boasted that he would fight without weapons and would cleanse the hall. He carries out both boasts; the dislocations between intent and fulfilment are only minor. The hall is still threatened (Grendel's mother, the evil of the retainers, foreign enemies), but no longer defiled. His decision not to use weapons is ironic, as the good sportsmanship he proposes accidentally coincides with the only means by which Grendel can be killed. Before the fight with Grendel's mother, he vows to avenge Æschere: 'Selre bið æg-hwæm, / þæt he his freond wrece' (1384-5); at the mere, he vows to win glory with Hrunting or die (1490-1). Here the dislocation is greater. He kills the mother to avenge Æschere, but, since Æschere is not his friend, he performs an act that is the duty of Hrothgar. He gains no glory with Hrunting, but because he finds another sword, he also does not die.

In the dragon fight, the speech which finally ends with such boast as he can formulate (2510-37) is characterized by a desperate searching for a comprehensible mode of action and fulfilment. His initial attempt is broken by the conditional clause: 'gif mec se mansceaða / of eorðsele ut geseceð.' (2514-15) His uncertainty about how to come to grips with his boast is contained in his apology for fighting in full armour. He acknowledges the uneasiness he feels by directly naming Wyrd:

> Nelle ic beorges weard
> oferfleon fotes trem,   ac unc furður sceal

weorðan æt wealle,   swa unc wyrd geteoð,
Metod manna gehwæs.   (2524-7)

He is acutely conscious that he stands in the narrow place from which
he is not likely to escape. He does not speak of cleansing the land of the
dragon ('fælsian' dominates the first fight) nor of vengeance for the
dragon's burning ('wrecan' dominates the second fight). The closest he
comes in this speech to the traditional boast is in his final words before
battle: to win the gold or die. In terms of subsequent events, his analysis
of the alternatives is inaccurate. He and the dragon both die. He wins
the gold briefly, but loses it as the reserve of wealth with which he
thought to have secured his people's continuance in power and freedom.
They immediately bury it again with his body.

Beowulf had fought his first fight to earn the esteem of Hygelac; he
fights the second to win fame. The third he fights for the mercilessly accurate judgment of Wyrd, which is after all the only way men know God.
Because of his violent determination to face this unfaceable power, for
the moment, the moment which becomes the eternity of his heroism, he
breaks the barrier of his own error and touches the order of the universe
once more. In the end, however, Beowulf feels the same sweeping power
that has taken lesser men:

ealle wyrd forsweop
mine magas   to metodsceafte,
eorlas on elne;   ic him æfter sceal.   (2814-16)

In the remainder of this essay, I will consider the nature of the choice,
the act, the error that brings the kings of *Beowulf* into the realm of
Wyrd. As far as human society is concerned in the poem, the patterns of
obligation are determined by the heroic code which is analogous to the
'wheel of Wyrd.' As with the wheel, there is with the code a strain of
the inexorable demand that its requirements be met. The code, like the
wheel, binds men together, provides the standards for determining the
directions of good and evil action, of aspiration and failure. Men and
monsters are seen in relation to it. The laws of the code, like Wyrd, provide the balances for human inadequacies and failures. The human lord
is the centre of the society which circles about him; in terms of the metaphor, he is the axle to his retainers' wheel. The best men are closest to
him and receive his greatest favours. To attain a measure of security, a

life that is balanced, this society must consist of a king and retainers acutely conscious of their quintessential need of one another's powers.

The two functions of the code which we witness consistently in the poem are connected with war and the rituals of the meadhall, which are, in a sense, the rituals to preserve the tension of war in the passivity of peace. The bond of those who belong to this fellowship, kings and retainers alike, is total allegiance to the members of the band, the obligation to fight for it, to avenge its wrongs by killing or the exaction of wergeld, to reward its members with esteem and gifts. The pattern of obligation in this fellowship is that of the family, in particular, father-son, uncle-nephew, brother-brother. In the comitatus (the larger group made up of members not necessarily related), obligation and hierarchy is ritualistically established by the giving and receiving of treasure, which becomes under these auspices the symbolic equivalent of blood.

The ties of human society, however, are little more than a shadow of the absolute relationships which govern the universe. The heroic code, even if followed at the highest of all ethical levels, is not sufficiently inclusive to materialize clearly the divine order of things for men to follow. The men whose society the code defines in addition weaken its efficacy by making no effort to follow it at all. The inadequacies of the code and of the men who follow it are found in primarily two areas in the poem: 1/ the momentary stresses that occur in connection with war and 2/ the continual stresses that occur in response to the demands of peace. Only the latter attract the power of Wyrd.

The moments of crisis created by war and killing provide some of the most intense parts of *Beowulf*; the historical digressions are frequently founded on events which are too complex for the code and its verbal system of allegiances. What results is uneasy silence: the silence of Hengest and Finn through the bloodstained winter about the vengeance the code demands they carry out against each other:

Ða hie getruwedon   on twa healfa
fæste frioðuwære.   Fin Hengeste
elne unflitme   aðum benemde,
þæt he þa wealafe   weotena dome
arum heolde,   þæt ðær ænig mon
wordum ne worcum   wære ne bræce,
ne þurh inwitsearo   æfre gemænden,
ðeah hie hira beaggyfan   banan folgedon
ðeodenlease,   þa him swa geþearfod wæs;

gyf þonne Frysna hwylc frecnan spræce
ðæs morþorhetes myndgiend wære,
þonne hit sweordes ecg seðan scolde. (1095-1106)

There is the silence of Onela and Weohstan about the vengeance the
code demands that Onela, as uncle of Eanmund, take against his slayer
Weohstan: 'no ymbe ða fæhðe spræc, / þeah ðe he his broðor bearn
abredwade.' (2618-19) There is the allusion to the implicit silence of
Hrethel and Hæthcyn in the face of the code's demand that a father
avenge himself on his son's slayer, and its equally strong demand that he
protect, with his own life if necessary, anyone who is blood-kin to him
(2435 ff). There is the implicit silence of Beowulf and the Swedish
kings: with Onela, against whom the code demands Beowulf's vengeance
for the Swedes' killing of Heardred (2379 ff), and later with Eadgils
from whom the code exacts the duty of vengeance for his brother Eanmund against Weohstan, who comes to Beowulf's court after the third
Swedish war (2391 ff; 2611 ff).

This silence, a hiatus in the temporal sequence of allegiances and obligations, is eventually filled by some inadequate makeshift, by the renewed violation of sworn oaths and blood kinship, by exile, by delayed
vengeance, by the acceptance of the seething frustration which eventually kills Hrethel. These makeshifts are not however sufficiently powerful in their disruption of things to attract the attention of Wyrd. There
is even a kind of acquiescence in these immoral or inadequate compen-
sations. The Danes survive their time of troubles because of the energy
of men like Hrothulf (Hrolf kraki),[8] who, though their tactics are evil
in the given context of the code, nevertheless are evil in a very circum-
scribed way; they stay, as it were, on the wheel of Wyrd.

But those who violate the central symbolic relation between men
and God at the heart of the code fare worse. The centre of the fellowship of the comitatus, the gift-giving, is man's daring imitation of God's
gifts to men. Like Alfred,[9] the *Beowulf* poet associates God rather than
Wyrd with the goods of the earth (Hrothgar's sermon); they are his pro-
vince and it is man's chief duty to learn to use them to satisfy his spiritual
and creative needs. The injunction in *Beowulf* that attends the giving of
gifts is: 'Bruc ealles well! ' (2162; see also 1045, 1216, 2812). To use
the gifts well, man must not hoard them; he must also pass them on with
an accurate feeling for the deserts of the receiver, his proved worth, and
his potential for an equally adequate use of it. Gold, material possession
par excellence, requires that givers emulate the divine knowledge of

God, that receivers show themselves ready to take on this stature at need. But men can misuse the gifts or fail to use them adequately (again judged against an ideal but to man all but incomprehensible standard).

The result is that great wealth (this includes all material of the universe: gold, talents, kingdoms) creates a kind of tragic ambivalence in the poem. To keep life vital men, kings in particular, must use the wealth in creation, but they are blocked by their humanity and the intractable nature of the universe from accurate estimates about consequences of their actions. It is not only that men lack foresight, they also, unlike God, do not have Wyrd to balance out the deviations from the ideal standard which the recipients' freedom inevitably allows to them. Men have only their energy, their wisdom, their courage with which to compensate for the imbalances and vacuums of a universe indifferent to their hunger for creation and the fragility of their bodies.

Peace is the problem that provokes the perpetual crisis of men. The kings of the poem whose activities are presented with sufficient scope for comment, encountering the code's inability to supply a means of proceeding when the bloodshed is over, are faced with the task of employing their material, their men, their treasure, in some constructive way. But with this leisure, they succeed only in creating an artificial world that interferes with the true order of things and brings retaliation in the form of monsters and of Wyrd.

Hygelac's decision as he rides on the high wave of his success in the first Swedish war and perhaps too of the treasure Beowulf has brought from Hrothgar is to create an artificial state of war: to raid. His choice is so poor that even his monster is artificial; the Franks neither attack the nation, as the other monsters do, nor are they anything other than men (Dæghrefn alone supplying a note of monstrous hope). The first account of Hygelac's raid is mentioned in connection with Hrothgar's gift to Beowulf of the necklace of the Brosings; the juxtaposition of his fall and the loss of the necklace highlights Hygelac's misuse of the gift. The punishment: 'hyne wyrd fornam, / syþðan he for wlenco   wean ahsode, / fæhðe to Frysum.' (1205-7) We hear on three other occasions of Hygelac's fall and each time we are reminded of the general absurdity of his commitment to fight the Franks, and more important, as Bonjour has pointed out,[10] of his inadequate relation to treasure. There was no reason to attack the Franks except the base one of booty, no sense in wearing a magnificent necklace on a raiding expedition, no intelligence in remaining in the rearguard when a whole nation's warriors could be expected to be in hot pursuit.[11] Hygelac is the example in the poem of the floundering imagination. He never discovered the issues, symbolic or otherwise, which are worth grappling with, the absolute values of the world's reality. He did not draw forth a monster as did Hrothgar and Beowulf in their attempts to follow out the tenets of the code at the most generous of all possible levels. He tried to imagine one elsewhere; and, in legend, he became one himself.[12] He asked for it, and Wyrd takes him as it took Grendel.

Hrothgar and Beowulf, similarly, must decide what to do when they find themselves so powerful that no neighbouring king will come against them. Their freedom and power lead them to set up a utopia which in both cases ignores an essential requirement of the code. If Hygelac violates the code's underlying contempt for irresponsible, aggressive energy exerted in the use of and search for treasure, Hrothgar's choice ignores the requirements which the power politics inherent in his system of government place upon reward. Hrothgar, at the height of his success, proposes to build the great hall Heorot and in joyful contemplation of this endeavour resolves to distribute all his wealth to young and old alike:

> Him on mod bearn,
> þæt healreced   hatan wolde,
> medoærn micel   men gewyrcean
> þonne yldo bearn   æfre gefrunon,
> ond þær on innan   eall gedælan
> geongum ond ealdum,   swylc him God sealde,
> buton folcscare   ond feorum gumena.   (67-73)[13]

And later he carries out his promise: 'He beot ne aleh,   beagas dælde, / sinc æt symle.' (80-1) The poet at once juxtaposes the allusion to the burning of Heorot (82-5).

Hrothgar, in these lines which should be footnoted with the same meticulousness as the first scene of *King Lear,* makes the Lear-like error of disregarding the hierarchy which keeps evil in check. This democratic use of the gold which ought to be reserved for the ritualistic distribution of the gift-giving destroys the hierarchy where the best are highest in the court, the worst without fame or power. It is apparent that not all is well in Denmark when the ominous figures of Unferth and Hrothulf sit at the feet of the lord of the Danes, not Æschere. Hrothgar's reaction is to recognize his error and adjust to the situation, to adjust even to the monster with whom he must share the rule of his hall. While Hrothgar, walking the narrow line of his humiliation, is no longer heroic, no longer confronts the space before him, he, in his wisdom, also does not bring Wyrd against him.[14] It is his retainers who, trying in their futile fashion to regain control of the hall, feel its power.

The error that takes Beowulf into the realm of Wyrd is more complex than that of Hrothgar or Hygelac, which destroys the kingly efficacy of the one and the life of the other. With Beowulf more clearly than with these kings, we face a terrible and incomprehensible world. The misuse of 'treasure' figures as a cause in the Danish episodes and the raid on the Franks, and may be said to be the central issue in the dragon fight. But while it is immediately apparent what Hygelac and Hrothgar should not have done with treasure, it is not at all apparent that Beowulf could legitimately have done anything else with his. If he held to the ceremony of the hall and the ethical requirements of the code, protected his retainers beyond the common wont of kings, he obviously did so in preference to conquest and raiding which would have charged the ceremony with new life, but would have led to continual physical death of his men and others. If he saw as the centre of the meadhall boasting the preparation of men for total freedom, rather than merely a limited and disciplined playing out of the drama of stress and crisis, he obviously did so in the hope that higher aims create a better world. In order to do anything more noble than he did as king, Beowulf would have required a new heaven and a new earth. His human world provided no images adequate to his energy and his visions. While one may speak of Hygelac's rashness and of Hrothgar's weakness, one must speak of Beowulf's tragedy.

The final episode of the poem opens at the end of fifty years of Beowulf's peaceful reign. The events of his kingship are described to us in flashback and the conclusions we draw about his error must be based largely on the events that occur the day he dies. On this day what he fails to do in terms of the code is to recognize the necessity for the reciprocity between king and retainers, to recognize that the axle performs its function only when the wheel turns on it and supports its weight. For, to borrow Alfred's full metaphor, no matter what concessions the Axle is prepared to make, the wagon of the universe will only move forward if the Wheel performs its function. If man will not see to this necessity, then Wyrd will.

Through the words of Wiglaf, we hear that Beowulf has maintained the ceremony of the hall, the boasting and the gift-giving, with a generosity that leads him to seek far and near for those treasures which will give his retainers most pleasure (2864 ff). He has earned their adulation as is abundantly apparent in their tribute to him after his death (3180-2). But he does not recognize the absolute human necessity for engaging them in a vital heroic commitment to assembling the jagged pieces of naked primary experience. On this day, Beowulf does not force his retainers to fight the dragon with him, either by threat of his superior strength, or by insistence that they fight whether they understand or not, or even by descending to the elementary form of challenge which Hrothgar had offered to him earlier before the fight with Grendel's mother: 'sec gif þu dyrre!' (1379) While he takes them with him, he in effect gives them only another empty ceremonial honour; speaking to them as 'swæse gesiðas' (2518), he yet does not allow them to experience their commitment.

> Nis þæt eower sið,
> ne gemet mannes, nefne min anes,
> þæt he wið aglæcean eofoðo dæle,
> eorlscype efne. (2532-5)

Beowulf's extraordinary strength and kindness blots out in his mind the fated necessity for keeping alive that reciprocal commitment for the edge of doom which must underlie the relation of the king and those with whom he celebrates in the meadhall. In his fearful knowledge that it is his sin that brings the dragon, he ironically protects again the men for whom his former concern has made the unreal kingdom of the dragon's eternal earthhall the mirror of his own.

With such kindness, Beowulf, in his fifty years of peaceful reign, has created a utopian world ultimately more dangerous than the worlds Hygelac and Hrothgar tried to create with much more limited success, for Beowulf's powerful choice had the tragic result of destroying the possibility for his kingdom's survival. When the secure warm world he had created for his retainers is shattered by his death, they are too protected to take over the responsibility for putting the world together again.

At their moment of preliminary decision, the council that precedes the battle with the dragon, they fail to understand the reasons for fighting the monster. Wiglaf, and his supporters, thought that the dragon would not return again and should be left alone.

> Ne meahton we gelæran leofne þeoden,
> rices hyrde ræd ænigne,
> þæt he ne grette goldweard þone,

lete hyne licgean,   þær he longe wæs,
wicum wunian,   oð woruldende.   (3079-83)

The battle has not changed Wiglaf's mind: 'Oft sceall eorl monig anes willan / wræc adreogan, swa us geworden is.' (3077-8) The readiness with which the messenger immediately produces elaborate forecasts of the disasters that will befall the Geats now that Beowulf is dead (2900 ff) suggests another strain of argument at that council: Beowulf as talisman for the security of the land of the Geats should not fight the dragon because it might kill him.

Much of the power and the terror of the ending of the poem is created by these two retainers avoiding an assessment of the demand for heroic confrontation of the world before them. In their ceremonial shielding of themselves, they contemplate their own death and are stirred to action only to celebrate the past, to build a great barrow to Beowulf. They attempt to return things to the way they were before, at least in externals. They get rid of the dragon, bury the gold again, build a monument in worship of Beowulf, and when we last see them they are engaged in the ritual order of the funeral. Wiglaf has not had the power to understand his experience in the fight; the other ten men ran from it; the rest waited in an enclosure up over the edge of the cliff. The Geats, like children unable to handle the plague, return to their game of Ring-around-the-Rosey. The symbols of this episode, as anyone knows who has dealt intensively with them, are terrifying. I do not mean to suggest that anyone, without comprehending what Beowulf does in the dragon fight, would have done any better, or that there is not a certain beauty in their elegiac choice. But when we compare like things to like, when we place them beside the retainers of *Maldon*, who also face the terror of their lord's death and in addition immediate death for themselves, the retainers of Beowulf are hollow men.

Wyrd destroys Beowulf in the final episode of the poem, not because of his age, not because he now lacks the strength and courage to confront the dragon, the most terrible of all challenges; it destroys him because the universe, Wyrd in particular, gives little credit for unmaterialized human dreams. The conflict between what man in his humanity aspires to do and what Wyrd allows him to do is the central conflict of the dragon fight. While space does not allow a full assessment of the poem's complex final episode, perhaps a few skeletal concluding remarks about the relation of Wyrd and Beowulf's heroic determination are in order.[15]

Beowulf does not at any point succeed in assessing the nature of the error that brings the dragon against him. He is instantly certain that the error is his own:

> wende se wisa, þæt he Wealdende
> ofer ealde riht ecean Dryhtne
> bitre gebulge. (2329-31)

He is certain that he must fight the dragon. Before the speech on the headland (2426 ff) where he attempts to solve the problem that confronts him, he restlessly senses the presence of Wyrd, and the poet tells us that it eventually kills him (2419-24). After this speech, he determines to face Wyrd directly, the 'Metod manna gehwæs' (2527) and to fight for the gold:

> Ic mid elne sceall
> gold gegangan, oððe guð nimeð,
> feorhbealu frecne frean eowerne! (2535-7)

With this choice, he chooses to fight for that substance which provides the highest potential for human benefit: 'fremmað gena / leoda þearfe' (2800-1), he says afterwards, as he looks at the treasure Wiglaf brings him from the dragon's cave.

In choosing to fight for the gold he affirms his commitment to his vision of the point of human effort. In the first segment of the fight, the poet tells us that Wyrd did not create triumph for Beowulf on this day (2574-5), but we may notice that it also does not create instant defeat, as it had done for Hrothgar's thanes, Grendel, and Hygelac. The net result of these decisions which manifest the titanic courage of a hero willing to endure the dragon's fire for what he believes in is to produce one of those rare pinnacles of pure elation in heroic literature, the open space where the hero's effort triumphs for a moment even, it would seem, over the force that waits to kill him. Beowulf's vision of the ideal relation of men materializes for a moment as Wiglaf proves capable of joining him in man's most terrible battle and brings him both freedom and victory.

But with the dragon dead, the gold in sight, Wiglaf frightened of its power, the tangible image of success crumbles and Beowulf dies, victorious, it is true — such briefness is the extent of human victories — but once more in the power of Wyrd (2814-16; see also 2420 ff). As the end of the poem makes all too apparent, Beowulf's victory makes no more alteration in his retainers' understanding than the dragon's defeat makes upon his gold. Like Alfred's God, Beowulf has given his men freedom, has extended his trust of them and their potential as far as his mind can reach. He has fought for the dragon's gold to increase the scope of his giving even further. But, unlike God, he cannot compensate for their hesitant small-heartedness in any way except with his own courage. He holds his own commitment to the bitter end. He does not recant; he does not condemn them in even their most abysmal failure. This strength is both his greatness as a hero and his tragedy as a man.

Men encounter Wyrd, then, not because they violate the tenets of the code in some obvious way which momentarily strains the *lex talionis*, but because in their attempt to extend the confines of the established boundaries of society and to create other worlds whose dimensions they lack the power to realize fully, they tangle with forces that have no respect for their efforts. Wyrd is the weight man's noblest efforts are anchored to; the heroic imagination, his highest form of perception and commitment, is all that gives him freedom in the face of the knowledge that what he strives for will, in the end, be seen as inadequate.

NOTES

1 For discussions of Wyrd, see, for instance, the following: Ladislaus Mittner, *Wurd: das Sakraler in der altgermanischen Epik* (Bern 1955); Dame Bertha S. Phillpotts, 'Wyrd and Providence in Anglo-Saxon Thought,' *Essays and Studies by Members of the English Association* 13 (1928) 7-27; Alan H. Roper, 'Boethius and the Three Fates of Beowulf,' *Philological Quarterly* 41 (1962) 386-400; B.J. Timmer, 'Wyrd in Anglo-Saxon Prose and Poetry,' *Neophilologus* 26 (1941) 24-33, 213-28. I draw freely on my book, *King Alfred and Boethius* (Wisconsin 1968), in particular on the chapters: 'Alfred's Idea of Freedom,' 39-77, and 'Wyrd, Fortuna, and Fatum,' 78-108. I would like to thank Professor J.D.A. Ogilvy for allowing me to read his forthcoming article 'Alfred and *Beowulf*,' the first part of which deals with Wyrd.

2 There are various words for fate in the poem: 'gewif' ('what is woven,' 697), 'gebyrd' ('what one is born to,' 1074), 'gescipe' ('what is shaped,' 2570), 'gifeðe' ('what is given,' 3085). Each appears once and refers to dimensions established from the beginning, the fixed outlines of the life of a man, a dragon, an event, rather than the living experience of the human consciousness with the intractable, which can take place only in the present moment and the present event, the experience 'Wyrd' describes.

3 All quotations from King Alfred's adaptation of the *Consolation* are taken from

W.J. Sedgefield, *King Alfred's Old English Version of Boethius* (Oxford 1899); page and line numbers will be given in the text.

4 This is an eventuality which Alfred mentions on two occasions: 57.7-8; 98.11 ff.

5 The word 'Wyrd' is used directly in the context of the Breca passage, but only at the beginning of the episode of Grendel's mother (1234). The patterns of the two passages parallel one another strongly, imminent defeat which is unexpectedly turned to victory by Beowulf's courage.

6 All quotations from *Beowulf* are taken from F. Klaeber, *'Beowulf' and 'The Fight at Finnsburg'* (3rd ed., Boston 1950).

7 1/ 455; 2/ 572; 3/ 734, 1056, 1233, 2420, 2526, 2574; 4/ 477, 1205, 2814

8 For the relation of Hrothgar and Hrothulf in the poem and later legend, see Klaeber, xxxi ff.

9 For instance: 'Sume uðwiotan þeah secgað þæt sio wyrd wealde ægþer ge gesælða ge ungesælða ælces monnes. Ic þonne secge, swa swa ealle cristene men secgað, þæt sio godcunde foretiohhung his walde, næs sio wyrd' (131.8-12); for discussion, see Payne, 88-9, 95-7.

10 Adrien Bonjour, 'Jottings on *Beowulf* and the Aesthetic Approach,' in *Old English Poetry*, ed. Robert P. Creed (Providence 1967), 179-92; 'The Problem of Dæghrefn,' in *Twelve Beowulf Papers* (Neuchâtel 1962), 77-88

11 For historical accounts of Hygelac, see Klaeber, xxxix-xl; Dorothy Whitelock, *The Audience of Beowulf* (Oxford 1951), 38 ff. For an analysis of his lack of wisdom, see R.E. Kaske, '*Sapientia et Fortitudo* as the Controlling Theme of *Beowulf*,' in *Anthology of Beowulf Criticism*, ed. Lewis E. Nicholson (Notre Dame 1963), 290 ff.

12 Whitelock, 46, quotes the following passage from the *Liber Monstrorum*: 'And there are monsters of a wonderful size; such as King Higlacus who ruled the *Getae* and was killed by the Franks, whom from his twelfth year no horse could carry. His bones are preserved on an island in the Rhine, where it flows forth into the ocean, and are shown to those who come from afar as a miracle.'

13 Line 73 would suggest that Hrothgar preserved something, but we are not sure what the folkshare was, nor whether the rest of the line means that there were royal slaves who were not distributed or whether it merely sets life in opposition to material possessions. Klaeber (cvii) found the line unnecessary and thinks it possibly a 'corrective addition.' In that case it would have been written by someone who could not believe that Hrothgar gave away both halves of the apple.

14 For a discussion of Hrothgar's lack of courage, see Kaske, 279 ff.

15 In its original form this article was followed by an additional section entitled the 'Heroic Imagination,' which dealt with the five challenges Beowulf meets in the course of his life. The major share of this section was taken up with an analysis of the dragon fight. I hope to publish this at a later time.

HARRY BERGER, JR
H. MARSHALL LEICESTER, JR

Social structure as doom:
the limits of heroism in *Beowulf*

This essay is less a full-scale interpretation of *Beowulf* than a qualifying
and occasionally critical extension of some recent readings of the poem
to which our approach is heavily indebted. Our view of *Beowulf* owes
much to Edward B. Irving, Jr's fine studies, *A Reading of 'Beowulf'* and
Introduction to 'Beowulf,' with an assist from John Halverson's essay,
'The World of *Beowulf.'* We propose to navigate along a line of inquiry
somewhere between those struck by Irving and Halverson, for in significant ways these two interpretations contradict each other and can
therefore be made to complement each other. We shall try to sketch out
the various positions by considering some critical responses to a particular incident, Hrothgar's raising of Heorot.

The building of Heorot is the climax of Hrothgar's career, a turning
point from his years of active military conquest to a phase of stability
and 'cultural' leadership. Like Beowulf's barrow in years to come,
Heorot will be the site and source of continuing group life; a widely visible centre of protection, solidarity, reciprocity, and celebration; a
seemingly permanent symbol of achieved Scylding glory. Hrothgar's aim
may be simply to settle down and enjoy the fruits of long battle-years,
but the passage describing the raising of Heorot poses some questions
about this:

>   Him on mod bearn,
> þæt healreced   hatan wolde,
> medoærn micel   men gewyrcean

þon[n]e yldo bearn   æfre gefrunon,
ond þær on innan   eall gedælan
geongum ond ealdum,   swylc him God sealde
buton folcscare   ond feorum gumena.
Ða ic wide gefrægn   weorc gebannan
manigre mægþe   geond þisne middangeard,
folcstede frætwan.   Him on fyrste gelomp,
ædre mid yldum,   þæt hit wearð ealgearo,
healærna mæst;   scop him Heort naman
se þe his wordes geweald   wide hæfde.
He beot ne aleh,   beagas dælde,
sinc æt symle.   Sele hlifade
heah ond horngeap;   heaðowylma bad,
laðan liges;   ne wæs hit lenge þa gen,
þæt se ecghete   aþumsweoran
æfter wælniðe   wæcnan scolde.
Ða se ellengæst   earfoðlice
þrage geþolode,   se þe in þystrum bad,
þæt he dogora gehwam   dream gehyrde
hludne in healle.   (67-89)[1]

It came to his mind that he would command men to construct a hall,
a mead-building large[r] than the children of men had ever heard
of, and therein he would give to young and old all that God had given
him, except for common land and men's bodies. Then I have heard
that the work was laid upon many nations, wide through this middle-
earth, that they should adorn the folk-hall. In time it came to pass —
quickly, as men count it — that it was finished, the largest of hall
dwellings. He gave it the name of Heorot, he who ruled wide with his
words. He did not forget his promise: at the feast he gave out rings,
treasure. The hall stood tall, high and wide-gabled: it would wait for
the fierce flames of vengeful fire; the time was not yet at hand for
sword-hate between son-in-law and father-in-law to awaken after mur-
derous rage.

   Then the fierce spirit painfully endured hardship for a time, he who
dwelt in the darkness, for every day he heard loud mirth in the hall.[2]

   Like other readers, we detect a faint echo of the building of the tower
of Babel in this passage. But unlike some Christian and allegorizing
critics, we don't infer from this that Hrothgar is a spiritual son of Cain

and Heorot an emblem of the earthly city. Nor are we persuaded by the cooler argument of R.E. Kaske, who views Hrothgar's flaw through patristic glasses as a failure of *fortitudo* which affects the old king's otherwise exemplary *sapientia*: 'he is no longer at his best when facing decisions involving violence or the prospect of it,' and this accounts for 'such mistakes as the marriage of Freawaru to Ingeld and, apparently, the unwise toleration of Hrothulf at the Danish court.' His courage having waned with age, 'he now relies chiefly on counsel, kingly munificence, diplomacy, and wise endurance — all valuable means in themselves, but indifferent substitutes for *fortitudo* as a defense against the forces of naked violence.'[3] Thus Kaske sees Grendel 'as the product of the present Danish situation' (287), that is, as an allegorical projection of *fortitudo* breaking loose from *sapientia*'s control and joining forces with *malitia*.

Both Halverson and Irving have persuasively argued against such Christian and ethical critiques of part I.[4] They defend Hrothgar and Heorot as good, not bad. 'The point,' observes Irving, 'is that Heorot is not a false good in the poem; it is not something like Pandemonium or the Tower of Babel in *Paradise Lost,* an assertion of Satanic pride and arrogance.' This view, he continues, may be encouraged by lines 81b-5 describing the splendour and doom of Heorot; yet the passage only implies that Heorot, mighty as it is,

> will one day perish. But the tone of this passage is far from the smug I-told-you-so of the Christian moralizer; it is rather a tone of deep regret for the instability of all human things, even the greatest. The sons of Cain in the poem are the Grendels, not the Hrothgars. In terms of the dominant heroic values of the poem, Hrothgar's Denmark is represented as very nearly the height of human achievement.[5]

Given so difficult a world, this achievement is bound to be less than perfect, and Irving's studies contain many perceptive passages describing the weaknesses and instabilities of Danish institutions.

We agree with Irving that the poet is not by any means presenting Hrothgar as an example of human pride or of the failure of courage. We see no ethical disapproval in the sense of criticism directed by the poet either at the intentions of this individual or at the sinfulness of fallen man aspiring to divine status. But we might well ask an 'ethical' question at another level: has the society 'done wrong'? — and not the Danes only, since the poem clearly embraces pan-Germanic institutions. It is here, for the poem as a whole, that Irving and Halverson part company. Irving often notes the inability of such institutions as vendetta and marriage to provide satisfactory solutions to the 'powerful and centrifugal forces [that] must always have been felt in a society so dedicated to aggressive behavior and the strutting niceties of personal honor,'[6] but his response to this is expressed in casual and discrete observations that reflect nothing so much as the sense of the world held by the characters themselves.[7] Like Hrothgar and Beowulf, Irving tends to bury the specific institutional bases of conflict and disorder in the purely ethical and universal terms of the opposition between the heroic individual and cosmic doom: the hero is all the nobler because he confronts so dark a world.

In this connection, some of Halverson's brief suggestions about social organization in the Dark Ages point to a more specific set of polarities existing in what might be called the middle range between hostile cosmos and hero:

> The way to stability ... is through closer social ties and greater common effort. This is implicit in the *treow*-ethic, but conflicts with heroic individualism. ...
> The Dark Ages period is an heroic age, the time of the individual hero. Everything depends on 'the will of one man.' ... It is the great men who, by force of personality and military capacity, alone keep together the fabric of civilization, and when they die the order they have established soon disintegrates. ...
> The code of loyalty ... expresses the intent of cooperation. Why does it fail? Because of individualism. The 'cowardice' of the retainers is simply an expression of the priority of the individual over the group. ... Beowulf, the greatest of heroes, is loved and revered by his nephew [sic], but the heroic solution is not always the best solution. It is not Beowulf's pride that brings about the ultimate catastrophe, but precisely his heroism. He is not a victim of ego inflation; he simply cannot see other alternatives to his own way. He is a victim of the heroic milieu; he is molded gloriously and inflexibly by his world.[8]

Where Irving tends to agree with the more reflective characters in the poem (Hrothgar and Beowulf) that the source of man's doom lies in the universal human condition, Halverson steps back behind the poet to suggest a specific historico-social cause in conflicting institutional ideals. He suggests a level at which ethical considerations are irrelevant because we are dealing with structural patterns operating for the most part beneath the consciousness of the characters in the poem. They may well feel the stresses and strains their society imposes on them, but the institutions that cause them are taken for granted, and are not subject to analysis by the characters, who tend rather to ascribe their troubles to fate, God, pride, the way of the world, the 'instability of all human things,' and other generalized perceptions of this sort. At this level Halverson provides a perspective complementary to Irving's, but his explanation of the tensions in the poem centres on the problem of individualism and fails to account for the ways in which other institutions — raid, feud, marriage, feasting, gift-giving, and the rituals for magnifying honour — equally contribute to the difficulty of life in heroic society.[9] He seems to accept at face value the poet's apparently positive attitude toward the social order of the Danes, perhaps because he assumes that only modern readers and historians can identify institutional contradictions of this kind. For example, he tends — along with Irving — to overpraise Heorot in defending it.

Both critics appeal to Mircea Eliade's mythography of the sacred centre, which leads Halverson to see Heorot 'as a repetition of the original cosmogonic act': just as God 'brought form out of chaos, light out of darkness, so the king brings order to his world and maintains it. ... The lord's hall defines meaningful reality.'[10] And Irving invokes Eliade to support the idea that the scop's 'Song of Creation serves to exalt the significance of the building of Heorot by associating divine creativity ... with the purely human creativity of the Danish civilization.'[11] But surely we are meant to distinguish the viewpoint of Hrothgar and his scop — which the two critics here adopt — from that of the *Beowulf*-poet: the scop's song, itself a bright island of praise, is followed immediately by the poet's dark sequel which we, but not the Danes, hear. If God himself in the midst of his leafy new world wove kinstrife as well as kinlove into the primal family structure, how could Hrothgar do less (or more)? To create a family, a society, a dynasty, or a gift-hall is to create those conditions which are inseparable from, and have no meaning apart from, social order: treachery, envy, isolation, and exile. To create an Inside is to create an Outside, but an Outside existing within the bonds of hall and family as well as beyond them.

The Babel echo, then, suggests something about the latent consequences, the doom, built into the meadhall and — if we may extend the reference — into all the interwoven institutions of Germanic society, and it is at this point that we part company from both Halverson and Irving. If the latter tends to stay too close to the characters, and therefore to miss or occlude those patterns in the poem of which they are not conscious, the former tends to distance himself too fully from the critical perspective of the poet, and therefore to simplify the trouble with Germanic society by failing to hear what the poet is telling us about institutions other than that of heroic individualism. In the following sections we shall take up and develop some of the clues offered by our two critics, and try to articulate a more consistent or at least explicit account of the negative aspects of social structure, treating these as specific causes of the problems which confront the hero. Our argument turns on the hypothesis that while the characters focus on ethical behaviour — ideal heroic consciousness — as the key to order, the poem and the poet direct our attention to fundamental conditions of social structure which operate beneath or beyond consciousness, and which constrain heroic behaviour in ways not discernible by the characters.

These latent conditions, as presented in the poem, have certain resemblances to the motivational and structural bases of tribal society which one anthropologist has characterized in terms of Hobbes's primitive state of 'Warre,' the war 'of every man against every man':

> Individuals and subgroups of tribal society maintain the certain right and potential inclination to secure by force their safety, gain, and glory. ... Warre exists, but mainly in the form of an underlying circumstance. In *fact*, tribesmen live in kin groupings and communities within which feuding is usually suppressed, and they have benefit too of economic, ritual, and social institutions conducive to good order. To speak of Warre, then, is to uncover by analysis tendencies ordinarily concealed by powerful impositions of the cultural system. Primitive anarchy is not the appearance of things. It is the unconscious of the system. Yet as the outward behavior of a person may not be intelligible except as the transfiguration of unconscious desires, so the objective organization of tribal society may only be understood as the repressive transformation of an underlying anarchy. Many of the special patterns of tribal culture became meaningful precisely as defense mechanisms, as *negations of Warre*.[12]

If we ignore the misleading Freudian metaphor, we can more easily adapt this description to the different conditions of post-tribal Germanic society by noting that assertions of Warre in that society are as important as negations. Feuding is less fully suppressed in heroic society than in those of which Sahlins speaks. It is in fact a necessary institution. Germanic society is post-tribal in being centred on the *comitatus* more than on actual kingroups. Kinstrife widens as 'kin' relations are extended to, or augmented by, the bonds of the *comitatus*. The society has to channel and constrain violence chiefly because it values and encourages it. The kingroup gives way, or is extended, to the *comitatus*,[13] because the latter is a more efficient means of protection against raid and vengeance. Yet the *comitatus* relies on raiding for economic purposes, and therefore encourages 'ellen' and honour-seeking, which in turn provide a heroic context of motivation for the acquiring and redistributing of treasure. The reliance on honour and performance supplant the more 'automatic' ascriptions of function and role prescribed by kinship patterns in tribal societies. But honour is *zêlos*, as jealous and proud as it is zealous, and the ceremonial publicity attending the reward for performance may stir up envy and discontent, ultimately dishonour and treachery (e.g., Unferth). All this naturally keeps alive the very dangers which the *comitatus* is organized to fend off. Intertribal feuds simmer for generations, providing the environment of Warre in which the men of heroic societies pass their lives, for example, the predicted fate of the Geats at the hands of their old enemies, the Franks, Frisians, and Swedes.

The same ambivalence and contradictions inhere in peace-weaving institutions. Wergeld is substituted for vendetta to reduce bloodshed and bring feud under jural control; but it also diminishes the opportunity for enhancing and preserving honour through aggressive behaviour. The ironic references to Grendel's refusal to pay wergeld set the stage for the hero to enter and win glory. As the Finn and Ingeld episodes suggest, marriage brings into close contact groups which would otherwise be enemies at a distance, thus exacerbating tensions and increasing the chances that sooner or later peace-weaving will become war-making. As in exogamy, kingroups and warbands have both an economic and a metabolic need of outsiders in order to guarantee the continuing supply or circulation of women, children, protective alliances, treasure, honour, risk, and potential corpses. The structure of heroic institutions is such as to require and therefore to create enemies and victims as well as the heroes who thrive on them.

The backlash from the *comitatus* is felt within dynastic kingroups. Kinstrife is intensified. Hrothgar's sons and Onela's nephews are threatened because the stakes are higher, the crown more attractive, the sanctions against kinmurder less potent in the setting provided by large warbands and 'international' politics. Hygd is rightly uneasy about Heardred. Wealhtheow's double uneasiness — about Beowulf (1169 ff) and

Hrothulf (1216 ff) — testifies to the dilemma posed by the necessity and danger of having heirs in such a setting. Yet the alternative exemplified by Beowulf, who died childless (and, perversely, by Grendel's mother, who died heirless), proves to be even worse.

It is this institutional network, or rather tangle, which in our view supplies the limiting conditions of the heroic world, and not merely the single conflict between heroism and common effort (as Halverson would have it) nor the extra-social grimness of cosmic fate (as Irving would have it). 'The edge of the grimpen' is an edge created by those who make boundaries. In the following sections we shall explore some aspects of the doom created by heroic institutions.

THE MUNIFICENT KING AND THE MEADHALL

Hrothgar has spent most of his life doing everything right and now finds himself suffering for it. He 'was given success in warfare, glory in battle, so that his retainers gladly obeyed him and their company grew into a great band of warriors' (64 ff). He built the biggest and best of mead-halls, acquired an exemplary wife and peace-weaver from the Helmings, displayed great liberality and piety, is known abroad as a wise and good king. Why, then, should he be humiliated by Grendel and castigated by critical Christians? What can the alien 'mearcstapa' possibly have to do with him? Where did he come from, and why? We know more than the Danes do on this score, since it isn't clear that they have been filled in on Grendel's ancestry. Grendel is less an outsider than he seems.

But the poet suggests through his language even more intimate re-lations between Grendel and Heorot. Consider once again lines 82-9 in the passage quoted earlier (p. 38 above). Grendel, still nameless, begins his career in the poem interwoven with Heorot, Hrothgar, and Ingeld. This convergence is produced in the first reference to him, 'ellengæst,' and is intensified if we momentarily hear or think 'ellorgast': Grendel is not yet alien; for a moment he shares the 'ellen' of bold warriors like Hrothgar and Ingeld. That 'earfoðlice' can mean 'impatiently' as well as 'painfully' assimilates his present inactivity to 'the time not yet at hand for sword-hate.' Grendel and Heorot are creatures 'conscious' of wait-ing; they 'know' what conscious men do not. They wait for burning or booty together, and momentarily Grendel's spirit melts into that of the son-in-law Ingeld, or into the fierce feuding spirit that joins Hrothgar wit Ingeld in war, in marriage, and again in war. All manifest the spirit of kin strife. Presumably at this moment the feud between Danes and Heatho-

Bards is temporarily pacified by the promised gift of Freawaru. Yet even if ferocity only smoulders, even if it sleeps, the contentious spirit holds the marches of consciousness and waits for the inevitable dawn of kin-strife. Grendel will break forth first, Ingeld later, no doubt because Grendel as a walker-alone is relatively free, while Ingeld is subject to the constraints and displacements by which human institutions·delay or temper violence while recreating it in new and more complex forms: the incestuous monsters are ultimately self-destroying in their blind violence, but the simple immediacy of their relationship is clean of the kinds of anxiety, distrust, betrayal, and deeply cleft loyalties generated by the intertribal dialectic of raid, feud, precarious peace-weaving, and the symbiosis of honour and resentment. The spirit of Cain is never too far away.

Both destroyers, and both dangers to Heorot, are verbally presented as consequences of the building of the hall: its doomful future is built into it as surely as its conspicuous splendour and iron reinforcements, as surely as the 'dream' of feasting, gift-exchange, and honour rituals which Heorot magnifies. These illustrious activities, brightened by the meadhall, work like a magnet to draw envious raiders and outsiders. Greed, competition, and distrust are intensified among kinsmen and retainers. And why should they not be? The poet clearly describes the building of Heorot as Hrothgar's culminating display of power. It is an heroic deed, another act of conquest topped off with a 'beot' — promise or threat — of implacable prestation.[14] And this is presented as Hrothgar's plan: 'Him on mod bearn' that he would command men to build ('gewyrcean') the hall; no sooner thought than done — 'weorc gebannan' on many peoples, it rose quickly, and he whose word-sway was wide over men gave it its name. 'Gewyrcean' and 'weorc' here imply mighty achievement, painful or difficult accomplishment: the magical speed combined with the difficulty of the labour imposed on many tribes reflects the magnitude of Hrothgar's deed. Its likeness to the fiat of God is sealed by the scop's song of creation. Heorot is the embodiment of heroic aspiration. And it is not only the sequel to years of contention and violence; it is itself the product of a contentious spirit — not Hrothgar's alone, but that built into his social order.[15]

If contentiousness and violence, the fear of kinstrife, the perpetual uneasiness of the 'Warre ... of every man, against every man,' are at the roots of human association, they must somehow be put to use. Contentiousness must be made to enhance group solidarity. Thus, among the benefits that flow from the gracious nature of a liberal king like Hrothgar are bloody occasions. Thanes are under obligation to their lord for the chance to fight and kill or die nobly, to contend with others in manliness and compete for the position, treasure, and honour, by which valour and loyalty are rewarded. Hrothgar shares with the poet a clear and consistent understanding about the two-phase temporal pattern of ideal lordship, a pattern enunciated in the old king's long sermon (1700-84) as well as in the passage under consideration: first you spend most of your time fighting, then you spend most of your time giving and rewarding. The building of Heorot must seem to Hrothgar to signify the happy end of his initial raiding career, and the peaceful beginning of a more positive way to express and share his heroic being. Perhaps also, after years of contention, of tensed and always ready awareness, there can be a tempered détente, a de-tensing just sufficient to allow more expansive hall-joys among which the savouring of the glorious past will no doubt be a prime source of renewed pleasure and solidarity. Thus Beowulf tells Hygelac that the old Scylding was accustomed to speak 'of times far-off,' and 'of his youth, his battle-strength' (2105, 2112-13).

The trouble with this 'dream' is that its creators and participants are asleep to the latent motives and consequences which necessarily alter its character. For fighting is not the only mode of contention. As the language of our passage reveals, gift-giving and reciprocity are equally contentious. Lords and thanes strive to outdo each other in service and reward, and in the expressions of love, loyalty, and obligation. The contentious nature of gift-giving is discussed at length in Marcel Mauss's *The Gift*; for example:

> Between vassals and chiefs, between vassals and their henchmen, the hierarchy is established by means of ... gifts. To give is to show one's superiority, to show that one is ... *magister*. To accept without returning or repaying more is to face subordination, to become a client and subservient, to become *minister*. ... The aim is to be the first, the finest, the luckiest, strongest, and richest.[16]

This personalistic economics provides the basis for the reciprocity that structures the social relations of lord and retainers. Its basically competitive character is stressed in the description of the building of Heorot as an appropriately ornate setting for a liberality so heroic that it must surely lay all who approach the 'gifstol' under uneasy obligation. 'Charity,' observes Mauss, 'wounds him who receives,' and 'the gift not yet repaid debases the man who accepted it.' (63) This theme is not explicit in *Beowulf*, yet its presence must be felt wherever political relationships among individuals are welded to ethical concepts — honour and shame — and are fluid enough, free enough from kinship prescription, to depend upon reciprocal performance. The king's gift is not only a reward for service done but also a challenge to match munificence and avoid shame by further service. Kings like Hrothgar depend on the potential wound charity can inflict to tighten the bonds of loyalty and fellowship.

Prestation is a giving which is lending, a challenge to be met by counter-prestation or some other reciprocating act.[17] Heorot is a challenge — a 'beot' — to the rest of the world as well as a gift to the Danes, and a glance at some responses to Hrothgar's demanding generosity will help establish the institutional rather than ethical character of the trouble in Denmark. The range of responses is bounded by the extreme cases of Beowulf and Grendel: Hrothgar for once finds it hard to match with treasure the generous heroism of Beowulf; and he is unable to give Grendel anything at all not merely because Grendel will not reciprocate or will not deign to receive, but because God will not let him approach the 'gifstol' to receive treasure (168-9) — this, it should be noted, might be a problem for Hrothgar as well as for Grendel. Whatever else Grendel represents, he is by pedigree the product of faulty giving, descended from one who stirred up kinstrife because his own gift-giving was less acceptable to God. To see the evil and rancour and exile of Cain's brood of walkers-alone as the effect of defeated or rejected gift-giving is to understand both how important Hrothgar's special art is to group solidarity and how precarious is the psycho-social atmosphere which such an art creates.

This uneasiness is exacerbated by the presence of Beowulf. The alternate definitions of his mission which he and Hrothgar give constitute a verbal duel. First Beowulf tells the guard (258 ff) that he has come to help the 'protector of the people,' teach him how to conquer his enemy, and ease him of his affliction: 'Or else ever after he will suffer tribulations, constraint, while the best of houses remains there on its high place.'[18] When Beowulf's presence is announced to the old king by Wulfgar, the terms of his answer tend to diminish the hero's overpowering image: Hrothgar remembers Beowulf as a boy, he knows his father received a home and wife through the generosity of Hrethel, and now Ecgtheow's 'eafora' has come here, 'sought a fast friend' ('sohte holdne wine') in Hrothgar. Beowulf is a good man sent by God, and Hrothgar will reward him well with treasure, repay him for his 'modþræce' (372-85). Against this carefully reductive picture of the hero as a proper ob-

ject for the king's friendship and munificence, Beowulf's address to
Hrothgar (407-55) threatens to swell his ethos and the value of his offer,
his risking of life, beyond the limits of adequate repayment. During this
speech, and before his 'beot,' he reminds Hrothgar that Heorot 'stands
empty and useless,' and says he came because the 'best wise earls' of the
Geats, knowing his strength, advised him to volunteer his services to the
king. Hrothgar meets this with a different account (457-72), reminding
him of a prior obligation, for Hrothgar had settled a feud between Geats
and Wylfings by paying the wergeld for a Wylfing whom Ecgtheow had
killed. Against Beowulf's emphasis on his own singular power and generosity — the claim on Hrothgar is heightened by Beowulf's vivid image
of the less likely prospect, Grendel's victory feast (445-55) — he affirms
the principle that sons should honour the debts incurred by their fathers.
Not long after, when stirred to another account of his feats by Unferth's
insult, Beowulf's taunt to the fratricide is generalized to include all the
Danes (595-601): Grendel 'has noticed that he need not much fear the
hostility, not much dread the terrible sword-storm of your people, the
Victory-Scyldings. He exacts forced levy, shows mercy to none of the
Danish people; but he is glad, kills, carves for feasting, expects no fight
from the Spear-Danes.'[19]

Thus in his own way Beowulf threatens Heorot — or what it stands
for — as much as Grendel, and Hrothgar is pressed to pre-define the
hero's promise and achievement so as to keep it within the bounds of
reciprocity. It is in this latent manner that we feel the presence of the
problem articulated by Mauss: 'charity wounds him who receives.'
Hrothgar is arming himself against that possible wound. And when Beowulf's conquest of Grendel is celebrated, the poet's account of the
treasure-giving stresses two features: the heroic quality of Hrothgar's repayment, and the uneasiness that lurks beneath the joyful surface of the
ceremony (1020-62). Irving comments on the fact that gift-giving must
be public and ostentatious:

> Gifts must not only change hands but must be seen to change hands.
> Many watched ... as the wargear was brought into the hall; Beowulf
> had no need to feel ashamed of these gifts in front of all the warriors.
> ... [The poet] voices approval of Hrothgar's manly generosity, re-
> marking that no one can find fault with it (with the suggestion im-
> plicit that it is always open to public criticism).[20]

But the negative implication seems to us to be a little stronger than that:

'no man will ever find fault with them — not he that will speak truth according to what is right' (1048-9). This conspicuously suppresses the opposing thought: that someone might find fault — for example, some one of those fighting men before whom Beowulf had no need to be ashamed. The public nature of the ceremony is such as to tempt onlookers to envy and fault-finding as well as gratitude and admiration. The institution in this fashion demands control and watchfulness not only from heroic giver and receiver, but from all those lesser comrades who depend on them. The poet emphasizes this need a few lines later in his sententious conclusion to the gift-giving which is also a transition to the account of the doomed hall-joys of Hildeburh and Finn: 'Yet is discernment everywhere best, forethought of mind. Many a thing dear and loath he shall live to see who here in the days of trouble long makes use of the world.' (1059-62)

The ambivalence of gift-giving is stressed in the Finn and Freawaru episodes and, in a somewhat lower key, in the network of passages tracing the necklace, breast-armour, and standard from Wealhtheow and Heorogar through Beowulf and Hygd to Hygelac, who wore and lost them all, along with his life, 'when for pride he sought trouble, feud with the Frisians' (1201-14). Mauss observes that 'the theme of the fateful gift, the present or possession that turns into poison, is fundamental in Germanic folklore. The Rhine Gold is fatal to the man who wins it.' (*The Gift*, 62) Freawaru, and probably Hildeburh, are gifts who become poison; their very presence and situation generate anew the anxieties they are intended to alleviate. Irving draws from such entanglements the lesson that 'gifts are obvious symbols of human success and felicity, but they cannot govern the future, they cannot keep people alive or ensure that their expectations will always come true' (*Reading*, 143). This again seems to skew the message, which is not that gifts fail to govern the future, but that gift-giving governs the future only too well; it bears within itself the destructive possibilities that cancel its manifest function. The pattern of reversal, 'edwenden,' about which Irving has many good things to say, derives less from the general unreliability of life than from the excessive reliability of heroic institutions which sooner or later impose on men both sides of their character. The point to be made about 'edwenden' is that it is, emphatically, a pattern; a predictable structure dynamically at work beyond the consciousness of the men locked into it, and revealing itself to them only in their perpetually uneasy consciousness of 'wyrd,' the doom, what happens because life and the world are the way they are.

This uneasiness is nicely caught by Mauss, who describes how, in primitive societies, men in times of feasting and ceremony 'meet in a curious frame of mind with exaggerated fear and an equally exaggerated generosity,' because 'there is no middle path. There is either complete trust or mistrust,' therefore festival and warfare lie very close together. In 'setting up the will for peace against rash follies' of violence, tribesmen 'succeed in substituting alliance, gift and commerce for war, isolation and stagnation' (79-80). And in *Beowulf*, these substitutions retain their original contentiousness and danger in transformations that keep them alive as sleepers.

THE MEADHALL AND THE MONSTER

In Hrothgar's munificence the substitution has the same aggressive valence and may be understood to produce the same latent anxieties. There is another reason for this: consider, for example, the brief reference to the Franks plundering the Geat bodies after the death of Hygelac, and taking with them the vaunted neck-ring and armour given him by Beowulf (1212-14). Consider also the related reference to Hama, who apparently stole another neck-ring from Eormenric and 'got eternal favor' (1198-1201). Consider finally the more extensive speculation of Beowulf that the gift of Freawaru will lead to a situation in which the Heatho-Bards will rankle at the sight of the Danes wearing the 'gomelra lafe' of Ingeld's people (2032 ff) — that is, the booty taken in previous raids and redistributed by Hrothgar. These allusions remind us that the treasures Hrothgar hands out must come from somewhere; the poet refers only twice to human smithies. Hrothgar's gift-giving is a challenge full of latent strife because the other side of giving is taking. If the Danes seem to have few active enemies, Hrothgar's thirty-eight or so years of successful war must have produced a host of ill-wishers — those, for example, on whom the burden of building Heorot was laid, as well as those whose treasures he plundered: and maybe the building of Heorot is simply to be understood as the positive or honorific side of that dark coin.[21]

This notion suggests the appropriateness of introducing Ingeld and Grendel together with the building and doom of Heorot. The extent of the king's munificence and the hall's magnificence may also be the measure of how many enemies lurk — like Grendel — 'dreamum bedæled' and 'bealohydig' (721, 723), embers under ashes. And Grendel may himself be a caricature in which are gathered all those deprived and festering spirits, those wounded and angered souls, whose 'mod' is abstracted from the network of human creatures and social institutions containing it in both senses of that term – producing and domesticating the 'ellengæst,' allaying and reviving Grendelian rancour. Grendel taking his thirty thanes home is 'huðe hremig' (124), like a plundering warrior. As taking is the other side of giving, and contention the other side of generosity, so Grendel shadows the darker antecedents and consequences latent in Hrothgar's good works.[22] But this is not, we repeat, to be construed in terms of ethico-psychological categories, for example, 'unconscious pride,' to which Christianizing critics appeal when attributing the gilded rottenness in Denmark to our old stock, or to pagan *vanitas*. Nor is Hrothgar a Germanic version of the fisher king, though there are some structural similarities in his dilemma: the presence of an evil intrinsically connected to the 'land' – that is, the society – and therefore eradicable only by one who is an outsider, and who is singular or 'touched' in some magical or religious sense.[23] Hrothgar's good works are exemplary of the best in heroic society generally; what is good or bad in the poem is pan-Germanic. And the deep-structural ambivalence, the 'edwenden,' of hall-building, gift-giving, honour-seeking, and peace-weaving – with raid, plunder, slaughter, feud, vengeance, envy, resentment, and treachery finely woven into them – is presented as the practical basis which both supports and constrains the way men live, behave, act, choose, and think. With one possible exception,[24] Grendel does not appear as an allegorical projection of something specifically wrong with Hrothgar and the Danes. He and Heorot are causally linked crystallizations of the bad and good features of heroic institutions. If the defeat of Grendel does not spell the end of Danish troubles, the burning of Heorot does not end either the Scylding dynasty or the Danish people.

This aspect of Grendel's significance is persuasively brought out by Irving's descriptions of his human and social dimension:

> He is the rebellious exile, the *ymbsittend*, the neighbor who cannot be tamed, will not pay tribute, refuses to be brought within the frame of social order by force of arms or rule of law. (*Reading*, 93)

> Grendel seems representative at times of an evil and arrogant individualism that is wholly destructive in its effects on society and has some connection thematically with the feuds smoldering below the surface of the poem or with a figure like Heremod, type of the self-willed and wicked king. (111)

> If Grendel has had originally a human kind of strength like Cain's, it has now blurred and become almost unrecognizable; he is a disturb-

ingly alien creature who will no longer fit our familiar categories. But he is never totally unrecognizable. The poem succeeds in giving the figure of Grendel its memorable power precisely by keeping him flickering in that half world on the edge of the human, *manncynne fram,* far out away from mankind, and yet part of mankind. (*Introduction,* 48)

At once an 'ellorgast' and a 'mearcstapa,' he is not only arrogant, not only — as Kaske would have it — an embodiment of 'purely malicious violence.'[25] He is a joyless creature ('wonsæli wer,' 105) who endured distress ('þrage geþolode,' 87) when he heard the hall-joys; a despairing walker-alone ('angengea,' 165) forbidden to touch or receive treasure; one deprived of joy ('dreamum bedæled,' 721)[26] who 'Godes yrre bær' (711) — an odd phrase, suggesting that Grendel brought to others the divine wrath he felt (perhaps as his own) and under which he suffered. Cain's crime and exile followed his contentious effort to please his lord with gifts, and the lord's rejection of this effort. Grendel is thus no purely malicious outsider but an exile from the 'cynn' of man to which his ancestors belonged. His hatred springs from the pain of the have-not, the violent knocker at the door who wants to return and possess or destroy the forbidden hall-joys that torment him.

In these brief ethical references to his underlying helplessness and fatedness, the poet links hatred, anger, and violence in a general way to a deep human fear — the dread of losing existence, freedom, security, favour, and companionship. The structural 'edwenden' of heroic institutions continually jeopardizes these necessities of life in the process of sustaining them. Like Grendel, who is doomed to bear Cain's mark and God's anger, the institutions seem to have the spirit of kinstrife woven into them. Yet, unlike Grendel, they do not make themselves known. Or rather, they make themselves known only as Grendel (and his mother). Grendel serves as a kind of decoy, drawing the fear of the Danes and the wrath of the hero toward himself. And the poet shows the significance of this diversionary function by changing the characterization of Grendel as the poem proceeds. We now turn to explore these changes.

Irving's interpretation offers an approach to the changes, but in vague germinal form which remains undeveloped. Along with other critics, he remarks on Grendel's dull-wittedness, his misplaced expectations, and the self-destructive 'combination of passionate juggernaut will and dimmed intellect' which make him seem 'as much a blind victim of fate as an agent of it.' (*Reading,* 111) He shows how the poet presents Grendel's defeat in a comic and derisive light, and concludes that 'to expose the essential incongruity of Grendel, half bogey and half outlaw, by bringing him into the sunlit world of laughter is a powerful exorcism, perhaps the most powerful of all. The devil cannot endure to be mocked.' (111) But he fails to distinguish this narrative mode of helplessness from the deeper helplessness described above, and he misses the real point of the comic exorcism, which is that it diverts attention from more proximate and permanent dangers. The story of Grendel is like those narrative myths which, in primitive and traditional societies, serve to block further explanations by giving definite answers that set the curious or anxious mind at rest — and serve often to distract it from the underlying insoluble sources of social stress.

The initial helplessness Grendel externalizes is that of an embittered 'wræcca,' a victim of ancient kinstrife and rebellion against a munificent lord; an exiled soul doomed to privation, isolation, and violence as a way of life, roused to envious rage by the presence of all he desires but cannot share. After being introduced in momentary conjunction with Heorot and Ingeld, he is extricated from that complex and given his own alien being. Like a scapegoat, he bears the mark of Cain beyond the border into the non-human world. But his Old Testament genealogy keeps his human meaning before us and suggests how Irving's appeal to Grendel's more universal significance is to be understood:[27] as an evil transcending this or any individual monster, sown in the world with the generation of the first human family, and therefore never to be finally purged by the heroic solution of single encounter. Through line 189, Grendel retains this universal significance as an enemy of mankind, reflecting the kind of spiritual and psychological evil connected with transgressions against the social order and customs of the Danes (150 ff). Grendel is psychologically most powerful when he possesses the hall and its occupants — when his assaults communicate his own despair to his victims who, in their helplessness, turn to heathen sacrifices and pray for deliverance from the 'gastbona.'

What happens to Grendel after Beowulf arrives is that his humanity becomes increasingly physical and social. While the introduction of his eerie habitat adds strangeness to his being, intensifies his alien quality, by line 1258 he has become a member of a truncated kingroup. Just as Grendel had materialized from the Heorot-Ingeld complex, so his mother appears in close connection with Wealhtheow's uneasy references to her sons' future, following the scop's song of Hildeburh. This introduces a new set of themes as Grendel's 'mother, woman, and monster wife' emerges from nowhere to become his nuclear family and jural avenger. Hrothgar now explains (1345 ff) that there were two such 'mearcstapan,' both human in form, and when Beowulf penetrates the depths of the mere, that alien place suddenly changes into a mirror image of the human hall and hearth. Thus as Grendel and his mother become stranger and more monstrous to the other characters in the poem, the evil they embody appears to us increasingly to reflect locally specific problems inherent in Germanic society: problems of feud and vengeance; the recurrent outbreak of violent disorder — the power, in Kaske's terms, 'of even defeated violence to spawn further violence'; and the problems of succession and perpetuation implied by the fact that Grendel and his 'aglæcwif' are the last survivors of their particular branch of Cain's brood. Hildeburh and Grendel's wife represent opposing extremes: the former a passive political object, the latter a usurper of the male avenger's role. Between these extremes, Wealhtheow feels the pressures and dilemma of the woman's role as wife and mother, feels hovering over her perhaps the spectre of the same ultimate doom that frustrates the Grendel dynasty. But the actual assault on the hall by Grendel's wife has the effect of diverting everyone to an episode which, however grim its onset, falls clearly within the consoling category of adventures for the invincible hero.

By conveniently locating and distancing these problems in the hateful outsiders, the poet prepares them for easy disposal by Beowulf. Thus poet and hero co-operate in exorcising and destroying the enemies, and in bringing on another happy ending. Or so it appears to the Danes, for we see something different, namely, that the embodiment of evil in monsters diverts the characters from the true intra-psychic and -social sources of more abiding trouble. As a condensed and melodramatic version of the trouble, the monstrous manifestation followed by the happy ending provides the Danes with a deceptively skewed exemplum of evil and its conquest. The poet consistently distinguishes the messages received by his characters from those received by us, never more than when his characters are moralizing.[28] Hrothgar's sermon provides a beautiful example of this. After receiving from Beowulf the hilt of the giant sword, the old king praises his wisdom as well as his strength, foreseeing a successful career for him as leader of the Geats — if he will learn by the example of Heremod to keep up his guard against 'unsnyttru' and 'oferhygd.' Heremod's career in its beginning was similar to Hrothgar's: God gave him power and strength, set him up over all men, but, unlike Hrothgar, Heremod neglected to 'give rings to the Danes for glory.' What follows develops the contrast. God gives wisdom, land, and

earlship to mankind, makes the kingdoms of the world so subject to a
man of illustrious family

> þæt he his selfa ne mæg
> his unsnyttrum   ende geþencean.
> Wunað he on wiste;   no hine wiht dweleð
> adl ne yldo,   ne him inwitsorh
> on sefa(n) sweorceð,   ne gesacu ohwær
> ecghete eoweð,   ac him eal worold
> wendeð on willan: he þæt wyrse ne con — ,
> oð þæt him on innan   oferhygda dæl
> weaxeð ond wridað;   þonne se weard swefeð,
> sawele hyrde;   bið se slæp to fæst,
> bisgum gebunden,   bona swiðe neah,
> se þe of flanbogan   fyrenum sceoteð.
> þonne bið on hreþre   under helm drepen
> biteran stræle   — him bebeorgan ne con — ,
> wom wundorbebodum   wergan gastes;
> þinceð him to lytel,   þæt he lange heold,
> gytsað gromhydig,   nallas on gylp seleð
> fætte beagas,   ond he þa forðgesceaft
> forgyteð ond forgymeð,   þæs þe him ær God sealde,
> wuldres Waldend,   weorðmynda dæl.   (1733-52)

... that in his unwisdom he may not himself have mind of his end.
He lives in plenty; illness and age in no way grieve him, neither does
dread care darken his heart, nor does enmity bare sword-hate, for the
whole world turns to his will — he knows nothing worse — until his
portion of pride increases and flourishes within him; then the watcher
sleeps, the soul's guardian; that sleep is too sound, bound in its own
cares, and the slayer most near whose bow shoots treacherously. Then
is he hit in the heart, beneath his armor, with the bitter arrow — he
cannot protect himself — with the crooked dark commands of the
accursed spirit. What he has long held seems to him too little, angry-
hearted he covets, no plated rings does he give in men's honor, and
then he forgets and regards not his destiny because of what God, Wielder of Heaven, has given him before, his portion of glories. (30-1)

It seems unlikely that Hrothgar is thinking of Grendel. Grendel's body
is out there somewhere, dead; his head is on display in the hall. 'The ac-

cursed spirit' is probably the devil whose ambush was set up by his soul-Quisling, the pride that makes a conquering ruler covetous and niggardly. The poet's language, however, ought to remind us of Grendel chiefly because of the image of sleep. The victims of Grendel and his mother were all men who fell asleep in the hall after feasting, celebrating, and drinking. There are some nine references to the unhappy hall-sleepers,[29] a more general reference to man's soul which must seek 'the place where, after its feasting, one's body will sleep fast in its death-bed' (1008), and two references to Beowulf's watchful waiting (660 and 1268). These sleepers and wakers do not enact an allegory of pride and alertness in the sense defined by the example of Heremod. On the contrary, the sleepers are all beneficiaries of Heremod's implied counter-example, Hrothgar himself. Their sleep is the consequence of his careful liberality, a consequence of golden Heorot. The good king gives them their 'dream,' and therefore the evil monster takes their lives.

The institutional double bind is apparent in the way the two messages cut athwart each other: Heremod dramatizes the message, 'if you try to keep it, you lose,' while the latent message is, 'if you share it, you lose.' The Grendelian spirit stands behind each act of giving in two ways. 1/ It is neutralized in that the taking which aroused that spirit, or which depends on it, is placated by the act of giving what has been taken. The more you give, the more you ought to be able to neutralize the effect of the prideful spirit within you and within those to whom you give. Yet, 2/ the more you give, the more you arouse contention by your conspicuous success and wealth, by the charity that threatens to wound and the riches tempting to greed. Furthermore, the neutralization in 1 is actively centred in the most important of social functions, feasting in the mead-hall. The purposes of feasting are to renew solidarity and tighten social bonds; to give treasure or gifts; to bestow praise and honour; to pledge help or vengeance; to define status and value or impose one's charismatic presence on others; and to commemorate past deeds and heroes, often by way of celebrating a more recent triumph. As the poem reveals in more than one place, feasting and beer-drinking may bring on shame, envy, and strife. But its manifest function in *Beowulf* is to heighten the sense of group security. Its latent disfunction is therefore that it may lull the members of the warband into the sleep of false security. They may look in the wrong places for the sources of trouble. The rhythm of fighting and feasting may produce the false sense of the happy ending. At the same time, the various hall-scenes also suggest the lurking uneasiness which qualifies the notion that feasting merely lulls warriors to sleep.

We may also feel in those scenes, as a desperate undercurrent, the insistence that the hall-celebration should be compact of 'dream' — somewhat like keeping a bad party going by insisting that one is really having a good time, and proving it by drinking oneself to sleep.

Whether the tension is reduced because the feasters believe they are in a safe place, or exacerbated because they are never sure it is safe, the sleep that invites Grendel is certainly not the ethical sleep exemplified by Heremod. As individual figures, both Grendel and Heremod are distractions who prompt the Danes to locate the source of their trouble in corrupt forms of consciousness in bad men and monsters. The self-destructive behaviour of the outsiders conceals from the Danes what it reveals to us, the potentially destructive aspects of heroic institutions even at their best.

The continuation of Hrothgar's sermon reveals a mounting uncertainty in his own mind. He exhorts Beowulf to keep himself from Heremod's wickedness but then goes on to itemize other dangers not ascribable to ethical failure, and he concludes with a vague, perhaps puzzled, reference to his own predicament. Evil, he begins, befalls the evil man:

Hit on endestæf   eft gelimpeð,
þæt se lichoma   læne gedreoseð,
fæge gefealleð;   fehð oþer to,
se þe unmurnlice   madmas dæleþ,
eorles ærgestreon,   egesan ne gymeð.
Bebeorh þe ðone bealonið,   Beowulf leofa,
secg betsta,   ond þe þæt selre geceos,
ece rædas;   oferhyda ne gym,
mære cempa!   Nu is þines mægnes blæd
ane hwile;   eft sona bið,
þæt þec adl oððe ecg   eafoþes getwæfeð,
oððe fyres feng,   oððe flodes wylm,
oððe gripe meces,   oððe gares fliht,
oððe atol yldo;   oððe eagena bearhtm
forsiteð ond forsworceð;   semninga bið,
þæt ðec, dryhtguma,   deað oferswyðeð.
  Swa ic Hring-Dena   hund missera
weold under wolcnum   ond hig wigge beleac
manigum mægþa   geond þysne middangeard,
æscum ond ecgum,   þæt ic me ænigne
under swegles begong   gesacan ne tealde.

Hwæt, me þæs on eþle   edwenden cwom,
gyrn æfter gomene,   seoþðan Grendel wearð,
ealdgewinna,   ingenga min;
ic þære socne   singales wæg
modceare micle.   (1753-78)

In the end it happens in turn that the loaned body weakens, falls doomed; another takes the earl's ancient treasure, one who recklessly gives precious gifts, does not fearfully guard them.

Keep yourself against that wickedness, beloved Beowulf, best of men, and choose better — eternal gains. Have no care for pride, great warrior. Now for a time there is glory in your might: yet soon it shall be that sickness or sword will diminish your strength, or fire's fangs, or flood's surge, or sword's swing, or spear's flight, or appalling age; brightness of eyes will fail and grow dark; then it shall be that death will overcome you, warrior.

Thus I ruled the Ring-Danes for a hundred half-years under the skies, and protected them in war with spear and sword against many nations over middle-earth, so that I counted no one as my adversary underneath the sky's expanse. Well, disproof of that came to me in my own land, grief after my joys, when Grendel, ancient adversary, came to invade my home. Great sorrow of heart I have always suffered for his persecution. (31)

Perhaps God sent Grendel because Hrothgar dropped his guard, was too sure of himself, swallowed a drop from the cup that undid Heremod. At any rate, the lesson has been learned, the Almighty has supplied a saviour, and for this happy ending there will be 'joy of the glad feast' and many 'treasures will be shared when morning comes.' (1782-4)

The passage incidentally suggests how the reckless giver began as a taker, and reinforces with ethical justification the first of the two phases of the good ruler's career. But when he mentions how a similar, if less extreme, plague visited the good ruler himself, he falters and offers Beowulf a brief aphorism which, while ethical in tone, is diffuse and cryptic in meaning. For ethical explanation is irrelevant. What happened to him happened because he did everything he was supposed to do. And this problem, this irrelevance, will pursue the hero into part II.

HOARD AND HERO

Heroic generosity demands reciprocity — demands it in two senses: as
the repayment in loyalty and service through which munificence attains
its objective of strong group solidarity, and as a contentious response to
the challenge inherent in giving. In his sermon, Hrothgar takes note of the
practical dimension of gift-giving and alertness, viewing them in ethical
perspective. But a good king may fail as well as a Heremod, and the consequences of his failure for his people may be as grave, or even graver.
The ethical focus of Hrothgar's sermon is quite irrelevant to part II of
Beowulf and in this fact lies the most complex and moving aspect of the
last part. Nor is it enough merely to say that in part II the good king
somehow fails. Rather, he fails precisely because he is so good a king.
Thus we return to Halverson's insight: 'It is not Beowulf's pride that
brings about the ultimate catastrophe, but precisely his heroism.' Once
again, if this reintroduces 'ethical' issues it does so at a level beyond that
of the sphere of conscious choice and action to which ethical analysis
normally applies.

Beowulf is the best of men in the poem, Hrothgar the second best.
Hrothgar and Beowulf have both been seen as figures of the good king,
but the ideal includes Hrothgar more completely than Beowulf. Beowulf
in part II fuses two different roles, hero and king, yet this is only one reason why he is atypical. Readers have always felt this atypicality, and
though the analogies to Christ are ludicrous they suggest one aspect of
the kind of feeling Beowulf inspires. Irving speaks of 'that vital extra
margin of power which distinguishes the hero as individual and unique
force from the hero as representative man,' and of 'that special blend of
wild daring, restless strength, alert intelligence, luck, and divine favor
that makes a hero.' (*Reading*, 121) But the poem suggests even more
than that: a kind of *mana* attaches to this hero, a misty and superstition-
ridden aura of the uncanny, the 'unheimlich.'

This comes through in the references to his special relation to the
ocean, the watery depths, and water-monsters.[30] It comes through also
in the folktale of the bear-son hovering in the background and recalled
by his name (Bee-wolf), by the narrative elements of the two Grendel
adventures, and by the reference to his deviance as a youth (2183 ff). In
the early parts of the poem his presence gives off a power edged with
menace. Under his self-possessed and well-minded demeanour lives the
'mod' for terrible violence evident in the tone and substance of his first
address to Hrothgar and in his reply to Unferth. We have seen Hrothgar's

verbal efforts to control this power and keep the hero's offer of help within the limits of reciprocity.

In the fight with Grendel his eagerness for battle and his tremendous energy burst forth with such fury as to make the two enemies momentarily indistinguishable. Both equally threaten Heorot: 'Yrre wæron begen, / reðe renweardas. Reced hlynsode,' so that it was a wonder the wine-hall did not fall to the ground (769-72). Grendel's grasp affixed to the wall is a dark admonitory image of the hero's handgrip. Both are walkers-alone and both are outsiders, Beowulf even more than Grendel.[3] If only as a cancelled possibility, the fury of Grendel smokes the contours of the hero's bright outline. When the scop who praises his exploit recalls the glory of Sigemund and the infamy of Heremod, his account of the latter (901-15) resonates with an odd tone, somewhere between a *caveat* ('Beware, Beowulf, strength and courage are not enough') and an exhortation ('Please, Beowulf, strength and courage are not enough'). However domesticated and benign the bear-son has become, his presence in the hall adds a touch of uncertainty to the general uneasiness communicated by the poet in his account of the gift-giving ceremony.

The edginess about Beowulf is partly a function of the situation: the helpless and humiliated Danes are forced to place themselves in the hands and in the debt of an outsider. In order to help themselves trust him they have to try to persuade him to be good. The outsider is necessary because the evil that ravages the Danes is partly generated by their own social structure. The meadhall attracts hero and monster together. Thus the hero is not only limited in his role: he can only provide a temporary cure by ridding the Danes of this particular manifestation of their problem. He is also a potential threat who may evoke Grendelian feelings in others if not in himself. In his final speech, Hrothgar is still working on him, trying not only to bind him as a potential ally but also to neutralize the possible threat of a Geat attack. Hence the curious reference — the first and only one in the poem — to the 'sacu' and 'inwitniðas' which the Danes and Geats had practised on each other in the past (1856 ff), and his concluding words which promise a continuing supply of gifts, and appeal to the blameless character of the Geats in indirect exhortation (1859-65). That this carefulness coexists with Hrothgar's deep and fatherly affection for Beowulf (1870-6) points not only to the ambivalence inherent in the role of alien hero but also to Beowulf's 'unheimlich' charismatic power.

Beowulf's strangeness attaches to his being, not to his consciousness, which is singular in a more familiar manner: he is ethically the best of all possible men. In part II this combination, as we suggested, becomes the source of failure. Two reasons for this are anticipated in the contrasting image of Scyld which opens the poem: 1/ A son was born to Scyld, 'a young boy in his house, whom God sent to comfort the people: He had seen the sore need they had suffered during the long time they lacked a king.' (12-16) 2/ While still young, a man should give gifts 'to make sure that later in life beloved companions will stand by him, that people will serve him when war comes.' (22-4) It seems only a logical consequence of his uniqueness that Beowulf leaves no heir (2730-2); his brief reference to that fact adds resonance to his earlier comments on Hrethel and the father of the hanged man (2430 ff), and to his concluding remark about Hrethel: 'To his sons he left — as a happy man does — his land and his town when he went from life.' (2470-1)

Beowulf's relation to his cowardly retainers, and his motives for attacking the dragon by himself, raise further questions. Institutional contradictions are most strongly felt in these passages. In their reflective and past-minded mood, the poet and Beowulf together express inconsistent sentiments about the coming encounter. The poet first speaks in his own voice, and Beowulf later amplifies the same sentiments and subjects in his long soliloquy. The effect of this peculiar reiteration is to intensify the sense of inevitable doom, to put it off by reviving the past in order to prepare for the doom, and to set the dragon fight in an extraordinarily complex tissue of past and future feuds, shifting attitudes and alliances, and social dilemmas (2324-509). Beowulf's consequent decision to charge the dragon single-handed comes almost as a relief.

The poet first tells us that Beowulf was confident of winning, and so 'scorned to seek the far-flier with a troop, a large army.' (2345 ff) At line 2419b, however, we are told that 'his mind was mournful, restless and ripe for death' — as if, having 'survived every combat, every dangerous battle' (2397-8), he had fought and lived long enough. Beowulf himself communicates this feeling in a sympathetic remark about Ongentheow's death: 'his hand remembered feuds enough, did not withstand the life-blow.' (2488b-9) But remembering his past deeds on behalf of Hygelac and Hrothgar seems to give him new spirit. He is tempted to replay his conquest of Grendel and, though the dragon's fiery blast prohibits hand-to-hand combat, he will at least engage the foe in single encounter; therefore he orders his retainers not to help him (2512-37). But when Beowulf is pressed, Wiglaf urges them to help their king, ignoring his order (2633-60), and rushing to the barrow himself delivers the first blow that makes the dragon's fire subside (2700 ff). Afterwards, he and the poet blame the retainers for their disloyalty and cowardice (2846b-9 and 2864-91), but at line 3077 Wiglaf articulates the nearest thing in the poem to a criticism of the hero:

> 'Oft sceall eorl monig   anes willan
> wræc adreogan,   swa us geworden is.
> Ne meahton we gelæran   leofne þeoden,
> rices hyrde   ræd ænigne,
> þæt he ne grette   goldweard þone,
> lete hyne licgean,   þær he longe wæs,
> wicum wunian   oð woruldende.

Often many a man must suffer distress for the will of one man, as has happened to us. We might by no counsel persuade our dear prince, keeper of the kingdom, not to approach the gold-guardian, let him lie where he long was, live in his dwelling to the world's end.   (53)

This tends retrospectively to accentuate the heroic self-concern of such remarks as the following, addressed by Beowulf to his retainers: 'This is not your venture, nor is it right for any man except me alone that he should spend his strength against the monster, do this man's deed. By my courage I shall get gold, or war will take your king, dire life-evil.' (2532b-7) In the end, however, the heroic assertion ('ne gemet mannes, nefn(e) min anes') is frustrated by Wiglaf's 'eorlscype,' just as his request to Wiglaf to distribute the treasure (2799-801) is frustrated. The request is itself tonally weighted with the weariness of being a ruler, the ripeness for death:

> Nu ic on maðma hord   mine bebohte
> frode feorhlege,   fremmað gena
> leoda þearfe;   ne mæg ic her leng wesan.

Now that I have bought the hoard of treasures with my old life, you attend to the people's needs hereafter: I can be here no longer.   (49)

With this brief glance toward 'leoda þearfe' — the phrase is vague and generalized, the sentiment remote — he turns away from the cares of kingship to speak with more buoyant energy of his barrow (2801-8). His final words are not about the grim future of his 'leode' — he has shifted that responsibility to Wiglaf — but about the end of his own line; he and his kinsman are the last of the Wægmundings (2813-16).

The cumulative effect of these passages is to stress the conflict, identified by Halverson, between 'heroic individualism' and the code of loyalty and reciprocity which lead to 'closer social ties and greater common effort.'[32] Halverson's admirable account of this dilemma prompts us to add that the poet reveals it not only in the relations between Beowulf and his retainers but also within Beowulf himself: the justifiable self-concern of the hero is shown not to square with political concerns of the ruler. In the collapse or fusion of the two roles, the second gives way to the first. The king is old and weary of life, but the hero fulfils his long career by dying in glory. Beowulf embarrows himself, and the Geats along with him (2804).[33] The future offers no consolations but those provided by the past. His death is made easier by the sight of the ancient 'laf' and by the memory of his long career. His mind dwells on these, turns inward and backward, from the Geats to his immediate kinsmen and from their continuing life-needs — 'þearfe' — to his memorial. Halverson observes that 'in an altogether personalistic era, the center of order is conceivable only as a person. One cannot yet say, "The king is dead, long live the king," but only "Beowulf is dead — what will happen now? "' (607) One *can* say, however, 'the king is dead, long live the hero,' and this seems closer to the sentiments expressed by Beowulf.

Halverson finds Wiglaf's criticism of Beowulf just, since the king's death means 'the disintegration of the Geatish nation. ... The king has greater responsibility than the warrior.' (607) This is an important insight, yet there may be more to Beowulf's dilemma than the conflict in values generated by the appearance of the dragon, and more than the general 'excess of individualism' from which the Dark Ages suffered. The problem raised by particularistic conceptions of socio-political roles — king, hero, vassal — is one thing. The problem raised by conflicting roles and values — between king and hero, individualism and common effort — is another. There is only a vague historical similarity between Beowulf's dilemma and that of such powerful men as 'Clovis, Offa, Penda, Charlemagne, Alfred,' whose 'kingdoms rise, flourish briefly, and decline with the deaths of their creators.' (607) After all, the Danes outlast Hrothgar, and in the poem the Swedes outlast Ongentheow. We know about the Danes and the Swedes. But who has heard of the Geats? Klaeber's summary of the evidence shows how scanty and confused it is.[34] Outside of *Beowulf* there are only a few scattered Scandinavian references to them. If we put this together with his remarks that Beowulf 'is a solitary figure in life,' that 'he dies without leaving any children,'[35] and that he does not 'play any real part in the important events of his time,' and if we add to this the 'curious fact that Beowulf himself is never mentioned in the surviving Germanic heroic literature of Scandinavia and the continent,'[36] Beowulf's dilemma may take on a complexion more specific than that which can be explained by the particularism of the Dark Ages.

That is, his dilemma may owe less to 'an excess of individualism' than to 'an excess of Beowulf.' Consider, in addition to his childlessness, the cowardice of his retainers, noted by the poet as well as by Wiglaf. Consider also the instant demoralization reflected by the Geatish messenger and woman. Our account of the effects of Hrothgar's liberality on his sleeping thanes suggests to us that the failure of Beowulf's retainers may be intended to reflect on his leadership as well as their cowardice. There is only one passage in the poem which supports this hypothesis, but it seems to us to be significant. It is Beowulf's dying *apologia* (2736-43), which Halverson cites to show that Beowulf is satisfied that 'he has lived up to the code, protecting his people, true to his oaths, faithful to his kinsmen,' so that 'he can die content' because he has honoured 'the traditional contractual obligations.' (606) But Halverson neither quotes the immediately preceding lines (2733b-6a), nor comments on their implications. Beowulf says that he 'heold' the Geats fifty winters, that no neighbouring kings 'dared approach me with swords, threaten me with fears. In my land I awaited what fate brought me, held my own well, sought no treacherous quarrels.' Therefore God 'need not blame me for the slaughter of kinsmen when life goes from my body.' (48) Earlier, the poet had told us that Beowulf had come through many battles after purging Heorot but his subsequent remarks suggest that most of these occurred in the early part of his reign, ending with the victory over Onela (2349b-400). Beowulf himself confirms this impression in lines 2511-15.

From these clues we draw the implication that his unparalleled successes produced the kind of détente futilely sought by Hrothgar in building Heorot. Beowulf was the Heorot of the Geats. What he fashioned and gave with such generosity was himself. And in so doing, he unwittingly but unavoidably took something too: his unique and charismatic being made reciprocity impossible — worse, it made reciprocity unnecessary. Giving too much, he therefore gave too little. The role of hero, intensified by Beowulf's uncanny singularity, contains in its structure the same pattern of 'edwenden' as the other heroic institutions. In effect, he absorbed so much 'ellen' from the surrounding atmosphere that too little was left to nourish his people. He created something like a power or energy vacuum, de-tensing his warband in a world where tension, alertness, and uneasiness are basic to survival. Like Hrothgar's, his success turned warriors into sleepers. Hence the behaviour of his retainers and the choric sense of helplessness expressed by the messenger and the figure of the wailing woman. In the vast temporal perspective of the second part of the poem, Beowulf's fifty years as king — one for each foot of dragon-length — pass like a whisper, collapsing between the past and future Swedish raids,[37] and serving mainly to suggest the double bind that confronts the great hero as ruler: if by his excellence he holds fearful aggressors in abeyance, keeps raid and feud to a minimum, he erodes the Geat warrior ethos; if, on the other hand, he wages continual warfare every trophy he wins creates new enemies and lust for vengeance; in both cases the others, the 'ymbsittend,' 'painfully endure hardship for a time' (86-7), and when he dies his people become losers. The hero becomes the only winner, the only 'laf' bequeathed by his people to the world.

Among the Geats, all that remained of the will to fight ('wig') was concentrated in his kinsman, appropriately named Wiglaf. And even this fact reflects indirectly on the problem, for Wiglaf's sword and courage are pointedly derived from his father, and connected with Weohstan's participation in the anti-Geat campaign of Onela. Weohstan's change of allegiance is like Hrethel's insoluble wergeld dilemma: these, together with the analogy of the father whose son is hanged, suggest the increasing complexity and confusion, the imminent breakdown, produced by institutional 'edwenden.' The poet ironically and pointedly notes Onela's politically inspired violation of feuding customs (2611 ff). He suggests a general crisis in which the wider bonds of the warband are weakening, so that only political expediency or the more primitive and intuitive bonds of real blood relationship keep men together (cf. 2600-1). Thus only another Wægmunding comes to Beowulf's aid.

This hypothesis differs from Halverson's in suggesting that the disintegration of the Geats is a consequence of Beowulf's total career, and not merely the consequence of his decision to meet the dragon in single encounter. Our interpretation might be metaphorically focused by means of two phrases which the poet applies to Beowulf, and which seem in our opinion to suggest certain points of resemblance between Beowulf and the dragon. At line 2422 the poet tells us that the fate was very close which should come to seek Beowulf's 'sawle hord'; and at line 2791 f, when Wiglaf returns to attend the dying king, a 'wordes ord' broke through Beowulf's 'breosthord.'[38] Like the dragon, the hero is a hoarder. His soul's hoard consists of the riches of heroism, the hero's power and charisma, his ability to hold a warband together by his prowess, generosity, courage, and shining example. Theoretically, this should communicate itself to his people and quicken all their solidary institutions. But actually his singular powers are not communicable to ordinary men; failing to provide his retainers with the need (and therefore ability) to reciprocate, his 'eacen' spirit produces an enervating imbalance in the social bonds that hold the Geats together.

Strange resonances bind the two old hoarders together even as they differentiate them. Each is a solitary 'weard,' an old guardian wise in winters (2209, 2277), Beowulf an 'eþelweard,' 'folces weard,' and 'þeodcyning' (2210, 2513, 2694), the dragon a 'hordweard' (e.g. 2293) and 'þeodsceaða' (2688). Another 'hordweard,' Hrothgar (1047), predicts that Beowulf will become a good 'hordweard' (1852) of the Geat treasure. At line 2273 f the dragon is described as a 'nacod' night-flier 'fyre befangen.' At line 2585 Beowulf is failed by his war blade, 'nacod æt niðe,' and as a result he who before had 'folce weold' was 'fyre befongen.' (2595) We read the 'nacod' at 2273 metaphorically as 'unsheathed.' The dragon takes the air at night and burns when he flies, his barrow is his hall, his 'hordwynn' (2270) his hall-joy. Unlike Grendel, he is not described as a predator but remains sheathed (and sleeping) until disturbed in his barrow, at which point he becomes hot and fierce-hearted, and exults in the thought of war, an enemy of living men.[39] Beowulf too was like this, he awaited what fate brought him and sought no treacherous quarrels (2736 ff); his sword was 'nacod æt niðe,' unsheathed in response to hostility but not otherwise. In death the two lie side by side, and after death a curious interchange is suggested: the dragon is pushed into the watery depths in which Beowulf had been so much at home — his element — and Beowulf, now a barrow-dweller, is consumed by the dragon's element.

Why these correspondences, which suggest that the dragon may in some manner be the double as well as the antithesis of the hero? Beyond their connection with hoarding, we have no answer. We might speculate, however, that it has something to do with the theme of oblivion. The dragon is an ancient 'uhtsceaða' (2271), which could mean 'an enemy of the dawn' (as well as the more usual translation, 'enemy at dawn'): he presides over the 'laf' of dead societies, keeps them unused and forgotten in darkness. As Irving has suggested,[40] his hoard contains objects which embody the customs and institutions of heroic society: cups, rings, helmets, and a gold standard (2760b-9a), synecdoches of hall-joys, honour and reciprocity, protection and attack. The symbolic value that glints from the hoard-objects suggests those activities whose 'edwenden' leads inevitably toward the kind of confusion and breakdown stressed throughout part II. When the dragon is aroused, his rage 'is directed unselectively against ... whatever lives. He obliterates men, halls and all.'[41] He presides over and sustains the oblivion of that which has been obliterated. No names, no famous heroes, are connected to his hoarded 'laf.' The dragon's hoard is collective, whereas Beowulf's is singular.

It may be that the dragon himself, emerging from that welter of institutional confusions, condenses them into his mythic and monstrous form, making them ripe for heroic disposal. He may be linked to the fate that settles down on old societies. The oblivion and fate Beowulf fights might then be that which threatens his own people. But his battle is necessarily in vain, since the fate of the Geats emerges as much from his own breast-hoard as from the dragon's barrow. His own riches are blessed/cursed no less than those guarded by the dragon. Because the dragon kills Beowulf, the Geats will no longer be able to survive as a people; the treasure will not be recirculated. Because Beowulf kills the dragon, the Geats will escape oblivion. But they will be remembered only for Beowulf. His glory is the best and only 'laf' they bestow on the future; theirs is consumed in his; along with the treasure, their future lies in his barrow. Thus in the special sense defined by the meanings of this poem, the haunting refrain of *Deor* permeates the desolate world of the Geats: 'þæs ofereode; þisses swa mæg.'

CODA: THE *BEOWULF* POET AND THE BARROW

There are three barrows in *Beowulf*. The dragon's is one. The hero's is the second. The poem is the third. The dragon is a doom-sitter, his barrow oblivion, his hoard the golden and rusting artifacts of dead societies. The poet's time-calipers span a thousand years in part II, and in this perspective the doom of whole peoples and ways of life is the sad and central theme. It may seem dry, academic, and anachronistic to speak of this as an institutional doom, but from another standpoint that only increases the sadness. Looking back, we see that men are trapped by the order they have made. The world of human artifice includes not only swords, cups, standards, and halls, but also kingroup and *comitatus*, good and evil, gift-giving and honour-seeking, marriage, raid, and feud, and such roles as hero, king, and monster. The 'edwenden,' the double bind, produced by the complex interaction of these structures and processes is bewildering in appearance but sure in its doom.

The splendid things men do — their conscious acts of heroic will, endurance, and generosity — they do in the setting of this doom, and against its drift, yet ultimately, unwittingly, in its behalf. Since their social order is not the product of conscious artifice, but is the nonconscious or 'crescive' work of generations of culture, men experience it as part of the reality which appears to them to be given, grim, and unalterable. They can only, as Hrothgar does, give ethical counsel and try to act according to the norms and values prized by heroic consciousness. Yet these very acts and norms and values and consciousness have the doom woven into them and bring it on. Our modern sadness is not quite that of the early English poet: he does not speak of institutions as if they were 'artifacts' of human culture transposed into reality. For him they are not the Frankenstein's monsters that our institutions have seemed to become during the last three or four centuries. And yet — as we hope we have demonstrated — he clearly locates the doom in the processes of social order and just as clearly shows that his characters are baffled by this, that their institutions conspire to divert their attention by misleading symptoms and solutions. It is the poet who presents us with an old-time world in which the institutional doom is no less apparent and no less real than the doomed monsters.

The movement from part I to part II which Irving has so well described[42] strongly suggests the working of this pattern of 'edwenden.' To centre attention on Hrothgar, Heorot, Beowulf, and the monsters is to stress human skill and control, the excellence of what men do and make, their ultimate conquest over the forces of evil. The treatment in part I is, figuratively, spatial: the monsters are 'out there,' the Finn episode is not only long ago but also elsewhere, and Heremod is so exemplary as to be timeless. Except for occasional ominous asides, most evils are of the past, which is itself consoling, but they are present in the poem as analogies or antitheses visualized in some spatial or quasi-logical relation to the bright centre of Danish life. The effect of the transitional section — from the end of Hrothgar's sermon to the beginning of part II (1789b-2199) — is to intensify foreboding by orienting us toward the future. The poem looks ahead in time at threatening possibilities in existing arrangements: the possibility of enmity between Geats and Danes, Hrothgar's premonition that he will not see Beowulf again, the long account of the Danes and Heatho-Bards which occupies nearly a third of

Beowulf's report to Hygelac. His final touching words to Hygelac ('ic lyt hafo / heafodmaga nefne, Hygelac, ðec,' 2150b-1) anticipate a cluster of themes in part II: his childlessness and solitary nature, the desolate and sparsely inhabited landscape, the death of old men, loss of sons, and killing of kinsmen.[43]

In part II these themes are caught up in the dense interweaving of various Geat feuds which cover over two generations and which — through the poet's repetition, amplification, narrative dislocation, and vivid description — produce the image of an embattled society on the edge of chaos. It is as if the lurking dangers swept under the rug of Heorot had broken loose in Geatland to envelop Beowulf's people. The predicament is generalized by the arrival of the dragon, and the dramatic increase in the poem's time scale: the doom threatens not only the Geats but all societies founded on the values and accomplishments which Beowulf and the dragon, in their different ways, hoard. That this doom is the product and not merely the fate of heroic society has been shown by Irving in the one passage in which he clearly defines the accountability of heroic institutions, his study of the battle of Ravenswood.

Irving notes there that 'as the kind of heroic achievement that *Beowulf* represents nears its end in Beowulf's own death, the kind of self-destructiveness the feuds represent — the negative side of the heroic ideal — comes into clearer and clearer focus.' At Ravenswood,

> as everywhere in the poem, we can perceive the central tragic fact about the society that heroic poetry reflects: that in its very strength and beauty, in its cohesive loyalties and allegiances, lie inevitable forces of destruction and anarchy. Hygelac's action in honoring the slayers of Ongentheow is impeccable heroic etiquette, yet it plants the seeds of disaster; the greater the Geatish triumph, the more violent the predictable vengeful reaction on the part of the Swedes. Like the story of Finnsburg, the account of the battle of Ravenswood has an ostensibly happy ending, but both stories are fundamentally tragic prophecies in their contexts.[44]

The 'central tragic fact' is generalized by a feature of part II which readers of the poem have always noticed: the mythical or typical quality produced by the application of animal-names to persons and places. Irving views the animal theme as symbolizing the failure of control: the fighters in Ravenswood are released from any burden of rational choice or self-discipline by the animal necessity of survival. Brought to bay, they fight like animals. ... Two men named Wolf and Boar drag down the mighty Ongentheow in the Wood of the Ravens, and the Messenger's speech ends with a dialogue between Raven and Eagle,[45]

a dialogue in which Raven mentions the co-operation of Wolf in despoiling future Geat bodies. Immediately after the messenger's speech, the Geats go to the foot of Eagle Cliff to gaze on the bodies of Beowulf and the dragon. Wood and cliff join the birds in becoming symbols of battle and devourers of carrion. The messenger foresees no scop in the future except the raven, no audience except the eagle. But raven and eagle, wood and cliff are not merely agents of cosmic fate. As symbols of battle and death they are consequences of social forces, the recipients of meanings generated by human 'laf.' And the penetration of animal being into the human world signifies not only death but also oblivion. Eagle and raven are tributaries of the dragon. Beneath the heroic self-assertion of great lords and warriors works the anonymous 'edwenden' threatening them with the namelessness of carrion in a time when there will be no more companions to collect, embarrow, and remember the dead, only animals to despoil them.

The dragon's arrival three hundred years ago in Geat territory is a prophetic sign of this general and anonymous fate. He waits and sleeps until his moment comes. That moment is itself significant, and deserves our attention, because it reinforces the theme of social breakdown and anonymity. It is brought about by a combination of accident and symptoms of social stress. A slave (or captive) stumbled on the hoard ('Nealles mid gewealdum ... sylfes willum') while fleeing from his lord's 'heteswengeas' (2221-4). The poet describes him as 'hygegiomor' (2408) and 'synbysig' (2226); Donaldson translates the latter as 'guilty of wrongdoing' (39), but it may also mean 'distressed by (another's) hostility or crime.' He is first called a thief (2219) but later the poet says of his successful escape with the cup, 'So may an undoomed man who holds favor from the Ruler easily come through his woes and misery.' (2291-3) The indefinite references to the man (twice specified by the term 'nathwylc'), his anonymity yet narrative importance, assume a choric dimension. Questions of praise and blame, guilt and innocence now appear more complex and more irrelevant. Whether the slave is guilty or not others will suffer the consequences of his theft. He steals the cup to bring his master a peace-pledge ('friobowære,' 2282), and whatever the cause of the breach the generalized sense of strained social relations is only increased by his insignificance and anonymity. As one of those who accompany Beowulf, his reluctance to return to the barrow anticipates the cowardice of the others. This nameless man's resonance deepens as we look at him, for he becomes a figure of man in the society which Beowulf has 'heold' for fifty years — a figure of social man shrinking in the shadow of oblivion. When Beowulf first learns of the dragon he blames himself, thinking he had in some way angered God by offending 'ofer ealde riht.' (2330) But once again the ethical concern is irrelevant; at that level he finds out that it was not his fault. It is 'his fault' only at the deeper level to which praise, blame, and ethical consciousness do not penetrate.

The poet lays bare in part II what he had persistently hinted at in part I — that men suffer the consequences of the dilemmas inherent in the dynamic of their institutions — and shows that although everyone perceives and feels these consequences, the only way they can cope with them is to continue behaving, thinking, and judging according to the very norms by which they are being destroyed. Beowulf unavoidably does the dragon's work and thus, at his death, replaces the dragon as embarrowed doom-sitter. Since the dragon is dead, his barrow defeats oblivion. Yet the poet's treatment of the hero's burial most movingly bathes this triumph in the tenebrous ambivalence of the second part. What he discloses is not quite the triumph that Irving sees:

> The barrow is the objectification of memory and admonition. It is typical of this hero's practical altruism that he intends his grave to be a landmark and an aid to navigation. But it is to be an aid to moral navigation as well. ... The Geatish sailors on the dark sea of the world ... will orient themselves by the name and story of Beowulf.[46]

But Beowulf's words place the emphasis of the purpose clause not on the ships driven over the mists of the seas but on the sailors' recognition of his barrow: 'þæt hit sæliðend syððan hatan / Biowulfes biorh' (2806-7). And later the poet merely notes that it was '(wæ)gliðendum wide g(e)syne' (3158). Neither Beowulf nor the poet explicitly stresses its navigational function but rather its character as a 'wide-seen' memorial. His emphasis, and that of his people in the final lines of the poem, is on the hero's marker placed high in everyone's view, a beacon of inestimable brightness speaking of what has passed: 'þæs ofereode; þisses swa mæg.' And if, as Irving rightly observes, we are 'watching the fu-

neral of an entire nation,' if the Geats themselves are right in sensing tha
their dead king presages 'the fact of their own death,' then the provision
of navigational aid to Geatish sailors — nautical or moral — is hardly to
the point. If this is what Beowulf intends by the puzzling phrase 'to
gemyndum minum leodum' (2804), his good intention will be thwarted, just like his wish to distribute treasure, by his unwitting contribution to the dragon's work of doom. The barrow beams forth into the
darkness to announce his death to Franks, Frisians, and others, and in
that sense too it may stand as an omen, perhaps a cause, of the nation's
funeral.

Beowulf's funeral itself is divided into two parts, cremation and burial, and moves from a lament over the effects produced by the fiery dragon to a sorrowful but more positive eulogy to the hero. Burning his
bonehouse, the Geats lament 'their heart-care, the death of their liege
lord,' and the Geatish woman prophesies 'invasions of armies, many
slaughters, terror of troops, humiliation, and captivity.' That the poet
immediately adds, 'Heaven swallowed the smoke,' may be meant to
suggest the fulfilment of her dire prediction. Ten days later, after building the mound, twelve warriors circle it singing dirges. They 'mourn
their king' and 'speak of the man,' praising his 'eorlscipe,' 'ellenweorc,'
and 'duguð.' Finally, they say that he was of 'wyruldcyning(a)' the
'mildest of men and the gentlest, kindest to his people,' and 'lofgeornost,' 'most eager for fame' (3171-82 [55]). Their eulogy moves back
and forth between the king and the hero, but ends firmly fixed on the
latter. The poet approves their acts (3174-7), yet the poem ends in indirect discourse with the poet paraphrasing their words, not quite allowing their perspective fully to fuse with his.

In his own conclusion, Irving observes that the cremation with its
accompanying 'realization of annihilation ... must remain subordinate
to the intense and unswerving focus of attention on Beowulf.' And he
comments as follows on the tone of the final lines:

> The Geats mourn the passing of their king, but in words that rise to
> something close to triumph, in praises out of the heart of love that
> point to Beowulf's own affectionate and kind nature. To the extent
> to which they can courageously face their own destruction, they will
> draw their courage and their dignity from their love for their dead
> king, the incarnation of the heroic spirit and the radiant center of
> the poem.[47]

All true; and yet there is something else, since the heroic spirit has other, darker avatars in the poem, and indirectly the Geats draw their courage and dignity from the source of their destruction. It is not exactly that the dual structure of the ritual constitutes a kind of heroic or stoic evasion; they may be said to flinch from the spectre of annihilation and cling to the only 'laf' they can expect to bequeath the future, the hero's 'lof.' But a more cautious appraisal is that their desperate fixing of the eyes on the barrow is simply the other side of everything they do not, cannot, see.

What they cannot see is the deep doom-structure which the poet reveals to us. Assuredly he shares their feeling and joins them in the sentiments of which he approves. But between his sense of the occasion and theirs lies the whole of *Beowulf* as a poem. Like their eulogy, the poem is an act of commemoration. That is, it is in part a ritual burial, an embarrowing of the hero. More effectively than the mourning Geats, this poet has told a tale to thwart the raven as well as the dragon. If Beowulf's barrow sends its message across the seas, even across Jutland to England, the poet's literary barrow transmits it across time. Beowulf himself leaves little behind. Heroes and their societies propel themselves toward some inevitable grave and their 'laf' — cursed or useless, golden or rusty — remains to haunt the souls of children, romantics, and antiquaries in later times. It is the scop who revives the heroic image, polishes and preserves it, cleans away rust and restores it to later communities both as example and as warning.

There is a strange moment near the end of the poem when the poet, who otherwise approves the heroic burial, briefly abandons that attitude to comment on the old treasure: 'þær hit nu gen lifað / eldum swa unnyt, swa hi(t æro)r wæs.' (3167b-8) There it 'now still lives,' useless to men. The emphatic 'nu gen' directly connects the past act of burial with the present of the poet and his audience. 'Lifað' is not merely the neutral 'dwells,' as Donaldson translates it; as if it only sleeps, the treasure still has life, may still be revived and restored to men. And since the hero's ashes are mingled with the treasure, perhaps the phrase may be extended to Beowulf. Does the poet mean that Beowulf and the treasure are useless because they can't be unearthed, that their only use was in life, and that God (the true king of victories) has not appointed one fit to unearth and revive them? If so, the burial is being criticized because something important to men is being denied them now — perhaps the image of heroic consciousness and its undeniable virtues as a workable ideal which hard-pressed contemporaries might do well to emulate. Or does the poet mean that Beowulf and the treasure would be useless to men if unearthed, and therefore had better remain buried? If so, the burial is important because the hero's soul-hoard and the 'laf' of old societies are finally useless in their original form. They cannot be restored to living men unless they are significantly altered.

The poet's ambivalent attitude toward heroic society suggests that we combine these two responses. We said earlier that the scop revives the heroic image, but 'revives' insufficiently describes his act. He revises the image, sees it anew and sees it differently. To us the poem conveys an implicit message: that the hero may perform his most useful social function not in his 'historical' but in his literary role — not during his life but after his death in the work of the scop. If this echoes the sentiment, the hope, shared by the Geats and their 'lofgeornost' lord, the negations expressed in the previous sentence cast it in a very different light. Beowulf, the dragon, Grendel, and Heorot are 'wundorlic' not merely in the manner of old legends and fairy tales; this very quality lends them the more fatal attraction of dragongold, of the gift that may become poison. For what does it mean to 'unearth' Beowulf, what or who is being unearthed, what can he do for us, or to us?

As a primitive and uncanny figure (the bear-son), he seems less an historical personage than a creature of the folk imagination, while as hero he is more ideal, a better and purer example of the heroic ethos than figures who, like Hygelac and Hrothgar, are presumptively more historical. In his career through the poem he moves from the first of these qualities to the second, becoming more human and fallible, more 'milde' and 'liðe' — the potentially dangerous outsider who first confronts Hrothgar is, by the end of the poem, domesticated into a beloved culture hero. Taming that wildness, like conquering Grendel, is exchanging bad dreams for good. Of what use is it to bring forth such dreams from the earth, or from the folk imagination with its powerful longing for mystery, terror, beauty, and peace? Beowulf appeases the folk longing; his strange but consoling image answers the dread and passivity, dispels the ennui, that gave rise to it. A dream of Beowulf might relax and enervate the poet's audience just as Beowulf unstrung the Geats and Hrothgar the Danes. Between the scop and his subject matter, between the audience and the poem, reciprocity has to be possible. The scop reciprocates by revising, and we reciprocate by remaining alert, refusing to be lulled by the heroic dream, listening attentively for the sounds of doom working within the social order.

This interpretive reciprocity distinguishes our relation to the *Beowulf* poet from the relation of the Danes to Hrothgar's scop. The *Beowulf* poet seems to share with his Danish scop the inclination as well as the ability to tell a story of times far off, a strange story told in accordance with what is right or customary ('rehte æfter rihte,' 2110), a story which might please an old king by harking back to the ways of youth and battle-glory. Yet the magnetic influence exercised by the hero yearning forward on the audience yearning pastward may be worse than useless if the tale does not at the same time depict the 'soð ond sarlic' contradictions in heroic society. We are not to respond to *Beowulf* as the Danes responded to the tale of Finn, and perhaps too we are to take note of the omissions that deceptively illuminate the scop's tale of the triumph of Sigemund. By what he reveals in his poem, the *Beowulf* poet offers us a view of the scop and his function which contrasts with that which he ascribes to the scop in heroic society. We might say that he contains within himself the impulses of the heroic scop as the innocent heart of his own more sophisticated and self-conscious activity, that the poem by giving full play to those impulses arouses and then tempers them in its audience, and that in this way the heroic past is both glorified and exorcised, both celebrated and embarrowed, within the 'vicarious' boundaries of literary experience. As one of the institutions of heroic society, the role of the scop shares in the fundamental ambivalence attendant on feasting and hall-joys. The *Beowulf* poet embodies in his poem a revised version of that role by centring on the ambivalence which the work of the heroic scop tends to ignore.

NOTES

The authors wish to express their gratitude to Professor Edward B. Irving, Jr, who read the essay and made many helpful suggestions both substantive and editorial.

1 All passages of text quoted from Fr. Klaeber, *'Beowulf' and 'The Fight at Finnsburg'* (3rd ed., Boston 1950)
2 *Beowulf*, trans. E. Talbot Donaldson (New York 1966), 2-3. Future references refer to this translation.
3 R.E. Kaske, *'Sapientia et Fortitudo* as the Controlling Theme of *Beowulf,'* in *An Anthology of Beowulf Criticism*, ed. Lewis E. Nicholson (Notre Dame 1963), 285
4 See esp. John Halverson, *'Beowulf* and the Pitfalls of Piety,' *UTQ* 35 (1966) 260-78.
5 *A Reading of 'Beowulf'* (New Haven and London 1968), 92

6 *Introduction to 'Beowulf'* (Englewood Cliffs 1969), 23

7 With one exception: the treatment of the battle of Ravenswood (cf Irving, *Reading*, 189), to be discussed on pp. 69-70. This statement of the theme, however, is not expanded to the rest of the poem in an operational manner.

8 'The World of *Beowulf*,' *ELH* 36 (1969) 606-8

9 This is because he reads part I of the poem primarily as 'the contrast and conflict of two worlds — inside and outside, the world of man and the world of monsters, the world of order and the world of chaos' (Halverson, 'The World of *Beowulf*,' 601). This perspective keeps him from exploring the ways in which the major problems are 'inside' the world of man, and projected 'outside.'

10 Halverson, 'The World of *Beowulf*,' 596-7

11 Irving, *Reading*, 90

12 Marshall Sahlins, *Tribesmen* (Englewood Cliffs 1968), 7-8

13 The inadequacy and instability of unextended kinship organization could be exemplified by our First Parents and their feuding sons, and, more perversely, by the Grendel family (in reference to which the term 'unextended' is a hyperbole).

14 Klaeber (cvii) speculates that line 73 — 'buton folcscare ond feorum gumena' — might be a legalistic addition to the text. If so, this may suggest that Hrothgar's eagerness to give was felt by at least one scribe as extreme and in need of some editorial constraint.

15 In an odd way, Kaske's mistaken idea that Hrothgar is being accused of insufficient *fortitudo* (cf note 3 above) supports our opinion because it presupposes that the aggressive and contentious spirit is essential to survival in the Germanic world, and that it is not to be confused with prideful self-assertion. But Hrothgar does not simply depend on 'kingly munificence' as one of the 'indifferent substitutes' for the *fortitudo* he lacks: as we have just tried to demonstrate, he embraces it aggressively as a constructive mode of expression, at once glorifying himself, strengthening his dynasty and *comitatus*, and benefitting others. Hence his liberality — as we shall show — is the cause of ensuing violence rather than an ineffective defence against it.

16 Trans. Ian Cunnison (New York 1967), 72-3

17 The only use in the poem of the relatively rare word, 'leon' ('lend'), occurs at line 1456, when Unferth 'lah' his sword to Beowulf. But the general expectation of 'lean' ('reward'), and the convention of recompense, 'leanian,' makes every gift a loan.

18 In emphasizing Beowulf's tact and courtesy, Irving (*Reading*, 53 ff) seems to us to slight the way this section of the poem is structured to bring out the more aggressive but certainly conventional features of 'beot' and counter-'beot.'

19 Donaldson, 20. The verbal dual between Beowulf and Unferth is later followed by the loan and return of Hrunting. Although superficially this seems to signify a truce

to their bickering, the way both loan and return are described (1455 ff and 1807 ff) strongly suggests that the one-sided contest is being continued in the more positive expressive forms of prestation.

20 Irving, *Reading*, 131

21 The Danish coastguard's challenge to the landing Geats early in the poem dramatizes the uneasy watchfulness of Hrothgar's people, and tells us the Danes have potential enemies overseas. See especially 240 ff.

22 Irving puts this well, though he makes something else of it: 'what Grendel seems to represent is a rather complex objectification of antiheroic and antisocial forces intimately related by opposition to the positive heroic and social values of the poem, especially as they are embodied in the hero himself.' (*Introduction*, 48) This stresses his function as a counter-exemplum — like Heremod — which may be the way the Danes view him. Our emphasis is less on mere objectification than on allegorical displacement of the evil.

Both sides of Hrothgar's activity — giving and taking — are compressed into the word first used to describe his generous intention, 'gedælan,' which appears three times in the poem with two different meanings: to distribute, divide, and share out treasure (71); to sever, as when Grendel mentally 'gedælde' the men in the hall, hoping to divide lives from bodies (731); and, again, to sever, as when the dragon-fate approached Beowulf to seek his 'sawle hord' and 'gedælan / lif with lice' (2422-3), dividing that treasure not to share it out but to keep it from use.

23 On Beowulf's singular and uncanny quality, see p. 59 ff.

24 That is, lines 170-88, where the Danes' turning in despair to hell and the 'gastbona' is described in such a way as to suggest a Grendelian state: cf the later passages describing Grendel's death (756, 805 ff, 844 ff, 1002 ff). Their sacrifices and inability to praise God may echo passages about the Babylonians in *Daniel* but they may also call to mind the unacceptable offering of Cain — an ideological if not a verbal analogue.

25 Kaske, 280

26 In context this epithet is immediately proleptic in effect, but it also strikes us as generally descriptive.

27 Cf Irving, *Reading*, 93 f, 96, 111.

28 For example, the Danish scop's praise of Beowulf developed as a contrast between the good dragon-killer Sigemund and the evil Heremod. The point of Beowulf's connection with the former is apparently, for the scop and the Danes, that both are slayers of monsters. Just which of the elements of the enormously complex Sigemund-Volsung-Sigfrid-Nibelung saga the poet could have expected his audience to know we cannot say, but we may assume that the juxtaposition with Heremod controls the area of reference, and what we then notice is that by concentrating on the difference in 'lof' between the two exemplars the scop slides over the similar-

ities in their ends in darkness and betrayal. Though passing and unfocused reference is made to the wider context of Sigemund's tangled career (Wæls, Fitela and 'ellendædum uncuðes fela' [876]) the scop's focus makes what is traditionally the beginning of the hero's great deeds sound like the culmination of them, and therefore conspicuously excludes the darker elements of kinstrife, the curse on the hoard, etc, that were his later fate.

29 129, 640, 703, 729, 741, 1251, 1280, 1580, and less directly, 85 (which suggests that the feud-rage between Hrothgar and Ingeld still sleeps)

30 It is interesting that among the possible etymologies for 'Grendel' which Klaeber lists (xxviii f), one derives from '*grand,' ('sand,' 'bottom [ground] of a body of water'). The other possibilities — 'grind,' 'evil,' 'bolt' or 'bar,' and 'storm' or 'bellow' — may be combined with the first in a Spenserian mock-etymology to suggest the darker characteristics that lie at the root of what it means to be a man: the spirit of contentiousness, the capacity for angry and cruel violence, the dread yet need of others, the pain that erupts in vengeance. These potencies are most fully transformed in the figure of the hero, but their raw power is occasionally glimpsed. They are less fully transformed in the other institutions of heroic society.

31 That is, as our previous discussion of Grendel suggests, the monster has close connections with the family of man and, more specifically, with the social institutions of the beleaguered Danes.

32 Halverson, 'The World of *Beowulf*,' 606

33 The phrase 'to gemyndum minum leodum' (2804) is not unambiguous. Beowulf could mean that the barrow will be a memorial for surviving Geats to see when they sail by. Irving reads it this way (*Reading*, 233 ff) and Donaldson's translation, 'as a reminder to my people' (49), while noncommittal, implies a similar understanding. But the phrase could just as easily be read as a double dative, 'for a memorial to my people,' which suggests that Beowulf foresees his barrow as the most enduring monument to the Geatish people after they have perished or dispersed. Even if the hero means the first, the poem 'chooses' the second meaning.

34 Klaeber, xlvi-viii

35 Beowulf's comments on the probable doom of the Freawaru-Ingeld union have often been praised for their political astuteness. But they might as easily be viewed within the context of his own childlessness, and the lack of reference to any wife or immediate kin outside of Hygelac and Wiglaf. Perhaps the puzzling reference to Offa is meant to suggest an 'ideal of kingship' more responsible to the needs of history, less singular and mythic, than that exemplified in Beowulf's career. Offa was not only brave in war and gift-giving, widely honoured and wise; he domesticated and redeemed a cruel wife, and left an heir. Kemp Malone was led by the Thrytho-Offa vignette to wonder why the poet chose Beowulf rather than Offa as his hero, and decided it was because the poet 'found spiritual values in Beowulf's monster-

quelling which he could not find in Offa's man-[and woman-] quelling.' Malone quaintly remarks that Offa 'proved master of the situation at home as well as on the field of battle' (*'Beowulf,'* in Nicholson, *Anthology,* 148-9). These qualities may be meant to accentuate Beowulf's singularity by contrast.

36 Irving, *Introduction,* 12

37 See the fine discussion by Irving in *Reading,* 179-91 and 198-205.

38 Significantly, the only other use of 'breosthord' comes in a reference to another hoarder, Heremod (1719), though once again the irrelevance of the ethical failure of Heremod should be noted.

39 Irving notes that the dragon is described as a stingy king, in contrast to the generous Beowulf (*Reading,* 209). But again, stinginess as a defect of will, an ethical failure, is not the problem, and at the deeper level, where Beowulf and the dragon interchange qualities, 'stinginess' might be used as an inept — because ethical — metaphor to describe the inability of the singular hero to communicate or share his breast-hoard.

40 Irving, *Reading,* 208, 232

41 Irving, *Reading,* 214

42 Irving, *Reading,* 192 ff

43 Some phrases after Hrothgar's sermon have an ominous ring: the reference to night-fall (1789b-90), and to the sleeping guest and blithe-hearted raven (1800b-2). Beowulf's careful lie to Unferth sustains the sense of an uneasy atmosphere never fully secure in spite of the hero's triumph. In his report to Hygelac, he amplifies the account of Grendel's seizure of the Geatish victim, and his brief image of Hrothgar stresses the old king's age and nostalgia. In all these ways, the superficial character of the happy ending is framed in darker retrospects and anticipations.

44 Irving, *Reading,* 179, 189

45 Irving, *Reading,* 188

46 Irving, *Reading,* 234

47 Irving, *Reading,* 245-6

ROBERT B. BURLIN

Inner weather and interlace: a note on the semantic value of structure in *Beowulf*

Hengest ða gyt

wælfagne winter   wunode mid Finne
eal unhlitme.   Eard gemunde,
þeah þe he ne meahte   on mere drifan
hringedstefnan;   holm storme weol,
won wið winde,   winter yþe beleac
isgebinde,   oþðæt oþer com
gear in geardas,   swa nu gyt deð,
þa ðe syngales   sele bewitiað,
wuldortorhtan weder.   Ða wæs winter scacen,
fæger foldan bearm.   (1127b-37a)[1]

In these lines from the Finn episode of *Beowulf* we find the Old English poet in obviously brilliant command of his resources. To mark the temporal transition which leads to the climax of this terse and allusive narrative, he selects judiciously from his repertoire of formulae and with a notable change of pace evokes tellingly the change of the seasons and the 'inner weather'[2] of the protagonist as well. 'Winter locked in the waves with a bond of ice' (1132b-3a) recalls the image of binding, as analyzed by Edward Irving in the *Wanderer*,[3] metaphorically extended from the external landscape to the psyche of the speaker. Here, the impassable sea, rendering immobile man and waves alike, is both cause and mirror of the agon of Hengest, frustrated as much by his conflicting obligations to revenge and to his contract with Finn as by his inability to act. Or as T.A. Shippey has put it: 'These clashes of storm and ice, of change in the year set against an unchanging purpose, brilliantly express a contorted state of mind, built up from Hengest's opposing desires and from the unexpressed implications of the contract and burning.'[4] By the introduction of a few carefully chosen, though commonplace, details of this 'slaughter-stained winter,' the poet has extracted the maximum poetic charge from the passage, effecting the movement in time and simultaneously reflecting in concrete terms the quality of the hero's dilemma.

Though the passage defines a transition in time, the impression we receive of its temporal extremities is very different. In the lines cited, the word 'winter' (1128, 1136) creates an envelope for the description; its opposite is denoted only by its absence (1136b) or the bland 'gear.'[5] The components of winter are specified — storm, wind, ice — and its verbs conjure up a swift and decisive battle against the waters — 'weol,' 'won,' 'beleac,' ('-gebinde'). In contrast, the new season is characterized only by two very general adjectives — 'wuldortorht' and 'fæger.' The coming of spring occupies as much 'verse space' as does winter in this passage, but its introduction occurs in a flat, trite clause padded with a gnomic expression, understandably characterized by Klaeber as 'a trivial statement of a matter-of-course fact':[6] 'until another year came, as it still does, the gloriously bright weathers which always observe the (proper) season.'[7]

What, if anything, is one to make of this brief conflict of stylistic modes? One can forgive the poet a momentary lapse into vacuity and go on, or one can speculate upon his motives for calling attention to seasonal change as a recurrent and continuing phenomenon. Klaeber's note on the 'trivial statement' reminds us of an earlier occurrence: 'Metod eallum weold / gumena cynnes, swa he nu git deð.' (1057b-8) This blunt assertion of divine governance over the affairs of men is followed by some uninspired moralizing on the need for prudence in this life which offers, to anyone who endures, much of good and of bad. The whole passage rounds off the Grendel story and leads into that of Finn and Hengest. The poet has self-consciously donned his pseudo-vatic robes in order to utter pious truisms which do not begin to comprehend the complexity of moral vision which has characterized the preceding events. Perhaps, then, the simplistic terms of the seasonal transition also help to alert us to ironic disparities. The two passages affirm, with the aid of their common formula, an on-going pattern of order and stability apparent beyond the flux of everyday mortal concerns: God rules; nature renews itself. But the relation of the gnomic utterance to the context is no more straightforward in this instance than in the first.

The coming of spring means freedom for Hengest from the bondage of winter exile during which he 'eard gemunde.' But Hengest requires more than physical release from the forced hospitality of Finn:

> Fundode wrecca,
> gist of geardum; he to gyrnwræce
> swiðor þohte þonne to sælade ... (1137b-9)

And the episode concludes with the triumphant execution of Hengest's revenge. The fire, slaughter, and pillage were undoubtedly fair and gloriously bright to him and to the Danish audience listening to the lay, but these are hardly the traditional expectations of the season which had been blandly smuggled in by the transitional lines. As in the *Seafarer*, where the evocation of springtime renewal serves ironically as a reminder of mutability and the world's decay, so here there is a grim disjunction between the bright joyful pattern of regeneration after the struggle with winter and its implied correlate in human affairs. Man finds his release by asserting another pattern; his pleasure comes in revenge and destruction. This is perhaps the force behind the puzzling 'woroldrædenne' (1142): what Hengest does not refuse when he takes up the familiar sword is the accepted custom among men, the way of the world. In the encapsulated world view provided by the Finn episode, the beginning and the ending in fire and death far outweigh the sense of triumph. The whirligig of time may bring in 'wuldortorht weder,' but with it also come man's revenges.

But the aim of the episode is clearly not to cast blame — on Hengest or any one else. We are hard put to define with clarity any tribal law or heroic code that would cut through the Gordian knot of moral bewilderment and frustration on which the story depends. The emphasis is rather on the pity of it all, combined with an unflinching refusal to evade the fact that this is the way things are. The ironies of the spring passage work because there are similarities as well as differences. As in the regular procession of the seasons, there is in the affairs of men a pattern, a 'law,' which is immutable and beyond the control of human agency, though men are themselves the agents. Heroes and heroic codes may attempt to counter its force and occasionally meet with some success, but eventually they are borne down. In this world it goes as it will.

What I am describing is perhaps what was commonly meant in pre-Christian times by 'wyrd,' before its powers had been subsumed under a Boethian divine providence. The Finn episode and *Beowulf* as a whole achieve their elegaic power, the sense of *lacrimae rerum*, by pitting their magnificent pagan heroes against the force of the way things are, without the benefit of a transcendent metaphysical perspective. Their failures have a splendour precisely because these heroes had no other recourse but to define by the thrust of their resistance the sad condition of transitory human affairs. It is misguided to attempt to assign blame to them or their societies; the force which conquers them is beyond as well as within them. Such a vision of life does not submit tidily to reasoned categories. It can perhaps only be realized imaginatively, as in these lines of the Finn episode whose implications I have much belaboured. The essential mysteriousness of what shapes human lives compels even those who pride themselves on their rationality to resort to mythic analogies — from original sin to the Oedipal complex. Critics of a literature where so much must always remain unknown are perhaps overinclined to impose moral categories to assuage other uncertainties. Yet the most probing of poetic insights often renders moral judgments the most difficult.

Take, for example, Chaucer's narrative strategy in the 'Knight's Tale.' Palamon and Arcite love and do battle, and on one level seem to be fully responsible for their choices. Yet from the beginning, love is seen to be an uninvited force over which they have no control and which shatters their chivalric bond of brotherhood. The impulses of amorous and military aggressiveness are internal, but they have also an external existence in the planetary deities of Mars and Venus — the human psyche writ large in the heavens. The situation is complicated by the presence of Saturn whose destructive indifference to human affairs trips up Theseus' attempts to contain and civilize the young men's aggressions. In spite of the differences of genre, Chaucer's poem, like *Beowulf*, uses a pagan setting to propound a vision of human society which though it includes the morally iniquitous — Creon, Heremod — and the gratuitously inimical — Saturn, the monsters — is regulated by powers that are immanent in, yet transcend their mortal agents, powers that evade human control and defy human understanding and judgment.

In *Beowulf*, it is the larger structural patterns of narrative that contribute powerfully to a sense of the mysterious shaping of human events. Much, of course, has been written, before and after Tolkien, on the implications of the hero's fights with the monsters, and much, before and after Bonjour, about the background and thematic associations of the 'digressions,' but the full value of the poet's extraordinarily complex narrative procedure has too often been underestimated. The imaginative vision of *Beowulf* requires that the recurrent patterns within the major battles be apprehended concurrently with the fragments of historical interlude. To focus only on the hero or to be blinkered by the puzzling allusiveness of the subordinate material is to see only the pieces of bright mosaic glass and to miss the total picture. Every aspect of the style of *Beowulf* warns that we must step back to see the whole; the surface has been deliberately patterned to repel that absorption in the temporal continuum which is demanded by the realistic novel. With the larger narrative units as with the syntax of the poetic language, the proper response requires the kind of practiced memory that characterized illiterate audiences, the ability to recompose the spatial integrity of the scop's imaginative vision.

The total structure of *Beowulf* is best described by John Leyerle's term 'interlace,'[8] a pattern found in the visual arts, in manuscript illumination and sculptural relief, in which precisely calculated curves are interwoven with such frequence and complexity that the tangle seems either natural or unfathomable. The interlacing in *Beowulf* — the digressive material entangling the main plot — differs from that of its plastic analogues not only in that it is apprehended cumulatively, but in that there is also a distinct and significant acceleration. Of the three large and roughly equal sections, the first presents the central narratives without interruptions. The fight with Grendel is preceded by the introductions of the Danish dynasty, of the monster and the hero, with the flyting of Unferth and swimming match with Breca the only substantial interludes. After the fight, the 'digressions' are equally justified by the story proper as songs of praise and celebration — the Sigemund-Heremod lay and the Finn episode. The fight with Grendel's mother is also uninterrupted, and the second Heremod allusion, absorbed in Hrothgar's sermon, completes the Danish visit. But two substantial digressions add density to Beowulf's return to the Geatish court — the Thryth and Offa tale, puzzling though clearly positive in tone, and the Heathobard feud, a dark and deliberate echo of the Finn episode. In these major sections, then, the heroic action stands free of entanglement with the 'historical' world of imperfect beings and impure motives, but each concludes with a substantial evocation of a world in which heroic fame is dubiously achieved at an appalling cost in human life and emotional damage.

In the last section of the poem, the heroic fight with the dragon is relentlessly interlaced with glimpses into that darker mode of being, until they are finally knotted together in the messenger's speech on the death of Beowulf. The battle is broken into again and again as the political implications of Beowulf's new role as king are brought home. There are no less than nine major allusions to past events, and in this section all are seen to bear directly on the hero's situation. The tangled world of human affairs that had been reserved for moments of celebration or reflection has now woven itself into the central action. Three dominant motifs can be identified, and their sequence plotted as in a musical composition. As a kind of 'ground' which establishes the prevailing tone are the generalized, almost abstract, laments: that of the Last Survivor (2247 ff) and that of the Father (2444 ff) whose situation reflects that of the bereaved Hrethel. The second motif refers to a single event, the disastrous Frankish raid ('FR') of Hygelac, first mentioned early on (1212 ff) but here recalled ominously three times (2355 ff, 2501 ff, 2913 ff). The third motif, the Swedish Wars ('SW'), confirms our sense of the poet's deliberate and astonishingly complex method. It consists of four references to interrelated events involving three generations of Geatish and Swedish royalty, their internal as well as external conflicts, and the sequence is unfolded in roughly a reverse chronological order, following the bewilderingly enmeshed events back to the time of fierce and imposing grandfathers. The management of this material alone would testify to a master craftsman, but the whole pattern of interlace in the last 1000 lines of the poem is a feat of astounding virtuosity. The order is as follows: Lament-FR-SW^4-Lament-SW^2-FR-SW^3-FR-SW^1.

Such a display of narrative skill is clearly not without its imaginative force of semantic implications, the most immediately apparent of which is tonal. The last struggle of Beowulf is larded with sad tales of the death of kings: supported by the two 'abstract' elegies, one from the death of Herebeald, and the repeated allusions to the death of Hygelac in the Frankish Raid, the Swedish Wars toll the deaths of Heardred and Onela; Hæthcyn and Ongentheow; Eanmund; and Ongentheow again. Three generations of two royal houses are slaughtered, and when one looks back for an initial cause — and this seems to be part of the point of the reverse chronology — one is hard put to find any more substantial justification for the Swedish enmity than for Hygelac's attack on Frisia. Yet the last allusions to each conflict are coupled together within the messenger's speech and presage a continuation of the hostilities beyond the events of the poem. But Hygelac is not severely castigated within the poem for what seems to many modern critics a doubly foolish death;[9] and the Swedish War sequence concludes with an ambiguous scene that celebrates a Geatish triumph to hold against the gloomy future of the race, and yet gives pride of place to the fierce old Swedish king, brought down only by two brutish-named adversaries, falling with something like the weight of the old dragon itself. Amid all this grasping for wealth and power, this smouldering revenge, these repeated deaths, senseless but often splendid, the poet simply invites us to look on, with a dazed wonder that stupefies judgment, at the way things are.

And it is the way things are that has finally caught up with Beowulf in the form of the dragon. Many readers have felt the force of Tolkien's conception of the monster as 'the personification of malice, greed, destruction (the evil side of heroic life), and of the undiscriminating cruelty of fortune that distinguishes not good or bad (the evil aspect of all life).'[10] Most recently T. A. Shippey has amplified: 'The dragon is like Revenge. It sleeps, but can be woken; it is monstrously sensitive to the slightest of injuries. An Anglo-Saxon might not have seen quite such abstract connections, but he might well have been able to feel powerfully the ramifications of feud or vendetta ... The moral most obviously conveyed is the paradoxical and profitless nature of feud and malice.'[11] Revenge and malice are indeed the dominant forms taken by human forces of aggression and destruction in the poem, and the dragon symbolically partakes of them on a non-human level. But in the interlaced events, other actions, from the accidental slaying of Herebeald to the foolhardy expedition of Hygelac, shape disaster, and the dragon itself appears, in the poem and in the famous Cottonian gnome, as a natural force, merely doing what it is there to do. The interwoven events of the final section, like the dragon, stand for something that cannot be reduced to a convenient category like revenge or *malitia*, though these are some of the forms taken by what they comprehend. They are imaginative vehicles, one structural, the other symbolic, for the poet's vision of a greater reality which has many names but is finally mysterious.

It is in fact the coalescence of narrative methods which precludes simple moral judgments in *Beowulf*. The interlacing of historical associations presents the human faces of what the dragon embodies as an extra-human principle, just as Chaucer's planetary deities reveal the cosmic aspect of what moves Palamon and Arcite. But one cannot equate the dragon or Beowulf's responses to its challenge with the specific motives which generate the interlaced events. They can be identified only in terms of a more encompassing and ultimately unnamable vision of the way things are. Obviously the poet owes something of his ability to focus his poetic imagination as he does, to the Christian context in which he writes. But the world of *Beowulf*, like that of Chaucer's Athens, merely anticipates Christian revelation. The magnanimity of its hero gropes for a kind of fulfilment that is inevitably frustrated or destroyed in this world. It is precisely the poet's grasp of something beyond that enables him to imagine and create this world as he does. But he does not need to find some flaw — Augustinian or Aristotelian — in his hero or some inherent deficiency in the heroic society he embodies, to envision the death of Beowulf and its consequences. The tragic element is built into the very fabric of life itself and is as natural as the coming of spring or of a dragon and as inevitable as the interlacing of human events.

NOTES

1 The text is that of Elliott V.K. Dobbie, *Beowulf and Judith*, ASPR III (New York 1953).
2 Stanley Greenfield has used the term in his discussion of the 'Old English Elegies,' in *Continuations and Beginnings*, ed. E.G. Stanley (London 1966), 165.
3 E.B. Irving, Jr, 'Image and Meaning in the Elegies,' in *Old English Poetry*, ed. Robert P. Creed (Providence, R.I. 1967), 160 ff
4 *Old English Verse* (London 1972), 24
5 Of course in this context the word means 'spring, the time of new growth,' but only the context distinguishes this more specific from the general meaning, whose familiarity diminishes the word's evocative power. See Bosworth-Toller Supplement, 'gear,' III.
6 Fr. Klaeber, ed., *'Beowulf' and 'The Fight at Finnsburg'* (3rd ed., Boston 1950), 175
7 Dobbie's translation, 178
8 'The Interlace Structure of *Beowulf*,' *UTQ* 37 (1967) 1-17
9 I am grateful to my co-editor for the just reminder that line 1206 may be taken as critical of Hygelac: 'syþðan he for wlenco wean ahsode.' The second half-line, applied elsewhere by Beowulf to the sea-monsters he dispatched in his youth (425), I take to mean something like 'courted disaster.' 'Wlenco,' however, is difficult to assess. Within the poem, it is both unambiguously positive — in Wulfgar's interpretation of the Geats' motives (338) — and either ironic or pejorative — at the beginning of Unferth's taunt (508). The related adjective, 'wlonc,' is clearly positive on three occasions — describing Wulfgar (331), Beowulf (341), and Hygelac

(2953) — but, with a dependent noun, is twice applied to monsters 'glorying in' their spoils (1332, 2833). Elsewhere in Old English poetry, the connotations of 'wlenco' range from 'idolatrous pride' (in *Genesis* and *Daniel*) to 'abundance,' 'prosperity,' 'high honours' (favourably in Psalm 29:6, but threatened by fortune, pride, or death in the *Metres of Boethius*, 1:76, 5:31, 10:28) to the 'pomp and grandeur appropriate to the mighty' (in the Exeter *Maxim* 61: 'þrym sceal mid wlenco'). The adjective follows much the same pattern, but is also used to convey the splendour of such various items as horses (*Maldon*, 240, *Riddles*, 80:7), the Day of Judgment (Exeter *Day 1*, 50), and even the triune God (*Creed*, 48).

'Wlenco' seems to emanate from a sense of confident superiority and is powerfully reflected in physical appearance. We still speak of a 'high-spirited' horse or a rich man 'exuding prosperity,' but I find no appropriate word for the heroic contexts. The element of pride involved is morally objectionable to the authors of religious narratives, but this may simply reflect that Christian sensitivity which has made the words for 'pride' in most Western European languages potentially pejorative unless qualified: 'justifiable pride,' 'noble orgueil.' I believe that 'wlenco,' however, is morally neutral, as does T.A. Shippey, *Old English Verse*, 28-9: 'Old English heroes are not presented to be judged. They inculcate rather an uneasy awareness that good intentions can lead to evil results, that the same mental quality ("wlenco") may bring success or misery, depending on circumstance.' The second half of line 1206 certainly indicates what Hygelac's 'wlenco' will lead to, but the cluster of occurrences between 331-41, when the Coastguard recognizes in Beowulf that high quality he himself possesses, establishes clearly that a disastrous outcome is not necessarily consequent to the exhibition of 'wlenco.'

10 J.R.R. Tolkien, '*Beowulf*: the Monsters and the Critics,' *PBA* 22 (1936) 259
11 Shippey, 48-9

J.B. BESSINGER, JR

Homage to Caedmon and others: a Beowulfian praise song

Old English secular panegyrics in verse are scarce and late, so let us imagine an early one: Caedmon's Hymn secularized as a Beowulfian panegyric. We may do so not as sacrilege but for inquiry, somewhat as Friedrich Klaeber provided trial openings for the Beowulfian lays of Sigemund and Heremod,[1] or as Kemp Malone recomposed the first thula of *Widsith* to include King Hygelac;[2] in any case we need not linger long upon the medley itself. In homage to Caedmon, to the poet of *Beowulf*, and to John Collins Pope, who has told us so many useful things about them both, let us then make a new oral-traditional praise song for the heroic builder of Heorot. This is of course very easy if the Hymn is used as a frame, for it is already basically that kind of poem, a *preislied auf Gott*, in Klaeber's pregnant definition,[3] indeed in one sense the best example surviving from the OE period of an heroic praise song.

Nu sculon herian   *heall-ærnes* weard,
mann-dryhtnes meahta   and his mod-geþanc,
weorc *weorod-þeodnes*,   swa he wundra gehwæs,
eorla dryhten,   or astealde.
He ærest scop   ielda bearnum
Heorot to hrofe,   *helm scieldinga*;
þa *mæran heall*   *magu-dryhte* weard,
eorla dryhten   æfter teode —
firum *fold-bold*   frea *scieldinga.*

The italicized substitutions are Beowulfian in vocabulary (whether simply or in synthesis) and Caedmonian in prosody — or so I must hope, considering the triple dedication of this poem. Readers are invited to improve it with other substitutions. In the first off-verse, for example, one might borrow 'heah-burge,' (here and elsewhere a small grammatical adjustment is needed), 'heah-seles,' 'heah-stedes,' 'hord-ærnes,' 'hord-burge,' or 'hleo-burge' to replace Caedmon's 'heofon-rices,' regretfully leaving aside 'Heorotes' as metrically too light.[4] Rather like an older traditional poet in a precompositional exercise, one tests and discards his substitutions and their variations and repetitions,[5] probably to discover that Caedmon's plain formal balance, his proud if rather stiff parade of epithets for God, are firmly grounded in a meaningful structure; change a word and the poem is changed.

If suppletion has left the pseudo-poem reasonably true to both originals, however, we are reminded that Caedmon's Hymn and the Creation sequence in *Beowulf* both sing of a ruler's power, purpose, creative act, and adornment of his creation — for I shall argue that 'teode' in the Hymn must mean 'adorned' and not 'created,' as many have thought (it should be the equivalent of 'gefrætwode' [MS: 'gefrætwade'] at *Beowulf* 96a); and that this meaning has consequences for the themes and structures of the two OE poems and for an inquiry into a half-definable sub-genre, the heroic encomium praising a structure along with its builder. Not that the main genre — heroic panegyric — is easy to define, or to identify at all in early English literature.

The panegyric or encomium or praise song is a component form of traditional heroic verse in many ancient and modern societies. The Chadwicks, perhaps too rigorously, held that 'nothing of it survives among the remains of Teutonic and Greek heroic poetry.'[6] A heroic praise song, said Sir Maurice Bowra, perhaps a little too concisely, 'celebrates a great man's doings to his face.'[7] If, as seems reasonable and timely, we broaden the latter definition to include great women too (and so do not overlook the song of Deborah and Barak to the heroine Jael in Judges 5:24, or the reference to songs praising Ealhhild in *Widsith* 97-102), we still have no obvious English specimens.

The panegyrics scattered through the annals for the period 937-1065 (with occasional laments, sometimes in the same poem) are mostly mixed or debased examples; Dorothy Whitelock, with good reason, would not even treat some of them as verse.[8] *Brunanburh*, the best of the Chronicle poems, could not be called a panegyric according to Bowra's definition if only because the persons celebrated were not present at the

composition of a poem hardly intended for performance. By comparison, Caedmon's little doxology is almost an orthodox panegyric. The
person celebrated is by definition present, and the praise given the ruler
of heaven is both particular and oral-traditional in the heroic vein. Both
the Chadwicks and Bowra, however, were looking for secular poems.

Professor Pope has suggested that the building of Hild's great monastery at Streoneshealh may have played its part in the background of
Caedmon's composition,[9] which might be even more likely if the poet
had also heard some royal panegyrics containing architectural matter;
something like the ghostly macédoine of this essay. He is unlikely to
have heard any early, oral predecessor of the encomium urbis type, for
Margaret Schlauch has shown that the genre of Durham is a classical
borrowing into very late OE poetry.[10] Perhaps, though, he could have
heard, in English, poems like Úlf Uggason's Húsdrápa, 'A Praise Song
for the House,' composed for a marriage feast in a richly decorated Icelandic hall in the late tenth century.[11] The skaldic poem, which survives
only in fragments, was clearly a panegyric for an important person and
his new residence. Wide-flung literary and oral-traditional parallels might
be cited, from Pindar's first Pythian ode[12] to a humorous praise song for
a Bantu (Xhosa) chieftain and his new office building, recorded on 4
July 1970,[13] but this architectural sub-variety of the panegyric is not to
be found in OE poetry in a simple form. It exists instead as a metaphor
in Caedmon's Hymn and in other instances of the Creation theme in OE
verse, as well as in a remarkably expanded Creation sequence in Beowulf. We should now examine these poems more closely.

In the imaginary panegyric of Hrothgar above, the king is not praised
by name because the model forbids it in several ways, the least important of which is that his name never appears in Beowulf with a post-
positive epithet (the pattern demanded here) except in the vocative
case, and Caedmon's is not a praise-him-to-his-face poem;[14] strictly, this
would disqualify the poet from Bowra's panegyric court of appeals, but
let us carry the case farther. It is more interesting that God is not given
the name 'God' in Caedmon's Hymn, but rather is referred to by a famous series of heroic periphrases in a pleonastic tour de force. I think
the Beowulf-poet knew and admired this burst of thematic embellishment, for he seems to have imitated it, not indeed where one would
expect it, in the Creation song (90b-8), but, after an interval of violent
action, in lines 167-83, where his probable debt to Caedmon is more
challenging to our appreciation.

It will be noticed that the modern poem and Caedmon's similarly regard a domestic creation and a dynastic creator. So do the relevant passages in *Beowulf*. Caedmon describes the Creation, if I rightly understand his architectonics, as construction followed by decoration, rather as an early Anglo-Saxon church would be built and furnished: first [God made heaven as a roof for men, then he adorned the earth for men. If the sequential content of the parallel narrative in *Beowulf* is thoughtfully considered, then Heorot calls to mind a greater construction: Hrothgar created Heorot, then adorned it, whereupon in Heorot the scop sang of the creation and adorning of the universe.[15] The Danish scop's divine song generates Grendel's rage and the main action of the story, but the *Beowulf*-poet does not yet abandon his joint theme of divinity and praise. The difficult 'giefstol' passage (168-9)[16] and the passage on apostasy that follows it make a striking and well-connected finale to an expanded panegyric upon Creation and Heorot. What has sometimes been read as interpolation is climaxed by a high-flown, densely formulaic panegyric embellishment unusual for the *Beowulf*-poet — between lines 180b and 188 we hear the words 'meotod,' 'demend,' 'dryhten God,' 'heofona helm,' 'herian,' 'wuldres waldend,' 'dryhten,' and 'fæder,' which all but recapitulate the Caedmonian praise song and localize it once again, with a great difference, at Heorot. But a song of that type has not been far from the poet's mind since the introduction of the 'heall-ærna mæst' for which Hrothgar 'scop him Heorot naman,' at line 78, for he echoes Caedmon's reverent (and, if our composite creation song is any guide, thematically crucial) near-pun on 'scop' (the verb) and 'scieppend' with the sequence 'scopes ... gescop ... scieppend' (90, 97, 106) in his section on Heorot and its attacker; two Caedmonian variations for 'God' follow at once — 'ece dryhten' and 'meotod' (107, 110).[17] An encomiastic association between cosmic and worldly rulers and their creations therefore holds this part of the epic together, precisely where some readers find it suspiciously diffuse. Did what is for us the shadowy genre of a praise song for builders help the *Beowulf*-poet to make the association? Our play with a reconstituted song of this type is dispensable. We need now to show by a stricter philology that, in their creation poetry as we have received it, Caedmon's Hymn and *Beowulf* are significantly related. Not all scholars have thought so.

Klaeber, for instance, in a famous article on Christian elements that has been a landmark in *Beowulf* criticism, an article whose data we may now examine and partly reinterpret, thought the similarity between the two poems textually slight and uninteresting.[18] He found only one im-

portant correspondence between them, 'or astealde' / 'onstealde'
(Hymn 4b, *Beowulf* 2407b), a verse which in *Beowulf* has nothing to do
with the creation theme. But the verbal parallels between the Hymn
and its enlarged reflection in *Beowulf* 67b-188 are remarkable in sum
and in kind. Only two verses of the Hymn (3b 'swa he wundra gehwæs,' 4b 'or astealde') have no counterparts in that section of *Beowulf*
that comprises the creation and adorning of Heorot and the universe,
the intrusion of an ungodly monster into Hrothgar's wondrous creation,
and the poet's animadversions upon the Danish inability to praise God.
Of eighteen verses in the Hymn, sixteen share ideas or diction, or both,
with this part of *Beowulf*.

HYMN		BEOWULF	
1a	sculon herian	182b	herian ne cuðon
1b	heofon-rices weard	182a	heofona helm [*Hrothgar called* beag-horda weard 921b, rices weard 1390a]
2a	meotodes	180b	meotod
2b	his mod-geþanc	67b	him on mod be-arn
3a	weorc wuldor-fæder	69b	gewyrcan, 74b weorc, 92b worhte, 183a wuldres wealdend, 188 fæder
3b	swa he wundra gehwæs		
4a	ece dryhten	108	ece dryhten, 181 dryht-en god
4b	or astealde		
5a	scop	78b	scop, 97b gescop [90a swutol sang scopes]
5b	ielda bearnum	70a	ielda bearn, 77a ieldum, 150a ielda bearnum
6a	heofon to hrofe	182a	heofona helm [? 81b-82a sele hlifode / heah and horn-geap]
6b	scieppend	106a	scieppend
7a	middan-geard	75b	middan-geard
7b	mann-cynnes	110	mann-cynne, 164 mann-cynnes
8a	ece dryhten	108	ece dryhten, 181 dryht-en god

8b	teode	76a	frætwan, 96a gefræt-wode
9a	firum foldan	91a	frum-sceaft fira, 96b fol-dan sceatas
9b	frea ælmihtig	92a	se ælmihtiga

A doubter might grant more correspondence than Klaeber did and still object that there are merely salmon in both rivers, or mere necessary formulary fragments in both poems. The question is one of concentration, or of boundaries. Klaeber properly restricted his context to *Beowulf* 90b-8, the song of Creation in Heorot, to bring it parallel with other references to the Creation theme in the OE poetic corpus. The epical context, however, appropriately more ample than Caedmon's poem, frames the religious theme (which in *Beowulf* is not simply a praise song like Caedmon's, but a narration about another narrative concerning Creation) within a Caedmonian panegyric of Hrothgar for his creative act and a quasi-Caedmonian castigation of the godless Danes. The panegyric with its aftermath may be called Caedmonian because it follows the 'plot' of the panegyric Hymn, doubles the plot (two rulers create and decorate their creations for their peoples), and then dramatically inverts the religious message — Hrothgar's work is to be damaged by Grendel and destroyed by fire; God is not praised. Concurrently we discover the paragraph-balanced embellishments of the Hymn, its varied terms for God, rearranged in a crescendo.[19]

HYMN	BEOWULF 64-188
1 Let us praise the king of heaven (four terms) and his wonders.	1 Praise of Hrothgar for his successful military kingship.
2 He (four terms) created heaven as a roof for men and adorned the earth for men.	2 He had the greatest of halls made and adorned for men ('folc-stede frætwan,' 76a). It will be destroyed by fire; meanwhile Grendel is nearby (82b-9a). The scop sang: God (one Caedmonian term) created earth with sun and moon as lights for men, and adorned the earth.

3 The enemy of God (three
Caedmonian terms) attacks
the hall.
4 The terrified Danes did not
know how to praise God
(four Caedmonian terms
plus three others).

Some recollection or equivalent of Caedmon's Hymn appears to have
been reflected in *Beowulf* as an engrossing and original sequential theme
with its sub-themes and vocabulary remarkably intact, and with one
stunning climactic adaptation, the work of a master: 'We should praise
God' becomes 'They did not know how to praise God.' From what thematic repertory did the poet devise such a new sequence? (We leave
aside the problems of the origin of the poem as a whole, the sources
and analogues of the central fable or fables.) Presumably from the formulary commonplaces of the Creation theme in early OE poetry, as
gathered, with late examples also, in Klaeber's *Anglia* catalogues,[20]
conflated and presented here in a new arrangement:

Gen 92-234, esp. 92-4, *112-
17a, 135-8a, *206-15a
Exo 24-9 (with analogue to
Bwf 90-4 separately dis-
cussed by Klaeber in *MLN*
33 [1918] 221), 429b-31;
cf Crd 1-5a
Dan 362-408; cf Aza 73-161a
XSt 1-17a
And 324b-9a, 746b-50,
*769b-99
Ele 725-34a
Chr 222-8, 659
Glc 50b-8
Aza 73-161a; cf Dan 362-408
Phx 129b-31a (not in Latin
original)
Jul 111b-13a, 497b-500a
Sfr 104-5

Mxm I *25b-34
OrW 38-59a
Rdl 40 passim, esp. *1-7
Rsg 2b-5a (Klaeber's and
Grein-Köhler's 'Gebete IV')
Hom II 10b-11a
Bwf 90b-8
Jud 346b-9
PPs 73.16, 94.5, 95.5, 101.22,
103.18-19, 135.4-9 (cf Cæd
1-9), 145.5 and passim
MBo 4.1-2a, 11.1-7a, 17.7-15
and passim
Mnl 46-7
Glo I 16b-23
Crd 1-5a; cf Exo 429b-31
Cæd 1-9; cf PPs 135.4-9
MCh 1.64, 77b-9a

The reader scanning these themes in the *Anglo-Saxon Poetic Records* will quickly find that they consist largely of dutiful or cursory references to the Creation, sometimes with specification of the earth, sun, and moon, but seldom with any poetic spark. If space permitted a comparative study of the entire list, Caedmon's Hymn and *Beowulf* would stand out in a small group of non-stereotyped passages (these may be highly formulaic as to diction) in which the Creation theme serves some structural function within the poem, as is true, for instance, of the moving Creation-prayer that concludes *Judith* or the lively Creation-prayer and panegyric that the story makes central in *Daniel.*

We shall glance at five items only, those asterisked in the table above, not for their poetic evaluation but for the special reason that they distinguish the themes of creation and decoration or in various ways link them, and so help to certify the meaning of 'decorated, adorned' for Caedmon's 'teode,' whose structural function in the Hymn has already been hinted at. The lexical proposition is that the defectively preserved consonantal verb 'teon' / 'teogan' ('teode') meant 'adorn' as well as 'create (?), prepare, furnish,' which it should do for the theme or themes in the Hymn and *Beowulf* to be strictly analogous — for otherwise Caedmon's second verse-paragraph, lines 5-9, does not refer to decoration at all, but consists only of the two statements that God first created ('scop') heaven and then created ('teode') earth, an easy reading certainly. Evidence for the more difficult reading (God created heaven and then adorned the earth) may be found in the extended Beowulfian creation-scene already discussed, in some Latin writers to be noted shortly, and in the following OE poetic passages, cited from Klaeber's list.[21]

> Her ærest gescop   ece dryhten,
> helm eall-wihta,   heofon and eorðan,
> rodor arærde,   and þis rume land
> gestaðelode   strangum mihtum,
> frea ælmihtig.   Folde wæs þa gieta
> græs ungrene ...   (*Gen* 112-17a)

That is, colour was applied to the universe after its creation. No verb meaning 'decorate, adorn' is used, however.

> Þa sceawode   scieppend ure
> his weorca wlite   and his wæstma blæd,
> niwra gesceafta. ...

```
                  ...  Nealles wolcnu þa giet
ofer rumne grund  regnas bæron,
wann mid winde,       hwæðre wæstmum stod
folde gefrætwod.  (Gen 206-15a)
```

The new creation is decorated with greenery, as in *Beowulf* 96-7a, where the same verb 'frætwian' is used.

```
                       Scoldon hie þam folce gecyðan
hwa æt frum-sceafte      furðum teode
eorðan eall-grene      and upp-heofon,
hwær se wealdend wære    þe þæt weorc staðolode.  (And 796b-9)
```

The earth and its decorative colouring are created at once; 'teode' must here mean 'creatively adorned' or the like. Compare *Daniel* 204-16, where this verb is used for the setting up or furnishing of a (golden) image.

```
                     Beam sceal on eorðan
leafum liðan,       limu gnornian. ...
þy weorðeþ on foldan swa fela      fira cynnes,
ne sie þæs magu-timbres      gemet ofer eorðan,
gief hie ne wanige      se þas weorold teode.  (Mxm I 25b-34)
```

Leaves must fall; men would suffer over-population if he who created (and furnished, decorated?) the world did not diminish their numbers. The ecological theodicy here is perhaps more interesting than the possible secondary sense of 'decorated' in 'teode,' which, if it is there at all, depends on the Beowulfian collocation in the second line: 'limum and leafum,' *Beowulf* 97a.

```
Ece is se scieppend ...
He mec wrætlice      worhte æt frymþe,
þa he þisne ymb-hwyrft      ærest sette. ...
Ic eom fægerre      frætwum goldes. ...  (Rdl 40.1, 6-7, 46)
```

The universe both resembles an ornamented object and surpasses such an object in beauty. Here, as in the *Andreas* quotation above, creation and decoration are conceptually distinguished by the poet, but are thought of as simultaneous actions. Line 6 is a translation of Aldhelm's

De Creatura, 'Me variam fecit, primo dum conderet orbem.'[22]

In summary, creation and decoration are distinct ideas, sometimes presented sequentially in OE poetry, sometimes not; if 'teon' / 'teogan' and 'frætwian' are synonyms, an important thematic complex in OE poetry becomes more intelligible, but parallel citations do not entirely fix the synonymy, unless those in Caedmon's Hymn and *Beowulf* are thought to make it self-evident. To the support of purely textual arguments, however, we should add the testimony of early Christian writers in Latin.

The joint theme of creation and decoration in Christian poetry is apparently a reflex primarily of Genesis 2:1, 'Perfecti sunt coeli et terra, et omnis ornatus eorum,'[23] but also of some gloss like Ambrose's to Genesis 1:1, 'Primo fecit Deus, postea venustavit.'[24] It was this topos, we may believe, that Aldhelm reflected in his *De Creatura,* approximately during Caedmon's lifetime. If a patristic notion of such power and beauty were in the air it is not strange that a Caedmonian poem should echo it,[25] though perhaps odd that Bede's Latin paraphrase of the Hymn fails to certify it,[26] for Bede's own Latin poetry notices God's activity as a decorator: 'Deus ornavit orbem et aethera.'[27] One might assume that Bede was translating a version of the Hymn different from those now extant, or that his foreshortened Latin paraphrase of Caedmon's poem was careless in suppressing the decoration-motif,[28] or that the apparent reflection of this particular patristic notion in Caedmon's poem is a modern illusion.

That the Hymn and *Beowulf* have a Creation theme in common, whatever its etiology, is a truism for most modern commentators, even though Klaeber did not find them very similar: 'Vielmehr sind die beiden Fassungen so verschieden wie nur möglich.'[29] I have been trying to show a particularity in their common theme without comparing the two poems except in a few crucial details. Not surprisingly, two such different poems exhibit distinctive qualities even in their one close resemblance. *Beowulf's* cosmology is more free, more expansive (though less complete, since heaven is not created with the earth). Its verse in this section moves with a fluent lyric quality that was justly praised by Klaeber.[30] One may note as a curiosity that *Beowulf* is the less anthropocentric poem. The Hymn praises God for creating a roof and adorning a dwelling-place for mankind alone. In *Beowulf,* Hrothgar creates an ill-fated hall in which to practise the generosity God made possible for him, after the example of a God who created an English universe, a green and pleasant island, for all land-dwellers and living beings, among whom the non-human or sub-human Grendel is shortly to be noticed. While the Hymn's archaic restraint is relieved only by its march of epithet-ornaments, the much broader use of the creation-decoration topos in *Beowulf* seems by comparison boldly discursive and inventive, as in the striking presentiment of Heorot's burning just after its building is described. The typically Beowulfian thrust reaches us the more poignantly the more we are aware of an analogy or correlation between the two creations, universal and local. That predicted conflagration in the golden hall, somehow linked to a freshly made and decorated universe, comes to seem half legend, half eschatology. We are brought as close as OE poetry can bring us to a glimpse of the *Götterdämmerung,* or of 'the fire next time.'

As for Caedmon's Hymn, it is very hard at over a millenium's distance to settle finally upon the explanation of a short song attributed by Bede to an atypical singer a century before his own time, an oral-traditional amateur of uneasy genius who abandoned the harp to sing his songs for scribes to copy down. He was surely a most noteworthy transitional artist, but we know all too little of the transition within which he made his effect. Would such a man more naturally have composed a new Germanic doxology or a metamorphosed Christian praise song? Very possibly both, in some proportion beyond our analysis, but 'menn ne cunnon secgan to soðe.'

What is a little more certain is that the composer of the extended Heorot-Creation sequence in *Beowulf* responded to converging secular and religious elements in the tradition he inherited, and, we must believe, transformed. I conjecture that he was able to do this partly because he had heard in a Caedmonian praise song one staple of his own aesthetic creed that he shared with the Sutton Hoo goldsmith: creator and decorator are one.

In the major work that must one day be written on Anglo-Saxon aesthetics, there will surely be a chapter on functional ornament, decoration for use and show. 'Created for men, decorated for men.' A legendary hall had of course to be well-braced as well as gold-plated; a universe provided with a roof before it was embellished. The most splendid artifacts of the period betray an equally extravagant regard for ornamental utility. Among the Sutton Hoo treasures the sumptuously original Anglian jewellery serves as a matched set of seventeen fittings for the belt and shoulder-strap of some great man, like a 'Sam Browne' harness, the fittings of which are brass. The Sutton Hoo fittings are gold, inlaid and interlaced, and only three are unjewelled.[31]

This elegant decoration of a basic fabric must have seemed equally appropriate, where the means were available, for other kinds of craftsmen, including poets. Pondering the thematic construction and decoration of Heorot and the religious music sung there, one thinks of Benedict Biscop, who lived in the time of the Sutton Hoo artist, Caedmon, and Aldhelm, and of his progressive decoration of the new churches at Wearmouth and Jarrow from 670 to 684. Bede's *Historia Abbatum* describes Benedict bringing masons and glaziers from Gaul, and importing, eventually in no fewer than six journeys to Rome, 'ornamenta uel munimenta,' specified as books, relics, sacred vessels, vestments, and paintings, 'ad ornandum aecclesiam ... quam construxerat.'[32] 'First he built it,' certain poets might have noted with understanding and respect, 'then he adorned it.'

NOTES

1 *'Beowulf'* and *'The Fight at Finnsburg'* (3rd ed., Boston 1950), 158, note to 867b-915

2 'Widsith, Beowulf, and Brávellir,' in *Festgabe für L. L. Hammerich* (Copenhagen 1962), 161

3 'Die christlichen Elemente im *Beowulf*,' *Anglia* 35 (1911) 113. Cf Morton W. Bloomfield, 'Patristics and Old English Literature: Notes on Some Poems,' *Comparative Literature* 14 (1962) 36, who provides what is at first sight an opposed definition: '... a short example of a favorite ancient Christian literary genre, the poetic biblical paraphrase of an hexaemeral cast.' The present essay will explore the possibility that it is both, at second hand, to be sure, in both cases. All students of the Hymn are doubtless familiar with the most important modern studies of it, those by Wrenn, Magoun, Malone, and Blake, all cited in John C. Pope's *Seven Old English Poems* (Indianapolis 1966), 52-3, itself an admirably balanced and comprehensive survey of the Hymn and various scholarly topics that have grown up about it.

4 Texts for all poems cited in this essay are normalized — to remove for my readers a distraction that the early poets could not have comprehended — from George P. Krapp and Elliott V. K. Dobbie, eds., *The Anglo-Saxon Poetic Records*, 6 vols. (New York 1931-53). I am naturally indebted also to Klaeber's *Beowulf* and to John C. Pope's *The Rhythm of Beowulf* (rev. ed., New Haven 1966), with a specimen notation for Caedmon's Hymn, 214; Pope's normalization of the Hymn in *Seven Old English Poems* gave me 'meahta,' line 2, and the punctuation for my praise song.

5 This exercise owes much to Robert P. Creed, 'The Making of an Anglo-Saxon Poem,'

ELH 26 (1959) 445-54, and to William Whallon, 'The Idea of God in *Beowulf*,' *PMLA* 80 (1965) 19-23, and I now agree with their independent conclusions, after learned discussion of formulaic interchanges and substitutions, that the original texts contain 'the best of all possible *combinations of formulas*' (Creed, 454) and that 'the phrases are best in the text as it stands' (Whallon, 21). If I were as gifted as Creed I should have been more sensitive, no doubt, to the possibilities of certain new juxtapositions; if I were as bold as Whallon, I should have handled Caedmon's epithets for deity more drastically — that is, left some of them untouched to assert earthly kingship for the Danish king.

6 H.M. and N.K. Chadwick, *The Growth of Literature* (Cambridge 1932), I, 42
7 *Heroic Poetry* (London 1952), 8
8 *The Anglo-Saxon Chronicle*, rev. trans., ed. Dorothy Whitelock, with David C. Douglas and Susie I. Tucker (New Brunswick, N.J. 1962), for example, *s.a.* 975. See my review in *Manuscripta* 7 (1963) 176-8.
9 Pope, *Seven Old English Poems*, 53
10 'An Old English *Encomium Urbis*,' *JEGP* 40 (1941) 14-28
11 The account is found in the *Laxdæla saga*, 29. See Lee M. Hollander, *The Skalds* (Princeton 1947), 49-54. The fragments of the house-poem are tantalizing, for they describe heroic stained carvings on the wainscoting and roof timbers 'so excellently well executed that the hall looked more magnificent when the hangings [of tapestry] were not up' (Hollander, 49); cf *Beowulf* 994b-6 and Klaeber's note on the tapestries in Heorot. The skald's poem incorporated ancient tales based on the carvings, stories of the Brísing's necklace, Thor's fight with the Midgard serpent, and Baldr's funeral pyre. Collectors of Beowulfian analogues may wish to take notice of this Icelandic panegyric for a great man and his new dwelling, in a setting of wealth and social promise that soon turns to tragedy (the marriage of the chieftain's daughter and his new son-in-law ends fatally in the saga's next chapter amid circumstances involving an accursed sword). However, in the saga the hall Hjardarholt survives; it was 'larger and better than any that men had seen' (ch. 29); cf *Beowulf* 69-70: '... medu-ærn micel   men gewyrcan / þanne ielda bearn   æfre gefrunon.'
12 Sir John Sandys, ed. *The Odes of Pindar* (New York 1915), 152-67. Upon his victory in the chariot-race of 470 BC, Hieron of Ætna is praised as founder of a city and victor in war. The lyre-playing in his court is part of a cosmic music, and the monster Typhos, underground nearby, hears and shudders at it. See C.M. Bowra, *Pindar* (Oxford 1964), 41. Another Beowulfian analogue? This classical panegyric resembles *Beowulf* at least as much as the Virgilian lines sometimes cited: Klaeber, *Beowulf*, note to 90-8; Tom Burns Haber, *A Comparative Study of the Beowulf and the Aeneid* (Princeton 1931), 132-3, referring to *Aeneid* I.740-6, VI.724-9. The song of Iopas at Dido's court in I mentions the moon, sun, and other luminaries and the origin of living beings, rain, and fire, without mention of a creator or a creative

act; in VI the shade of Anchises gives a moralized anatomy of the cosmos. Haber believes the *Beowulf*-poet knew Caedmon's Hymn but took his setting and 'inspiration' from Virgil.

13 Jeffrey Opland, 'Two Xhosa Oral Poems,' *Papers in African Languages* ([Cape Town] 1970), 86-98; a fascinating account of the *imbongi* (or praise-singer) Zamumzi Sinqoto, a road gang labourer aged 23, is found on 93 ff. For a general study of Bantu praise-singing see Trevor Cope, *Izibongo: Zulu Praise-Poems* (Oxford 1968). Cope's poems concern chiefs who died before 1884, and the collector treats them as memorized poems (Opland, 87). As Opland's study makes plain, the Xhosa *imbongi* composes extemporaneously.

14 Cf 'Hroþgar leofa,' 1483, 'glæd-mann Hroþgar,' 367, 'þeoden Hroþgar,' 417. In Caedmon's alliterative and syntactic framework, which we are following arbitrarily for the composite poem, the king's name would be restricted to the main stave in lines 1 and 6, where Caedmon's 'h——es weard' will not accommodate it. One could of course recompose more freely: 'Nu sculon herian   Hroþgares ærn,' etc, or, abandoning both Caedmon's Type E off-verse rhythm and Beowulfian epithet-usage, 'Nu sculon herian   Hroþgar cyning,' etc; which would be like playing tennis without a net.

15 I am indebted here to Edward B. Irving, Jr, *A Reading of Beowulf* (New Haven 1968), 89-90, and to Alvin A. Lee, *The Guest-Hall of Eden: Four Essays on the Design of Old English Poetry* (New Haven 1972), 175-9, but my treatment of the two creations differs from that of either scholar in being limited to a relatively simple structural matter.

16 If the 'gief-stol' is a decorated throne (cf *Mxm* I.68 'gief-stol [sceal] gegierwed standan') or an object precious and valuable by association with the gift-giving promised and fulfilled by Hrothgar in his decorated hall (*Beowulf*, 71-3, 76a, 80-la, 167 ['sinc-fage sæl,' immediately before the crux]), it forms part of a decoration theme and is less likely to be an interpolation or lapse of poet or scribe: 'Grendel could not approach (or attack) the (decorated) gift-seat of Hrothgar, that precious object, because of God's protection'; but this to be sure gets us only three-quarters of the way through the crux, and the decoration theme does not help with 'ne his myne wisse.'

17 I take for granted that 'scop' ('poet-singer') and 'scieppan' ('shape, create') were heard as related terms by OE poets and audiences, whether through popular etymology or as acoustic puns; but they are apparently not related. See Alois Walde, *Vergleichendes Wörterbuch der indogermanischen Sprachen*, ed. Julius Pokorny (Berlin 1927-30). The synonymy of OE 'scop' with other words for 'poet' is another question; see Norman E. Eliason, 'The Þyle and Scop in *Beowulf*,' *Speculum* 38 (1963) 267-84.

18 Klaeber, 'Die christlichen Elemente,' 114; *Beowulf*, note to 90-8

19 This *Beowulf* passage uses eleven epithets for deity (twelve if 'for meotode,' 169a refers to God), eight (or nine) of them Caedmonian. The Hymn's 'weard,' 'wuldor-,' and 'frea ælmihtig' appear elsewhere in *Beowulf* but not in this passage; *Beowulf*'s 'demend,' 'heofona helm,' and 'wealdend' do not appear in the Hymn.

20 Klaeber, 'Die christlichen Elemente,' 113-61. Titles are adjusted from the editions cited by Klaeber to those in Krapp-Dobbie, and listed in the order of the Krapp-Dobbie volumes. Line references are sometimes corrected or expanded, and I have added a few references to Klaeber's list. Abbreviations are those given by F.P. Magoun, Jr, in *Études anglaises* 3 (1955) 138-46. Five references touching on the decoration theme, to be discussed below, are marked with asterisks.

21 Unhappily, the easy reading is vouched for by Bede's prose paraphrase, in which 'creauit' governs both 'caelum' and 'terram' in the poem's last sentence; this would make both 'scop' and 'teode' mean 'created.' See Charles Plummer, *Venerabilis Baedae Historiam Ecclesiasticam* ... (Oxford 1886), I, 260. Professor Pope, *Seven Old English Poems*, 52, notes that Bede's paraphrase, 'by deliberately avoiding the repetition and shortening the second section' of the poetic summary, obscures the poem's symmetry; OE lexicography and literary study have been affected by Bede's sentence also. No meaning 'adorn' appears for the appropriate verb in Joseph Bosworth and T. Northcote Toller, *An Anglo-Saxon Dictionary* (London 1898), or in Toller's *Supplement*; users of Bosworth-Toller may choose from among 'to make, frame, create, ordain, arrange, contrive, bring about, construct,' a list which is more rationally subdivided, with allowance for 'adorn' also, in J.R. Clark Hall, *A Concise Anglo-Saxon Dictionary* (4th ed., Cambridge 1962). *Beowulf* editors, glossing the word at lines 43 (where it certainly means 'furnish, provide') and 1452 (where it could mean 'adorn') have generally followed Bosworth-Toller; so Klaeber (1922-50 editions) and Else von Schaubert (1949), with A.J. Wyatt and R.W. Chambers (1914) relenting to allow 'adorn' as one possible meaning. C.L. Wrenn (1953, 1958) did not gloss the word at all. For the verb in the Hymn, Professor Pope, in *Seven Old English Poems*, glosses 'adorn, prepare, create,' but Professor Dobbie's edition in *Anglo-Saxon Minor Poems* (New York 1942) translated 'teode' as 'created.' Of modern authorities, only A.H. Smith, *Three Northumbrian Poems* (London 1933), 40, unequivocally and simply translates 'adorn.'

22 Frederick Tupper, Jr, ed., *The Riddles of the Exeter Book* (Boston 1910), 162

23 Klaeber, 'Die christlichen Elemente,' 115

24 Bernard F. Huppé, *Doctrine and Poetry* (Albany 1959), 99-130. I cite here from the reprint in Martin Stevens and Jerome Mandel, eds., *Old English Literature* (Lincoln, Nebraska 1968), 131.

25 Bloomfield, 43

26 As noted by Smith, 40, n. 7

27 Bede, 'Hymnus de opere sex dierum,' cited by Klaeber, 'Die christlichen Elemente,' 115

28 But see again Pope's remarks about Bede's paraphrase, cited in note 21 above.

29 Klaeber, 'Die christlichen Elemente,' 114

30 Klaeber, *Beowulf*, note to 90-8: 'The rare note of joy in the beauty of nature contrasts impressively with the melancholy inspired by the dreary, somber abode of Grendel.'

31 Charles Green, *Sutton Hoo* (New York 1963), 78

32 Plummer, 369

STANLEY B. GREENFIELD

'Gifstol' and goldhoard in *Beowulf*

As a tribute to John Collins Pope it would be satisfying to be able to
offer something as substantial and persuasive of general acceptance as
his own contributions to the study of Old English literature have been.
I cannot aspire to such substantiality and definitiveness, however; still
I hope the following observations on the meaning of the dragon's hoard
in *Beowulf* may be deemed not unworthy as a 'hygeweorðung' for the
distinguished scholar this volume seeks to honour.

Attempts at valuation of the hoard have been many, and its wildly
fluctuating critical market suggests it has not yet been pegged at its
true rate. There are obvious reasons for this critical state of affairs:
cruces of interpretation haunt individual words and lines (for example,
lines 3074-5), and conflicting testimonies in the poem about the provenance and status of the treasure do not lend themselves to ready ac-
commodation. Also, the generic expectations critics bring to the poem,
their differing aesthetic responses to tonal quality, and different meth-
odological approaches have in no small way contributed their share to
the various overlapping, and more frequently incompatible, significations
assigned the treasure. Michael Cherniss has noted that such assignations
conveniently polarize into favourable or unfavourable, good or evil.[1]
Quite so, but this reductive categorization does scant justice to the
range of proposed symbolic values: honour and men's worthiness; the
social good; worldly *sapientia*; transience; the vanity of worldly
wealth; avarice and cupidity; spiritual death and damnation[2] — to mention but a few. It would seem that while the poem's treasure led to

Beowulf's death and was useless to the Geats, it has gained a life of its own in, and some value for, critical controversy.

I should like to argue in this paper that the context of the poem has deposited upon the hoard a contrariety of functions that render attempts to find an overriding signification unconvincing. For the hoard is a nucleus of different meanings, so much so that Edward Irving suggests

> it would be well to admit that we cannot recapture all [of them] now. For it seems likely that even the pre-Christian attitude towards treasure must have contained its own inherent complexities; when a Christian point of view (and which Christian point of view?) is super-imposed on it without entirely replacing it, we have rich possibilities for ambiguity, if not for genuine confusion.[3]

Nevertheless, I think some of these possibilities, particularly in the pre-Christian attitude, can be clarified, even if all confusion cannot be un-confounded.

Let us begin with the function of the treasure in the narrative line of *Beowulf*. Whereas in part I the hero's motivation and goal were clearly defined by a single moral imperative — the elimination of a marauder (Grendel, Grendel's mother) to avenge a feud — in part II they are, at least superficially, disparate: the moral burden of revenge to be taken upon the dragon for his destructive attack on the one hand, and the acquisition of a treasure on the other. But dragons and buried treasure were in a way inseparable to the Anglo-Saxon mind: we have frequently been reminded in this connection of Cotton *Gnomes* 26b-7a, 'draca sceal on hlæwe, / frod, frætwum wlanc.'[4] Further, there is the suggestion in part I that the deed of derring-do which kills a dragon and takes his treasure is indeed a single act of heroism, one which has positive value for the poet and his audience: I refer, of course, to the Danish scop's jubilant account of Sigemund's dragon fight and his winning 'selfes dome ... beorhte frætwa.' (884b-97) Most critics have seen in this recitation an implicit favourable comparison with Beowulf.[5] Certain other parallels between parts I and II have not to my knowledge, however, been sufficiently acknowledged; and these parallels contribute in different ways to the positive value of the hoard.

We may note in the first place that Beowulf's Danish exploits are not without their material rewards. Though the hero undertakes his venture against Grendel out of true nobility of spirit, with perhaps some thought to repay Hrothgar for his earlier kindness to his father Ecgtheow,[6] the concept of reward for such favours rendered is obviously implicit in the heroic ethos, and Hrothgar makes it explicit when he finally accepts Beowulf's offer: 'Ne bið þe wilna gad, / gif þu þæt ellenweorc aldre gedigest.' (660b-1) When Beowulf performs as promised, Hrothgar not only wishes to adopt him as a son, but again states that he will give him treasure (946b-50); and at the banquet that evening he does so, the poet describing the gifts in some detail (1020-49). The same pattern holds in the Grendel's mother episode: promise before action in 1380-2, promise again after action in 1706b-7a and 1783b-4, and actual giving in 1866-7. Now, if we look carefully at the order of events in part II, we see that Beowulf resolves to fight the dragon because of the devastation he has wrought before he even knows there is a treasure involved:

> Hæfde ligdraca   leoda fæsten,
> ealond utan,   eorðweard ðone
> gledum forgrunden;   him ðæs guðkyning,
> Wedera þioden   wræce leornode.   (2333-6)

It is not until after he has had the iron shield made and has set off on this expedition that we are told

> hæfde þa gefrunen,   hwanan sio fæhð aras,
> bealonið biorna;   him to bearme cwom
> maðþumfæt mære   þurh ðæs meldan hond.   (2403-5)

Although the use of 'þa' following an initial verb in an independent clause is a common syntactic feature of Old English poetry in general and of *Beowulf* in particular, usually to be translated 'then' or not translated at all, the context of these lines suggests that 'þa' here means 'by that time'; and the whole passage unmistakably indicates that this knowledge about the origin of the feud has come to Beowulf only after his decision to avenge that feud. Thus Beowulf's motive in this case, although more personal, is no less noble or 'pure' than it was in his earlier ventures. But, despite the selflessness of motivation, the heroic pattern, as we have noted above, calls for a reward. In the Danish instances, Hrothgar was at hand to provide the 'expected' bonus; here Beowulf, in fulfilment of that pattern, becomes his own gift-giver. For this purpose the dragon's treasure will serve. So the hero can with propriety subsequently say,

>   'Ic mid elne sceall
> gold gegangan,   oððe guð nimeð,
> feorhbealu frecne   frean eowerne!'   (2535b-7)

That the poet has told us 'næs þæt yðe ceap / to gegangenne   gumena ænigum' (2415b-16) and that the hero will die in the attempt is, in the context of the poem, tragically ironic, but this result in no way demeans Beowulf's motive and procedure.

Beowulf, however, is not just a hero in part II, he is king,[7] and as he lies dying he gives voice to his concern for his people, telling Wiglaf to attend to their needs (2800b-1a) and glorying in his having won the treasure for their benefit (2794-8). This concern leads me to the second parallel I would entertain between parts I and II as layering the hoard with strands of positive meaning: that between Hrothgar and Beowulf as kings in their moments of greatest crisis. Each in effect has lost his 'gifstol,' the latter by the dragon's breath, the former by Grendel's mouthed defiance. Each, therefore, finds the act of gold-giving, so central to his function as a good king,[8] frustrated. Here we touch upon the thorny problem of interpretation of lines 168-9, and we must pause to consider this passage and its context in greater detail.

The word 'gifstol' occurs in *Beowulf* only on two occasions: in the description of conditions in Heorot due to Grendel's visitations and in that of Geatland ravaged by the dragon. In the former instance, after a great amount of uncertainty, critics seem today largely to accept a reading in which lines 168-9, 'no he þone gifstol   gretan moste, / maþðum for Metode,   ne his myne wisse,' refer to Grendel, who cannot 'approach (or attack) the throne of Hrothgar (or/and God), nor know God's (or Hrothgar's) love (or mind or purpose).' The many explanations and rationalizations for this line of interpretation, involving such concepts as the sanctity of the throne and Grendel as an anti-thane,[9] are reasonable enough, up to a point; but in the end I find them less than satisfactory. Such an uneasiness, centring around the referent of the word 'þæt' which begins line 170, prompted Arthur G. Brodeur in his *Art of Beowulf* to argue at length for an interpretation that sees the 'he' of line 168 refer proleptically to Hrothgar, who is then focussed upon in line 170 as 'wine Scyldinga.'[10] As Brodeur recognized, a major difficulty with this position is that it involves a sudden switch of reference from Grendel to Hrothgar by means of the pronoun when the

king has not been mentioned since line 152a; but he adduced a number
of syntactic and contextual parallels or similarities that would allow,
easily enough, for such a reading. Nevertheless his argument has not
won devotees, and a recent interpretation of these lines does not even
mention the possibility that the 'he' may refer to Hrothgar and not to
Grendel.[11] Yet if we view Hrothgar's position in this part of the poem
as parallel to Beowulf's later dilemma (a structural feature unfortunately not considered by Brodeur), then it makes excellent sense to see
lines 168-9 referring to Hrothgar's inability to approach his 'gifstol'
while Grendel occupies the hall at night. Under these circumstances
Hrothgar cannot distribute treasure properly, as a good king should: as
he had promised on the inception of Heorot he would (71-3), and as
he had dutifully performed (80-1a) 'oð ðæt an ongan' to render the
gift-seat nocturnally unusable. It is this negation of his function as a
gold-giver (perhaps as much symbolic as literal) that is a 'breaking of
spirit to the friendly lord of the Scyldings.' If we read the passage this
way, we avoid the awkward parenthesis around lines 168-9 (Klaeber
text), and the difficulty of referent for 'Þæt'; and we achieve not only
a more straightforward narrative account but a clearer reading for 'ne
his myne wisse.' We thus would have the following (the punctuation is
my suggestion):

> Swa fela fyrena   feond mancynnes,
> atol angengea   oft gefremede,
> heardra hynða;   Heorot eardode,
> sincfage sel   sweartum nihtum.
> No he þone gifstol   gretan moste,
> maþðum for Metode,   ne his myne wisse:
> þæt wæs wræc micel   wine Scyldinga,
> modes brecða.

Thus (in summary of what has up to this point been detailed about
Grendel's behaviour) the enemy of mankind, the terrible lone-goer,
often performed many crimes, terrible injuries; he occupied Heorot,
the treasure-adorned hall, on dark nights. Not at all might he (Hrothgar) approach the gift-throne, (that) treasure before God, nor did he
understand his purpose (in so depriving him): that was a great distress, a breaking of spirit, to the friendly lord of the Scyldings.

The poet then continues immediately with the description of how 'many a mighty one sat in council' to seek a solution to the problem of Grendel, and how many turned to pagan ritual in their confusion.

In this reading, as I indicated above, 'ne his myne wisse' offers little difficulty: it refers to Hrothgar's failure to understand God's purpose in so depriving him of the substance of his kingship.[12] It is only through his continuing experience of misfortune, which lasts twelve years, that he reaches a position where, at the end of that time, he can lecture the young Beowulf about the pitfall awaiting that man arrogant enough to assume that he is so powerful that he is exempt from all enmity and change for the worse (1772b-3). It is Beowulf's advent on the scene that gives hope to the aged king for an 'edwenden' of his troubles, hope that the treasure-adorned hall ('sincfage sel') may become once again a place for distributing 'sinc.' When the hero performs what he promises, Hrothgar, with his 'gifstol' made functional once again, can be lavish in bestowing treasure upon his deliverer.

When Beowulf in turn in 'ufarum dogrum' is deprived of his ability to be a good king by the total destruction of his 'gifstol,' it is no wonder that he, like Hrothgar before him, experiences disquietude, feels he does not understand God's purpose in this wanton and seemingly senseless havoc, wonders whether he has not offended God 'ofer ealde riht' (2327b-32).[13] (I think it important to stress again that Beowulf's distress of mind occurs before he discovers the role of the hoard in the feud.) But Hrothgar's gift-seat had remained at least physically intact; all he needed was a champion to remove the barrier between himself and that literal-symbolic seat in order to resume his powers. Beowulf, on the other hand, is in need of more drastic remedy. I suggest that the dragon's hoard, when he is made aware of its existence, offers itself to his eyes as a 'maþðum' to replace his destroyed 'gifstol,' as a prospective redistribution and rehabilitation 'centre' after he avenges the feud. I realize the poet does not make this *quid pro quo* explicit (or I would cite the lines), but the hypothesis does not seem to me unreasonable if we accept a perspective on the hero as a model of deportment, however much he may be wrong as to the value the treasure will have for his nation. Some recent criticism holds that Beowulf's decision to fight the dragon and win the treasure reveals an obstinacy of mind, a foolish trust in his own strength ('Nis þæt eower sið / ne gemet mannes, nefne min anes,' 2532b-3), a denial of reliance upon God, and an ignoring of his followers' 'cease and desist' entreaty 'Ne meahton we gelæran leofne þeoden, / ... / þæt he ne grette goldweard þone,' 3079-81);[14] but this is to ignore the heroic expectations of the measure of the hero[15] which is so much a part of the poem's fabric.

The hoard is thus, in its positive meaning, not only the focal point and stimulus of heroic exploit — it is as well a symbol of some thematic consequence. By concentrating on this value of the treasure and its dual relation to treasure-giving, we can with Cherniss see the hoard as representative of men's worthiness and honour through their deeds and its reburial with the dead Beowulf as a symbol of the Geats' dishonour and unworthiness in their defection. Such an interpretation is attractive, and I am tempted to push it a bit farther by suggesting that the rusted and ultimately useless hoard is an analogue for the cowards themselves, their honour gone to rust, and that the still-gleaming standard that lights the ground-plain for Wiglaf inside the mound (2767-71a) similarly is an analogue for Wiglaf, the retainer in whom the heroic light still shines. Such a single-minded interpretation can only be maintained, however, at the expense of ignoring other manifestations of the hoard's being and essence. For there are obvious negative associations that the poet has been at some pains to foreground.

Throughout the poem he has vilified the hoarding of wealth: he has praised the practice of its antithesis, from Beowulf I's distribution of treasure 'on fæder bearme' through Hrothgar's dispensation of rewards; and he has condemned it outright in the twice-told exemplum of Heremod and in Hrothgar's warning to Beowulf to eschew the path of miserliness. The treasure hoard by its very essence is 'hoarding' and 'notgiving'; in the poem's context it cannot avoid the implications of niggardliness. It is indeed a fitting symbolic counterpart to its anti-king 'agend,' the dragon.[16] But it should not be confused with treasure *per se* or with gold-giving: Hrothgar's sermon is not directed against gold as such, only against an unremitting accumulation of it.

With its negative and positive implications of meaning, the hoard pulls in two directions at once, and the narrative features of part II reflect this double direction. Beowulf's desire to gain it, his eagerness to see it before he dies so that he may die the easier by his view of it (2749b-51), and his hope for it as his people's salvation are concomitants of its positive thematic role.[17] The hoard's elegiac burial by the last survivor, the unrightful behaviour of the dragon ('unrihte,' 3059a) in keeping it hidden, its reburial and uselessness to the Geats — these belong to its negative meaning. But there is a further possibility on the negative side, embodied in the poet's Christian perspective. How potent this perspective is for meaning depends upon the critic's generic view of the poem and his consequent understanding of Hrothgar's sermon and its relation to Beowulf's later actions, the second account of the hoard's burial, and the poet's explicit remarks about buried treasure.

We might legitimately expect that an Anglo-Saxon Christian poet and his audience would see in the buried rusting earthly treasure an intimation of a heavenly treasure beyond the ravages of time. Yet the poet has done remarkably little in an explicit way to encourage response to such an overtone of meaning. There is Hrothgar's admonition to Beowulf to choose 'ece rædas' (1760a); there is the curse on the hoard which involves mention of 'domes dæg,' 'synnum scildig,' and 'hell-bendum fæst,' phrases which show 'that the poet is not really thinking in heathen terms'[18] despite the narrative context of the curse; there is the poet's interpolation of lines 2764b-6:

> Sinc eaðe mæg,
> gold on grund(e)   gumcynnes gehwone
> oferhigian,   hyde se ðe wylle;

and there is the poet's comment on the uselessness to men of the hoard reburied: 'þær hit nu gen lifað / eldum swa unnyt,   swa hi(t æro)r wæs.' (3167b-8)

On the first of these possible explicit encouragements, I would mention only that the meaning of 'ece rædas' has been disputed: at least one interpreter who sees the poem in Christian terms considers the words to refer to everlasting fame in this world rather than to life after death and advice to the hero to seek the proper relationship with God.[19] The second point, the curse, is a very sticky problem and may well be, as Margaret Goldsmith suggests, an artistic blemish.[20] Or perhaps we may view it in terms analogous to those by which E.G. Stanley shows us we should view 'realistic' description in the elegies;[21] that is, as conventional objective correlatives for mental and emotional states — so that the curse should not be understood literally but as a conventional theme or topos by which the poet conveys unmistakably the hoard's negative implications. As for the poet's intrusive comment on the overpowering effect of gold in the ground in lines 2764b-6, I would note that, whatever the precise meanings of 'oferhigian' and 'hyde' may be, the words do not have the same explicit Christian pointing of lines 100-2 of The Seafarer:

> ne mæg þære sawle   þe biþ synna full
> gold to geoce   for Godes egesan,
> þonne he hit ær hydeþ   þenden he her leofaþ.

Moreover, consider for a moment the passage in which the *Beowulf* poet's comment appears; it is descriptive of what Wiglaf sees when he enters the mound at his dying lord's request:

> þær wæs helm monig
> eald ond omig,   earmbeaga fela
> searwum gesæled. —   Sinc eaðe mæg,
> gold on grund(e)   gumcynnes gehwone
> oferhigian,   hyde se ðe wylle! —
> Swylce he siomian geseah   segn eallgylden
> heah ofer horde ...   (2762b-8a)

If lines 2764b-7a were omitted, along with the following transitional verse, the sense and metrical requirements would not be affected at all: we would simply have a continuation of the enumeration of treasures which Wiglaf sees! (I would not press this 'interpolation' theory, but it is worth noting as a possibility.) Finally, on the poet's statement about the gold being 'as useless to men as it had been before' in lines 3167b-8, I would suggest that it need be no more than a factual observation about the literal value of this particular hoard in the narrative.

Of course the contention of critics who would interpret the gold as a temptation to sin and an invitation to spiritual damnation does not rest on these somewhat problematic explicit passages but on presumed parallels between *Beowulf* and exegetical commentary, based on the assumption of a tacit understanding between poet and audience as to how to listen to or read poetry.[22] I do not wish to explore my reservations on this position here: I have recently said something about this matter elsewhere apropos of Beowulf's behaviour in the dragon fight,[23] and not too long ago Bruce Mitchell argued with some force against it vis-à-vis the meaning of the dragon.[24] Mitchell's arguments have not deterred subsequent assays in this direction, nor do I expect mine to do so. Nevertheless, they must be made, and may give some critics pause.

In this essay I have been chiefly concerned with the positive and negative meanings for the goldhoard within the heroic ethos, but have not ruled out the existence of a Christian overlay of meaning (though not too weighty a one) that complicates or increases the treasure's negative quality. It is this perspective which leads me to conclude that it is better that we view the significance of the treasure as a problem that will forever remain unresolved — though the tension in meanings is nonetheless effective in the aesthetic of the poem — than that we try obstinately to achieve a consistent evaluation of less than true currency.

NOTES

1 'The Progress of the Hoard in *Beowulf*,' *PQ* 47 (1968) 473-86
2 See Cherniss; Edward B. Irving, Jr, *A Reading of Beowulf* (New Haven 1968), 208; R.E. Kaske, '*Sapientia et Fortitudo* as the Controlling Theme of *Beowulf*,' *SP* 55 (1958) 448; Margaret E. Goldsmith, *The Mode and Meaning of Beowulf* (London 1970), 94 (as symbol of transience) and 96 (as symbol of cupidity); Kemp Malone, 'Symbolism in "Beowulf": Some Suggestions,' in *English Studies Today*, 2nd series, ed. G.A. Bonnard (Bern 1961), 90; and Alvin A. Lee, *The Guest-Hall of Eden* (New Haven 1972), 216.
3 Irving, 207
4 Textual quotations are from *The Anglo-Saxon Poetic Records*, 6 vols. ed. G.P. Krapp and E.V.K. Dobbie (New York 1931-53), except for *Beowulf*, where I have used Fr. Klaeber's 3rd edition (Boston 1950).
5 For a critic who sees the dissimilarities as more prominent and thus a negative reflection on Beowulf, see H.L. Rogers, 'Beowulf's Three Great Fights,' in L.E. Nicholson, ed., *An Anthology of Beowulf Criticism* (Notre Dame 1963), 254, originally in *RES* 6 (1955) 339-55. Goldsmith, 227, would deny any necessary connection between the dragon fight and the acquisition of treasure.
6 So Adrien Bonjour, *The Digressions in Beowulf* (Oxford 1950), 15-16
7 John Leyerle, 'Beowulf the Hero and the King,' *MÆ* 34 (1965) 89-102, would use this distinction to condemn Beowulf's actions in part II as wrong or misguided within the heroic ethos.
8 The best exposition of this relationship between gold-giving and kingship is by Ernst Leisi, 'Gold und Manneswert im *Beowulf*,' *Anglia* 71 (1953) 259-73.
9 See, e.g., Robert M. Estrich, 'The Throne of Hrothgar,' *JEGP* 43 (1944) 384-9; Irving, 110-11, 209.
10 *The Art of Beowulf* (Berkeley 1959), 200-4
11 Betty S. Cox, *Cruces of Beowulf* (The Hague 1971), 56-79, who would see the 'gifstol' as related to the Ark of the Covenant
12 See Leisi, 263.
13 On this phrase, see Morton W. Bloomfield, 'Patristics and Old English Literature,' *Comparative Literature* 14 (1962) 39-41.
14 I refer to Goldsmith's *Mode and Meaning* in particular, and have argued against

these various points in *The Interpretation of Old English Poems* (London 1972), 18-20, 136-7, 156-7.

15 See Daniel G. Calder, 'Setting and Ethos: The Pattern of Measure and Limit in *Beowulf*,' *SP* 69 (1972) 21-37, esp. 30 ff.

16 On the dragon in this light, see Irving, 209.

17 An interesting parallel of a sort may be found in the *Life* of St. Wilfrid of York who, when he felt death nigh, requested the treasury of Ripon, with its gold, silver, and precious jewels, brought before his eyes. The anonymous re-teller of Eddius's account in John Henry Newman's *Lives of the English Saints* (London 1900), I, has the comment: 'A strange sight, surely, for a dying Saint! but it was not to feast his eyes with pride, as Hezekiah had done when he paraded the ambassador through his treasure-house' (430). Wilfrid, of course, then asked for the treasure to be divided into four heaps, one for the churches of St Mary and St Paul in Rome, another for the poor for his soul's redemption, a third for the priors of Ripon and Hexham, and the fourth for his former companions-in-exile; but this incident in a saint's life tends to support, I believe, a positive reading of Beowulf's attitude towards the dragon's treasure when he asks to view it and then thanks God that he has acquired it for his people (2794-8). I am most grateful to Fred C. Robinson for having called this parallel to my attention.

18 Goldsmith, 230

19 Charles Donahue, '*Beowulf* and Christian Tradition: A Reconsideration from a Celtic Stance,' *Traditio* 21 (1965) 82; Goldsmith argues against this reading on page 206 of her book.

20 Goldsmith, 95

21 'Old English Poetic Diction and the Interpretation of *The Wanderer, The Seafarer* and *The Penitent's Prayer*,' *Anglia* 73 (1955-6) 413-66

22 See Bernard F. Huppé, *Doctrine and Poetry: Augustine's Influence on Old English Poetry* (New York 1959).

23 See note 14 above.

24 'Until the Dragon Comes — Some Thoughts on *Beowulf*,' *Neophilologus* 47 (1963) 126-38

FRED C. ROBINSON

Elements of the marvellous
in the characterization of Beowulf:
a reconsideration of the
textual evidence

Elements of the marvellous are not uncommon in *Beowulf*. A fire-breathing dragon, sea monsters, and magically protected ogres from the race of Cain are but some of the fabulous wonders that the poet has admitted to his story. But in general the wonders are carefully restricted to the devil's party. Against these superhuman (as well as many human) adversaries the hero Beowulf can pit only his man's strength and his man's courage.[1] True, he is not an average man — 'se þe manna wæs mægene strengest / on þæm dæge þysses lifes' (789-90)[2] — but he is *only* a strong man, and the poem thus reveals how the best of human beings might comport themselves in their struggle against the hopeless odds of the enemy. If the poet had been indiscriminate in his use of the supernatural, if he had lavished fabulous powers on ogre and champion alike, then the hero would have become a kind of monster himself, and *Beowulf*, instead of being a heroic poem, would have been a romantic fable describing the conflict between good monsters and bad monsters.

The poet's concern to portray Beowulf as a man rather than as superhuman is revealed in his repeated allusions to the hero's physical limitations and vulnerability. Most memorable, perhaps, is the account of Beowulf's suffering and death in the last part of the poem, a subject which is discussed with characteristic eloquence in John C. Pope's essay for the Meritt Festschrift.[3] But there are earlier reminders of human fallibility. In lines 739 and following we see that Beowulf is incapable of preventing Grendel from killing and devouring the Geatish warrior Hondscioh, and later he confesses to Hrothgar (960-2, 967-70) that he lacked the strength to hold the monster in the hall and kill him there, as he wanted to do. The poet tells us that Beowulf all but died in his struggle with the hag (1550 ff), a fact which the hero himself acknowledges in his reports to Hrothgar (1655-7) and to Hygelac (2140 ff). In the dragon fight, only Wiglaf's intervention saves Beowulf from an instant and ignominious death.[4] The inadequacy thus demonstrated was sensed by the hero earlier when he apologized for having to use a sword and armour in his last adventure (2518 ff). Here as elsewhere in his closing speeches, 'the sense of his own vulnerability seems to draw him closer to the period of boyhood dependency,'[5] and we are reminded that throughout the poem he has been portrayed as a man, not a demigod.

But is it true that in characterizing Beowulf the poet systematically eschews elements of the marvellous? Doesn't he in fact sometimes allow the hero's physical powers to grow embarrassingly far beyond human dimensions? Beowulf remains underwater for hours — or perhaps for an entire day — as he descends to the bottom of Grendel's mere. Alone, he carries thirty suits of armour from the battlefield in Frisia and swims with them through the North Sea and the Skagerrak to Geatland, a distance of some five hundred miles. In early life he swam for five to seven days with his companion Breca, slaying sea monsters by night. At these points in the narrative it would seem that the distinction between the powers of men and the powers of his supernatural adversaries becomes quite indistinct.

At least two critics of the poem have perceived just how important these lapses are for our understanding of the nature and meaning of *Beowulf*. Citing the three episodes just mentioned, Rodney Delasanta and James Slevin point out that such feats temporarily remove Beowulf from the category of 'high mimetic hero' and mark him instead as a 'romance hero,' one who is superior not only to other men but also to his environment.[6] By applying Northrop Frye's terms to *Beowulf*, Delasanta and Slevin bring into clear focus the tensions between epic and romance qualities which seemed to trouble W.P. Ker: 'There was a danger that Beowulf should be transformed into a sort of Amadis,' he muses, and concludes uncertainly, 'this danger is avoided, at least in part.'[7]

It is my purpose in the present essay to argue that, if we return to the text of *Beowulf* and examine each of the three occasions where Beowulf seems to be temporarily endowed with supernatural powers, we will discover a strange insubstantiality in the evidence for such endowments. In fact, I am convinced that the supposed evidence for a superhuman Beowulf is largely a fiction of editorial interpretation and comment and that Beowulf throughout is conceived of as a heroic man and not as a romance hero. The reason for the supernaturalizing misinterpretations, I shall further suggest, is that in reading the poem scholars may have been excessively influenced by its folktale analogues and so have sometimes read back into the sophisticated text of the poet a wild extravagance which he had carefully purged from the material he adopted.

THE DESCENT INTO GRENDEL'S MERE

In his account of Beowulf's fight with the ogress the poet is at some pains to explain that the conflict does not take place under water but rather in a dry chamber where no water could reach the combatants:

>   Ða se eorl ongeat,
> þæt he [in] niðsele   nathwylcum wæs,
> þær him nænig wæter   wihte ne scepede,
> ne him for hrofsele   hrinan ne mehte
> færgripe flodes.   (1512-16)[8]

Thus localized, Beowulf's exploit is one which we could imagine a human being performing, and as the fight progresses and he begins to lose ground, we are prepared to believe that the hero is indeed fighting desperately for his life.

This careful circumscription of the hero's power is completely undercut, however, by the standard interpretation of the lines describing Beowulf's descent through the water:

>   brimwylm onfeng
> hilderince.   Ða wæs hwil dæges,
> ær he þone grundwong   ongytan mehte.   (1494-6)

The surging water closed over the warrior. Then it was *the space of a day* before he could see the bottom of the mere.

This is the sense supplied by early editors and translators. Later editors, apparently embarrassed by the hero's holding his breath and swimming downward for an entire day, endeavour to reduce the time spent sinking to the bottom: 'hwil dæges,' says Klaeber (186), means '"a good part of the day," not "the space of a day,"' and most modern scholars have agreed.

But it is strange that there is no mention elsewhere of the hero's fantastic ability to travel underwater for hours on end, and stranger still that the poet proceeds immediately to contradict himself by depicting the distance from the surface of the mere to the bottom not as a day's journey but as a very short space. For in lines 1588 and following, when Beowulf beheads the monster, spilling his blood into the water, we are told that men standing above the mere immediately ('sona') see the gore churn up to the top:

> Hra wide sprong,
> syþðan he ...
> hine þa heafde becearf.
> Sona þæt gesawon   snottre ceorlas,
> þa ðe mid Hroðgare   on holm wliton,
> þæt wæs yðgeblond   eal gemenged,
> brim blode fah.   (1588-94)

And the hero's own ascent to the shore seems a matter of moments (1618-24) rather than a day's journey. Such apparent inconsistencies certainly justify R.W. Chambers' exasperation: 'We may render this phrase [i.e., 'hwil dæges'] either "a large part of the day" or "the space of a day," as we will ... unreason like this is possible in *Beowulf*, though one wonders how so farfetched an idea ever occurred to anybody.'[9]

But is the farfetched idea really in the text, or is it only in the minds of the commentators? 'Hwil dæges,' I believe, does not mean either 'the space of a day' or 'the large part of a day' but simply 'daytime,' and all the poet is saying is that by the time Beowulf reached the bottom of the mere it was already daylight. S.O. Andrew suggested this interpretation briefly in his *Postscript on Beowulf* (Cambridge 1948, 99), but E.V.K. Dobbie dismissed the idea without argument,[10] and so far as I am aware it has never been advocated since. An examination of the phrase 'dæges hwil' in its occurrences throughout Old English poetry, however, suggests that Andrew was almost certainly correct:

þa wæs on þam ofne,   þær se engel becwom,
windig and wynsum,   wedere gelicost
þonne hit on sumeres tid   sended weorðeð
dropena drearung   on dæges hwile,
wearmlic wolcna scur.   *(Daniel* 345-9)

Then, when the angel came, it was airy and pleasant in the furnace, most like the weather in summer, when the dropping of rain, the warm shower from the clouds, is sent in the daytime.

... þonne on sumeres tid   sended weorðe
dropena dreorung   mid dæges hwile.   *(Azarias* 63-4)

[From the same context as *Daniel* 345-9] ... when the dropping of the rain is sent during the daytime.

                hord eft gesceat,
dryhtsele dyrnne   ær dæges hwile.   *(Beowulf* 2319-20)

He [i.e., the dragon, who flies only at night] returned to his hoard, his secret dwelling, before daylight.[11]

A parallel phrase is used in the poet's statement indicating that the dragon flies by night:

                lyftwynne heold
nihtes hwilum   *(Beowulf* 3043-4)

he held sway in the joyous air by night.

The manifest meaning of the phrase 'dæges hwil' (and 'nihtes hwil') in these passages would seem to indicate that the only reasonable interpretation of *Beowulf* 1495-6 is 'Then it was daytime before he could get to the bottom.' This reading not only preserves the human dimensions of the hero but also conforms with the poet's carefully marked time-sequence throughout the episode. Grendel's mother raids the hall at night, and Hrothgar is notified immediately (1279-1309). Beowulf is summoned, and he reaches Hrothgar's chamber 'samod ærdæge' (1311) — that is, in the early hours of the morning before daybreak.[12] It is growing light as the warriors proceed toward the mere, for they are able to see the bloody track of the ogress over the moor (1402-4). In 1495 the poet says it was broad daylight ('hwil dæges') when Beowulf plunged to the bottom of the lake. The struggle is arduous, and the Danes seem to wait a long time before giving up their watch at 'non dæges,' that is, at mid-afternoon (1600). It is just then, however, that Beowulf overcomes the hag and beheads Grendel. He swims quickly to the top of the mere, rejoins his comrades, and they repair to the Danish hall, where Beowulf's triumph is celebrated until night falls and the banquet ends (1789-90). The poet's marking of the passage of time is exceptionally clear –

> 1311-12   Samod ærdæge / eode eorla sum ...
> 1495   Ða wæs hwil dæges ...
> 1600   Ða cwom non dæges ...
> 1789-90   Nihthelm geswearc / deorc ofer dryhtgumum ...

– provided we understand 'hwil dæges' to mean 'daytime' and not 'the space of a day' or 'the large part of a day.'[13]

Once these factors are all taken into account, the meaning 'daytime' rather than 'space of a day' seems so inevitable that one wonders what could have given rise and longevity to the erroneous interpretation. The answer, I suspect, is implied in the comment with which Klaeber annotates the passage:

> 1495. hwil dæges, 'a good part of the day,' ... A long time is required for the same purpose in several corresponding folk-tales, see Panzer 119.

Panzer does indeed provide examples of such descents requiring twenty-one days, a year, and even three years. But neither here nor in other parts of *Beowulf*, so far as I am aware, does the poet show himself to be such a slave to folktale sources that he cannot alter an inappropriate detail when he wishes. I suspect that it is not so much his judgment as the judgment of modern scholars which has been overmastered by the folktale sources.

THE RETURN FROM FRISIA

Lines 2359b-68 of *Beowulf* are generally supposed to tell the story of an astounding *geste* performed by the hero after Hygelac's defeat in Frisia:

> Þonan Biowulf com
> sylfes cræfte,   sundnytte dreah;
> hæfde him on earme   (ana) þritig
> hildegeatwa,   þa he to holme (st)ag ...
> Oferswam ða sioleða bigong   sunu Ecgðeowes,
> earm anhaga   eft to leodum.

R.K. Gordon, who fairly represents all the translations of this passage which I have seen, renders the lines, 'Beowulf came thence by his own strength; swam over the sea. Alone he held on his arm thirty suits of armour when he set out on the sea ... The son of Ecgtheow swam over the stretch of the gulfs, the hapless solitary man back to his people.'[14]

Several years ago I published a study of this passage in which I argued that the actual words of the manuscript (before editorial intercession) say less than has been generally assumed. In particular I was concerned to show that there is no clear statement that Beowulf held thirty suits of armour on his arm when he set out or that he leapt into the sea with whatever it is that he *was* holding in his arm. The most that can be gathered from the transmitted text, I suggested, is that he was in possession of an unspecified amount of war-gear when he left the field of battle.[15] Recently Karl P. Wentersdorf has carried this analysis further, arguing that not only is there no basis for assuming that Beowulf swam to Geatland with thirty suits of armour; indeed, there is no evidence that he swam anywhere at this time.[16] The unique phrase 'sundnytte dreah,' he points out, can be pressed into no more specific meaning than 'he made the sea trip,'[17] and the verb 'oferswimman' clearly did not have the meaning 'swim over,' as a speaker of Modern English would expect, but meant to pass over the water by any one of various possible means of locomotion. This broad semantic range of Old English 'swimman' is recognized in the standard dictionaries and is amply illustrated in Bosworth-Toller, *Dictionary* and *Supplement*. Among documentations of the verb referring to a ship's movement through the water, a particularly clear specimen is that in Vercelli Homily XIX, which is not represented in the dictionaries: 'þa sona swa þa menn þe on þam scipe wæron ut on þære sæs dypan gesegled hæfdon, þa onsende God mycelne ren 7

strangne wind 7 grimme yste on þa sæ, swa þæt þæt scip ne mihte
naþer ne forð swymman ne underbæc ...'[18]
   A conflation of Wentersdorf's conclusions with my own would
yield this interpretation of the verses quoted above: 'From there
[i.e., from the battle] came Beowulf by means of his own physical
strength — undertook a journey on the sea. He had held battle-gear[19]
on his arm when he moved toward the sea ... Then, alone and wretched, the son of Ecgtheow crossed the expanse of ocean, returning to
his own people.' This cautious translation is better founded, I believe,
than previous ones based on the old editorial reconstructions and ad
hoc interpretations of word-meanings. There is nothing in this translation about fantastic swimming feats, it will be noted, although there
is no dearth of them in Panzer's collection of parallels (269-70).[20]

THE SWIMMING FEAT WITH BRECA

The story of Beowulf's exploit with Breca differs in kind from the
two events discussed above. It does not take place in the poem's present time but is reported as something which occurred years earlier.
This temporal distance gives the adventure a slightly different valence
from that of the central narrative actions, one linking it as much with
the remembered deeds of Hrethel, Heremod, and Scyld Scefing as
with those of the mature Beowulf.[21] In another sense too the Breca
episode is different: it never comes to us with the direct authority of
the poet's own voice but is reported in two contrasting versions by
characters within the poem — first by Unferth after he had drunk
deep of the beer and wine (531, 1467) and then by the indignant Beowulf. Either the hostile circumstances of the telling or the temporal
remoteness of the events described leads to a curious inconsistency
and vagueness in the reports. Beowulf's counter-version plays down
certain aspects of Unferth's initial account. He and Breca were together on the sea for five, not seven nights; they wore protective
arms, and although the winds were cold, Beowulf does not say it was
winter. Also, whereas Unferth makes it appear that the two contes-
tants set out swimming ('eagorstream   earmum þehton ... mundum
brugdon'), Beowulf uses the verbs 'rowan' ('to go by water, row,
sail'),[22] and 'fleotan' ('to float, drift, flow, sail').[23] (The only other
occurrence of 'fleotan' in the poem clearly has the meaning 'sail':
'fleat famigheals   forð ofer yðe,' 1909.) It is only during the last
night of the Breca episode that Beowulf describes himself as actually

being in the water (553 ff), and that is when he grapples with the 'merefixas.' But even here the possibility of a raft or boat being present cannot be completely ruled out, although I consider this unlikely.[24] The setting is also somewhat unclear in Beowulf's account. Usually he agrees with Unferth in locating the action on the open sea, but in line 568 he indicates that the monsters he fought were denizens of the fords.[25] Perhaps there is a rationale for these variations: Unferth exaggerates the dimensions of the episode in order to emphasize Beowulf's foolhardiness in undertaking it, and so Beowulf, in rebuttal, represents it as a somewhat less prodigious undertaking. But whatever the reason, Beowulf's version, which, I presume, we are expected to credit more seriously than we are Unferth's, presents the events of the swimming feat in terms less imposing and more noncommittal than is the case with Unferth's jeering account.[26]

However problematical these details may be, such local probings ignore the great overriding uncertainty of the Breca episode — the mystery as to who Unferth is and what is the nature of the entire exchange between Beowulf and the 'þyle.' It is this enigmatic quality of the 'Unferth Intermezzo' that leaves scholars undecided as to whether the tale of Beowulf and Breca should be interpreted as sober history, a boisterous flyting, or 'whopping lies.'[27] Therefore, in the remaining pages of this paper I shall turn to the problem of Unferth, trying to determine afresh what we know and do not know about his character and how we are to interpret the story which his report introduces into the poem.

Although interpretations of Unferth's character have been richly diverse, in general they fall into two broad categories, those which conceive of the 'þyle' as a serious and powerful figure and those which see him as essentially a source of diversion or an object of ridicule in the Danish court.[28] Critics who view him as serious or sinister usually assume that the contest with Breca is to be taken more or less at face value. Those who view him as playing a lighter role often interpret the tale of the Breca swim as an exaggeration or a joke. Neither view has been firmly established or is like to be. Quite possibly the 'þyle' represented for the audience of the poem some social role involving a combination of grave and playful elements which is now beyond our ken, the institution itself having eluded precise record. Recently, however, it seems to me that increasing evidence has come to light which gives support to the less serious interpretations of Unferth and weakens the case for the sombre readings.

I shall review and supplement that evidence here.

Most critics have assumed that the designation 'þyle' marks Unferth as holder of the solemn office of king's spokesman or counsellor, but the entry for 'þyle' in Bosworth-Toller, *Dictionary*, points out that the gloss 'ðelum' to 'scurris' suggests rather that 'his [Unferth's] function was something like that of the later court jester, and the style of his attack on Beowulf hardly contradicts the supposition.'[29] Recent studies have added force to this suggestion.[30] Another fundamental datum for the advocates of a serious Unferth is his sinister name, for if we assume a certain amount of distortion in the letters and sounds, it can be construed as 'Unfrið,' 'discord, un-peace.'[31] But, as I have suggested elsewhere,[32] the meaning of the name in its attested form without distortion has at least as much to recommend it: 'un-ferð' to the unbiased eye would seem to mean 'unintelligence' or 'folly' rather than 'discord.' (Cf 'leas-ferhð(nes)' ['levity, folly'], 'ungemynd' ['distraction or confusion of mind'], 'ungewitt' ['folly'], 'ungeræd' ['folly'], 'unræd' ['folly'].) Unferth's name and his official title point at least as much in the direction of a jeering, risible performer as they do of a serious one.

But is such a role consonant with the motivation which the poet gives for Unferth's railing attack?

> wæs him Beowulfes sið,
> modges merefaran, micel æfþunca,
> forþon þe he ne uþe, þæt ænig oðer man
> æfre mærða þon ma middangeardes
> gehede under heofenum þonne he sylfa. (501-5)

Surely this clear statement justifies Bonjour's inference that Unferth is 'jealous of his own glory' and that only a man 'of his prominent position,' 'a distinguished and glorious thane,' would harbour such concern for his martial reputation?[33] So it would seem, but the cited passage will bear scrutiny before the point is granted. As quoted, the passage says that Unferth was unwilling to admit that 'any other man on earth should perform glorious deeds.' But this meaning is achieved only by means of an emendation of the verb 'gehedde' to 'gehede,' which is then interpreted as preterite subjunctive of 'gehegan' and assigned the unique meaning 'to perform (deeds).' Elsewhere in Old English the verb always occurs with 'þing,' 'seonoð,' 'spræc,' or 'mæðel' as its direct object and means 'to hold (a meeting).' Left in its original manuscript form, 'gehedde' would be preterite of 'gehe-dan' ('heed, care for') (see Klaeber's glossary s.v. 'hēdan'). If the sentence is read this way, then Unferth emerges as a character with a most unheroic, Falstaffian attitude toward heroic deeds: he did not want to grant that other men cared for glory or for deeds of glory ('mærða') any more than he himself did. This is not an inappropriate sentiment for a man who, the poet later tells us, willingly 'forleas ellenmærðum' (1470-1). Perhaps there is more than a little of the swaggering coward in Unferth, and the speech reminding Beowulf of a past failure is motivated by a desire to scare the hero out of his commitment to face Grendel. If the speech is successful, then Unferth will have shown the Danes that he is not alone in his distaste for derring-do.

The accusation of fratricide (587 ff, 1167 ff) has widely, though not universally, been taken as a charge of cowardice against Unferth, and it is this interpretation that consorts best with the reading 'ge-hedde' just advocated. Unferth was such a craven that he would not even fulfil the thane's duty to fight alongside his closest kin when they were in desperate straits. But if this is so, how are we to justify the vehemence and gravity of Beowulf's statement, 'þæs þu in helle scealt / werhðo dreogan'? More than one critic has been troubled by the apparent excessiveness of this dark curse. Chambers suggested that Beowulf's taunt may be merely a 'countercheck quarrelsome' to the abusive 'þyle.'[34] Charles Donahue says, 'It is unlikely that Beowulf is referring here to a Christian *infernum*' since the hero who is elsewhere characterized as a pious pagan could hardly have knowledge of damnation in Christian terms.[35] He translates 'helle' as 'in the [pagan Germanic] realm of the dead.' Donahue's point is well taken, and his translation, which mollifies Beowulf's taunt considerably, may be right.

Before interpreting the text, however, it is instructive once again to look at the words as they appear, or do not appear, in the manuscript. An examination of the facsimiles of Cotton Vitellius A.XV will show no trace of a word 'helle' in the manuscript, and the commentaries of Zupitza and Malone confirm that the only vestige of a word at this point is a final '-e,' which is now covered by the leaf binding. Modern editors have inserted the word 'helle' solely on the authority of the Thorkelin transcripts, and these too merit scrutiny. Looking at Thorkelin's own copy (Thorkelin B), we find that the word 'helle' has been inserted 'on an original blank in another ink.'[36]

Evidently Thorkelin was unable to make out anything in the manuscript at this point and so left the space blank; later, he must have copied the word from Transcript A into his own transcription. It is likely, then, that Thorkelin A constitutes the sole authority for this reading.

The testimony of Thorkelin's copyist is not to be treated lightly, of course, and yet this is a peculiarly delicate case. Except for the covered '-e,' there is no sign of a word 'helle' in the manuscript today, and when Thorkelin examined the manuscript there was not enough there for him to make anything out. Surely the copyist, whose transcript preceded Thorkelin's 'by a few months or weeks only,'[37] must have based his reading 'helle' on manuscript evidence which was already quite deteriorated. Considering how much difficulty the copyist had in transcribing accurately even those words which are perfectly clear in the manuscript today (especially in the first part of the poem where he was struggling with an unfamiliar script), we might reasonably think of his 'helle' as little more than a game try at reconstructing lost characters from the vestiges which he descried at the crumbling edge of the folio leaf.

One of the chronic errors in A's transcription is the adding or omitting of letters in a diphthong. Only four words after the moot 'helle' he writes 'þeaeh' for the manuscript reading 'þeah.' Conversely, he writes 'halle' for 'healle' in line 89 and 'hald' for 'heald' in line 2247. He sometimes miswrites the 'ea' diphthong as 'e,' as in 'bedwa' for 'beadwa' (709) and 'begas' for 'beagas' (3105), and he starts to write 'pelhpeon' for 'wealhþeon' (629) but 'corrects' this to 'pealhpeon.' In the light of this latter tendency and of his earlier misreading of the diphthong in 'healle,' I conceive the disturbing possibility that the original word was 'healle' rather than 'helle' in line 588, in which case the passage would read 'þæs þu in healle scealt / werhðo dreogan': 'for that you must endure condemnation in the hall.' It is not my concern here to promote this reading, although some might find it preferable on several counts to the 'helle' of the transcripts. I want only to illustrate the tenuity of the hitherto unquestioned 'helle,' which has been thought to introduce such seriousness into Beowulf's retort to Unferth.[38]

How then are we to interpret Unferth's character? If pressed insistently for an opinion, I would say that he seems to be a blustering, mean-spirited coward who does not enjoy the respect of his comrades[39] and who seeks to bolster his self-esteem by decrying Beowulf's past performance and present qualifications. Beowulf imperturbably answers his hostile jibes, first by giving a more modest and convincing version of the boyhood experience which Unferth recounted and then by alluding pointedly to the cowardice of the 'þyle' and to his deficient 'wit,' 'hige,' and 'sefa' (589-94). The Danes are amused and impressed by the hero's perceptiveness in seeing Unferth for what he is, and they rejoice that such a resourceful champion is prepared to assist them (607-11: 'Ða wæs on salum   sinces brytta ... Ðær wæs hæleþa hleahtor'). Unferth resumes his accustomed state of disesteem in Heorot. But as the narrative progresses, Beowulf gradually regenerates the worthless Unferth into a man of some dignity and value in the court (an act of generosity which has been remarked by more than one student of the poem). By allowing Unferth to supply the sword needed for his second fight, the hero imparts a measure of reflected glory to the lesser man, whose pusillanimity nonetheless stands in effective contrast to the valour of Beowulf. Later, when he refuses to blame Hrunting for its failure and returns it to Unferth ceremoniously and with high praise (1659-60, 1807-12), Beowulf confers the most dignity he can upon the 'þyle,' who is no longer called 'Unferth,' but only 'sunu Ecglafes.'[40]

This hypothesis as to what Unferth's character and his relation to Beowulf may be would accord with my reading of the Breca-tale as a semi-serious affair and also has a certain inner consistency. Moreover, the relation I suggest here between hero and poltroon is much like that described in another narrative of the Danish court in Hrothgar's time — the *Hrolfs saga kraka*, chapter 23. There we are told that the royal house at Leire is plagued by a nocturnal monster, and when the bear-like hero Boðvarr Bjarki arrives on the scene prior to doing battle with the monster, he encounters the despised coward Hottr. Boðvarr treats Hottr roughly, but eventually, in the course of purging the Danish court of the monster, he regenerates the coward, just as Beowulf regenerated Unferth. In an incident involving the lending of a sword called 'Gullinhjalti' (which scholars have noted is cognate with the 'gylden hilt' of *Beowulf* 1677), Boðvarr contrives to gain some esteem for Hottr from the monster-slaying, and the erstwhile buffoon gains a new reputation and a new name. Conceivably we have here a remote echo of the interplay between Beowulf and Unferth.

The characterization of Hottr in the saga demonstrates that a Germanic author could conceive of a relation such as I have suggested for Beowulf and Unferth, but it should be apparent from the sceptical

treatment which I have given to analogues in the first part of this
paper that I would be unwilling to regard the parallel as probative
evidence of the Old English poet's intentions. Indeed, as I have said
before, I find the data insufficient to warrant any definitive interpretation of Unferth. He may be, as some have thought, a serious,
sinister character, but the evidence for this is weak, and it is at least
as likely that he is a kind of jester, as Bosworth-Toller suggests, or
that he is a fellow of low reputation in the court like Hottr in the
saga. Given the uncertainty as to his character, it is impossible to
argue with much conviction from the evidence of the swimming-tale
which he introduces into the poem. It is conceivable that the Breca
story is serious, but it could also be a wild yarn spun by the envious
'þyle,' or a flyting, or Unferth's effort to start a lying match.

The undue importance which has been accorded the Breca episode
in the past is in part a legacy of the early mythologizing critics like
Müllenhoff and Sarrazin, who viewed the swimming feat as a slightly
veiled *Naturmythus* and hence thought it comparable in importance
to the dragon fight and the contests with the Grendel kin.[41] The pre-
disposition to see the Breca adventure as much bigger than life may
have been nurtured by Panzer's carefully collected saga-parallels.
Troubling aspects of the Unferth episode as a whole could always be
shrugged off with the explanation that 'they must be looked upon as
an inheritance from the older legends which had come down from a
ruder age,'[42] and this attitude may have discouraged close scrutiny of
the textual mainstays of the received interpretation — such as the
name and office of Unferth as well as his motivation, the precise
terms in which Beowulf describes his own feat, and the manuscript
evidence for his threat of hell in his retort. If the earlier interpretations of these matters have not been replaced here with indubitably
surer and superior ones, I believe they have at least been shown to be
less certain than scholars had previously assumed. If so, this must
qualify one's interpretation of the evidence for astounding feats in
the Breca episode, just as the textual realities of lines 1494-6 and
2354-68 must be taken into account in assessing the supposedly marvellous elements earlier in the poem.[43]

NOTES

1 Of course this does not mean that he was ineligible for divine favour. Just as
Achilles enjoys the patronage of Athene and Hera, Beowulf occasionally receives

the support of a God whom he but little knows or understands. In a Christian view such favour would not set him apart from other men.

2 All quotations from *Beowulf* are from Klaeber's edition, *'Beowulf' and the 'Fight at Finnsburg,'* (3rd ed., Boston 1950), except that I have dispensed with Klaeber's macrons and other diacritics. Quotations from other Old English poems are taken from *The Anglo-Saxon Poetic Records,* ed. G.P. Krapp and E.V.K. Dobbie (New York 1931-53).

3 'Beowulf's Old Age,' in *Philological Essays: Studies in Old and Middle English Language and Literature in Honour of Herbert Dean Meritt,* ed. J.L. Rosier (The Hague 1970), 55-64

4 Wiglaf's speech in 2663-8 is a fitting emblem of the poet's tactful merging of Beowulf's pre-eminence with his human limitations:

> Leofa Biowulf,   læst eall tela,
> swa ðu on geoguðfeore   geara gecwæde,
> þæt ðu ne alæte   be ðe lifigendum
> dom gedreosan;   scealt nu dædum rof,
> æðeling anhydig,   ealle mægene
> feorh ealgian;   ic ðe fullæstu.

Invoking the king's youthful boasts as a means of urging him on to a last desperate effort is fine, but best is the lexical play by which Wiglaf emphasizes that even in his own youth he is inferior to the mighty king: only Beowulf can 'perform'; Wiglaf can but 'supplement the performance' ('læst eall tela ... ic ðe fullæstu'). Klaeber's note here that 'there is a singular lack of propriety in making young Wiglaf administer fatherly advice to Beowulf' seems to me to overlook the studiously respectful tone of the speech.

5 Pope, 60

6 *'Beowulf* and the Hypostatic Union,' *Neophilologus* 52 (1968) 409-16. I disregard a fourth element of the 'marvellous' which the authors mention ('his voyage from Geatland to Denmark, although not miraculous, is surrounded by an aura of wonder and majesty') since this is a matter of interpretation. I also disregard here the main concern of the article, which tends toward theological explication. What I have found valuable is the authors' perceptive formulation of the apparently mixed quality of the characterization in the narrative.

7 *Epic and Romance* (2nd ed., London 1908), 175. Cf Frank Beaumont, *'Beowulf,'* *Proceedings of the Royal Philosophical Society of Glasgow* 38 (1906-7) 201-33, esp. 210-17.

8 Comparable settings are indicated in Norse analogues, of course; cf R.W. Chambers, *Beowulf: An Introduction* (3rd. ed., Cambridge 1959), 52-3 and 451-85.

9 Chambers, 465

10 *Anglo-Saxon Poetic Records,* IV, 196

11 Dobbie's suggested translation of 'dæges hwile' as 'a [good] part of the day

[had passed] ' (196) must have been arrived at without reference to the passages here cited from *Daniel* and *Azarias* and in the hope of offering some support for the traditional interpretation of 1495b in *Beowulf*. All the translations I have consulted agree in rendering *Beowulf* 2320b 'before daytime / the time of day / daybreak / daylight / dawn' rather than 'before a [good] part of the day [had passed].'

12 'ærdæg' appears to be equivalent to 'uhta' (*Beowulf* 126: 'on uhtan mid ærdæge'; cf *Andreas* 235, 1388; *Elene* 105) and both words are used to translate Latin 'matutinus.' In the Cleopatra Glossary appears the explanation 'Matutinum, uhttid, siue beforan dæge' (Wright-Wülcker 450:3). Cf F. Tupper, *Anglo-Saxon Dæg-mæl* (Baltimore 1895), 37. The phrase 'somod ærdæge' occurs again at *Beowulf* 2942, referring, presumably, to the pre-dawn hour at which Hygelac's troops arrived and saved the Geatish raiding party from being destroyed by the Swedes 'on mergenne' (2929).

13 In addition to satisfying the time-sequence in the poem, the mention of daylight in 1495 would also accord logically with the immediately ensuing context, if I understand it aright: *because* it is broad daylight when Beowulf reaches the bottom of the mere, *therefore* the ogress is able to observe his arrival instantly ('Sona þæt onfunde'). This logical relation could be clearly displayed through a repunctuation of the passage if one were willing to accept S.O. Andrew's principles for interpreting introductory 'Ða-'clauses (*Postscript*, 11-12): 'As it was daylight before he could gain the bottom, the ravenous, greedy one who had occupied the watery region for fifty years perceived immediately that a man was exploring the realm of monsters from above.'

14 *Anglo-Saxon Poetry*, selected and translated by R.K. Gordon (London 1954), 47

15 'Beowulf's Retreat from Frisia: Some Textual Problems in Ll. 2361-2362,' *SP* 62 (1965) 1-16

16 'Beowulf's Withdrawal from Frisia: A Reconsideration,' *SP* 68 (1971) 395-415

17 Wentersdorf, 402-3. That 'sund-' in 'sundnytt' means 'sea' rather than 'swimming' seems to me particularly likely when we note that in every other nominal compound with 'sund-' attested in the poetic corpus ('sundbuend,' 'sundgebland,' 'sundhelm,' 'sundhengest,' 'sundplega,' 'sundreced,' 'sundwudu') the first element means 'sea' and not 'swimming.' Further, in the other two Old English nominal compounds with 'nytt,' the first element is in both cases a noun denoting the location of the act, not an abstract noun of means: 'cyricnytt,' 'weoroldnytt.' 'Sundnytt,' then, would appear to mean 'use of the sea' and the poetic phrase 'sundnytte dreah' 'he made use of the sea' or, as Wentersdorf suggests, 'he made the sea trip.'

18 Paul E. Szarmach, 'Three Versions of the Jonah Story: An Investigation of Narrative Technique in Old English Homilies,' *Anglo-Saxon England* 1 (1972) 186.

The use of 'swim' to refer to the progress of a boat over the water continues in Middle and early Modern English. (See Wentersdorf, 403-7.) Shakespeare uses the word in this sense in *Julius Caesar*, V.i.67, and in *As You Like It*, IV.i.40 ('... you have swam in a gondola').

19 As I point out in 'Beowulf's Retreat from Frisia,' the customary translation of 'hildegeatwe' as 'suits of armour' and the emendation 'ana' are incorrect, and the numeral XXX is not to be trusted. See especially 2-7.

20 Wentersdorf's linguistic critique, to which I have referred here, is but a part of his argument. His article subsequently explores analogues in Old English and cognate literatures which suggest that the *Beowulf* poet probably conceived of his hero as making his way from Frisia through the Skagerrak by ship.

21 This may seem a shadowy distinction, but I believe it is a real one. Many readers would have been troubled, for example, if the author had introduced giants and the fabulous Weland as royal smiths at Hygelac's court, but it does not seem unfitting that Beowulf's heirloom armour is 'Hrædlan laf, Welandes geweorc,' or that he wields an ancient sword called 'the work of giants' (1558, 1562, 1690, etc; cf 2616, 2979). So long as they do not intrude into the poem's present time such fabulous elements seem to leave undispelled our sense that the characters are human beings.

22 C.L. Wrenn, in his edition of the poem (195), notes that '*Rowan* "swim" does not occur *in that sense* in poetry outside *Beowulf*.' In his glossary he defines the word '*row*, hence *swim*.'

23 Bosworth-Toller, *Supplement*, records two prose occurrences of 'fleotend' used specifically to modify 'fisc' in the formula 'fleotende fixas and fleogende fugelas,' but there are no instances of the word being used to describe men swimming.

24 The earliest editor of the poem conceived that a vessel was present in the adventure – not through one of his many misunderstandings of the text but through retention of the manuscript reading 'wudu weallendu' in 581, which he translates '*lignis spumantibus*.' See G.J. Thorkelin, *De Danorum rebus gestis ...* (Havni 1815), 46. Zupitza's note to 581 in the EETS facsimile says, '*wudu* not *wadu* without the least doubt; an *a* open at the top does not occur so late in English MSS.' Subsequent editors uniformly emend to 'wadu weallendu' in order to bring the line into conformity with 546a, although the formula occurs nowhere else. Syntactical considerations and the similarity of phrases like 'brim weallendu' (*Beowulf* 847) seem to me to argue strongly for the traditional emendation 'wadu.' But it should not be forgotten that it is an emendation.

25 Alistair Campbell, 'The Use in *Beowulf* of Earlier Heroic Verse,' in *England before the Conquest: Studies in Primary Sources Presented to Dorothy Whitelock*, ed. Peter Clemoes and Kathleen Hughes (Cambridge 1971), 284, calls attention to the odd appearance of 'ford' in this context and questions whether it should

be emended to 'flod.' Campbell also remarks the odd application of 'rowan' ('row') to swimmers. Unferth (512) as well as Beowulf uses 'rowan' in describing the feat.

26 Beowulf's only heightening of the details of the episode would seem to be his introduction of the sea-monsters, and such prodigies, as we have seen, are a given in the poet's portrayal of the hero's adversaries. A further departure from Unferth's account, one which I have not mentioned above, is Beowulf's statement in 541-3 that he would not swim far from Breca, nor could Breca swim far from him. Prevailing opinion has it that this is an explicit contradiction of Unferth's statement that the adventure began as a race. Possibly, but there is a simpler explanation: perhaps the gallant hero intended to remain close to the weaker Breca until they were near their goal, at which time he would outstrip him and win the race without ever being beyond call if his companion should need help. Once again, the cryptic mode of the narrative here does not permit certainties.

27 The last phrase is that of Norman E. Eliason, 'The Þyle and Scop in Beowulf,' Speculum 38 (1963) 272. This article is a valuable and provocative re-examination of the entire question of Unferth's character.

28 It is generally agreed, of course, that Unferth serves an important purpose within the economy of the poem in that he tests the hero at a crucial point in the narrative. This function is served whether he is a statesman or a poltroon.

29 The gloss occurs in the Cleopatra Glossary as 'de scurris · hof ðelum.' I agree with Bosworth-Toller that 'hof' represents 'of' (with inorganic 'h-') rendering Latin 'de.' The associations of 'scurra' and 'þyle' in Old English are expertly treated in James L. Rosier's 'Design for Treachery: The Unferth Intrigue,' PMLA 77 (1962) 1-3.

30 See especially the articles by Rosier and Eliason.

31 The most persuasive and influential statement of this view is that of Morton W. Bloomfield, 'Beowulf and Christian Allegory: An Interpretation of Unferth,' Traditio 7 (1949-51) 410-15.

32 'Personal Names in Medieval Narrative and the Name of Unferth in Beowulf,' in Essays in Honor of Richebourg Gaillard McWilliams, ed. Howard Creed (Birmingham, Ala. 1970), 43-8

33 Adrien Bonjour, The Digressions in Beowulf (Oxford 1950), 17-22. See further the important modifications of Bonjour's analysis in his Twelve Beowulf Papers (Neuchatel 1962), 129-33.

34 Chambers, 28

35 'Beowulf and Christian Tradition: A Reconsideration from a Celtic Stance,' Traditio 21 (1965) 92

36 Zupitza, 29

37 The Thorkelin Transcripts of Beowulf in Facsimile, ed. Kemp Malone, Early Eng-

lish Manuscripts in Facsimile, I (Copenhagen 1951), 4

38 A.G. Brodeur, *The Art of Beowulf* (Berkeley 1959), 155, speaks for many when he observes that 'no one can ... ignore the weight of Beowulf's assertion that the penalty Unferth must pay for his brothers' death is damnation in hell.'

39 The statement in 1165-6 that the men in the hall trusted in Unferth's 'ferhþ' (probably a pun on his name) and 'mod' means, I take it, that in the joyous atmosphere of the victory celebration good will was extended to even the meanest of the company. The statement is preceded by the allusion to the temporary good will between Hrothulf and Hrothgar and followed by the reminder that Unferth had failed his brothers 'æt ecga gelacum.'

40 Whether it was the Danish courtiers who conferred the demeaning name 'Unferth' on the 'þyle' or whether he acquired it elsewhere cannot be determined from the text with certainty. It is to be noted that Beowulf's sympathetic concern for rehabilitating Unferth takes on special poignancy when we recall that the hero himself was once held in low esteem by his fellow men (2183 ff).

41 See W.W. Lawrence, *Beowulf and Epic Tradition* (Cambridge, Mass. 1928), 151-2. Cf Klaeber, 147, note 2.

42 Lawrence, 153

43 I wish to thank Professors Stanley B. Greenfield and Edward B. Irving, Jr, for reading this essay and offering suggestions for improvement.

INDEX OF TEXTUAL INTERPRETATIONS

Beowulf 505 'gehede.' Restore MS 'gehedde' ('heed, care for') 128-9
539 'reon' = 'rowed, sailed'? 126
542 'fleotan' = 'float, sail'? 126
581 'wadu.' Restore MS 'wudu' ('wood,' i.e. 'boat')? 135 note 24
588 'helle.' Read 'healle'? 130
499, 530, 1165, 1488 'Unferð' = 'nonsense, folly' 128
1495 'hwil dæges' = 'daytime' 121-4

E.G. STANLEY

Some observations on
the A3 lines in *Beowulf*

Where such reapers as Sievers, Hans Kuhn, A.J. Bliss, and John Pope
himself[1] have been harvesting it is presumptuous to hope for gleanings:
when they have reached no certainty, certainty may not be attainable.
Every analysis of versification, however, takes a different line from a
different point of departure. Mine began with multisyllabic initial dips
in the half-lines of *Beowulf*, with Kuhn's great article as a theoretical
and practical basis; but it soon became apparent that even such a very
limited survey, confined to, in Sievers's terminology, A3, B and C lines
(as well as a small number of others), all with three or more syllables in
the initial dip, would be very bulky. Moreover, since A3 lines are confined to the first half-line whereas all others occur in either half, A3
lines must be considered separately, away from a consideration of the
peculiarities of the initial dip of the second half-line. In considering
A3 lines, one more name is to be added to the list of those who have
done original and useful work, that of Erich Neuner who has not been
given the attention his work deserves.[2] Since in this study I confine myself to A3 lines I have included not only those with multisyllabic initial
dip (which are common), but also half-lines of only two unstressed
syllables before the single alliterative stress: such half-lines are comparatively rare (see *Rhythm*, 83 ff).

It is a feature of the work of Anglo-Saxon metrists that their various
findings cannot be reconciled. On the whole Bliss's analysis, with Sievers as a foundation, seems the most helpful for the very limited aims
of this study. I differ from Bliss, however, on the double alliteration

involving verbs in the first stressed position of the A half-line, in spite of his very careful discussion in *Metre*, §20. His view involves a tightening of Kuhn's *Satzpartikelgesetz* to cover what Kuhn himself explicitly exempted from the operation of the 'law' (*PBB* 57 [1933] 11).

It seemed at first sight an attractive proposition to regard lines listed by Sievers as bearing full stress on medial syllables (cf *Altgermanische Metrik*, §78) as expanded A3 lines of the type X X $\underline{/}\backslash$X, that is, with the medial syllable bearing half-stress, not full stress, such half-stress being the expansion (as in Sievers's A*, $\underline{/}$X | $\underline{/}$X is expanded to $\underline{/}$X | $\underline{/}\backslash$X). Examples of such lines include 'Gewāt ðā nēosian' (115), 'Ful oft gebēotedon' (480), 'hraðe hēo æþelinga' (1294, unless transverse alliteration were thought to make it a D line), all of which have been carefully considered by Professor Pope in his analysis of C lines (see especially *Rhythm*, 293-6). In the end I abandoned that view, partly because such half-lines occasionally occur with only a single unstressed syllable in the first dip ('Swā rīxode,' 144; 'Swā bealdode,' 2177) which would make one wish to class them as a type D with single lift rather than as type A; and chiefly because there seems to be no good reason why very similar half-lines (e.g. 'þāra þe hē cēnoste,' 206b;[3] 'þæt ic mē ǣnigne,' 1772b; 'þæt hē Wealdende,' 2329b; and with monosyllabic first dip 'þā sēlestan,' 3122b) should have been tolerated in the second half-line if they had been felt by the poets to be at all like A3 lines used by them in the first half-line only (cf *Metre*, §88). Furthermore, as Professor Pope says (*Rhythm*, 295-6), the subsequent history of the language as seen in the scansion and rhymes of Middle English[4] supports the assumption of full stress in ordinarily half-stressed syllables, where the metre requires full stress.

The following considerations, which I put in the form of questions, underlie the shape of this study of A3 lines in *Beowulf*:

1 Does the stress (which takes the alliteration) fall A/ on a noun, adjective, adverb, numeral, 'heavy' pronoun, or B/ on a verb (which may be an infinitive or a participle forming part of a verb-group)?
2 What word does the initial dip begin with, a connective,[5] or a verb, or what?
3 Has the alliterating word an unstressed prefix?
4 Is the alliterating stress resolved?
5 Does the alliterating stress come on a short syllable followed by only one unstressed syllable?
6 Is the syllable following the alliterating stress overweighted?
7 Could the half-line involve cross alliteration or transverse alliteration?

8 What is Klaeber's punctuation before and after the half-line?

1 and 2 provide a rough classification, A and B depending on where the only stress of the half-line goes, and then there are further sub-divisions in alphabetical order of the initial unstressed word of the half-line. 3 to 6 lead to my providing some prosodic details for the stressed word. As far as I can tell, no systematic conclusion is to be drawn from these listed details, except that, as might be expected, unstressed prefixes are very common when the stress falls on a verb (that is, in category B), and rare otherwise (examples of prefixes coming on words other than verbs do, however, occur in lines 544, 1626, 1628, 1721, 1732,[6] 1998, 2075, 2221, 2630, 2804, 2994, 3058, 3104); the greater frequency in the case of verbs is presumably merely the result of the frequency of verbal prefixes, especially 'ge-.' The relative frequency of type A3 with short alliterative stress, elicited by 5, is a fact much discussed by metrists.[7]

Complications of alliteration are discussed under 7. Question marks indicate doubt; thus single ? means that, though I am not sure, I think the alliteration could have been introduced by the poet deliberately; double ?? means that, though I myself think the alliterative complication is fortuitous, some people might think that it has been introduced deliberately. Half-lines introduced by the connective 'oð þæt' provide a good example of the kind of doubt I felt. As has been remarked before,[8] 'oð þæt' can begin a numbered section, and in that position and often elsewhere (where 'until' makes unsatisfactory sense) it may be translated as an adverb with some such meaning as 'at length.' Of the 32 occurrences of 'oð þæt' in *Beowulf*, 23 come at the beginning of the second half-line. 12 of these 23 occur in half-lines alliterating on vowels: that is a high proportion. Clearly, in such lines 'oð þæt' cannot share in the alliteration (double alliteration in the second half-line[9] being against such rules as have been established for Old English in the last hundred years or so). This is merely a troublesome statistical fact. Nine of the occurrences of 'oð þæt' come at the beginning of the first half-line, and of these all except 1414, 1640, and 1801 occur in A3 lines (1414 and 1640 are of the kind where the stress falls on a word which I have discussed above, that is, a trisyllabic word ordinarily stressed _/\X_). Six A3 lines are listed below, and it is puzzling that four of them (9, 219, 1740, 2934) have vocalic alliteration, so that, if 'oð þæt' is thought capable of sharing in alliteration, they could be regarded as having double alliteration. Professor Pope believes that this double alliteration is accidental (*Rhythm*, 251, 265-6), and on the whole I am inclined to agree because I look upon the similar double alliteration in the second half-line as fortuitous likewise. In the list such lines are, therefore, marked with a single question mark: I do not believe that there is double alliteration in these lines, but I do not think such a belief unreasonable.

I am not entirely convinced that transverse alliteration is ever more than fortuitous. In his important listing of alliterative patterns,[10] R.B. Le Page gives eighty examples of cross alliteration in *Beowulf* and 29 of transverse alliteration. Line 2615 (which lies outside the present study) is as clear an example of transverse alliteration as we find in *Beowulf*: 'brūnfāgne helm,   hringde byrnan,' but even that has been emended out of existence *metri causa* by some.[11] At the other end of the scale of certainty, I should not have thought that transverse alliteration can be involved in lines 355, 535, 813, 1721, 2385, 2406, 3081; for I doubt if words so slight as the following can carry alliteration: 'ðē' (rel.), 'wit' (pers. pron.), 'þæt' (three times), 'hē' (and 'hine'), 'sē' — unless for some special purpose, as in the repeated 'on þǣm dæge / þysses līfes' (197, 790, 806) or 'þegnes þearfe, / swylce þȳ dō-gore' (1797). That still leaves over twenty cases of likely, or at least not very unlikely, transverse alliteration. 1933 with initial 'nǣnig' seems pretty certain; and so does 1892 with 'nō.' Where the verb comes first, I am also inclined to think that it may be involved in transverse alliteration, 1184, 1573, 1732 (though I recognize that it falls under the heading of breaches of Kuhn's *Satzpartikelgesetz*, discussed by Bliss, *Metre*, §20), 2158, 2337, 3180. The adverbial phrase 'Nū hēr' (2053) could well carry additional weight, and therefore allow of transverse alliteration. Initial 'swylce' is involved in alliterative complications on several occasions, and may be involved in transverse alliteration in line 1482 'swylce þū ðā mādmas,   þē þū mē sealdest,' one of three lines in the poem in which 'mē' alliterates, but 2490 indicates that that does not enable us to infer anything from it about transverse alliteration in 1482. (The third line is 563.) Line 3164 is discussed below for vocalic transverse alliteration; it seems very unlikely that 'swylce ... swylce' should be involved in some further alliterative complication. 'Hwīlum' seems to be involved in transverse alliteration on the two occasions the word comes in an A3 line (1728, 2020), and in double alliteration elsewhere (175, 864, 2107); and at 1828b it bears the alliteration. The use of 'gif' in transverse alliteration (and also perhaps in double alliteration, 1846) has to be considered, because the proportion of A3 lines with initial 'gif' together with possible alliterative complications is high; even so, it is doubtful if the word is heavy enough for transverse alliteration at 1826 and 1836. The exclamation 'Hwæt' is not involved in alliteration in Old English verse,[12] and, therefore, transverse alliteration is not likely in line 1652. At 2442b the connective 'hwæðre' alliterates, but in that line it comes as the first element of the group 'hwæðre swā þēah,' quite different from the occurrence at line 2377, so that there is no clear parallel in *Beowulf* to lead to the assumption of transverse alliteration involving 'hwæðre' in line 2377. The matter is made more complicated by the emendation of manuscript 'him' (with horizontal stroke above 'i' for 'm') to 'hine' in a context where a direct object is required for the verb 'hēold'; recent editors (see especially E.v. Schaubert's excellent note) have, however, retained the manuscript reading here. If we emend to 'hine' and at the same time believe that 'hwæðre' is involved in transverse alliteration we have one more unstressed syllable between 'hwæðre' and 'folce' in the half-line 'hwæðre hē hine on folce' than elsewhere in the poem (according to Bliss, *Metre*, 125, type 1A*1c in his scansion is the longest sequence of unstressed syllables; there is no 1A*1d). If we believe in transverse alliteration here we must not emend (or we produce a line without parallel metrically); if we do not believe in transverse alliteration here we are free to emend. There seems even less justification for thinking that in lines 1535, 2669, and 3058 the connectives 'þonne,' 'æfter,' and 'þā' are involved in transverse alliteration.

Lines 779, 2651 (which is not listed by Le Page), and 3164 have to be considered further for transverse alliteration. 779 should perhaps not be included in this study at all, but scanned as a B type with resolution and unusual alliteration: 'þæt hit ā mid gemete   manna ænig' and that is where Professor Pope places it (*Rhythm*, 285-6); but he is inclined to emend the second half-line to 'ænig manna' because of the unusual alliteration.[13] The only reason for regarding the half-line as a short A3 is that the peculiarities which come together in it have more and closer parallels among the half-lines listed in *Rhythm*, 273-4, than among the half-lines listed as B3 in *Rhythm*, 285-6. It is most unlikely that in line 2651 cross alliteration of 'micle' with 'mīne' is involved or that 'mē' is somehow involved too: 'þæt mē is micle lēofre, þæt mīnne līchaman,' for possessive adjectives preceding their noun in the same half-line do not alliterate — cf 1007, and note 812, 1754, 3177 for the sufficiency of 'līchoma.' *Andreas* 1563 has a somewhat similar use of 'mycle,' clearly outside the alliteration: 'Is hit mycle sēlre, þæs þe ic sōð talige,' and it seems best to regard the possibility of cross alliteration in the *Beowulf* line as accidental, perhaps even the result of scribal addition of 'micle.' The third remainder, line 3164, involves even greater alliterative complexity: 'eall swylce hyrsta, swylce on horde ǣr,' words in both half-lines beginning with vowel, 's' and 'h.' Correlative 'swylc(e)' does not, however, participate in alliteration in the poem (see 1249, and note that the more common correlative 'swā' never shares in alliteration). In line 3164, therefore, 'swylce' is used unstressed in both halves. Stressed uses of 'swylc' (e.g. 582, 996, 1347, 2231, 2798) are quite different from correlative uses as in 3164. Under 'swā' in the list of A3 lines given below I mark the possibility that it could be involved in double alliteration with two question marks for lines 1092 and 1223, but do not mark possible cross alliteration for 943 and 1283. Line 1223, 'efne swā sīde swā sǣ bebūgeð,' provides the evidence that 'swā' in the second half-line cannot alliterate, and, though it is not conclusive for the first 'swā,' that makes it reasonable to suppose that the first 'swā' is unstressed too.

In the listing of A3 lines, Klaeber's punctuation, considered under 8, is indicated in parentheses before and after the half-line. Empty parentheses () indicate that Klaeber has no mark of punctuation; where Klaeber has a new paragraph beginning with the half-line listed the mark of punctuation preceding the half-line is followed within the parentheses by the letters n.p.; and where a new canto begins with the half-line the canto number is given as in the manuscript if manuscript, or within square brackets, as in Klaeber, if editorial.[14] It seems that A3 lines frequently opened cantos: about a quarter of the cantos in the poem begin with A3 lines. Editorial punctuation is, of course, not certain, and editorial practice differs. Klaeber's practice in general conforms to the rules of punctuation for Modern German with some compromise in the direction of Modern English practice; Dobbie's punctuation is lighter. Even so, like Rudolph Willard and Elinor D. Clemons, I have preferred to rely on an excellent editor's view of the sentence structure of the poem rather than adopt my own, for I found that, like Willard and Clemons, I was inclined to the view that A3 lines commonly begin the sentence, that being a corollary of Kuhn's *Satzpartikelgesetz* and his *Satzspitzengesetz*;[15] and I was tempted to repunctuate some of the lines of the poem to make the sentence structure agree better with this notion of where A3 lines come. In view of the frequency, however, with which relative clauses begin with an A3 line (or consist entirely of an A3 line) it is doubtful if we can generalize, and say that A3 lines are inceptive: in fact, I doubt if we can add to Professor Pope's cautious

statement 'that type A3 is employed very frequently as a light introduction to the weighty verses that follow' (*Rhythm*, 82).

That statement draws attention to what follows the A3 line, and
here it is clear that in the vast majority of cases Klaeber has no mark of
punctuation at the end of the A3 line — that is, in my notation the half-
line is followed by (). Some of the differences between Klaeber's punctuation and Dobbie's lighter (and less consistent) punctuation are systematic. Klaeber uses a comma when a dependent relative clause follows
the (A3) main clause; Dobbie usually does not; Klaeber uses a comma
before the second 'swa' or 'swylc(e)' of a pair of correlatives; Dobbie
usually does not. Dobbie is far more sparing than Klaeber in his use of
commas before noun clauses introduced by 'þæt.'

Apart from sporadic use of commas in these three groups in Dobbie's
edition (as well, of course, as in Klaeber's), there are several A3 half-
lines followed by a comma when the A3 half-line includes a verb, but
there is only one case of such a comma when the A3 line does not include a verb; both editions agree in their punctuation in these cases.
The one example of a comma at the end of an A3 line without verb is
1652, where the sentence is interrupted by two phrases of address:
'Hwæt, wē þē þās sǣlāc,   sunu Healfdenes, / lēod Scyldinga,   lustum
brōhton ...' Punctuation at the end of an A3 line is more common when
that A3 line contains a verb, stressed or unstressed. Again Dobbie punc-
tuates more lightly than Klaeber, systematically so before relatives (but
cf 506, 3009, for exceptions), and before noun clauses introduced by
'þæt' (but cf 290, 1671, 1846, for exceptions because of antecedent
'hit' or 'þæt'), and also before other kinds of clauses, whether sub-
stantival or adverbial, like 1188 and 2403 (but cf 798, 1392, 2976, for
exceptions).

It is obvious that editorial punctuation is not a reliable guide to the
sentence structure of *Beowulf*; it tells us only how a modern grammar-
ian, taking German or English as punctuated in his time as his norm,
thought it best to punctuate *Beowulf* for modern readers. We can make
assumptions about what forms a structural unit regardless of editorial
punctuation. We may feel that a structure is interrupted (as at lines
1652-3), or that some dependent clauses are so closely attached to
their main clause that Dobbie's English lack of punctuation accords better with what we feel is right than Klaeber's commas; but we have no
means of testing the validity of that feeling. When the main clause is
expressed by an A3 line the most we can say is that such main clauses
give the impression of leading forward to their dependent clauses with-

out interruption. That impression, however, is based on what we should feel in similar cases in Modern English. Some sentence structures require marking off by commas in modern practice, especially phrases or clauses thrust into the middle of a structural unit and felt to be separable from it. Vocatives (e.g. 429, 2000), interjected prayers (e.g. 435), interposed explanations (e.g. 706, 967, 2550), or other inclusions (e.g. 731, 1508, 2124, 2855) are punctuated by the editors as they would be in Modern English; and though poetic variation has no commonly occurring counterpart in Modern English, it is near enough to the concept of adjuncts (appositional, or seriate in other ways) to be punctuated similarly, that is, marked off by commas. It is, however, noteworthy that such poetic variation and other forms of (non-substantival) parallelism are found in *Beowulf* only after those A3 lines which have a verb in them, usually with the stress on the verb.[16] Variations and parallelisms (including verbal parallelisms) of this kind are found in the following lines: 361, 386, 1292, 1573, 1612, 1626, 1782. Seriation of short clauses is close to some forms of parallelism. An A3 line consisting of a self-contained simple sentence is unique in *Beowulf* (1232), punctuated with a full stop before and after the sentence. There are other cases of an A3 line consisting of a simple sentence, but, though the editors treat 316 and 1322 as self-contained (though both could be looked upon as introducing what follows), they treat 2609 differently. 316 is troublesome: we should expect 'mǣl' to be stressed and alliterate in 'Mǣl is mē tō fēran.' In the similar 'Sorh is mē tō secganne' (473) both the noun and the infinitive alliterate (and cf the second half-line of 700, 1322, 1703, all with participles, not infinitives, but otherwise similar; and all alliterating on the initial noun).[17] 1322 is a simple sentence, a command, the abruptness of which is, no doubt, a deliberate stylistic device. In Klaeber's punctuation, 2609 is punctuated with a comma after the A3 line;[18] but Grein's edition of 1857 and Dobbie, nearly a hundred years later, have a colon and a semicolon respectively; the half-line is the first of a sequence of three simple sentences.

We may perhaps, therefore, generalize about the sentences in which we find A3 lines to the extent that, on the whole (and as might be expected as a consequence of Kuhn's *Satzpartikelgesetz* and of his *Satzspitzengesetz*), A3 lines come very often at the beginning of sentences, and usually lead straight on to the second half-line; except that, when the A3 line includes a verb, the continuity of the sentence structure is not infrequently broken by an inclusion. Very occasionally A3 lines consist of one self-contained simple sentence, which may come as the first of a sequence of such sentences.

LIST OF A3 LINES IN BEOWULF[19]

A The stress falls on a noun, adjective, adverb, numeral, or 'heavy' pronoun

The first element is (or contains) a connective (other than a negative or a relative pronoun)

ac
(,) ac hine se mōdęga ( ) 813
(;) ac him on hreþre ( ) 1878
(,) ac hē him on hēafde ( ) 2973 (tr. allit. *ac*??)

æfter
(! ' n.p.) Æfter þǣm wordum ( ) 1492
(.' n.p.) Æfter ðām wordum ( ) 2669 (tr. allit. Æfter??)

ǣr (cf nō below)
(,)[20] ǣr hē þone grundwong ( ) 1496   /\

būton
(, −) būton hit wæs māre ( ) 1560
(,) būton þone hafelan ( ) 1614   ⌣/×x

efne, see swā, swylc(e), etc

for-ðām
(;) forþan ic hine sweorde ( ) 679
(.) Forþan bið andgit ( ) 1059   /\
(,) forþan hē tō lange ( ) 1336

ful oft, see oft

gif
(,) gif ic æt þearfe ( ) 1477
(.) Gif ic þonne on eorþan ( ) 1822
(.) Gif him þonne Hrēþrīc ( ) 1836   /\   (tr. allit. *Gif*??)

hraþe
(.) Hraþe wæs tō būre ( ) 1310

(.) Hræþe wearð on ȳðum ( ) 1437

hūru
(.) Hūru þæt on lande ( ) 2836
(.' n.p.) Hūru se snotra ( ) 3120

hwæþre
(;) hwæþre him sīo swīðre ( ) 2098
(;) hwæðre hē hine on folce ( ) 2377 (tr. allit. hwæðre?)[21]

hwīlum
(.) Hwīlum hē on lufan ( ) 1728   ⟋✕   (tr. allit. Hwīlum?)
(.) Hwīlum for (d)uguðe ( ) 2020   ⟋✕✕   (tr. allit. Hwīlum?)

nū
(?) Nū hēr þāra banena ( ) 2053   ⟋✕✕ (tr. allit. Nū?)

oft
(.) Ful oft ic for lǣssan ( ) 951[22]

ond
(,) ond þǣr on innan ( ) 71 (d. allit. ond??)[23]
( ) ond þē tō gēoce ( ) 1834
(,) ond wē tō symble ( ) 2104
(—,) ond hī hyne þā bēgen ( ) 2707

oð þæt
(,) oð þæt him æghwylc ( ) 9   ⟋＼   (d. allit. oð?)
(,) oð þæt ymb āntīd ( ) 219   ⟋＼   (d. allit. oð?)
(—, XXV) oð þæt him on innan ( ) 1740 (d. allit. oð?)
(—,) oð þæt hē ðā bānhūs ( ) 3147   ⟋＼   (cr. allit. -hūs??)[24]

siððan
(,) siþðan him Scyppend ( ) 106
(,) syðþan hīe þæs lāðan ( ) 132
(!) Siððan þā fǣhðe ( ) 470
(,) siðþan hē under segne ( ) 1204 (d. allit. siðþan?)[25]
(,) syþðan hē for wlenco ( ) 1206
(,) syðþan hē hine tō gūðe ( ) 1472
(,) syþðan hē æfter dēaðe ( ) 1589

(,) syð∂an ic on yrre () 2092
(,) syð∂an hyne Hæð cyn () 2437   / \
(,) syð∂an ic for dugeð um () 2501   ⌣××
(,) syð∂an hīe tōgædre () 2630   × _/×

sōna
(;) sōna mē se mǣra () 2011
(.) Sōna him se frōda () 2928

swā
(. n.p. VIIII) Swā mec gelōme () 559   × _/×
() efne swā hwylc mægþa () 943
() efne swā swið e () 1092 (d. allit. *swā*??)
(,) efne swā side () 1223 (d. allit. *swā*??)
() efne swā micle (,) 1283
(,) efne swā of hefene () 1571   ⌣××
(.) Swā wæs on ð ǣm scennum () 1694
(.) Swā wē þǣr inne () 2115
(,) efne swā hwylcum manna (,) 3057

swylc, swylce
() efne swylce mǣla (,) 1249
(;) swylce þū ð ā mādmas (,) 1482 (tr. allit. *swylce*?)
(;) gē swylce sēo herepād (,) 2258   ⌣× \
(,) eall swylce hyrsta (,) 3164 (tr. allit. *e*all?)[26]

sym(b)le
(;) symle ic him on fēð an () 2497

þā[27]
(. n.p. I) Ðā wæs on burgum () 53
(.) Ðā wæs on ūhtan () 126
(;) þā wæs æfter wiste () 128
(.) Ðā wit ætsomne () 544   × _/×
(! ' n.p.) Þā wæs on sālum () 607
(. n.p. XI) Ðā cōm of mōre () 710
(. n.p. XIII) Ðā wæs on morgen () 837
(,) ð ā hēo under swegle () 1078
(.) Ðā wæs on healle () 1288
(.) Ðā wæs of þǣm hrōran () 1629

(.) Þā wæs be feaxe () 1647
(.) Þā wæs on gange () 1884
(.) Þā wæs on sande () 1896
(.) Þā wæs be mæste () 1905
(.) Þā wæs æt ðām geongan () 2860
(.) Ðā wǣron monige (,) 2982 ⌣/XX (tr. allit. wǣron??)²⁸
(. n.p. XLII) Þā wæs gesȳne (,) 3058 X /X (tr. allit. Þā??)

þǣr
(,) ðǣr git for wlence () 508
(;) þǣr mē wið lāðum () 550
(.) Ðǣr wæs on blōde () 847²⁹
(,) þǣr him nænig wæter () 1514 ⌣/X
(,) ðǣr wē gesunde () 2075 X /X
(,) ðǣr hē þȳ fyrste () 2573

þæt (conj.)³⁰
(,) þæt hine on ylde () 22
(,) þæt wē hine swā gōdne () 347
(,) þæt ic mōte āna () 431
(,) þæt hit ā mid gemete () 779 X ⌣/X³¹ (tr. allit. ā?)
(,) þæt ðū hine selfne () 961
(−,) þæt hē þone wīsan () 1318
(,) þæt hēo þone fyrdhom () 1504 / \
(,) þæt hire on hafelan () 1521 ⌣/XX
(,) þæt hire wið halse () 1566
(,) þæt hine sēo brimwylf () 1599 / \
(,) þæt hē þæs gewinnes () 1721 X /X (tr. allit. þæs?? or even þæt??)
(,) þæt ic on þone hafelan () 1780 ⌣/XX
(,) þæt hē þone brēostwylm () 1877 / \
(,) þæt ðǣr on worðig () 1972
(,) þæt ðū þone wælgæst () 1995 / \ (cr. allit. -gǣst??)³²
(,) þæt hē mid ðȳ wīfe () 2028
(,) þæt hē tō Gifðum () 2494
(,) þæt se mǣra () 2587
(,) þæt mē is micle lēofre (,) 2651 (cr. allit. micle?? and even mē??)³³
(,) þæt hē þone nīðgæst () 2699 / \
(,) þæt him on brēostum () 2714
(,) þæt hē bī wealle () 2716
(,) þæt hē þone grundwong () 2770 / \

(,) þæt him for swenge () 2966
(,) þæt gē genōge () 3104   X _/X

þēah
(—,) þēah ðū þīnum brōðrum () 587

þenden
(,) þenden hīe ðām wǣpnum () 2038

þonne
(.) Ðonne wæs þēos medoheal () 484   _/X _\
(,) þonne hē æt gūðe () 1535 (tr. allit. *þ*onne?)
(.) þonne bið on hreþre () 1745
(,) þonne hē mid fǣmnan () 2034
(.) þonne cwið æt bēore () 2041
(;) þonne wæs þæt yrfe () 3051

The first element is a negative

næs, nealles
(.) Nalæs hī hine lǣssan () 43
(.) Næs hīe ðǣre fylle () 562
(;) nealles ic ðām lēanum () 2145
(. n.p. XXXII) Nealles mid gewealdum () 2221   X _/X
(;—) nalles hē ðā frætwe () 2503
(.) Nealles him on hēape () 2596
(.) Nalles æfter lyfte () 2832

nefne
(,) næfne hē wæs māra () 1353

nē
(,) nē þǣr nǣnig witena () 157   _/XX

nō
(;—) nō hē þone gifstōl () 168   _/ _\
(;) nō hē mid hearme () 1892 (tr. allit. *nō*?)
(;) nō ðȳ ǣr hē þone heaðorinc () 2466   _/X _\

The first element is a pronoun³⁴

Relative or demonstrative pronouns
(,) ðē mē se gōda () 355 (tr. allit. ðē??)³⁵
() þāra þe of wealle () 785
(. n.p.) Sē wæs wreccena () 898³⁶ (d. allit. wæs??)
(,) ðē wē ealle () 941
(;) þæs wǣron mid Ēotenum () 1145³⁷
(,) hwæt wit tō willan () 1186 (d. allit. wit??)
() þāra þe ic on foldan () 1196
(,) þæs þe hī hyne gesundne () 1628 ×_/×
(,) þæs ðe ic ðē gesundne () 1998 ×_/×
(:) 'þæt is undyrne (,) 2000 ×_/×
(,) þone þīn fæder () 2048 /×
(,) þone þe ðū mid rihte () 2056
(,) þone þe him on sweofote () 2295 /××
(,) þē hē wið þām wyrme () 2400
(.) Sē wæs on ðām ðrēate () 2406 (tr. allit. Sē?)
(,) sē ðone gomelan () 2421 /××
(;) þæt wæs mid eldum () 2611
() þām ðāra māðma () 2779
(;) sē scel tō gemyndum () 2804 ×_/×
(.') þæt wæs þām gomelan () 2817 /××   (tr. allit. wæs??)
(. n.p.) þæt ys sio fǣhðo () 2999

'Heavier' (object) pronouns
(.) Nǣnigne ic under swegle () 1197
(:) 'Fela ic on giogoðe () 2426 /××

Personal pronouns (other than subject personal pronouns immediately preceding their verb)
(!) Ic þē þā fǣhðe () 1380
(;) ic þǣre sōcne () 1777
(.) Hē mec þǣr on innan () 2089
(.) Mē þone wælrǣs () 2101 /\
(.) Ic ðā ðæs wælmes (,) 2135
(;) hē þǣr [f]or feorme () 2385 (tr. allit. hē??)³⁸
(.) Hē ðā mid þǣre sorhge (,) 2468
(. n.p.) Ic him þā māðmas (,) 2490

(.) Hyne þā mid handa () 2720 (d. allit. *H*yne?)[39]
(.) Hē ðā mid þām māðmum () 2788
(–:) 'Ic ðāra frætwa () 2794

The first element is an interjection

(:) 'Hwæt, wē þē þās sǣlāc (,) 1652 _/ _ (tr. allit. *H*wæt??)[40]
(.) Hwæt, mē þæs on ēþle () 1774

The first element is a verb (or a verb preceded by a negative or a subject personal pronoun)[41]

(.) Fand þā ðǣr inne () 118
(.) Hæfde se gōda () 205
(.) Wæs mīn fæder () 262 _/_×
(!) Habbað wē tō þǣm mǣran () 270
(.) Bēo ðū on ofeste (,) 386 _/_××
(;) gesaga him ēac wordum (,) 388
(.) Geslōh þīn fæder () 459 _/_×
(–:) 'Eart þū sē Bēowulf (,) 506 _/ _ (cr. allit. -*w*ulf??)
(.) Gespræc þā se gōda () 675
(!) Cōm þā tō recede () 720 _/_××
(.) Geseah hē in recede () 728 _/_××
(,) nam þā mid handa () 746 (tr. allit. *þ*ā??)
(. ') Hwearf þā bī bence (,) 1188
(. ' n.p.) Ēode þā tō setle (.)[42] 1232
(.) Setton him tō hēafdon () 1242
(. n.p.) Cōm þā tō Heorote (,) 1279 _/_××
(.) Gang ðā æfter flōre () 1316
(!) Wearð him on Heorote () 1330 _/_××
(. ') Āhlēop ðā se gomela (,) 1397 _/_××
(.) Gesāwon ðā æfter wætere () 1425 _/_××
(:) 'Geþenc nū, se mǣra () 1474
(;) hwearf þā be wealle (,) 1573 (tr. allit. *h*wearf?)
(. n.p.) Cōm þā tō lande () 1623
(.) Ēodon him þā tōgēanes (,) 1626 ×_/_× (tr. allit. *þ*ā??)
(,) seleð him on ēþle () 1730

(,) gedēð him swā gewealdẹne ( ) 1732 X _/X   (tr. allit. ge*dēð*?)
(;) þinceð him tō lȳtel (,) 1748
(!) Gā nū tō setle (,) 1782
(;) hēt [h]in*e* mid þǣm lācum ( ) 1868
(. n.p. XXVII) Cwōm þā tō flōde ( ) 1888
(. n.p. XXVIII) Gewāt him ðā se hearda ( ) 1963
(,) wolde *se* lāða ( ) 2305
(;) hæfde him on earme ( ) 2361[43]
(,) lēt ðone bregostōl ( ) 2389 _/X _\
(.) Gesæt ðā on næsse ( ) 2417
(. n.p. XXXV) Gewīteð þonne on sealman (,) 2460
(!) Geseah ðā be wealle ( ) 2542
(.) Lēt ðā of brēostum (,) 2550
(;) sceolde willan ( ) 2589[44]
(.) Gemunde ðā ðā āre (,) 2606
(.) Bīo nū on ofoste (,) 2747 _/XX
(. ') Dyde him of healse ( ) 2809
(.) Gewāt him ðā se gōda ( ) 2949
(.) Lēt se hearda ( ) 2977 (tr. allit. *Lēt*??)
(,) sealde hiora gehwæðrum ( ) 2994 X _/X
(.) Fundon ðā on sande ( ) 3033
(;) ālegdon ðā tōmiddes ( ) 3141 X _/X   (tr. allit. ðā??)
(.) Ongunnon þā on beorge ( ) 3143

With initial negative
(;) nāt hē þāra gōda (,) 681
(.) Ne gefrægẹn ic þā mǣgþe ( ) 1011
(:) 'Ne frīn þū æfter sǣlum (!) 1322 (tr. allit. *Ne*??)
(.) Næs þæt þonne mǣtost ( ) 1455
(.) Ne nōm hē in þǣm wīcum (,) 1612
(.) Ne meahte ic æt hilde ( ) 1659
(;) næs ic him tō līfe ( ) 2432
(.) Ne þynceð mē gerysne (,) 2653 X _/X
(.) Ne meahte hē on eorðan (,) 2855
(.) Ne meahte se snella ( ) 2971
(.) Næs ðā on hlytme (,) 3126

Verb preceded by subject personal pronoun[45]
(.) Hēo wæs on ofste (,) 1292
(.) Ic wæs þǣr inne ( ) 3087 (d. allit. *Ic*?)[46]

Verb heads main clause occupying only part of half-line
(;) wēne ic þæt hē mid gōde () 1184 (tr. allit. *wēne?*)[47]
(.—) Hȳrde ic þæt þām frætwum () 2163

B The stress falls on a verb

THE STRESSED VERB IS AN INFINITIVE OR A PAST PARTICIPLE[48]

Without preceding finite verb
(,) ond þonne geferian () 3107   ×⌣×× (tr. allit. *ond??*)

With preceding finite verb

The first element is a connective

ac
(;) ac hē hafað onfunden (,) 595   × ⁄×
(;) ac hīe hæfdon gefrūnen (,) 694   × ⁄×

hēr
(:) 'Hēr syndon geferede (,) 361   ×⌣××

nū
(.) Nū gē mōton gangan () 395

sym(b)le
(.) Symble bið gemyndgad () 2450   × ⁄×

þā
(. n.p. [XXXVIIII] Ðā wæs gegongen () 2821   × ⁄×

þonne
(.) Þonne bīoð (āb)rocene () 2063   ×⌣××

The first element is a noun[49]

(:) 'Mǣl is mē tō fēran (;) 316

The first element is followed by an interjection

(—:) 'Þæt, lā, mæg secgan ( ) 1700
(—:) 'Þæt, lā, mæg secgan ( ) 2864

The first element is a finite verb

(.' n.p.) Gewiton him þā fēran (,—) 301
(.) Wille ic āsecgan ( ) 344   X _/X
(.) Hæbbe ic ēac geāhsod (,) 433   X _/X   (d. allit. ēac??)
(.) Hæfde þā gefǣlsod ( ) 825   X _/X
(.) Hafast þū gefēred (,) 1221   X _/X
(.) Hæfde ðā forsiðod ( ) 1550   X _/X
(.) Hafast þū gefēred (,) 1855   X _/X
(;) (h)afað þæs geworden ( ) 2026   X _/X
(! n.p.) Mæg þæs þonne ofþyncan ( ) 2032   X _/X   (d. allit. þonne??)
(;) wæs ðā gebolgen ( ) 2304   X _/X
(.) Heht him þā gewyrcean ( ) 2337   X _/X   (tr. allit. Heht?)[50]
(;) hæfde þā gefrūnen (,) 2403   X _/X
(.' n.p.) Hēt ðā gebēodan ( ) 3110   X _/X

With initial negative
(;) ne mihte ðā forhabban (,) 2609   X _/X
(.) Ne meahton wē gelǣran ( ) 3079   X _/X

Verb preceded by object pronoun
(:) 'Ēow hēt secgan ( ) 391

THE STRESS FALLS ON A FINITE VERB

The first element is a connective (other than a negative or a relative pronoun)

ac
(;) ac mē geūðe ( ) 1661   X _/X   (d. allit. ac??)[51]
(,) ac hē hyne gewyrpte (,) 2976   X _/X

ǣr
(.) Ǣr hī þǣr gesēgan ( ) 3038   X _/X

for-ðām þe
(,) forþon þe hē ne ūþe (,) 503

gif
(.) Gif ic þæt gefricge () 1826 X _/X (tr. allit. *G*if??)
(,) gif þæt gegangeð (,) 1846 X _/X (d. allit. *g*if??)

hūru
(.) Hūru ne gemunde () 1465 X _/X

hwæþre
(!) Hwæþere mē gesælde (,) 574 X _/X
(;) hwæþre him gesælde (,) 890 X _/X
(;) hwæþre hē gemunde () 1270 X _/X

ond
(,) ond gē him syndon () 393
(,) ond him gesealde () 2195 X _/X
(,) ond þone gebringan (,) 3009 X _/X

oð þæt
(,– [XXVIIII-XXX]) oð ðæt hīe forlæddan () 2039 X _/X
(,) oð ðæt hī oðēodon () 2934 X _/X (d. allit. *o*ð?)

siððan
(,) syððan hīe gefricgeað () 3002 X _/X

sōna
(.) Sōna þæt onfunde () 750 X _/X
(.) Sōna þæt onfunde () 1497 X _/X

swā
(.) Swā hē ne forwyrnde () 1142 X _/X
(,) swā hē ne mihte (–) 1508

þā
(.) Þā gȳt hīe him āsetton () 47 X _/X (tr. allit. *g*ȳt?)
(.) Þā mē þæt gelærdon () 415 X _/X (tr. allit. *m*ē??)
(.–) Ðā þæt onfunde () 809 X _/X
(.) Ðā hīe getruwedon () 1095 X ⌣/XX (tr. allit. *h*īe??)
(,) ðā hyne gesōhtan () 2204 X _/X (tr. allit. ð*ā*??)

þæt
(,) þæt ðū mē ne forwyrne (,) 429   x _/x
(,) þæt hīe ne mōste (,) 706
(,) þæt hē ne mētte () 751
(,) þæt hē ne mehte () 1082
(,) þæt hīe oft wǣron () 1247[52]
(,) þæt hīe gesāwon () 1347   x _/x
(,) þæt ðū ne ālǣte () 2665   x _/x
(,) þæt hē ne grētte () 3081 (tr. allit. *þæt*??)

þēah
(,) þēah þe hē meahte () 1130[53]

þonan
(.) Þanon hē gesōhte () 463   x _/x
(;) ðonon hē gesōhte () 520   x _/x

þonne
(,) þonne wē gehēton () 2634   x _/x

The first element is a negative

nōðer
(.) Nōðer hȳ hine ne mōston (,) 2124

The first element is a pronoun

Relative pronouns
() ðāra þe ne wēndon (,) 937
() ðāra þe hē geworhte () 1578   x _/x
(,) þæs ðe ic mōste () 2797

Personal pronouns
   Subject[54]
(;) hi hyne þā ætbǣron () 28   x _/x
(.) Ic þæt gehȳre (,) 290   x _/x
(:) 'Ic hine cūðe () 372
(;) ic þæt þonne forhicge (,) 435   x _/x
(.) Wit þæt gecwǣdon () 535   x _/x   (tr. allit. *Wit*??)

(:) 'Ic þæt hogode (,) 632　ⵑ××
(.) Hīe þæt ne wiston (,) 798
(;) ic hine ne mihte (,) 967
(.) Ic hit þē gehāte (:) 1392　×_/×
(.) Ic hit þē þonne gehāte (,) 1671　×_/×
　Object
(.) Mē man sægde (,) 1175
(. n.p. XLIII) Him ðā gegiredan () 3137　×ⵑ××

'Heavier' subject pronouns
(.) Nǣnig heora þōhte (,) 691
(;) nǣnig þæt dorste () 1933 (tr. allit. *nǣnig?*)

Preposition followed by pronoun
(;) on him gladiað () 2036　ⵑ××

The first element is a verb

Verb heads main clause occupying only part of half-line
(;) mynte þæt hē gedǣlde (,) 731　×_/×
(;) cwæð þæt hyt hæfde () 2158 (tr. allit. *cwæð?*)
(,) bæd þæt gē geworhton () 3096　×_/×
(;) cwǣdon þæt hē wǣre () 3180 (tr. allit. *cwǣdon?*)

NOTES

1 E. Sievers, 'Zur Rhythmik des germanisches Alliterationverses,' *PBB* 10 (1885) 209-314, 451-545, of which 220-314 are specifically on *Beowulf*; also *Altgermanische Metrik* (Halle 1893). H. Kuhn, 'Zur Wortstellung und -betonung im Altgermanischen,' *PBB* 57 (1933) 1-109, summarized in English by D. Slay, 'Some Aspects of the Technique of Composition of Old English Verse,' *TPS* (London 1952) 1-14. A.J. Bliss, *The Metre of Beowulf* (Oxford 1958). John Collins Pope, *The Rhythm of Beowulf* (New Haven and Oxford 1942, rev. 1966).
  　Other investigations of metre used by me include: A. Heusler, *Deutsche Versgeschichte*, I (Berlin and Leipzig 1925, repr. 1956); W.P. Lehmann and T. Tabusa, *The Alliterations of the 'Beowulf'* (Austin, Texas 1958); R.B. Le Page, 'Alliterative Patterns as a Test of Style in Old English Poetry,' *JEGP* 58 (1959) 434-41; R. Willard and E.D. Clemons, 'Bliss's Light Verses in the *Beowulf*,' *JEGP* 66 (1967)

230-44. I have profited from W.J. Sedgefield's appendix I, 'Old English Versification,' in his third edition of *Beowulf* (Manchester 1935), 149-55, S.O. Andrew's *Syntax and Style in Old English* (Cambridge 1940) and *Postscript on Beowulf* (Cambridge 1948).

The text of *Beowulf* used is that of Fr. Klaeber's third edition (Boston 1950); his appendix 'Metrical Observations' (278-82) has been used often. Other editions, referred to below similarly by the editor's name, have been found especially useful for their notes on textual and metrical matters: E.V.K. Dobbie, in *ASPR*, IV (New York 1953); E. von Schaubert, 2. Teil: Kommentar, seventeenth edition of Heyne-Schücking's *Beowulf* (Paderborn 1961). *A Concordance to Beowulf*, by J.B. Bessinger, Jr, and P.H. Smith, Jr (Ithaca, N.Y. 1969), has been used very frequently.

Many of these works, especially those by Klaeber and Professors Pope and Bliss, have been referred to by me throughout, more often than the references to them might seem to indicate.

2 *Ueber ein- und dreihebige Halbverse in der altenglischen alliterierenden Poesie* (Diss. Berlin 1920)

3 Since this study is about A3 lines (which are confined to the first half-line, a-lines) only b is used, viz. to mark second half-lines, leaving a-lines unmarked.

4 Evidence of this kind is perhaps to be found as early as the *Chronicle* poem AD 1036C rhyming 'wunode' and 'lyfode' without alliteration and, with alliteration, 'hamelode' and 'hættode' (and cf AD 1086, last couplet 'mildheortnisse' perhaps rhyming with 'forgifenesse').

5 Cf Kuhn's use of the term *Bindewort*, PBB 57 (1933) 51.

6 'gewealdene,' past participle, is, of course, verbal.

7 See Pope, 272-4; and, especially for references to earlier work, Klaeber, 278 §17).

8 See, for example, von Schaubert's note on line 56.

9 See Klaeber, 280-1 (§28).

10 See above note 1.

11 See Klaeber, 98 footnote; Pope, 315; von Schaubert, note on line.

12 See von Schaubert, note on line 1. Old Saxon subsidiary alliteration, relevant because of *Heliand*, 2550, may be a different matter, on which see E. Martin, *Der Versbau des Heliand*, QF 100 (Strassburg 1907) 16-17.

13 Cf M. Kaluza, *Studien zum germanischen Alliterationsvers*, 2 Der altenglische Vers, ii *Beowulf* (Berlin 1894) 66 (Typus 36); Klaeber, 278 (§18); von Schaubert, note on line 779.

14 But note line 2039 without canto number, though a new canto is indicated by the large initial — see Klaeber, c-ci (and fn 7).

15 Kuhn defines the *Satzpartikelgesetz* at PBB 57 (1933) 8, the *Satzspitzengesetz*, a few pages later, at 43.

16 I have not investigated whether this is a peculiarity of *Beowulf* (and also perhaps of some of the other 'metrically exact' Old English poems), or whether it extends more widely.

17 It is probably best not to adduce 2093 ('Tō lang ys tō reccenne ') as a parallel, because that half-line seems to be metrically anomalous; see Bliss, §47. This anomaly involves the anacrusis 'Tō,' and is a separate problem from that of whether or not infinitives were originally inflected, on which see Klaeber, 78 (fn), 277 (§12), Pope, 310, Bliss §87.

18 Thus most editors, following Heyne's edition of 1863 and Grein's edition of 1857. Cf 386, where the editors have a comma at the end of the first half-line; in this line also two imperative simple sentences follow each other.

19 The following abbreviations are used in this list: allit. = alliteration, the various types being described as cr. = cross, d. = double, and tr. = transverse; n.p. = new paragraph (cf p. 144 above). Headwords are spelt as in Klaeber's glossary.

Unless the lines marked as having possibly (marked ?) or conceivably (marked ??) double or cross alliteration are thought to exhibit some form of subsidiary alliteration which is non-functional, recognition of proper double or cross alliteration in them would remove them from the body of A3 lines. I myself cannot believe in non-functional alliteration in Old English, not even in the case of transverse alliteration, and am, therefore, inclined to think that transverse alliteration is dependent on meaningfully stressed words, like all alliteration. Cf A. Heusler, in Hoops, *Reallexikon*, IV (Strassburg 1918), s.v. 'Stabreim,' §37 (page 239).

20 Dobbie has no punctuation. As a rule, I have not marked editorial differences in punctuation; cf pp. 144-6 above.

21 Pope, 268, describes transverse alliteration here as 'very doubtful'; cf pp. 142-3 above.

22 'ful' in the phrase 'ful oft' is weakly stressed in *Beowulf* 1252b.

23 See Pope, 265-6.

24 See Pope, 267.

25 Pope, 251, regards this line firmly as an A line with double alliteration, not as an A3 line. Bliss, 143 (and cf 123 and 125), on the other hand, regards it as his type a1e (of which there are 57 examples in the poem), not as his type 1A*1c with double alliteration, of which there are only two examples in the poem, presumably 1230 and 1859, that is, the other two lines given by Professor Pope as metrically like 1204 (but Bliss has left out the asterisk for 1859 in his table). If, however, a less precise matching of metrical patterns than Bliss's full system were thought sufficient (that is, if the number of unstressed syllables before the second stress were regarded as of no importance for the purpose of matching, thus aggregating all type 1A*1 lines as main type $\underline{/}\times |(\times\times)\times \underline{/}\times$), 1204 scanned with initial stress and double alliteration would be seen to belong to a very common pattern (of which Bliss has counted 308 examples in the poem).

26 See p. 144 above.

27 In view of the frequency with which adverbial 'þā' is followed by a verb, most commonly 'wæs' ('wǣron' 2982), but note 710, it might be thought better to list these lines under verbal first elements preceded by 'þā,' instead of under the connective. If that had been done, line 544 (and also 1078 with conjunction — not adverb — 'þā'), in which no verb follows the connective, would have had to receive separate treatment for which there is no real justification. And other connectives would have had to be treated similarly, for example, 'for-ðām'; for 1059 would have had to be separated from the other examples under that headword, because in 1059 initial 'Forþan' is followed by 'bið'; and similarly under 'hraþe' both, under 'þǣr' 847, under 'þæt' 2651 (and cf 431); and under 'þonne' 484, 1745, 2041 (with 'cwið'), and 3051; cf under 'būton' 1560, and perhaps similarly under the negative 'nefne' 1353. See also note 39 below.

Line 710 constitutes an exception to the general rule that 'þā' is followed by an unstressable word, usually 'wæs,' when 'þā' heads an A3 line, and that where a verb is more heavily stressed 'þā' follows it. A list of such lines is given by Willard and Clemons, 230-44, whose more far-reaching conclusions about stress in such lines seem, however, doubtful to me.

28 Transverse alliteration is unlikely here, since, as stated in note 27, it is the rule that adverbial 'þā' precedes its verb when the verb is unstressed.

29 If, as seems likely, 'þǣr' is like initial 'þā' in such lines, the verb following it is unstressed, and it is fortuitous that 'wæs' could be involved with 'weallende' in transverse alliteration. See notes 27 and 28.

30 For pronominal 'þæt' (lines 2000, 2817, 2999) see p. 152.

31 See p. 143.

32 See Pope, 267.

33 See pp. 143-4.

34 Lines the first element of which is a subject personal pronoun followed within the line by its verb are listed on p. 154.

35 See Pope, 265-6.

36 Pope, 295-6, lists this line doubtfully as a type C rather than A3, but points to the form 'wrecna'; cf A. Campbell, *Old English Grammar* (Oxford 1959), §617.

37 See Pope, 267, for 'Ēotenum'; and cf R.W. Chambers, *Widsith* (Cambridge 1912), appendix D, 237-41. If medial 'n' in the name is not merely the result of scribal confusion of 'Jutes' with 'etens' (but cf Campbell §610 [7]), the 'e' preceding it is likely to have been syncopated — 'Ēotenum.' Cf Bliss, §58; Klaeber, 233, fn 3.

38 See Pope, 265-6.

39 See Pope, 251, listing the line as an A line, not an A3. My doubts, viz. that 'Hyne' is too weak to bear alliteration, are not dispelled by the arguments advanced by Willard and Clemons, 243-4: the distribution of post-verbal 'þā' is not significantly

different in lines with double alliteration (30 out of 60) and single alliteration (38 out of 85), and though whatever follows initial 'þā' is weakly stressed, the converse, that when 'þā' is the second element of a half-line the element preceding it is strongly stressed, is not certain. Cf note 27 above.

) *Hwæt* is probably unstressed — see von Schaubert, note on line 1.

I See the important discussion of these lines by Willard and Clemons.

2 See p. 146.

3 Vocalic alliteration seems certain, but is, in fact, dependent on 'āna' in the second half-line; the word was first supplied by Grein (1857), the manuscript being damaged.

4 As Dobbie says in his note on the line, 'All recent edd. supply *ofer*, following Rieger, ZfdPh. III, 410'; but Grein-Köhler stuck to the unemended reading as late as 1914, and list it with the use of 'willum,' 1821, under 'willa' (see also Bosworth-Toller, s.v. 'willa,' VIII). That gives satisfactory or perhaps even better sense than the emendation (regardless of whether 'willan' is a singular or has '-an' for '-um,' plural): Beowulf's death was not easy but he went willingly as a good man should.

It should, however, be noted that 'sceolde willan' (unemended) is metrically unique in the poem, being an A3 line with only two syllables belonging to one single word preceding the alliterative stress. All other cases of only two syllables preceding the stress are with two words unstressed (see Pope, 83). It may be, therefore, that we must emend for metrical reasons, and that the choice lies between '[mid] willan' and '[ofer] willan'; the former seems preferable in sense.

5 For other lines with personal pronoun as first element, see pp. 152-3 above, and cf note 34.

6 See Pope, 250, where this line is listed as type A, not A3. The emphasis here is on Wiglaf's own witness of the events. That, however, is true also at 3090b where 'Ic' must be metrically unstressed ('Ic on ofoste gefēng'). Though it is unwise to regard the prosody of the two halves as sufficiently similar to allow the findings of a second half-line to apply to a first half-line, it seems best to regard 'Ic' at 3087 as unstressed, and only fortuitously alliterating.

7 See Pope, 268, where the transverse alliteration perhaps to be found here is compared with the double alliteration of 338. But double alliteration seems to me more firmly established than transverse alliteration, and the use at 338 is confirmed by that at 2172. In line 2163 'Hȳrde ic' does not participate in any alliteration.

8 Infinitives and participles rank in stress with nouns, etc; see especially A. Heusler, *Deutsche Versgeschichte*, I, sections 135-52. In this list the absence of present participles is, of course, the result of the fact that their form makes them elements of C lines, and, by definition, not of A3 lines; for examples, see 2218 (in the restoration accepted by Klaeber), and 2850.

9 See p. 146.

50 See Pope, 266.

51 See Pope, 265-6.

52 See Pope 234; Bliss, §27; and von Schaubert's note on the line.

53 The editors alter manuscript 'he' to 'ne,' or supply 'ne' after 'he' (thus avoiding somewhat unusual omission of subject pronoun in their emended reading); see Dobbie's note on the line. If the negative is supplied, Hengest dwells with Finn that winter, not voluntarily to avenge his lord before returning home, but because he could do nothing else. However, he seems to have got reinforcements through, and perhaps even summoned them. In such a difficult context it is perhaps wisest not to emend, but to understand 1129b-31a as introducing 1138b-41, with a little piece on the change of seasons and the growing longing for home intervening: his memory of home takes the form of plotting vengeance rather than voyaging back. See also von Schaubert's notes on these lines.

54 It is perhaps worth noting that the ten occurrences are all before Hrothgar's 'sermon,' or, looked at in terms of the scribes, all in the work of the first of the two scribes. It would, however, be rash to attempt to draw any conclusion from this distribution.

† KEMP MALONE

The rhythm of *Deor*

Admiration often begets imitation and this paper may be summed up as a try at doing for *Deor* what our jubilarian did so well for *Beowulf*. Both Pope and I have edited *Des Sängers Trost* (as the Germans call it), but neither included in his edition a full study of the poem's rhythmical features: Pope commented on verses 2b, 30b, and 39b[1] and I dealt briefly with 4a and 8a;[2] otherwise, we took up no particular cases and I contented myself with the general statement that 'the *Deor* poet wrote his verses in the conventional or standard Old English measure.'[3] Surely more is needed to do poem and poet justice, and in the following I will fill the gap as best I can.

I begin with a linear catalogue not unlike the one I gave in my revised edition of *Widsith*.[4] It differs from this chiefly in classifying the half-lines as Pope did in *The Rhythm of Beowulf*,[5] instead of simply specifying the type in terms of the five-type system of Sievers. Thus, I classify 'hæfde him to gesiþþe   sorge and longaþ' (*Deor* 3) as A77 for the on-verse, A5 for the off-verse. My catalogue takes shape in three columns, the first giving the line-number, the second the classification of the on-verse, the third that of the off-verse.

1	A7	D2	*6*	D33	B1	*11*	B2	A5
2	E1	E2	*7*	A5	A35	*12*	A5	C2
3	A77	A5	*8*	E7	B2	*14*	C3	A5
4	E17	D18	*9*	B55	B5	*15*	C2	A1
5	B7	A1	*10*	C11	C34	*16*	C26	D20

18	A28	A1		*28*	D11	A5		*35*	A70	A1	
19	E1	B16		*29*	C10	A1		*36*	B2	E5	
21	C22	A1		*30*	B3	E2		*37*	A1	C22	
22	E4	B2		*31*	A20	C23		*38*	C13	A1	
23	A3	C22		*32*	A1	A5		*39*	A1	B33	
24	D10	A5		*33*	A11	A5		*40*	E1	E1	
25	A2	A5		*34*	E1	B2		*41*	B3	A2	
26	C12	C11									

Most of the verses need no comment but some make more or less trouble for the would-be scanner. If the 'æ' of 'wræce'(1b) were long (so Grein-Köhler, Klaeber, et al.) the half-line would come under D40, but Bosworth-Toller and NED rightly enter the word with a short vowel. For the synonymous unrecorded OE '*wrǣcu' (fem.), an old '-in' stem cognate with Gothic 'wrekei' (see NED s.v. 'wreche,' where, however, the OE form is wrongly reconstructed). The second syllable of 'earfoþa' (2b) was originally long[6] and we may reasonably think that the secondary stress it took in proto-English was kept in traditional metrics after shortening came about in common speech. Alternatively it might be conjectured that this and parallel shortenings gave rise to a variant of type E with a weak second syllable. Compare the *Beowulf* poet's 'lissa gelong' (2150a) and 'rǣhte ongēan' (747b).[7]

In classifying 'wintercealde wræce' (4a) as E17, I go part of the way with W.P. Lehmann, whose study of the liquids and nasals of *Beowulf* came out in *Nordica et Anglica*, a book got out in honour of Stefán Einarsson.[8] Lehmann took it that the poet uttered 1, r, n, m as consonants in words like 'setl,' where the syllable is light, but as sonants in words like 'ādl,' where a heavy syllable precedes. That is to say, the liquid or nasal makes part of the light but not of the heavy syllable: 'setl' is monosyllabic whereas 'ādl' is disyllabic. For the evidence the reader is referred to Lehmann's paper. Here I will deal with OE 'winter' only. This word is cognate with Gothic 'wintrus' and the NED gives the hypothetical Germanic form as '*wentrus,'[9] seemingly a misprint for '*wentruz.' Here the r is clearly consonantal. The proto-English nominative singular form would presumably be '*wintr' and I agree with Lehmann that the r of this form would be sonantal, though I do not trace its sonancy back to pre-Germanic times. The recorded OE form 'winter' shows an 'e' which does not appear in the inflectional 'wintres,' 'wintra,' 'wintras,' 'wintru,' and 'wintrum.' I take it accordingly that the 'e' of OE 'winter' stands for a weak vowel which arose as a transitional sound. Whether the *Deor* poet said 'wintr' or 'winter,' he said it in two syllables, or so I think. Klaeber in his edition of *Deor*[10] underdotted for deletion the first 'e' of 'wintercealde,' his way of showing that in his opinion 'winter-' was monosyllabic, but there is no metrical need for so taking it and the disyllabic pronunciation strikes me as phonetically preferable. Doubts of the validity of the pattern E17 are not justified. A clear case is the 'swinsigende swēg' (1081a) of the OE *Genesis*, an on-verse which must be so scanned.

The off-verse 'wēan oft onfond' (4b) by its caesura is marked as a D type; the adverb goes with its verb. The on-verse of the next line, 'siþþan hine Nīðhād on,' is a B7 unlike the *Beowulf* on-verses of this pattern in that between its two main stresses comes a syllable which normally takes a secondary accent (it makes the second member of a compound) but here undergoes rhythmical weakening. In his discussion of on-verse B half-lines Pope lists eight cases of this kind[11] and I have found no others. Two of Pope's cases, indeed, must be stricken,[12] since OE 'inwid' or 'inwit' (OS 'inwid') is no compound; compare Latin 'inuidus' and 'inuidia' with the corresponding verb 'inuidēre,' where the prefix gives 'uidēre' a bad sense. We have no reason to think that the second syllable of OE 'inwit' was accented, whether as a simplex or as the first member of the compounds 'inwitnet' and 'inwitsearo.' Since all six of Pope's true cases come under B2, a pattern which (unlike that of B7) begins with a rest beat, we get an instructive contrast in the metrical practice of the two poets. It should be added that *Beowulf* has one off-verse, 2173b, with a B7 pattern like that of *Deor* 5a.

The verse 'þisses swā mæg' (7b) agrees in rhythm with Pope's A35 but in this pattern *Beowulf* always has a compound for second measure of the off-verse and I find no exact parallels in the on-verses either. The translation 'as regards this likewise it can' brings out something of the OE lift-pattern as well as making clear (clumsily enough) what the verse means: the infinitive 'ofergān' is to be understood and leaving it out throws more stress on 'mæg' than the word would normally take. In this setting 'mæg' may mean 'will' by meiosis, but I find it safer to translate literally.

C. Richter in his *Chronologische Studien*[13] misdivided line 8, coming thereby to metrical conclusions that I need not deal with here, since I have shown their falsity in my edition of the poem. The verse 'on sefan swā sār' (9a) shows a B pattern which the *Beowulf* poet seems to have restricted to the second half-line. The light measure of 'þæt hī sēo sorglufu' (16a) takes a rhythm with the stress on 'sēo' ('that') needed to bring out the meaning. It is noteworthy that *Beowulf* shows only one clear case of this C pattern, the on-verse of line 2148 ('ða ic ðē, beorncyning'). The scansion of verses like 'wē gēascodan' (21a) makes difficulties.[14]

The second syllable of 'wylfenne geþōht' (22a) takes a secondary accent (the OE adjectival suffix '-en' is cognate with Gothic '-ein'). The 'þæs' of line 26 is not the article but the demonstrative adjective and takes stress, light though it be. In my edition I took the 'þæt' of line 30 for the conjunction; hence my B3 for the on-verse. If 'þæt' is the pronoun the right classification is B2. Note that if we go by Pope's book *Beowulf* shows only three clear cases of B3 in the on-verse. But some of the ones that Pope puts under B2 can be read with B3 rhythm, for example, 1057a: 'ond ðæs mannes mōd' ('and that man's courage'). If 'þonne' (31) alliterates, the on-verse here is an A20, and so I take it; if not, the classification must be A74.

The off-verse 'sumum wēana dæl' (34b) makes trouble for traditional scanners, since 'sumum' here must take stress, contrasting as it does with 'monegum' in the line next before. Pope's system of scansion solves the problem neatly enough by giving a light stress to 'sumum.' The alternative, D17, carries with it a departure from alliterative orthodoxy which nobody would accept. My B33 for 'oþþæt Heorrenda nū' (39b) is orthodox indeed but leaves me unhappy. If one allows anacrusis in an E verse we have here a case parallel to *Beowulf* 501b, 662a, 1236a, and 2441a; A.J. Bliss gives these and several other examples, but rejects E and recommends B for them all.[15] In terms of rhythm B gives a poor fit here but orthodoxy must be served.

For a poem only 42 lines long, in which lines 7, 13, 17, 20, 27, and 42 are identical, frequency counts are not worth much, but here they are: of the on-verses, 13 are A's, 6 B's, 8 C's, 3 D's, and 7 E's; of the off-verses, 17 are A's, 7 B's, 6 C's, 3 D's, and 4 E's. Totals: 30 A's, 13 B's, 14 C's, 6 D's, and 11 E's. Both half-lines of the so-called refrain belong to the A type and if we count each occurrence of these the number of A types comes to 18 for the on-verse and 22 for the off-verse, or 40 all told. With these figures and a salute to John Collins Pope I make an end. Long may he live and make the music of our old poetry come alive.

NOTES

This essay, among the last written by Professor Malone, was received by the editors after his death. The annotation has been altered but the substance of the article remains unchanged.

1 *Seven Old English Poems* (rev. ed., Indianapolis 1966), 112, 116, 125
2 *Deor* (4th ed., London 1966), 19 ff
3 *Deor*, 19
4 *Widsith* (Copenhagen 1962), 65 f
5 *The Rhythm of Beowulf* (rev. ed., New Haven 1966), 247-373
6 See Karl Luick, *Historische Grammatik der englischen Sprache* (Stuttgart 1914-21), 277, and compare Gothic 'arbaiþs,' German 'Arbeit.'
7 On 747b, see esp. Pope, *The Rhythm of Beowulf*, 372, with xxxi of his revised edition.
8 'Post-consonantal l, m, n, r, and Metrical Practice in the *Beowulf*,' in *Nordica et Anglica*, ed Allan H. Orrick (The Hague 1968), 148-67
9 So also C.T. Onions, *Oxford Dictionary of English Etymology* (Oxford 1966), s.v. 'winter'
0 Fr. Klaeber, *'Beowulf' and 'The Fight at Finnsburg'* (3rd. ed., Boston 1950), appendix 4
1 Pope, *Rhythm*, 274-88
2 Presumably 'nealles inwitnet,' 2167, listed by Pope under B2, and 'ne þurh inwitsearo,' 1101, listed under B23 (Editors)
3 *Studien zur englischen Philologie*, ed L. Morsbach, vol. 33 (Halle 1910), 47
4 Pope's classification is followed; see *Rhythm*, 295 ff.
5 *The Metre of 'Beowulf'* (Oxford 1958), 43

R.W. BURCHFIELD

The prosodic terminology
of Anglo-Saxon scholars

This is one of a series of articles[1] in which the terminology of scholarly writings on Anglo-Saxon language and literature will be presented
in a historical manner after the style of the OED. It is based on a
reading[2] of a large number of books and articles on the subject written
in English from the eighteenth century to the present day. It seemed
appropriate to select the prosodic terms on this occasion since the
scholar to whom this volume is offered has himself made a distinguished contribution to the subject.

The systematic reading of sources for the OED was largely com-

---

1 Other studies will be concerned with the terms used for the Anglo-Saxon 'poet'
   or 'minstrel' ('bard,' 'gleeman,' 'scop,' etc), with types of poems (charm, enig-
   ma, epic, lay, lament, etc), with rhetorical terms (anacoluthon, ethopoeia, litotes,
   prosopopoeia, etc), and so on.
2 The greater part of the reading was done by two of my OED assistants, Miss Jean
   Buchanan and Mrs Juliet Field. At a later stage, when the entries were in first
   draft, I had a great deal of assistance from Miss Buchanan and from Mr M.W.
   Grose, bibliographical editor of *A Supplement to the OED*, with the verification
   of quotations and antedating of the drafted material. The 'List of Words Cited'
   was prepared by Mr Grose. Without their assistance this article could not have
   been completed. I am also indebted to Professors E.G. Stanley and Fred C. Robinson, who read the article in typescript and made a number of valuable suggestions, and to Mrs M.J. Blackler who typed it.

pleted by 1890 or so, that is before Anglo-Saxon became firmly established in the syllabuses of British universities. It is therefore not surprising that the terminology of Anglo-Saxon scholars is largely unrecorded in the dictionary. For prosodic terms, Dr Murray and his co-editors turned repeatedly to works on Greek and Latin metre for illustrative quotations, or, on occasion, to works concerned with the prosody of English writers like Milton and Shakespeare. Works on Anglo-Saxon poetry are very rarely cited.

In the list that follows the following conventions are observed:

1 For words treated in the OED the definition of the dictionary is retained. Comments on these definitions or on the currency, etc, of the terms are sometimes added, preceded by the symbol ⨎.

2 The symbol ‡ is used to mean 'not recorded in OED.' For such expressions a new definition is provided unless the meaning is obvious.

3 Within square brackets after each lemma a reference is provided, where relevant, to the corresponding word or sense in the OED. The date-range of the illustrative quotations in the OED is also indicated.

4 No indication of stressing and pronunciation is provided since these are available in the OED or are self-explanatory. For similar reasons etymological information is provided only for expressions that are not recorded in the OED.

5 The illustrative examples are arranged chronologically, and an attempt has been made in each instance to trace the 'first use' in print. (I should be pleased to receive details of any antedatings that readers may find.)

6 The titles of articles, books, etc, are omitted from the entries themselves but are readily available from the list of works printed at the end of the article. Thus '1958 BLISS 40' = 'page 40 of A.J. Bliss, *The Metre of Beowulf* (1958).'

7 Terms used of sectional divisions of Old English poems: canto, epilogue, exordium, fit, preface, prelude, prologue, stanza, strophe, etc, and of phrases or lines occurring at intervals at the end of stanzas: burden, chorus, refrain, etc, will be treated elsewhere.

8 The equivalent German terms (especially those used by Sievers) are provided where relevant, especially for those English terms that seem to be loan-translations.

accent *sb.* [OED 6, 1583-1871] The stress laid at more or less fixed intervals on certain syllables of a verse, the succession of which constitutes the rhythm or measure of the verse. $ Cf PRIMARY *a.*, SECONDARY *a.*, TERTIARY *a.* In quot. 1813 the 'wretched lines' are actually Latin.

1813 J.J. CONYBEARE 262 Of the substitution of accent or emphasis for quantity, the following wretched lines afford an example. 1823 BOSWORTH 220 It [*sc.* emphasis] is ... properly divided into syllabic emphasis, generally, but improperly, termed accent and verbal or sentential emphasis, commonly denominated merely emphasis. 1860 STEPHENS 22 Our ancestors grounded their verse on stave-rhyme and accent. 1910 SCHIPPER 16 Lachmann ... recognized a freer variety with two chief accents only in each section. 1942 POPE 43 The simple fact that five syllables in succession ... can hardly be spoken without differentiation of accent.

accented *ppl.a.* [OED 1837] Distinguished by or marked with accent or stress.

1826 W.D. CONYBEARE xxxviii The alliteration must always fall on the accented syllables. 1857 PATMORE 148 Each hemistich contains two accented syllables. 1932 CHADWICK I.21 Anglo-Saxon and early German poems have the same metrical form, each half-line containing two accented units.

accentual *a.* [OED 1610-1875] Of or belonging to accent; formed by accent, as distinct from quantity, [etc].

1838 GUEST I.174 What are the forms in which accentual rhythm made its first appearance amongst us. 1871 EARLE 552 Alliteration ... is an accentual reverberation. 1949 BAUM 158 By mixing the two molds of an accentual system and the classical quantitative system, Sievers laid himself open to certain contradictions.

‡ **a-line** Also *a* **half-line**, *a* **half-verse**, *a*-**verse**. The first half-line of a line of OE verse. Cf *b*-LINE.

[1891 BRIGHT 230 The superior letters *a* and *b* denote respectively first and second half-lines.] 1893 J. LAWRENCE 47 In the *a* half-verses ... there is ... no peculiarity ... to distinguish them from ordinary first half-verses with single alliteration. 1914 WILLIAMS 108 The *b* half-line contains the essential prose gnome, the *a* half-line representing ... an attempt at adornment. *Ibid* 130 Conceiving the *a*-line to be the end of the introduction, the *b*-line the beginning of the gnomes. 1918 KOCK 77 *Hronæs ban* is no verse at all, thus neither the beginning of a monstrous *a*-verse (Haigh and others), nor a *b*-verse (Wülker). 1935 BARTLETT 69

Sporadic instances of an expanded *a* verse with a normal *b* verse ... are not uncommon.

alliteral *a*. [OED 1850-64 (of African languages)] Characterized by alliteration. ⨎ No longer current.

1826 W.D. CONYBEARE xii The same alliteral letter obviously extends to the couplet as formed of the longer lines. **1866** E. KENNEDY 102 We do not claim for Saxon alliteral poetry any fixed principle of quantity.

alliterate *v*. [OED 1, 1816] *intr*. Of words: to begin with the same letter or group of letters, to constitute alliteration.

1857 PATMORE 148 In the first hemistich, the two accented syllables alliterate. **1888** TOLMAN 21 Two accented syllables of the first half-line, sometimes only one, must alliterate with one such syllable in the second. **1938** CAMPBELL 32 Both arses of the first half-verse alliterate in 38 cases. **1970** FAKUNDINY 138 The demonstratives alliterate with each other.

alliterated *ppl.a*. [OED 1776-1859] Composed with or characterized by alliteration.

1866 E. KENNEDY 103 The Anglo-Saxon ... concentrated his physical energies upon the alliterated words. **1892** BROOKE I.13 His voice rang out the alliterated words.

alliterating *ppl.a*. [OED 1846] Producing alliteration; beginning with the same latter as another word.

1842 THORPE 505 The alliterating words *sigor-lean sohtun*, and *secgað*. **1857** [see DISTICH *sb*.]. **1942** POPE 22 The second half-line contains by rule only one alliterating letter. **1970** FAKUNDINY 135 The verse clause opens somewhat unusually with an alliterating noun.

alliteration [OED 2, 1774-1871] The commencement of certain accented syllables in a verse with the same consonant or consonantal group, or with different vowel sounds, which constituted the structure of versification in OE and the Teutonic languages generally. ‡ **extra-alliteration** (see quot. 1959). ⨎ See also CROSS-ALLITERATION, CROSSED ALLITERATION, DOUBLE ALLITERATION, KEY-ALLITERATION, TRANSVERSE ALLITERATION.

1765 PERCY [see DISTICH *sb*.]. **1823** BOSWORTH 215 Alliteration, or the beginning of several syllables, in the same or corresponding verse, with the same letter, has been generally considered as one very particular and distinguishing feature of Anglo-Saxon poetry. 1857 [see ASSONANCE]. 1874 HOPKINS 284 Alliteration was an essential element in Anglo-Saxon or old English verse. 1928 W. W. LAWRENCE 40 Words like *sæ* and *heafo* ... are very loosely used in epic, partly in consequence of the demands of alliteration. 1940 TOLKIEN xxxiii The so-called 'alliteration' depends not on letters but on sounds. 1948 BAUM 87 Others ... based on the sound, as *eode eahte sum* / *under inwithrof*, which is pointed up by the extra alliteration in the second verse. 1959 LE PAGE 434 There are in Old English poetry generally numerous examples of what I have previously called 'extra-alliteration': of lines more heavily loaded with it, of couplets apparently linked by recurring alliteration, and of short passages of three or more lines where the same initial letter recurs frequently. 1962 CAMPBELL 17 In Old English epic verse the adjectives of indefinite quantity take the alliteration ... only in stock phrases.

alliterative *a.* [OED 1764-1865] Pertaining to or characterized by alliteration.
    1774 HENRY II.437 Their modes of versification ... chiefly of the alliterative kind. 1839 WRIGHT 8 Some Anglo-Saxon scholars ... have advocated the printing of the alliterative couplet in one line. 1903 ANDERSON 38 The tones of the harp were probably used to mark the emphatic alliterative syllables. 1939 LEWIS 119 It is a little remarkable that few have yet suggested a return to our own ancient system, the alliterative line. 1948 MALONE 21 Runes were used for some alliterative verses inscribed on the Franks Casket. 1970 FAKUNDINY 135 Almost any desired noun could be put in the first lift to fill alliterative requirements.

anacrusis [OED 1833-44] 'A syllable at the beginning of a verse before the just rhythm' (Kennedy). ‡ Also occas. **anakrusis**. ∮ The corresponding G word is *Auftakt*.
    1857 PATMORE 150 The 'anacrusis', or unaccented portion of a foot or bar, ... is the nearest approximation to Rask's idea of a 'complement' which the nature of metre will admit. 1870 MARCH 145 The common narrative verse ... may have four feet and an anacrusis in each section. 1894 HEATH 380 Anakrusis is oftener lacking than not. 1935 GIRVAN 17 The prefix *ge-* can be an anacrusis in the second half-line. 1948 MALONE 25 Both Heusler and Sievers began the half-line, on occasion, with an onset of one or more syllables reckoned as anacrusis.

anacrustic *a.* [OED Suppl. (1972), 1878] Characterized by anacrusis.
    1899 BRIGHT 352 The anacrustic beat is expanded in *þæt is on Hierúsalēm*. 1948 ANDREW 113 It is the weak anacrustic syllable which Sievers stresses in every line.

arsis [OED 2, 1834-76] In modern acceptation: the strong syllable in English metre (or classical metre as read by Englishmen), the strong note in barred music; thus identical with the modern meaning of L *ictus*. (A.J. Ellis) § Cf THESIS.

[1866 E. KENNEDY 102 The peculiarity of the intonation of the alliterated words was similar in its application to the 'ictus metricus', or 'arsis', in Greek metrical poetry.] 1870 [see THESIS]. 1877 REHRMANN 10 An arsis of a long line is formed in general by every syllable, the initial letter of which is, at the same time, the alliterative letter. 1910 SCHIPPER 28 Syllables with this secondary accent are necessary in certain cases as links between the arsis and thesis. 1942 POPE 49 Anacrusis derives its effect ... from being placed in the up-beat or arsis. 1970 CABLE 86 Alliteration would appear only in the second arsis.

assonance [OED 2, 1823-79] The correspondence or riming of one word with another in the accented vowel and those which follow, but not in the consonants.

1830 [see HALF-RHYME]. 1857 PATMORE 147 Alliteration is so essentially consonantal, that, in Anglo-Saxon and Icelandic poetry, in which this assonance has been cultivated as an art, there is properly no such thing as alliteration of vowels. 1888 COOK liii When the vowels are identical, and the following consonants or consonant combinations are dissimilar (assonance). 1910 SCHIPPER 63 Assonances, in which only the vowels correspond, as *wæf: læs* El. 1238. 1967 WRENN 36 As time went on ... to some extent rhyme and assonance were blended with alliteration.

a-verse = *a*-LINE (q.v.).

beat *sb.* [OED *sb.*[1] 5, 1885] The march of measured sound or of verse. (quot. 1892); ‡ also, in OE verse a stressed syllable, a lift. § Cf DOWN-BEAT, UPBEAT.

1892 BROOKE I.103 With the beat of his voice and of the hand upon his instrument at each alliterative word of the saga, he sings of the great fight with Grendel. 1894 HEATH 380 The OE verse ... in the short or half-line shows four beats. 1942 POPE 92 The assumption of the harp dispels the only practical objection to the theory of initial rests by enabling us to postulate a regular beat, not merely imagined but heard, as a complement to the voice. 1967 WRENN 40 This light syllable may combine with an immediately following light syllable to form in the pattern of the half-line a heavy beat or lift consisting of the two syllables 'slurred' together.

‡ *b*-line. Also *b* half-line, *b* half-verse, *b*-verse. The second half-line of a line of OE verse. Cf *a*-LINE.

1891 [see *a*-LINE]. 1893 J. LAWRENCE 47 The case is different ... as regards the *b* half-verses. 1914, 1918 [see *a*-LINE]. 1948 ANDREW 89 There are ... within the major actions, many minor transitions, which usually begin with a *b* verse. 1961 WHALLON 313 *sidfæþme scip* in the *b* half-line would seem dispensable in favor of *sægēap naca.*

cadence [OED 1, c 1384-1873] 'The flow of verses or periods' (J); rhythm, rhythmical construction, measure.

1805 TURNER IV.416 The words are placed in that peculiar rhythm or cadence which is observable in all the preceding extracts. 1813 J.J. CONYBEARE 259 I ... shall endeavour to show ... that the general rhythm and cadence of their verse is not altogether undiscoverable. 1929 LEONARD 7 The two cadences are in effect on the ear far more alike than many so-called 'subtypes' of any one of the orthodox five. 1970 LEHMANN 438 The cadence of the RP is more regular than that of any other OE poem of the period.

cæsura [OED 2, 1556-1841] In English prosody: a pause or breathing-place about the middle of a metrical line, generally indicated by a pause in the sense.

[1823 BOSWORTH 245 The whole ancient poetic art of the Northerns ... never in any way tolerates the division of verse (Cæsura), which is found in Greek and Latin Hexameters and Pentameters.] 1871 SWEET 3 Each long verse has four accented syllables ... and is divided by the cæsura into two short verses. 1935 BARTLETT 41 The position of the anaphora at the caesura, a position common in Anglo-Saxon verse. 1958 BLISS 37 The metrical significance of the cæsura has been merely asserted, never proved. 1970 FAKUNDINY 264 The separation of a sentence-part-particle from its related noun by a metrical caesura.

cæsural *a.* [OED 1783-1861] Of or pertaining to a cæsura.

1857 PATMORE 150 The supposition that this unartistic use of the cæsural dot reacted upon the practice of the poets. 1891 GARNETT 100 The sequence of thought is usually such that the rhetorical pause and the cæsural pause coincide. 1941 MENNER 133 Grein and Assmann made the same division of lines, but did not indicate caesural division. 1943 C.W. KENNEDY 18 A normal line of Old English verse was composed of two half-lines separated by a strongly marked caesural pause.

chronometric *a.* [OED 1830-81] Of or pertaining to chronometry; relating to the measurement of time. ∮ No examples of the metrical use in OED.

1958 BLISS 106 The current interpretation of modern English verse is that it is chronometric ... Recent interpreters of Old English verse, notably Heusler and Pope, have attempted to apply this theory to Old English. 1961 TAGLICHT 349 We may conclude ... that the metre has a quantitative or chronometric framework.

couplet [OED 1, 1580-1889] A pair of successive lines of verse, *esp.* when riming together and of the same length. ∮ In some writers a 'half-line' is called a 'line,' and a 'couplet' = two 'half-lines.'

1826 W.D. CONYBEARE xii Braces have been placed against the alliteral couplets. 1830 THORPE 160 We have ... in the first line of each couplet, three ictus, besides a number ... of short syllables. 1864 MORLEY 264 Germans who study Anglo-Saxon, differ from the usual custom of the English and the Danes by reckoning each couplet as a single line. 1957 LE PAGE 97 The lines must be regarded as a couplet, and not split up into half-lines. 1962 MALONE 61 In the other two thulas no stanzas occur; here we find only single lines and couplets.

cross-alliteration [OED Suppl. (1972) s.v. *cross-* 9, 1938 (not of OE verse)] = TRANSVERSE ALLITERATION. Cf next.

1910 SCHIPPER 25 If this cross alliteration [in line 1 of *Beowulf*] is intentional. 1938 CAMPBELL 32 Cross alliteration, in the form *abab*, occurs in 14, 33, 48 and 50. 1962 MALONE 73 The line has two staves, giving cross or transverse alliteration, with a pattern *abab* in line 44, *abba* in line 127. 1963 BESSINGER 28 The sequence is climaxed by a cross-alliteration in *sc-* and *w-*.

‡ **crossed alliteration** [OED *Crossed* adj.] = prec. ∮ Sievers used the corresponding G term *gekreuzte Alliteration* for the type *abab* and also for the type *baab*. J.C. Pope distinguishes *crossed alliteration* (abab) from *transverse alliteration* (baab).

1893 J. LAWRENCE 46 Crossed alliteration involves alliteration in the final arsis. 1900 EMERSON 127 The term transverse alliteration is chosen as least likely to cause confusion ... The name crossed alliteration, from Luick's 'gekreuzte alliteration' ... has never gained currency in English. 1940 TOLKIEN xxxv Crossed alliteration is occasionally found in the forms *ab|ab* and *ab|ba.* 1953 SLAY 4 More probably this is an attempt at a very unusual crossed alliteration *fr, f; fr, f.*

dip *sb.* [OED Suppl. (1972) lg, 1894-1961] An unstressed element in a line of OE verse. Opp. LIFT. Cf G *Senkung.*

1894 SWEET lxxxviii Each verse usually consists of four metrical elements, two lifts and two dips — that is, two strong- and two weak-stress elements. 1912 CHAMBERS 172 The second element may count either as secondary accent or as a dip. 1939 [see LIFT *sb.*]. 1966 STANLEY 120 The dip at the beginning of a half-line is a signalising position.

dipodic *a.* [OED 'In recent Dicts.'] Of the nature of a dipody; characterized by dipodies; as 'a dipodic measure.'

1918 LEONARD 120 Its tendency toward dipodic scansion awakens Germanic memories — ancestral reverberations long antedating the *Niebelungen* or *Beowulf.* 1949 BAUM 161 Dipodic verse has survived rather in oral tradition ... than as a literary form.

dipody [OED 1844-91] A double foot; two feet constituting a single measure.

1894 HEATH 384 If it is a sub-stressed syllable, and a Suffix, it can only bear a Verse Accent when, by so doing, it forms a Dipodie. 1929 LEONARD 6 A solemn and emphatic pronunciation ... echoed in the management of subsequent speech-material ... in the second dipody. 1948 [see *verse-unit*].

distich *sb.* [OED 1553-1891] A couple of lines of verse, usually making complete sense, and (in modern poetry) riming; a couplet.

1765 PERCY II.261 Their brethren, the Anglo-saxon poets, occasionally used the same kind of alliteration ... Skeop tha and skyrede / Skyppend ure ... But distichs of this sort perpetually occur in all their poems of any length. 1813 J.J. CONYBEARE 267 I do not recollect any instance of an attempt to carry on the same alliteration through a considerable number of lines together. It seldom ... extends beyond the distich. 1857 PATMORE 147 When the requisite number of alliterating consonants in each verse or distich cannot conveniently be produced, three words beginning with vowels are permitted to take the place of alliterating consonants.

‡ **double alliteration** [OED *Double* adj. 6] Alliteration of two stressed words in a half-line of OE verse (see also quots. 1900, 1937). Cf G *Doppelalliteration.*

1855 THORPE 2 The double alliteration, which rarely occurs in the second line of an alliterative couplet. 1900 EMERSON 127 Unfortunately, double alliteration has already been used in two distinct senses ... Sievers employed the term for two alliterating syllables in the half line, while Cook, followed by Crow among American editors, has used the same term for two, rather than three, alliterating syllables in the whole line of alliterative poetry. **1906** KRAPP xlvi Double alliteration in the first half-line is one fourth more frequent in *Andreas* than in Cynewulf. **1937** GORDON 44 Double alliteration also occurs in the pattern *abab* in 24, 63, 68, [etc]. **1958** BLISS 4 The phrase 'double alliteration' is here used to indicate that there are two alliterating words in the *a-* verse, not that there is alliteration on two distinct letters.

down-beat [OED Suppl. (1972), 1876-1955 (all non-metrical examples)] A downward beat; spec. in *Mus.*, (the downward stroke of a conductor's baton or hand, indicating) the first or most heavily accented note of a measure.

1942 POPE 49 We can reconcile rhythm and meaning ... by assigning each of these pairs to the up-beat ... of the first measure of its own verse, while we fill the down-beat or thesis of this measure with a rest. **1953** MAGOUN 458 The first down-beat or ictus in the off-verse does not here alliterate with the preceding on-verse.

drop *sb.* ǂ = DIP *sb.* Cf G *Senkung.*

1941 MALONE 74 A metrically heightened syllable may be called a lift (German *hebung*); a metrically lowered syllable may be called a drop (German *senkung*). **1953** WRENN 78 Prefixes are normally parts of the weakly-stressed portion of the half-line and form the dip or drop.

emphasis [OED 4] ǂ *spec.* = STRESS *sb.*

1823 [see ACCENT *sb.*]. **1830** FOX vi In these compositions ... trochaic feet predominate, and these are distinguishable by accent or emphasis. **1967** WRENN 37 Its two basic principles of metre are those of stress or emphasis ... and secondly of alliteration.

emphatic *a.* [OED 1b, 1837-9] Of a word or syllable: that bears the stress in pronunciation.

1847 LONGFELLOW 4 The short exclamatory lines, whose rhythm depends on alliteration in the emphatic syllables. **1883** H.M. KENNEDY I.21 A measure which belonged to the antiquity of all Germanic races; namely, the line with eight emphatic syllables, divided into equal parts by the cæsura. **1953** WRENN 79 In that kind of rhetorical declamation which the Anglo-Saxon scop would use, the emphatic syllables receive greater and clearer force than they would in ordinary speech.

end-rhyme [OED Suppl. (1972) s.v. *end* sb. 25, 1855-1953] = RHYME. Cf G *Endreim*.

1831 PALGRAVE 168 End-rhymes were not used. 1949 BAUM 153 End rhyme in the two verses of the long line occurs five times.

end-stopping [OED s.v. *End* sb. 25, 1881 (*-stopping*), 1877 (*-stopped*)] (Of blank verse) a division of the lines, such that they end with a pause or stop; so **end-stopped** *a.*; ‡ **end-stop**, such a pause or stop.

1932 CHADWICK I.61 The two Anglo-Saxon heroic poems which are not narrative [sc. *Deor* and *Widsith*] show end-stops. 1912 CHAMBERS 175 Whilst the proportion of end-stopped to mid-stopped lines is in *Beowulf* 385:282 ... it is ... in *Widsith* ... 29:0. 1948 MALONE 26 In the oldest linear verse the end-stopped style prevailed. 1912 CHAMBERS 174 In two groups of [OE] poems only do we find consistent and unbroken 'end stopping'. 1948 MALONE 26 One might have expected to find end-stopping used a good deal in the gnomic verses.

enjamb(e)ment [OED 1837-81] The continuation of a sentence beyond the second line of a couplet. [OED Suppl. (1972), 1929] Now applied less restrictedly to the carrying over of a sentence from one line to the next. ∮ None of the examples in OED is of OE verse.

1892 FOSTER 41 Our poet in tasteful variety uses 'enjambement', or a minor syntactical pause, at the close of the line. 1910 SEDGEFIELD 7 The interlocking by alliteration and *enjambement* makes for closeness of web and rapidity. 1958 BLISS 109 These shorter phrases ... serve to mark the division between the lines, a division which tends to be obscured by the characteristic Old English *enjambement*.

expanded *ppl.a.* ‡ Used of an abnormally long line of OE verse, hypermetrical.

1886 COOK li Expanded lines are employed in passages of peculiar elevation and solemnity or expressive of unwonted agitation. 1894 HEATH 386 Expanded lines, called by German scholars *Schwell-verse* or *Streck-verse*, are hypercatalectic. 1953 MAGOUN 462 The origin and special function, if any, of the expanded or hypermetric verses.

extended *ppl.a.* ‡ = prec. word.

1910 SCHIPPER 36 These extended hemistichs must be carefully distinguished from the hemistichs which have one or more unaccented syllables *before* the first accented syllable. 1946 DAUNT 61 The 'extended types' of Old English. Here the line shows an increased number of stresses and the 'pattern' can be regarded as an enlargement of one type or a mixture of two.

extra-alliteration see ALLITERATION.

‡ extrametric *a.* = next.

> 1942 POPE 19 If he is unafraid of extrametric anacrusis ... Leonard can follow Heusler in the establishment of two quadruple measures for each verse instead of the four simple ones.

extrametrical *a.* [OED 1863] Exceeding the number of feet or syllables proper to a metre; hypermetrical.

> 1958 BLISS 40 This extrametrical prelude to the verse is known as anacrusis. 1970 SWANTON 126 Grein supplied *and* at the beginning of the line, assuming it to have been lost ... and justifying it as an extra-metrical syllable.

falling *ppl.a.* [OED 2, 1844] Of a foot, rhythm, etc: decreasing in stress, having the ictus at the beginning. Opp. RISING *ppl.a.* ∮ An 1893 example of 'falling stress' is recorded in OED s.v. *Stress* sb. 8.

> 1894 SWEET xciv There is a tendency to combine different types in a line, the falling types A and D being most frequent in I, while in II the rising types B and C are preferred. 1962 BLISS 31 An increase in the proportion of rising rhythms at the expense of falling rhythms. 1967 WRENN 41 Two feet in falling rhythm, two in rising rhythm.

‡ five types. In the system of the German scholar Eduard Sievers (esp. in his *Altgermanische Metrik*, 1893), the five principal classes of rhythm observable in the surviving OE verse. Also *five-type* attrib.

> 1892 MATHER 100 He divides the five types into two classes. 1899 BRIGHT 354 The fixed laws of the five types of rhythm. 1946 DAUNT 59 What neither Sievers nor any other writers ... have ever pointed out, is that the 'five types' are language patterns not metrical patterns. 1958 BLISS 81 Sievers' five types really do exist. 1959 LE PAGE 435 For the purposes of definition and enumeration I have accepted Sievers' five-type theory.

foot *sb.* [OED II.6, c 1050-1846] A division of a verse, consisting of a number of syllables one of which has the ictus or principal stress. ∮ Examples referring to OE verse are given in OED (1846) and OED

Suppl. (1830-1942).

1735 SHELTON 17 They strictly observed Metre or the Quantity of Feet. 1813 J.J. CONYBEARE 262 The verses of the Anglo Saxons ... will be found to consist for the most part of feet of two or three syllables each. 1888 COOK 1 A normal hemistich contains two metrical feet. 1942 POPE 12 Sievers was only borrowing mistakes from contemporary metrical theory when he marked the 'feet' of his five types. 1958 BLISS 80 The vast majority of ... Old English verses consist of two 'feet' divided by a cæsura.

half *sb.* ‡ = HALF-LINE.

1892 BROOKE I. x The Anglo-Saxon line is divided into two halves by a pause. The first half has two 'measures'. 1940 TOLKIEN xxvii The Old English line was composed of two opposed word-groups or 'halves'. Each half was an example, or variation, of one of six basic patterns.

‡ **half-lift** A medium-stressed lift in OE verse. Cf LIFT and G *Nebenhebung, Nebenton.*

1894 SWEET xc To make up for the want of an accompanying dip, an extra medium-stressed half-lift is made obligatory. 1953 SLAY 7 In general he [*sc.* H. Kuhn] includes the half-lift *(nebenhebung)* under the lift. 1967 WRENN 38 Five basic combinations of stress or lift of the voice, half or secondary stress or half-lift, and unstressed syllables.

‡ **half-line** The portion of an OE line of verse that lies either before or after the cæsura. Cf LINE, *a*-LINE, *b*-LINE; G *Halbzeil.*

1864 MORLEY 251 The most important is a heroic poem ... extending ... to 6357 of the short Anglo-Saxon lines, or half lines, as they are usually printed. 1894 [see BEAT *sb.*]. 1906 [see DOUBLE ALLITERATION]. 1939 [see LIFT *sb.*] 1951 WHITELOCK 10 *God eaðe mæg* 'God can easily', always used as a second half-line with its object in the following line.

‡ **half-rhyme** An imperfect or near rhyme. ∮ Cf G *Halbreim*; also ON *skothending* which is usually rendered by 'half-rhyme' (e.g. G.P. MARSH *Lect. Eng. Lang.* [1860] xxv.553).

1830 THORPE 139 Line-Rime is when two syllables, in the same line of verse, have their vowels and the consonants following them alike, which is called perfect rime (consonances), or unlike vowels, and only the following consonants the same, which is called half rime (assonances). 1868 SKEAT xxii There are also half-rimes, as in '*sar* and *sorge*', '*his boda beodan*', &c.

‡ **half-stress** A secondary stress. Cf STRESS.

1938 CAMPBELL 24 Graz ... regarding *butu* as having a half-stress on the second syllable. 1961 TAGLICHT 345 Long and short syllables must be distinguished in scansion, when they bear either a strong stress or a half-stress.

‡ **half-verse** = HALF-LINE. ∮ 1711 example in OED s.v. *Hemistich*. Cf G *Halbvers.*

1876 SWEET xcviii There is often only one alliterative letter in the first half verse. 1907 BLACKBURN x Uncorrected errors are few, though occasional omissions occur, generally of a half-verse. 1938 CAMPBELL 16 It will be convenient to group its half-verses in the 'five types' of Sievers.

head-stave see STAVE *sb.*

heavy *a.* ‡ As a general term in OE prosody (opp. to LIGHT *a.*); *spec.* (see quot. 1958).

1893 J. LAWRENCE 46 Verses with double alliteration are as a rule heavier than those with single. 1948 BAUM 81 These heavy and extra-heavy verses, are the exceptions. 1958 BLISS 8 There are also many verses which contain three stressed elements instead of the normal two: blæd | wide | sprang 18b ... All verses of this kind are here termed 'heavy' verses.

hemistich [OED 1575-1839] The half or section of a line of verse, as divided by the cæsura or the like; also, a line of less than the usual length.

1823 BOSWORTH 246 [quoting J.J. Conybeare] The question, as to whether the two hemistichs shall be regarded as one or two lines, is evidently that of a writer or printer, not of a singer or reciter. 1857 [see ACCENTED *ppl.a.*]. 1888 COOK l The line of poetry consists of two hemistichs, separated by the cæsura. 1925 CLUBB xv The mark most consistently ... employed is the metrical point, indicating the pause between hemistichs. 1970 CABLE 86 One would not expect *þā* to provide the only alliteration in the second hemistich.

hypercatalectic *a.* [OED 1704-1886] Of a verse or colon: having an extra syllable after the last complete dipody. Also applied to the syllable itself. Formerly also = *hypermetric.*

1813 J.J. CONYBEARE 265 Of the Trochaic species, with the Hypercatalectic syllable, as, Ahte ic, ealdor, stol. 1894 [see EXPANDED *ppl.a.*].

hypermetric *a.* [OED 1, 1865-87] Of a 'verse' or line: having one or more syllables beyond those normal to the metre; having a redundant syllable or syllables. Also said of the redundant syllable.

1892 MATHER 100 It will be well to note the occurrences of hypermetric lines in the different poems. 1906 KRAPP xlvii *Beowulf* (which contains twelve hypermetric lines). 1958 BLISS 96 The distribution of hypermetric verses varies from poem to poem. 1970 SWANTON 61 Blocks of hypermetric verse used contrapuntally.

hypermetrical *a.* [OED 1751-1886] = prec.

1891 BRIGHT 238 These hypermetrical half-lines ... usually add dignity to the sense and movement of the passage. 1922 KLAEBER lxxi Groups of emphatic hypermetrical types are introduced three times. 1935 BARTLETT 70 The hypermetrical irregularities of the other Anglo-Saxon poems. 1958 BLISS 88 The vast majority of hypermetrical verses end with a group of syllables which is exactly equivalent to an ordinary verse.

ictus [OED 1, 1752-1871] Stress on a particular syllable of a foot or verse; rhythmical or metrical stress.

1823 BOSWORTH 246 [quoting J.J. Conybeare] The ear is satisfied, not by the number of syllables, but by the recurrence of the accent, or ictus, if one may call it so. 1888 TOLMAN 21 March ... declares that 'the time from each ictus to the next is the same in any section'. 1953 [see DOWN-BEAT].

isochronous *a.* [OED 1784-1822] Equal in metrical length.

1857 PATMORE 149 A metre which, totally abandoning the element of natural syllabic quantity, takes the isochronous bar for the metrical integer. 1942 POPE 9 Isochronous measures are the rule ... and it is easy to produce them in *Beowulf* by means of limited quantitative variation. 1948 BAUM 75 There is ... no reason to suppose that, *if* the *Beowulf* was chanted to a real musical accompaniment, the lines were therefore delivered in isochronous groups.

‡ isochrony [Formed as prec., after *synchrony*, etc] Isochronism; the character or property of being isochronous.

1961 TAGLICHT 342 There exist all sorts of musical rhythms very different from the isochrony which has dominated European music for so long a time. 1966 POPE x Isochrony and initial rests are ... vital, in my opinion, for the achievement of an adequate sense of order in opposition to the extraordinary variety of syllabic patterns in the verses.

‡ **key-alliteration** Alliteration of the ‡ key-letter, that beginning the first stressed word in the second half-line of a line of OE verse. Cf STAVE.

1875 WATSON 35 The key letter should begin the former of the two loud syllables in the second section of the line. 1940 TOLKIEN xxxiii The key-alliteration or 'head-stave' was borne by the first lift in the second half. 1948 BAUM 73 The dogma (Sievers' word) that the first metrical stress of the second half-line gives the key alliteration.

lengthened *ppl.a.* Extended in duration, prolonged, long, as ‡ *lengthened line, verse*, a hypermetric line.

1883 H.M. KENNEDY I.47 Such lengthened lines ... are especially frequent in the *Judith. Ibid* 85 The poet [of the later *Genesis*] is partial to the long-drawn lines designated ... as 'lengthened' verses. 1894 SWEET xciv There are also various forms of lengthened or three-wave verse, which are introduced only occasionally, generally in solemn, lyrical passages. 1915 BRADLEY 179 The shortest section [in *Judith*] has a larger proportion of lengthened verses than the other two.

lift *sb.* ‡ A stressed element in a line of OE verse. Opp. DIP. Cf G *Hebung.* Cf also HALF-LIFT.

1894 [see DIP *sb.*]. 1927 TOLKIEN 42 This accords with the employment of the conjunction (notably in the form *būton*) twice as a lift in *Beowulf.* 1939 LEWIS 121 The half-line consists of Lifts and Dips. 1961 TAGLICHT 345 Sievers's 'lifts' and 'dips' are not phonetic entities. 1970 FAKUNDINY 135 It occupies the second lift of an off-verse.

light *a.* [OED 12, 1887-1901] Of a syllable: unemphatic, of little weight or sonorousness. ‡ As a general term in OE prosody (opp. to HEAVY *a.*); *spec.* (see quot. 1958).

1893 J. LAWRENCE 46 So light a verse is very rare. 1948 BAUM 81 One or more light syllables may precede the first stress. 1958 BLISS 8 All verses which consist of only one stressed element are here termed 'light' verses.

line *sb.* [OED *sb.*² 23 e, 1563-1894] The portion of a metrical composition which is usually written in one line; a verse; *pl.* verses, poetry. ∮ Freq. interchangeable with HALF-LINE. Cf also next two words.

1813 J.J. CONYBEARE 262 The line 'That we motun' evidently consists of two trochees. *Ibid* Variety was produced ... by the admitting lines of different lengths from two to four feet. 1830 THORPE 137 In A.S. poetry the two lines connected by alliteration, need not ... be connected also in sense. 1948 MALONE 26 The short verse, the basic metrical unit, usually occurred by twos — that is, in lines, the two parts of which were linked by alliteration. 1951 [see HALF-LINE] 1957 LE PAGE 101 In *Beowulf* the line is the rhythmical unit, not the half-line.

long line, long-line ‡ In OE verse, two half-lines considered as a unit; spec. **long epic line** (see quot. 1892). Cf prec. and next word, and SHORT LINE; cf also G *Langzeile.* $ In OED only *attrib.*, 1755-1849, and not specifically of OE verse.

1868 SKEAT xxiv There has been much discussion as to whether alliterative poems should be printed in couplets of short lines, or in long lines comprising two sections. 1877 REHRMANN 9 All words of a long-line are fit for alliteration that distinguish themselves in the verse by natural gravity or grammatical accent. 1892 BROOKE II.283 That Cynewulf, having fixed himself down in the *Elene* to the short-epic line, should ... use in the *Dream* that solemn but various, dignified but rushing long-epic line which is found in the *Genesis, Exodus,* and *Judith.* 1929 LEONARD 7 The law of the meter remains, an eight-beat long-line. 1935 [see OFF-VERSE]. 1970 FAKUNDINY 133 The metrical division between two verses (hemistichs) of an alliterative long line.

‡ long verse, long-verse = prec. Cf SHORT VERSE.

1871 SWEET 3 Each long verse has four accented syllables. 1889 KENT 8 The so-called 'long-verse' consists of two hemistichs.

measure *sb.* [OED 16, c 1450-1869] Poetical rhythm, as 'measured' by quantity or accent; a kind of poetical rhythm; a metrical group or period; metre.

1774 HENRY II.432 The kinds and measures of their [*sc.* Saxon and Danish poets'] verses. 1802 SIBBALD IV.lviii In the same kind of measure [as the Fragment of the genuine Caedmon] are almost all the popular rhymes which still continue to be repeated by children in their ring-dances. 1873 MORLEY 20 There is one measure for Beowulf, Cædmon's Paraphrase, and all subsequent First English poems. 1877 REHRMANN 10 A foot or measure is made up ... of one accented syllable and its connected unaccented syllable, or syllables. 1942 POPE 44 According to Heusler, alliteration must introduce the first measure in the second half-line.

metric *sb.* [OED 1760-1905] *sing.* and *pl.* The science or art that deals with metre, esp. with the laws of versification in Greek and Latin.

1892 MATHER 100 Metrics and æsthetics must go hand in hand. 1941 GIRVAN 331 The metric is astonishing and cannot be paralleled in Anglo-Saxon poetry. 1970 CABLE 81 (*title*) Rules for syntax and metrics in *Beowulf.*

metrical *a.* [OED *a.*[1] 1, 1432-1855] Pertaining or relating to metre or versification; consisting of or composed in metre; having the characteristics of metre.

1807 TURNER II.294 This poem [sc. *Beowulf*] is certainly a metrical romance in the Anglo-Saxon language. 1813 J.J. CONYBEARE 259 The Anglo Saxon poetry does really differ from their prose by the usage of metrical divisons. 1826 W.D. CONYBEARE lxxix Metrical paraphrases of the Lord's Prayer. 1830 THORPE 150 The Anglo-Saxons ... in many M.S.S., carefully separate the verse by metrical points. 1840 PETHERAM 169 A metrical Hymn, in Anglo-Saxon, from MS. Cotton Vesp. D.VI, of the ninth century. 1855 THORPE viii It is ... a metrical paraphrase of an heroic Saga composed in the south-west of Sweden. 1897 FRYE 79 This regularity of arrangement holds only for the half line, the metrical unit. 1900 BLACKBURN 5 A conjecture must not violate established metrical laws. 1925 [see HEMISTICH]. 1946 [see FIVE TYPES]. 1953 MAGOUN 449 The discovery of ... the non-existence of metrical formulas in the poetry of lettered authors. 1963 QUIRK 159 Metrical units in variation.

‡ **off-verse** The second half-line of a line of OE verse.

1935 MALONE 291 The chief function of alliteration in OE poetry is that of binding together the two halves (i.e. the on- and off-verses) of the so-called long line. 1963 MAGOUN 134 These verses tend to be used as off-verses. 1970 FAKUNDINY 134 The Anglo-Saxon poets apparently preferred beginning new clauses with the off-verse.

‡ **on-verse** The first half-line of a line of OE verse.

1935 [see OFF-VERSE]. 1970 LEHMANN 438 Rime forces all final lifts in on-verse or off-verse into prominence.

pause *sb.* [OED 2, 1589-1824] A break occurring according to rule at a particular point in a verse, a cæsura; also, a break of definite length in a verse, occupying the time of a syllable or number of syllables.

1826 W.D. CONYBEARE xxxviii The monotony which would prevail if the pause generally coincided with the close of the alliteral system is avoided. 1838 GUEST I.148 In the Anglo-Saxon poems, we find the close of every sentence ... coincident with a middle or final pause. 1894 HEATH 382 Absence of Anakrusis is replaced by a Pause. 1948 MALONE 25 The weaker beat fell on an unstressed syllable, or on a pause (metrically a rest) in the prose rhythm.

prelude *sb.* ‡ (See quot. 1894) Also used somewhat more generally.
1823 BOSWORTH 224 It is regarded merely as a species of prelude or overture, which is gone over as hastily as possible. 1826 BOSWORTH 72 *And* is the prelude, and ... the verse first properly begins with *eálle þa.* 1894 SWEET xci Another licence is the prelude, that is, beginning a verse with a weak syllable which does not form an integral part of it, being uttered rapidly so as to be included in the pause at the beginning of the verse. 1948 BAUM 82 Along with the simple form 'on *flet boren*' 1657 ... occur the form with longer prelude ('anacrusis' is not the term here): þonne *wig* cume 23 ... and the very common light form.

primary *a.* [OED 3] Of the first order in any series, sequence, or process: ‡ spec. *primary accent, beat, lift, stress,* etc.
1888 COOK l Of the lighter syllables following or preceding a primary stress, one may, under certain circumstances, receive a secondary stress. 1910 SCHIPPER 19 Most of the partisans of the four-beat theory for the hemistich agree in making two of these beats primary, and two secondary. *Ibid* 25 The first element of the compound ... has the primary accent. 1942 POPE 21 Heusler postulated ... Every verse must contain two syllables capable of bearing primary accent. 1962 MALONE 61 In the rest of the poem we find ... many lines with a first lift that is not primary.

resolution [OED 6 c, 1884] In prosody, the substitution of two short syllables in the place of a long one. ∮ The corresponding G word is *Auflösung.*
1888 COOK l The substitution of two ... short syllables for a single long one is called resolution. 1925 CLUBB 63 Sievers ... first objected to the MS reading *cearum*, because it would give a shortened C-verse with resolution of the first arsis. 1969 DUNNING & BLISS 75 Resolution of a secondary stress is relatively much more frequent than in *Beowulf.*

resolved *ppl.a.* ‡ Of a syllable, etc: resulting from metrical resolution. Cf prec. word.

1891 BRIGHT 229 A resolved stress ... consists of two syllables of which the first is short and the second is light enough to combine with the first to produce with it the metrical equivalent of a long syllable. 1967 WRENN 42 We have a C-type half-line (with resolved first lift).

rest *sb.* [OED *sb.*[1] sense 7 b, 1612-1824] = PAUSE *sb.* Also ‡ *rest-beat.*

1883 VIGFUSSON & POWELL I.434 When a monosyllabic word is stressed and followed by no enclitic words before the next stress it is succeeded by a short interval of silence, which we call a rest. 1910 SCHIPPER 18 Where, in a verse, the *morae* are not filled by actual syllables, their time must be occupied by rests. 1929 LEONARD 2 Six speech-beats, three in each half-line, with a rest-beat at the end of each half-line. 1942 POPE 21 The place of this syllable may be filled by a rest. 1948 [see PAUSE *sb.*].

rhyme, rime *sb.* [OED 3 a, 1663-1871 (*rhyme*), *a* 1300-1868 (*rime*); 3 c, 1656-1867 (*rhyme*), 1599-1891 (*rime*)] Agreement in the terminal sounds of two or more words or metrical lines, such that (in English prosody) the last stressed vowel and any sounds following it are the same, while the sound or sounds preceding are different. (The term is sometimes extended to include assonance and even alliteration (*initial* or *head rime*).) Also, an instance of this. ∮ OED has separate entries for *rhyme* and *rime* though they are in origin merely graphic variations of each other.

1715 ELSTOB 68 Sometimes they use a kind of Rhime and Verses ending alike. 1774 MITFORD 157 The Anglosaxon poets ... generally used measures without rime. 1830 [see HALF-RHYME]. 1838 GUEST I.175 The advantages of the initial rhime or alliteration. 1861 WRIGHT II.159 Rhyme was never, properly speaking, in use in Anglo-Saxon poetry. 1868 SKEAT xxii There are some instances of full-rime in Cædmon. 1909 GUMMERE 16 His [*sc.* the *Beowulf* poet's] rhythm holds to that four-stressed verse with initial rimes which dominates all Anglo-Saxon poetry. 1949 BAUM 153 Rhyme, apart from initial rhyme or alliteration, occurs here and there in the *Beowulf*, but it is not functional and probably not intentional.

rhyme-letter [OED s.v. *Rime* sb.[1] 5, 1865] The distinctive initial letter in a line of alliterative verse.

1875 WATSON 35 The initial letters common to two or more of these loud syllables are called the rime-letters.

rhythm *sb.* [OED 4, 1560-1891] The measured recurrence of arsis and thesis determined by vowel-quantity or stress, or both combined; kind of metrical movement, as determined by the relation of long and short, or stressed and unstressed, syllables in a foot or a line.

1805 TURNER IV.414 The rhime used was ... quite distinct from the general metre or rhythm of the poem [sc. *Judith*]. 1823 BOSWORTH 218 Rhythm is formed by a periodical syllabic emphasis. 1942 POPE (*title*) The rhythm of Beowulf. 1961 TAGLICHT 349 In the treatment of syllabic length ... the verse rhythm is based essentially on the rhythm of speech. 1970 LEHMANN 441 The regular rhythm and the rime make the poem [sc. *Riming Poem*] closer to the expected music of current verse than does the pure alliterative line.

rhythmic *a.* [OED 1 a, *a* 1631-1889] = next word.

1892 GUMMERE 113 The rhythmic accent coincided with the syntactical or logical. 1936 TOLKIEN 273 There is no single rhythmic pattern progressing from the beginning of a line to the end.

rhythmical *a.* [OED 3 a, 1589-1872] Of language, verse: marked by or moving in rhythm; composed in rhythm; often, having a good, smooth, or flowing rhythm.

1813 J.J. CONYBEARE 271 It might also perhaps be questioned by some, whether the rhythmical system itself ... was originally the property of our northern ancestors [etc]. 1864 MORLEY 253 The long rhythmical, alliterative poem [sc. *Beowulf*]. 1909 LOTSPEICH 375 The old rule of rhythmical stress accent laid down by Sievers. 1957 LE PAGE 92 Even the best system of musical notation so far produced — that of Professor J.C. Pope — has itself led to overconcentration on the theory of a consistent rhythmical norm.

rising *ppl.a.* ‡ Of a foot, rhythm, etc: increasing in stress, having the ictus at the end. Opp. FALLING *ppl.a.* $ Cf sense 4 c in OED, 'increasing in pitch.' An 1893 example of 'rising stress' is recorded in OED s.v. *Stress* sb.8.

1894, 1962, 1967 [see FALLING *ppl.a.*]. 1970 FAKUNDINY 141 The verses formed are always rising types.

run-on *attrib. phr.* or *adj.* [OED s.v. *Run* ppl.a. 14, 1877] Continued into the next line, couplet, etc.

1903 TINKER 99 There is always a pause at the end of a line in Old English; run-on lines are uncommon. 1935 BARTLETT 111 The Latin hexameter may have influenced the run-on lines in Anglo-Saxon. 1962 MALONE 61 In the rest of the poem we find ... many run-on lines.

secondary *a.* [OED 1] Of the second order, or of less than primary significance, in any series, sequence, or process: ‡ spec. *secondary accent, beat, lift, stress,* etc. § OED records *secondary accent* from Guest *Eng. Rhythms* (1838); also a 1785 example s.v. *Stress* sb.8.

1888 [see PRIMARY *a.*]. 1899 BRIGHT 368 This secondary accent (as by analogy it may be called). 1910 [see PRIMARY *a.*]. 1938 CAMPBELL 19 Words of the type *gyldenne, bundenne* have a secondary stress on the second syllable. 1941 [see TERTIARY *a.*]. 1942 POPE 21 At the middle of each measure there is normally another syllable bearing secondary accent.

section *sb.* [OED 2 h, 1838] Used by Guest for: a member of a verse, esp. a hemistich of an OE or ME alliterative line.

1838 GUEST I.163 Our Anglo-Saxon poems consist of certain versicles, or, as we have hitherto termed them, sections, bound together in pairs by the laws of alliteration. 1870 [see THESIS]. 1910 SCHIPPER 30 The regular alliterative line or verse is made up of two hemistichs or sections.

‡ **short line** In OE verse, a hemistich, half-line; spec. **short epic line** (see quot. 1892). Cf LONG LINE; cf also G *Kurzzeile.*

1864 [see HALF-LINE]. 1868, 1892 [see LONG LINE]. 1902 W.W. LAWRENCE 251 The four short lines 3, 8, 17, 19, must arrest attention, such verses being unusual in Anglo-Saxon poetry.

‡ **short verse** = prec. word.

1830 THORPE 136 In short verses there occurs sometimes but one sub-letter. 1911 SKEMP 298 Of these ... thirty-four short verses, seventeen have alliteration concluded within the short verse. 1948 [see LINE *sb.*].

slur *sb.* [OED *sb.*[3] 5, 1861-98] A slurred utterance or sound. ‡ More precisely, in OE verse an unstressed syllable or syllables not essential to the basic rhythm of the line.

1883 [see SLURRED *ppl.a.*]. 1894 SWEET lxxxvi Two short syllables constituting a slur ... which must be uttered very rapidly.

slurred *ppl.a.* [OED 1746-1883] Run together, rendered indistinct, blurred, etc. ‡ More precisely, in OE verse, unstressed, unaccented.

1883 VIGFUSSON & POWELL I.433 In many lines there occur one or more unstressed syllables, which form ... the ... unmeasured part of the line; these, for want of a better term, we call slurred syllables, or, collectively, a slur. 1894 SWEET lxxxvi The first of which has strong stress, constituting a slur, which we denote by (ˇ) over the vowels of the two slurred syllables.

stave *sb.* ✝ spec. An alliterating letter in a line of OE verse. So head-stave (see quot. 1940). Cf G *Stab, Hauptstab,* ON *hǫfuð-stafr.* ∮ *Stave* in the sense 'verse, stanza' also occurs in works on OE prosody.

1894 SWEET lxxxv In our texts ... the letters or staves are in italics. *Ibid* We denote the first and second verse of each line by I and II respectively. II ... has only one stave called the head-stave, while I has either one or two called under-staves. 1940 [see KEY-ALLITERATION]. 1959 LE PAGE 434 The two alliterating staves, one in each half-line, have a definite structural function. 1962 MALONE 67 Grammatically *fela ic monna* makes a unit but because of the m-stave that binds the two halves of the line together the on-verse must be classified as D in spite of the f-stave.

stave-rhyme [OED s.v. *Stave* sb.[1] 8, 1888] Alliteration; an alliterating word in a line of alliterative poetry. Cf G *Stabreim.*

1860 STEPHENS 21 The Epic is of course in the Old-English stave-rhyme, the stately metre of our oldest verse. *Ibid* [see ACCENT *sb.*].

stichic *a.* [OED 2, 1886-1900] Consisting of successive lines of the same metrical form.

1888 COOK xlix Old English verse is rarely strophic, but almost without exception stichic; that is, consists of ungrouped lines, following each other as in Modern English blank verse. 1910 SCHIPPER 24 At a very early period this sung strophic poetry gave way to a recited strophic form. 1922 KLAEBER lxxi The stichic system of West Germanic verse ... appears in our poem in full bloom. 1962 MALONE 61 Instead of one-sentence lines, couplets, and stanzas we find a stichic system like that of *Beowulf.*

stress *sb.* [OED 8, 1749-1893] Relative loudness of force of vocal utterance [etc]. ∮ The OED examples are not all from prosodic contexts. OED records examples of *stress-rhythm* (1901) and *stress-syllable* (1847, 1901) but not with reference to OE verse.

1830 THORPE 136 The riming letters must always be found in those words which have the stress or tone on the syllable which begins with them.1883 VIG-FUSSON & POWELL I.433 In every line two stress-syllables at least, one in each half-line, must begin with a similar consonant or a vowel. 1904 CHILD xxi The Old English verse is made up of two half lines separated by a cæsura, linked by alliteration, marking the chief stresses. 1958 BLISS 61 Light verses are those which contain only one stressed element, and therefore (apparently, at least) only one full stress. 1961 TAGLICHT 344 We nowhere find signs regularly indicating the strong stresses or otherwise marking the metrical subdivision of the half-line.

stressed *ppl.a.* [OED 2, 1913] Marked with a stress, emphasized.
1883 VIGFUSSON & POWELL I.442 Stressed words in slur. **1922** KERSHAW 1
The ordinary quadruple-stressed alliterative verse. **1963** QUIRK 152 Alliteration
in Old English verse serves not only to connect stressed forms within the half-
line but also [etc].

tertiary *a.* Of the third order in any series, sequence, or process: ‡
spec. *tertiary lift, stress*, etc.
1941 MALONE 75 Not infrequently ... a regular four-lift pattern will take a
tertiary lift instead of one or both of the secondary lifts. **1958** BLISS 48 The
variety with tertiary stress is much more frequent in the *a*-verse then in the *b*-
verse.

thesis [OED 2, 1398-1879] By later Latin writers ... used for the
lowering of the voice in an unstressed syllable, thus practically rever-
sing the original meaning; hence in prevalent acceptation (from the
time of Bentley, 1726): the unaccented or weak part of a foot in
verse (classical or modern), or an unaccented note in music. ∮ Cf
ARSIS.
1870 MARCH 147 The regular Germanic epic line has four ... arses in each
section, each of which may have a thesis or not. **1888** TOLMAN 20 Only one accented syllable, out of the first sixteen in this poem [sc. *Beowulf*], has a syllable expressed as its thesis or senkung. **1910** [see ARSIS]. **1938** CAMPBELL 18
A dissyllabic second thesis seems not to be found in lines of type A. **1942** [see
DOWN-BEAT].

‡ **transverse alliteration** In OE verse, alliteration of the patterns *abab*
or *baab*; = CROSS-ALLITERATION, CROSSED ALLITERATION. ∮ See
note s.v. CROSSED ALLITERATION.
1900 EMERSON 127 (*title*) Transverse Alliteration in Teutonic Poetry. **1942**
POPE 154 Transverse alliteration occurs once with the whole-line pattern bx |
ax ‖ ax | bx. **1949** BAUM 146 The most interesting of these minor variations is
the crossed or transverse alliteration *ab ab*. **1962** [see CROSS-ALLITERATION].

unaccented *ppl.a.* [OED 1598-1893] Not accented or stressed; unem-
phasized.
1830 THORPE 162 Its first part consisting of an ictus, and several short or unaccented syllables. **1871** SWEET 3 The number of unaccented syllables is indif-

ferent. 1953 SLAY 8 As a heavy unaccented sentence particle it will be placed in the first dip of the clause.

unmetrical *a.* [OED (not defined), 1791-1885] Not conforming to the metrical conventions of a specified system.

1938 CAMPBELL 8 The unmetrical unsyncopated form *hremige.* 1953 MAGOUN 461 The becoming unmetrical of such a verse [*héan landes* for *héahan landes*] would have been a gradual process.

unstressed *ppl.a.* [OED (not defined), 1883] Not stressed.

1883 VIGFUSSON & POWELL I.433 In many lines there occur one or more unstressed syllables. 1953 SLAY 7 Unstressed words which belong only to one single word or part of the sentence are called sentence-part particles.

upbeat *sb.* [OED 2 a, b, 1883-99] a An anacrusis. b An arsis or stressed syllable.

1942 [see ARSIS]. 1948 ANDREW 120 Anacrusis is an introductory unstressed up-beat.

verse *sb.* [OED 1, c 900-1895] A succession of words arranged according to natural or recognized rules of prosody and forming a complete metrical line; one of the lines of a poem or piece of versification.

1715 ELSTOB 68 The Saxon Verses consist of three, four, five, six, seven, eight, or more syllables. 1830 [see METRICAL *a.*]. 1883 H.M. KENNEDY I.22 The sentence rarely closes with the ending of the verse. 1938 CAMPBELL 16 Sievers showed once and for all the combinations of accentual elements, which might be used to build a verse. 1948 BAUM 74 The simple 'principle' of two beats or emphasized syllables in each half-line or verse. 1958 BLISS 1 The term 'verse' is here used instead of the more cumbrous 'half-line' or 'hemistich'.

attrib. and *Comb.* as ‡ *verse accent* (also *-accented* [*adj.*], *-form, -pair, -rhythm, -stress, -unit*).

1894 Verse accent [see DIPODY]. 1892 GUMMERE 113 These verse-accented syllables must also be word-accented. 1906 KRAPP xlvi The distinctively epic verse-form. 1966 ROGERS 95 The [OE] verse-form (despite alliteration) is much less restrictive than the Homeric hexameter. 1953 MAGOUN 449 The recurrence of verses and verse-pairs in Anglo-Saxon poetry. 1942 POPE 22 In no case is it necessary to pass beyond the limits of accentual adjustment that verse-rhythm everywhere allows. 1894 HEATH 386 Expanded lines ... possess a larger number of Verse Stresses than the normal line. 1948 BAUM 77 When the character of the dipody, or verse unit, is examined, the first impression is one of extreme variation. 1966 ROGERS 96 The verse-unit, the half-line, was quite short.

versicle [OED 2 c, 1573-1893] A short or single metrical line.
1838 [see SECTION *sb.*]. 1860 STEPHENS 15 There are no points or commas ... scarcely a capital letter, and not even the usual dot after each poetical versicle!

LIST OF WORKS CITED

Anderson, L.F. *The Anglo-Saxon scop.* Toronto 1903 (University of Toronto Studies, Philological Series 1)
Andrew, Samuel Ogden. *Postscript on Beowulf.* Cambridge 1948
Bartlett, Adeline Courtney. *The larger rhetorical patterns in Anglo-Saxon poetry.* New York 1935 (Columbia University Studies in English and Comparative Literature 122)
Baum, Paull F. 'The meter of the "Beowulf,"' *MP* 46 (1948) 73-91; (1949) 145-62
Bessinger, J.B. '*Maldon* and the *Oláfsdrápa*: an historical caveat,' in S.B. Greenfield, ed. *Studies in Old English literature in honor of A.G. Brodeur.* Eugene, Oregon 1963. 23-35
Blackburn, Francis Adelbert. 'The *Husband's Message* and the accompanying riddles of the Exeter Book,' *JEGP* 3 (1900) 1-13
— ed. *Exodus and Daniel.* Boston 1907
Bliss, Alan Joseph. *The metre of Beowulf.* Oxford 1958
— 'The appreciation of Old English metre,' in N. Davis and C.L. Wrenn, eds. *English and medieval studies presented to J.R.R. Tolkien.* London 1962. 27-40
Bosworth, Joseph. *The elements of Anglo-Saxon grammar.* London 1823
— *A compendious grammar of the primitive English or Anglo-Saxon language.* London 1826
Bradley, Henry. 'The numbered sections in Old English poetical MSS.,' [read 24 Nov. 1915] *PBA 1915-1916* (1919) 165-87
Bright, James Wilson, ed. *An Anglo-Saxon reader.* New York 1891; London 1892
— 'Proper names in Old English verse,' *PMLA* 14 (1899) 347-68
Brooke, Stopford A. *The history of early English literature: being the history of English poetry from its beginnings to the accession*

of King Alfred. 2 vols. London 1892

Cable, Thomas M. 'Rules for syntax and metrics in *Beowulf,* '*JEGP* 69 (1970) 81-8

Campbell, Alistair, ed. *The battle of Brunanburh*. London 1938

— 'The Old English epic style,' in N. Davis and C. L. Wrenn, eds. *English and medieval studies presented to J. R. R. Tolkien*. London 1962. 13-26

Chadwick, Hector Munro, and Chadwick, Norah Kershaw. *The growth of literature*. 3 vols. Cambridge 1932-40

Chambers, Raymond Wilson. *Widsith: a study in Old English heroic legend*. Cambridge 1912

Child, Clarence Griffin. *Beowulf and the Finnesburh fragment*; translated from the Old English. Boston 1904

Clubb, Merrel Dare, ed. *Christ and Satan: an Old English poem*. New Haven 1925 (Yale Studies in English 70)

Conybeare, John Josias. 'Account [read 4 Feb. 1813] of an Anglo-Saxon paraphrase of the Phoenix ... in the Exeter Manuscript,' *Archaeologia* 17 (1814) 193-7

— 'Observations on the metre of the Anglo-Saxon poetry [3 Feb. 1813],' and 'Further observations on the poetry of our Anglo-Saxon ancestors,' *Archaeologia* 17 (1814) 257-74

— *Illustrations of Anglo-Saxon poetry*; edited with additional notes, etc by W. D. Conybeare. London 1826

Conybeare, William Daniel (1826) *See* Conybeare, J. J.

Cook, Albert Stanburrough, ed. *Judith: an Old English epic fragment*. Boston 1888

Daunt, Marjorie. 'Old English verse and English speech rhythm,' *Transactions of the Philological Society 1943-6* (1946) 56-72

Dunning, Thomas Patrick and Bliss, Alan Joseph, eds. *The Wanderer*. London 1969 (Methuen's Old English Library)

Earle, John. *The philology of the English tongue*. Oxford 1871

Elstob, Elizabeth. *The rudiments of grammar for the English-Saxon tongue*. London 1715

Emerson, Oliver Farrar. 'Transverse alliteration in Teutonic poetry,' *JEGP* 3 (1900) 127-37

Fakundiny, Lydia. 'The art of Old English verse composition,' *RES* 21 (1970) 129-42; 257-66

Foster, Sir Thomas Gregory. *Judith: studies in metre, language and style*. Strassburg 1892 (Quellen und Forschungen zur Sprach- und Culturgeschichte 71)

Fox, Samuel, ed. *Menologium; seu, Calendarium poeticum, ex Hickesiano thesauro; or, The poetical calendar of the Anglo-Saxons.* London 1830

Frye, Prosser Hall. 'The translation of Beowulf,' *MLN* 12 (1897) 79-82

Garnett, James M. 'The translation of Anglo-Saxon poetry,' *PMLA* 6 (1891) 95-105

Girvan, Ritchie. *Beowulf and the seventh century.* London 1935 (Methuen's Old English Library)

— 'Finnsburuh' (Sir Israel Gollancz Memorial Lecture 1941), *PBA 1940* (1943) 327-60

Gordon, Eric Valentine, ed. *The battle of Maldon.* London 1937 (Methuen's Old English Library)

Greenfield, Stanley Brian. *A critical history of Old English literature.* New York 1965

Guest, Edwin. *A history of English rhythms.* 2 vols. London 1838

Gummere, Francis Barton. *Germanic origins: a study in primitive culture.* New York 1892

— *The oldest English epic: Beowulf, Finnsburg, Waldere, Deor, Widsith, and the German Hildebrand, translated in the original metres.* New York 1909

Heath, H. Frank. 'The Old English alliterative line,' *Transactions of the Philological Society 1891-4* (1894) 375-95

Henry, Robert. *The history of Great Britain from the invasion of it by the Romans under Cæsar.* 6 vols. London 1771-93

Hopkins, Gerard Manley. *The journals and papers*; edited by H. House and G. Storey. London 1959

Kennedy, Charles William. *The earliest English poetry: a critical survey of the poetry written before the Norman Conquest.* New York 1943

Kennedy, Evory. 'On the principles and uses of alliteration in poetry,' *Afternoon Lectures on Literature and Art delivered in Dublin.* 3rd series. London 1866. 87-128

Kennedy, Horace M. (1883) *See* Ten Brink, B.

Kent, Charles William, ed. *Elene.* Boston 1889 (Library of Anglo-Saxon Poetry 3)

Kershaw, Norah, ed. *Anglo-Saxon and Norse poems.* Cambridge 1922

Klaeber, Friedrich, ed. *Beowulf and the Fight at Finnsburg.* Boston 1922; London 1923

Kock, E.A. *Jubilee jaunts and jottings: 250 contributions to the in-*

terpretation and prosody of Old West Teutonic alliterative poetry. 1918 (Lunds Universitets Årsskrift, n.s. 1, XIV)

Krapp, George Philip, ed. *Andreas and the Fates of the Apostles: two Anglo-Saxon narrative poems.* Boston 1906

Lawrence, John. *Chapters on alliterative verse.* London 1893

Lawrence, William Witherle. 'The first riddle of Cynewulf,' *PMLA* 17 (1902) 247-61

— *Beowulf and epic tradition.* Cambridge, Mass. 1928

Lehmann, Ruth P.M. 'The Old English *Riming Poem*: interpretation, text and translation,' *JEGP* 69 (1970) 437-49

Leonard, William Ellery. 'Beowulf and the Nibelungen couplet.' *University of Wisconsin Studies in Language and Literature* 2 (1918) 99-152

— 'Four footnotes to papers on German metrics,' in K. Malone and M.B. Ruud, eds. *Studies in English philology: a miscellany in honor of F. Klaeber.* Minneapolis 1929. 1-13

Le Page, R.B. 'A rhythmical framework for the five types,' *English & Germanic Studies* 6 (1957) 92-103

— 'Alliterative patterns as a test of style in Old English poetry,' *JEGP* 58 (1959) 434-41

Lewis, Clive Staples. *Rehabilitations and other essays.* London 1939

Longfellow, Henry Wadsworth, ed. *The poets and poetry of Europe.* Philadelphia 1847

Lotspeich, C.M. 'Musical accent and double alliteration in the *Edda*,' *MP* 6 (1909) 375-84

Magoun, Francis P. 'Oral-formulaic character of Anglo-Saxon narrative poetry,' *Speculum* 28 (1953) 446-67

— 'Béowulf B: a folk-poem on Béowulf's death,' in A. Brown and P.G. Foote, eds. *Early English and Norse studies presented to Hugh Smith.* London 1963. 127-40

Malone, Kemp. 'Alliteration in *Widsith*,' *ELH* 2 (1935) 291-3

— 'Lift-patterns in Old English verse,' *ELH* 8 (1941) 74-80

— 'The Old English period (to 1100),' in A.C. Baugh, ed. *A literary history of England.* New York 1948. 3-105

— ed. *Widsith.* Revised edition. Copenhagen 1962 (Anglistica 13)

March, Francis Andrew. *Introduction to Anglo-Saxon.* New York 1870

Mather, Frank Jennett. 'The Cynewulf question from a metrical point of view,' *MLN* 7 (1892) 97-107

Menner, Robert J., ed. *The poetical dialogues of Solomon and Saturn.* New York 1941

[Mitford, William]. *An essay upon the harmony of language, intended principally to illustrate that of the English language*. London 1774

Morley, Henry. *English writers. I: The writers before Chaucer*. London 1864

— *A first sketch of English literature*. London 1873

Palgrave, Sir Francis. *History of England. I: Anglo-Saxon period*. London 1831

Patmore, Coventry. 'English Metrical Critics,' *North British Review* 27 (August 1857) 127-61

Percy, Thomas, ed. *Reliques of Ancient English Poetry*. 3 vols. London 1765

Petheram, John. *An historical sketch of the progress and present state of Anglo-Saxon literature in England*. London 1840

Pope, John Collins. *The rhythm of Beowulf*. New Haven 1942

— Revised edition. New Haven 1966

Quirk, Randolph. 'Poetic language and Old English metre,' in A. Brown and P.G. Foote, eds. *Early English and Norse studies presented to Hugh Smith*. London 1963. 150-71

Rask, Rasmus Christian. *A grammar of the Anglo-Saxon tongue, with a praxis*; translated from the Danish by B. Thorpe. Copenhagen 1830

Rehrmann, Heinrich. *Essay concerning Anglo-Saxon poetry*. Lübben 1877

Rogers, H.L. 'The crypto-psychological character of the oral formula,' *English Studies* 47 (1966) 59-102

Schipper, Jakob. *A history of English versification* [translated from the German]. Oxford 1910

Sedgefield, Walter John, ed. *Beowulf*. Manchester 1910

Shelton, Maurice (1735) *See* Wotton, W.

Sibbald, James. *Chronicle of Scottish poetry from the thirteenth century to the Union of the Crowns*. 4 vols. Edinburgh 1802

Skeat, Walter William. 'An essay on alliterative poetry,' in J.W. Hales and F.J. Furnivall, eds. *Bishop Percy's folio manuscript. Ballads and romances*. London 1868. III xi-xliv

Skemp, A.R. 'The Old English charms,' *MLR* 6 (1911) 289-301

Slay, D. 'Some aspects of the technique of composition of Old English verse,' *Transactions of the Philological Society 1952* (1953) 1-14

Stanley, Eric Gerald, ed. *Continuations and beginnings: studies in Old English literature*. London 1966

Stephens, George, ed. *Two leaves of King Waldere's lay.* Cheaping-haven [Copenhagen] 1860

Swanton, Michael, ed. *The dream of the Rood.* Manchester 1970 (Old and Middle English Texts)

Sweet, Henry. 'Sketch of the history of Anglo-Saxon poetry,' in T. Warton. *The history of English poetry,* edited by W.C. Hazlitt. London 1871. II 3-19

— *An Anglo-Saxon reader in prose and verse.* Oxford 1876

— 7th edition. Oxford 1894

Taglicht, Joseph. '*Beowulf* and Old English verse rhythm,' *RES* 12 (1961) 341-51

Ten Brink, Bernhard. *Early English literature*; translated from the German by H.M. Kennedy [and others]. 3 vols. London 1883-96

Thorpe, Benjamin (1830) *See* Rask, R.C.

— ed. *Codex Exoniensis.* London 1842

— ed. *The Anglo-Saxon poems of Beowulf, The Scop or Gleeman's Tale, and the Fight at Finnesburg.* Oxford 1855

Tinker, Chauncey Brewster. *The translations of Beowulf: a critical bibliography.* New York 1903. (Yale Studies in English 16)

Tolkien, John Ronald Reuel. 'Philology: general works,' *Year's Work in English Studies 1925* (1927) 32-66

— 'Beowulf: the monsters and the critics' (Sir Israel Gollancz Memorial Lecture 1936), *PBA 1936* (1937) 245-95

— (1940) *See* Wrenn, C.L.

Tolman, A.H. 'The style of Anglo-Saxon poetry,' *Transactions of the Modern Language Association* 3 (1888) 17-47

Turner, Sharon. *The history of the Anglo-Saxons.* 4 vols. London 1799-1805

— 2nd edition, corrected and enlarged. 2 vols. London 1807

Vigfusson, Gudbrand and Powell, Frederick York, eds. *Corpus poeticum boreale: the poetry of the old Northern tongue, from the earliest times to the 13th century.* 2 vols. Oxford 1883

Watson, Robert Spence. *Cædmon, the first English poet.* London 1875

Whallon, William. 'The diction of *Beowulf*,' *PMLA* 76 (1961) 309-19

Whitelock, Dorothy. *The audience of Beowulf.* Oxford 1951

Williams, Blanche Colton, ed. *Gnomic poetry in Anglo-Saxon.* New York 1914. (Columbia University Studies in English and Comparative Literature)

Wotton, William. *Wotton's short view of George Hickes's Grammatico-*

critical and archeological treasure of the ancient Northern-languages; translated from the original Latin by M. Shelton. London 1735

Wrenn, Charles Leslie, ed. *Beowulf and the Finnesburg fragment: a translation into modern English prose by John R. Clark Hall.* New edition completely revised with notes and an introduction; with prefatory remarks by J.R.R. Tolkien. London 1940

— ed. *Beowulf with the Finnesburg fragment.* London 1953

— *A Study of Old English literature.* London 1967

Wright, Thomas. *An essay on the state of literature and learning under the Anglo-Saxons.* London 1839

— *Essays on archaeological subjects, and on various questions connected with the history of art, science and literature in the Middle Ages.* 2 vols. London 1861

EDWARD B. IRVING, JR

Exodus retraced

The recent reprinting of my edition of the Old English poem *Exodus*[1] must be the occasion of a little embarrassment to an editor reflecting on its many still unamended deficiencies. While I have already published a set of textual notes dealing with line-by-line problems,[2] such a format hardly permits any reconsideration of larger questions in the light of two decades of subsequent research. Hence this present essay may be regarded as a supplement to the original introduction to the 1953 edition, and will be organized under its headings.

MANUSCRIPT

There is unfortunately little new to add under this category; apart from a few faint hints, the early history of the text remains shrouded in the usual mystery. N.R. Ker suggests that the Junius 11 manuscript is 'possibly identical with the "Genesis anglice depicta" in the early fourteenth-century catalogue of Christ Church, Canterbury.'[3] Careful study of the location in the manuscript of such variant spellings as 'com(on) / cwom(on)' led Kenneth Sisam to venture tentatively that '*Exodus* and *Daniel* have not for long had the same transmission as *Genesis A* and *B*,'[4] and similar evidence inclined Robert J. Menner independently to the belief that 'the scribal history of *Exodus* and *Daniel* must have been somewhat different from that of ... *Genesis A*.'[5]

There has been further discussion of the possibility of some significance in the selection and arrangement of the various poems in Junius 11. J.W. Bright pointed out long ago that the first three (actually four) poems, *Genesis A* and *B, Exodus,* and *Daniel,* recount Old Testament events which are also a typological series in the liturgical service for Holy Saturday.[6] Others have since suspected some design in the manuscript order. Robert T. Farrell sees a possible thematic connection between *Exodus* and *Daniel;*[7] Alvin A. Lee would even associate the final poem in the manuscript, *Christ and Satan,* usually excluded from consideration of this kind, with a 'poetic and symbolic' unity of the manuscript as a whole.[8] Since we generally have difficulty establishing the principles governing the make-up of OE poetic anthologies, there seems little chance of consensus here, but one may at least conjecture that this manuscript may have been intended for use by lectors in monasteries.[9] G.C. Thornley has attempted to show that the accents and points in the manuscript reflect familiarity with the usage of liturgical recitative.[10]

TEXTUAL PROBLEMS

The century-old wrangle over whether the so-called 'Exodus B' (i.e., lines 362-445, the section dealing with Noah and Abraham) is an interpolation or not seems at last to have come to a full stop; it is encouraging to have one problem settled in this difficult poem. All modern scholars see the passage as an integral part of the poem, whether they defend its relevance strictly in terms of patristic theology[11] or in terms of internal literary structure.[12]

In my edition I boldly rearranged the text of the last 75 lines of the poem, placing lines 549-90 before 516-48, not so much in order to adapt the poem to modern tastes as to make the new conclusion resemble that of many OE poems in closing with a very general homiletic passage. I now think that this rearrangement was unnecessary and unjustified, perhaps an instance of scholarly 'ofermod,' and would agree with Neil Isaacs who concludes, after an able defence of the original order: 'Barring any *positive* evidence for transposed passages, one may assume that the manuscript order accurately carries the structure of *Exodus.*'[13] There is of course no physical evidence whatever of any transposition. Earl also offers a detailed defence of the manuscript arrangement, too long to summarize here.[14]

SOURCES

Liturgy
Bright's important article proposing the Holy Saturday or Easter Eve
baptismal service as a main source for *Exodus* (the scriptural readings
in this service containing not only the Red Sea narrative but also the
stories of Noah's flood and Abraham's sacrifice of Isaac) has received
recent support, although in 1953 I was unwilling to accept this service
as a certain model for the poem.[15] One of my remarks then has often
been quoted: 'While no one could deny that the [Holy Saturday] service is dominated by the theme of baptism, no sane reader would be
likely to call *Exodus* a poem about baptism.'[16] (I remember John
Pope once suggesting delicately to me that I might tone down that
statement, but I failed to take his good advice.) I now regret having
written it simply because it has proved so untrue as prediction; more
than one presumably sane reader has since implied or insisted that
Exodus is indeed a poem about baptism![17] Whether calling it that is
useful or accurate still seems to me highly questionable, if only because such a classification immediately directs us away from the
poem's grittily peculiar qualities and special achievements in favour of
a convenient labelling of it as One More Instance of the supposedly
uncontrollable impulse to allegorize to be found in all medieval poets.
It is better first, before prejudgment, to try to define more clearly
what *Exodus* is as a poem, as I shall attempt to do later in this essay.
The question of baptism, and of symbolic meaning generally, is discussed from two interestingly different points of view by two recent
commentators: Alvin A. Lee,[18] who stresses the typological background, and T.A. Shippey,[19] who regards *Exodus*, together with the
other Junius poems, as 'resistant to allegorical or figural readings.'
(153).

It is probably true, I now realize, that a liturgical model must have
inevitably given the poem some of its shape, though we must be wary
of simply transferring the full 'meaning' of the liturgy to the poem itself. Possibly some relatively obscure early liturgy, perhaps of Celtic
origin, rather than the more conventional ancestors of the modern
Roman rite, may have been familiar to the poet. Eleanor McLoughlin,
for example, has called attention to a few striking parallels between

Exodus and the *Antiphonary of Bangor*, a seventh-century Hiberno-Latin text,[20] and M.-M. Larès suggests that 'Liber I' of the Junius 11 manuscript reflects liturgical practices of the early community in Jerusalem, somehow brought to England during the early years of the conversion.[21] More investigation remains to be done in this interesting area.

Biblical sources, other than the immediate sources in Genesis and Exodus

Many individual details in the poem are ultimately derived from other parts of the Old Testament, as both the Edition and 'New Notes' point out, but special attention might be given here to the Psalter and the Book of Wisdom.

As Geoffrey Shepherd reminds us,[22] the Psalter was the part of the Bible most familiar to medieval ecclesiastics, and its influence on *Exodus* seems much more extensive than I had realized earlier. The escape from Egypt is of course the chief subject of several psalms (e.g., 104, 105, 113, 135 in the Vulgate) which provide some striking imagery for a poet's use. Furthermore, certain basic dramatic patterns found in *Exodus* are vividly present in other psalms which do not deal explicitly with the events of the Exodus from Egypt. Man trapped in death's snare calls out to God for help, and God arrives in earthquake and showers of fire to rescue him from 'many waters' (Ps 17); God gives courage and guidance to man in terror of his enemies (Ps 58, 141); man earnestly states his trust in the Lord's protection (Ps 32 and elsewhere).

The important specific images of *Exodus* appear in many psalms. God's powerful right hand is mentioned in a dozen places; God's freeing of the (chained) prisoner is often described (e.g., Ps 106:14, 115:16, 145:7); God's protective tent or *tabernaculum* (cf 'feldhusa mæst,' *Exo* 85) appears several times (e.g., Ps 26:5, 60:5). The metaphor of the *via*, the spiritual road or path (cf 'lifweg,' 104) is common: the psalmist begs God to lead him 'in via aeterna' (Ps 138:24), and pleads 'dirige me in semitam rectam' (Ps 26:11), even though God's way may lead through unexpected places ('in mari via tua, et semitae tuae in aquis multis,' Ps 76:20). But God has made the roads known to Moses (Ps 102:7).

Finally, a number of what were once puzzling details in the OE poem may have come from the Psalms. God's sword ('alde mece,' 495) is mentioned in Psalm 7:13; the 'suðwind' (289) as a manifestation of divine power appears in Psalm 77:26; God's use of coals of fire to punish sinners (cf 'hatum heofoncolum,' 71) is described in Psalms 10:7 and 139:11. Moreover, it might be noted that virtually all the Hebrew names in *Exodus* are also found in the Psalms, where (as we can see in the glosses to the Lambeth Psalter, for example) they were often furnished with significant etymologies from Jerome, some of which were clearly used by the poet.

Another possible source for some parts of *Exodus* is the Book of Wisdom, the concluding chapters of which demonstrate the operation of divine wisdom and justice in sacred history, particularly in the Exodus. Verses 15-20 of chapter 10 might almost serve as a brief summary of the Old English poem, and, like the poem, this passage contains two details not mentioned in the Book of Exodus, the cloud-pillar as *velamentum* and the capture by the *iusti* of the spoils of the Egyptians after the drowning in the Red Sea. A more interesting similarity is to be found in the last three chapters of Wisdom (17-19), where the author develops, with much elaboration of paradox, the contrast between the darkness surrounding the Egyptians and the light granted to the escaping Israelites, both in the vivid account of the death of the firstborn in the last plague and in the description of the drowning in the Red Sea. In Wisdom, these two events are mingled rather confusingly, just as they are in the first part of the poem, the death of the firstborn being seen as a prediction of the later catastrophe: 'Solis autem illis superposita erat gravis nox, imago tenebrarum quae superventura illis erat; ipsi ergo sibi erant graviores tenebris. Sanctis autem tuis maxima erat lux ...' (Wis. 17:20-18:1) Images of chaining and imprisonment in darkness occur (17:15-16, 18:4), as well as the idea of liberation (e.g., 10:15, 18:5, 19:9).

Wisdom 19:13-17 justifies the harsh punishment of the Egyptians in terms of their gross violation of hospitality toward strangers ('bonos hospites in servitutem redigebant') and their ingratitude toward their benefactors. There is some hint in the poem, in the passages just before and after the manuscript gap at line 141, that the poet was viewing the Egyptians in similar terms. Lines 137b-40a seem to stress the special cruelty of enslaving homeless people, and lines 144-53 (beginning with 'ealles þæs forgeton') certainly accuse the Egyptians of ingratitude.[23]

Geographical details
Several pages of the 1953 introduction discussed the possibility that the Greek geographer Diodorus Siculus may have been the source of

some of the curious details (e.g., a shield-like sun, a cloud-covered country) included in the poet's description of the country between Egypt and the Red Sea, but the likelihood of this now seems to me remote. Familiarity with the confusion of fact and allegory found in the glosses on place-names leads one to think that the poet was giving a local habitation and a name to allegorical abstractions rather than visualizing the kind of geographical terrain we would naturally think of.

Patristic sources
Most of the new evidence falls under this heading, the great bulk of it consisting of brief and isolated patristic and exegetical passages that seem to be reflected in the poem, with varying degrees of certainty. It need hardly be said that deciding where the poet found such exegetical commonplaces, most of them passed on from one commentator to the next during the patristic period and after, is virtually impossible, but a few highly probable identifications can be made.

In 1953, I mentioned Jerome and Josephus as likely sources for certain details.[24] New evidence, much of it resulting from the energetic researches of Fred C. Robinson, emphatically confirms this probability.[25] At least one passage from Josephus seems to be almost literally translated by the poet, and others seem also to be reflected.[26] The poet's heavy use of Jerome's etymologies of Hebrew names is remarkable.[27] Commentaries on the Old Testament and other works by Augustine,[28] Isidore,[29] and Ambrose[30] may also have been drawn on (though perhaps not at first hand). Commentaries on the Psalms by Cassiodorus[31] may also have been used. Some of these details are found in the anonymous commentary on the Pentateuch by 'Pseudo-Bede' which the poet may have known.[32] The detail about Judah being the first tribe to enter the Red Sea ultimately goes back to Jewish tradition, but is found nearer at hand in the commentary on the Epistle to the Hebrews at various times attributed to Pelagius, Primasius, and Haimo of Auxerre, but probably composed in Ireland between 650 and 800.[33]

It might also be mentioned that non-Vulgate texts of the Old Testament seem clearly to account for several minor variant readings in the poem.[34] Since most of the passages in question form part of the liturgy, where non-Vulgate texts were in use much longer than elsewhere, this fact is of no value as a criterion for dating the poem.

To sum up, it is conceivable that there was a single source for all or most of this miscellaneous exegetical material, but I have been unable to find it. My general impression, for what it is worth, is that the poet is certainly in one sense much more learned than I had once thought him to be. He is someone so familiar with the usual glosses and explications of Old Testament texts that he brings them into his poem almost unconsciously. On the other hand, he never seems to reproduce any extended or elaborate allegorical interpretation, though we may assume such texts were available to him. He freely borrows details, but not structures of meaning; on the larger scale, he makes his own poem.

DIALECT AND DATE

Study of the scribal errors in *Exodus* suggests strongly that the West Saxon scribe was unfamiliar with certain Anglian words and spellings and tended to corrupt them. This seems fairly good evidence that the poem was originally Anglian, though one might also argue that the first scribe of Junius 11 (or an earlier scribe) was merely unaccustomed to copying poetic texts with their high percentage of Anglian vocabulary. For instance, the Anglian-poetic element 'heoru-' seems to be mangled three times in the poem, appearing as 'heora,' 'here,' 'huru'; the chiefly poetic word 'cyrm' turns into the prose word 'cyre'; the Anglian word 'tane' becomes 'tacne,' and so on.[35]

Dietrich Hofmann has challenged the traditional assumption of a relatively early date for *Exodus*, arguing that evidence indicates that both *Genesis A* and *Exodus* were probably composed in the Danelaw in the late ninth or tenth century, since he believes he finds Old Norse influence in both poems.[36] In a detailed reply I stated my conviction that his evidence seemed far from persuasive.[37] One of his claims, for example, that the second element in 'hildecalla' (*Exo* 252) shows the influence of the common ON word 'kalla,' has since, I think, been refuted by the evidence for the native origin of the word collected by E.G. Stanley.[38]

STRUCTURE AND STYLE

As was pointed out above, the medieval interpretation of the Exodus and the crossing of the Red Sea as a prefiguration of baptism and salvation seems to have been taken by some readers to be, quite simply, the primary meaning of the OE poem. Even in the dark ages of 1953, just before the explosion of interest in the application of allegory to medieval literature, I was fully aware of the existence of this interpretation, but it seemed to me then applicable only in a small way to the vigorous heroic action of the poem, and by no means to be substituted for the meaning of that action. Twenty years later I feel the same way, and I am pleased to note that some recent comments on the allegorical approach to the poem offer some support for such a point of view.

Philip Rollinson, working within the definitions of early medieval rhetoric, discusses *Exodus* as an instance of an historically based heroic fiction, containing an exemplary meaning within the *sensus litteralis*, but disputes Huppé's claim that the '*sensus spiritualis* constitutes the intended, primary meaning of this fictional narrative.'[39] He concludes his brief analysis with this statement:

> The first purpose of the Old English *Exodus* seems to be to relate the exemplary (and exciting) story of a Jewish hero, of the heroic conflict between God's people and Satan's people, and of God's spectacular judgment, which decided that contest. The historical, literal level alone of the Old Testament account is re-presented in the heroic conventions and poetic expectations of a Germanic, if Christianized, tradition. In spite of the liturgical overtones, which could hardly be avoided, the essential meaning intended is surely not to emphasize the relationship of the poetic fiction to the rite of baptism. (18)

Stanley B. Greenfield cites (and seems to share) some of Rollinson's views in the chapter entitled, 'Generic Expectations and the Quest for Allegory,' in his recent book, where he argues sensibly for a less Procrustean kind of criticism by the users of allegorical exegesis.[40]

A similar view, though from another angle, is taken by T.A. Shippey, who points to some significant differences in the way Old Testament events are handled by the commentators and by this poet.[41] An example he offers is the poet's explanation (135 ff) of the motivations of the pursuing Egyptians, especially their jealousy at the Israelites' prosperity. 'This idea,' he writes, 'is certainly latent in the Bible itself (see Exodus 1:7-20), and is in itself plausible. But it is a sign of the poet's natural bent towards history that he includes it, while the concern for human motivation on a realistic level is markedly alien to the type of commentary most practised by Augustine and his followers.'

From a literary point of view, typology — and, strictly speaking, it is typology rather than allegory that we are examining — means a story that repeats or suggests a pattern found in other stories, or in The Story. But a narrative poem of this kind is aesthetically effective not because it obtrusively keeps drawing our attention to its similarity to another story but because it is first of all a vivid and 'true' literary experience in itself. We should certainly be aware, for example, that in the later cycle plays Cain is the type of Satan and Isaac the type of the sacrificed Christ, but to say only this is to say almost nothing about the actual plays where Cain and Isaac appear as intrinsically interesting characters in their own right. The Egyptians in *Exodus* are bullies and villainous treaty-breakers; it adds little to their dramatic reality as characters in the fiction to maintain that they are 'really' mankind's sins, to be washed away in the purifying baptismal waters.

It is rather our task to assess the OE *Exodus* as the poet wrote it, and thus to deal with an artifact that is not necessarily identical in form or purpose with any exegetical sources he may have consulted. Let us first ask these questions: what is apparently the poet's chief concern? Where does his poem take on a certain telltale life and excitement? The answer is scarcely unexpected, in the light of the poetic traditions in which he worked: he thinks primarily in terms of heroism, in terms of being alternately brave and frightened, in terms of faith or lack of faith in a leader's power and his ability to deliver what he promises to his followers. Very possibly Mediterranean Christians of the poet's own time might have found this a rather strange way to describe the events of the Exodus or to compose a 'poem about baptism,' if that was what they expected.

By stressing this heroic aspect, I surely do not wish to suggest that *Exodus* is a secular or only half-Christian poem; it is an extremely didactic poem in a Christian sense. It has an obvious message which takes two forms, the first directly stated at beginning and end, and the second indirectly stated in the whole narrative action of the escape from Egypt. The direct message, found in lines 1-7 and in the 'ece rædas' propounded by Moses after the crossing (516-48),[42] is simply the good news of salvation, addressed to all men ('we' in lines 1 and 529, 'us,' 531), who have the freedom whether or not to hear it. In line 7 what seems to be an old minstrel formula, 'gehyre se ðe wille,' is virtually forced by its context to echo also the pointed biblical admonition, 'he that hath ears to hear, let him hear.' The later passage (516-48) can be summarized as a brief homily stating that

God's mercy exists and that, even though we must eventually realize that earthly life is one of exile and misery, dominated by the fear of being imprisoned in hell, Judgment Day will come to liberate the righteous from this condition and will bring about their triumphant entry into the homeland of heaven. This message itself requires liberation, locked as it is in the mysterious language of scripture (perhaps specifically, as Earl suggests,[43] in the book of Deuteronomy), until the time when the keys of the Spirit can unlock meaning for us, that time when 'ræd forð gæð' (526) as the message of salvation makes its own exodus out of mystery.

The second message of the poem is contained in the main narrative action, an action that is presented dramatically and consecutively. The poet does not pause in his story to moralize (as does Cynewulf, for example, in *Christ II*) or to point out the explicit *significatio* of individual objects or events in the manner of exegetical commentators. What he has drawn from the exegetical tradition is built into his swift-paced narrative without interrupting it, as, for instance, the ideas or images derived from the etymologies of names (the Egyptians as 'dark' or 'darkness,' the journey from Etham onward as a voyage, Abraham as 'father of many nations'). Such material becomes inconspicuous and, in one sense, even unnecessary. It is not essential to identify subtle symbolic meanings in order to understand and respond to this poem. While we know nothing of the original audience, we may imagine that the poem might have been effective on two levels: for a relatively unsophisticated group and for a more learned group which may have appreciated recognizing many allusions, a group that had read, for example, of the symbolic meaning of the themes of imprisonment and liberation in the Exodus story. But the poet's impressive use of these themes as *poetic* devices, with strong and simple emotional connotations rather than merely rational theological ones, would have been clear to an attentive reader or listener with only the barest knowledge of Christian doctrine (and doubtless there were many like this even in a monastic refectory).

We can test this by looking at the use of such themes in *Exodus*. The action of the poem begins with the slaying of the Egyptian first-born (36-53), described in a passage still very difficult to make out in all its details and still eluding any scholarly consensus,[44] but with an undeniable focus on images of paralysis and impotence: sleep, falling, inert corpses, the locked hands of laughter-smiths, imprisonment foretold for the Egyptians as just return for their imprisonment of the

Israelites. These images are juxtaposed effectively to the quick power-ful movements of the escaping Israelites as they break out into hos-tile territory:

> Fyrd wæs gefysed,   from se ðe lædde,
> modig magoræ[s]wa,   mægburh heora;
> oferfor he mid þy folce   fæsten[n]a worn,
> land and leodweard   laðra manna,
> enge anpaðas,   uncuð gelad,
> oðþæt hie on guðmyrce   gearwe bæron
> (wæron land heora   lyfthelme beþeaht,
> mearchofu morheald).   Moyses ofer þa,
> fela meor[r]inga,   fyrde gelædde.

(Lines 54-62; the text quoted here, in punctuation and some read-ings, is that of 'New Notes' and differs somewhat from that in the edition.)

One may note that this burst of headlong movement is framed in the common envelope pattern ('fyrd ... lædde'; 'fyrde gelædde'), thereby receiving special emphasis. Here, as elsewhere in the poem, the effect is further underlined by a simple contrast between dark-ness and light: the slaying of the firstborn takes place 'æt middere niht' (37), while the Israelites come out into sunlight, indeed an ex-cess of sunlight, for the pillar of cloud appears here first in the form of a shelter against the scorching Ethiopian sun.

The Israelites see the cloud as being a shield, a net, a sail, a tent — something miraculously suspended over them. Each image has its symbolic dimensions, but dramatically the rapid series of images here stresses the fugitives' initial bewilderment: 'hæleð wafedon,' 78 — what *is* that up there? If a sail, a sail whose halyards and yardarm they cannot see; if a tent, it is one with no visible fastenings. By the very effort of trying to put it into familiar terms, they come quickly to know that it is miracle:

>   Fyrd eall geseah
> hu þær hlifedon   halige seglas,
> lyftwundor leoht;   leode ongeton,
> dugoð Israhela,   þæt þær Drihten cwom,
> weroda Drihten,   wicsteal metan.   (88b-92)

Note the alliterative stress on 'halige' and the unusual repetition of 'Drihten.' God now emerges from behind the images. We see the Israelites in the act of developing the faculty of symbolic vision, and the poet asks us to participate in this process.

As they follow the cloud-pillar on their journey, their progress is described as sailing and they are called 'sæmen' (105). Whatever this metaphor may suggest in other contexts (the church as ship or 'nave,' the Ark, etc),[45] in this immediate context it describes a new form of locomotion with its own strange and joyous power, in contrast with the fierce effort of the first forced march into the wilderness. Now they *sail* swiftly and magically through the desert and (eventually) across the dry sea-bed, freed from the very bonds of earth. Like the Seafarer, they can now experience what the proud man on land cannot imagine.

While this way of moving is a stage toward their liberation, the Israelites are not yet entirely free and confident. Even though the pillar of fire keeps darkness and its terrible 'westengryre' away from them during their overnight halt, it does not prevent the sheer panic that overcomes them the next day when they see that they are pinned against the Red Sea by the oncoming Egyptian army. The trapped fugitives can only sit, wait, anticipate their destruction, now in much the same paralyzed state (and psychological darkness) in which we saw the stricken Egyptians earlier.

At this stage Moses must intervene to restore their collapsed morale. To a limited degree, this excellent commanding officer succeeds in reducing their fear simply by ordering them to rise at the blast of trumpets, to arm themselves, and to fall into formation, twelve divisions of fifty companies each. The very numbers are definite and comforting, the images hope-bringing: dawn, picked men rising to their feet, a standard being raised, a herald springing forward to cry silence for the general's speech. So Earl Byrhtnoth marshals his men at Maldon, and perhaps the most useful general parallel for this scene is not a biblical passage but the account of Hygelac's rescue of the Geats at Ravenswood (*Beowulf* 2933-45).

Despite this response to military discipline, the Israelites are still frightened; Moses must begin his speech to them with the words 'ne beoð ge þy forhtran' (259). He must now sharpen their vision, so that they can see that the vast numbers of the Egyptians and the threat that they imply are simply illusory and meaningless, so close are the pursuers to being destroyed. The Israelites seem to believe firmly in what they see: they believed both in the guiding cloud and in the menace of Pharaoh's army. Now it is necessary for Moses to tell them to look — look with their eyes — at the great sudden miracle taking place before them.

That the poet departs rather strikingly from the biblical account here by allowing Moses to describe the parting of the sea rather than by himself describing it directly has troubled more than one reader of the poem.[46] This is an important literary change, for which no explanation is likely to emerge from the columns of the *Patrologia*. But I think the surrounding dramatic context may explain it. Unlike Moses, the Israelites have not seen God, and do not yet comprehend God's full power and benevolence; they have risen and formed their ranks only out of a faith in their leader. Thus it is the very intensity of this personal relationship between Moses and his people that demands that Moses himself must tell them of the miracle, show it to them, shift their trusting eyes from his gesturing hand to what is taking place in the sea.

When they have seen, they begin to act, now released from the paralysis of fear. Once again the poet describes the forming of military units, but this scene differs significantly from the scene just preceding Moses's speech. Then they were formed into impersonal 'feðan' and 'cista,' as numbered anonymous units; now they become named people, marching forward to take on great identities — they are Judah, Reuben, Simeon, they have 'name.' Judah carries as his standard the golden lion, 'deora cenost' (322), the epitome of animal courage like the boars on a Germanic warrior's helmet. That it materializes here to stand for his tribe's newly found bravery and selfhood seems more important dramatically than any of the myriad meanings the exegetes assigned to this famous symbol. Reuben's men now swagger down to the sea in the aggressive role of 'sæwicingas,' forgetting the old disgrace of losing their position of leadership. And, as Simeon and the other tribes swing into line and follow, the sun, 'Godes beacna sum,' rises over the sea, much like the light that blazes out in Grendel's 'hof' after Beowulf seizes and uses the giant-sword and, like that light, as much an approving response by divine powers to heroic initiative as a cause of it.

As part of knowing who they are, the tribes remember now that they are brothers in a mighty family, for 'him wæs an fæder' (353); they seem to be recalling Moses' admonition to think of the God of Abraham. Surely there are strong resonances here of the proud patronymics of epic poetry. As they begin to think of their ancestors, we are told old tales about them, those ancient Scyld-like heroes who acted and marched and sailed, as their descendants are now learning to do in their turn. Viewing this passage from such a point of view makes much smoother the apparently abrupt transition to Noah in line 362.[47] Noah once valiantly cruised the deepest of drowning-floods and, like any 'god cyning,' thus preserved for his descendants the greatest of all treasure-hoards. Like the fugitives from Egypt now, Abraham too once lived in exile, until he led his own greatest treasure, his only son, to the sacrificial altar, an act presented primarily as one of courage and unflinching faith in his king's command. Heroism and faith are rooted in both past and future. Abraham is both an ancestral model of behaviour and the receiver of the great promise of a future return from exile for his descendants, a promise wholly earned by his bravery.

It should be obvious that, in describing this sequence, I have deliberately stressed its resemblances to heroic poetry, but I am certainly not denying that the Christian typological pattern is also there, the same majestic series of great names one can find in the thirteenth chapter of Hebrews or in the liturgy. The two traditions fuse so well that one is tempted to invent a descriptive term like 'heroic typology.'

After the second manuscript lacuna at line 446, the text resumes with the Egyptians already wallowing helpless in the Red Sea. Their seemingly unstoppable forward motion has been completely blocked; indeed, when they turn back, they find that they cannot even move in retreat. Trapped and immobilized, just as we saw them prophetically at the opening of the poem, they can only scream as the sea's great darkness closes over them, chained as they are in the strong fetters of death.

> Him ongen genap
> atol yða gewealc,   ne ðær ænig becwom
> herges to hame,   ac behindan beleac
> wyrd mid wæge ...
> Heah ofer hæleðum   holmweall astah,
> merestream modig;   mægen wæs on cwealme
> fæste gefererod.   (455b-8a; 468-70a)

What, in their moment of panic, the Israelites had feared for themselves now happens to their enemies. As the Israelites prepare to march on toward the reward promised them by Abraham, the Egyptians receive their reward (called, punningly, a 'deop lean,' 507) on the sea-bottom. So stopped is all Egyptian movement that not a single man survives to carry the news back to Egypt. Our last sight of them is a panorama of lifeless bodies on the shore, helpless to prevent the eager hands of Israelite looters from stripping them of the treasure they had once looted from Joseph.[48] 'Werigend lagon / on deaðstede,   drihtfolca mæ[st].' (589b-90) As the Egyptians become finally locked into death's prison, the once enslaved Israelites are set free at last ('hæft wæs onsæled,' 584); their new freedom of movement finds expression both in the joyous antiphonal song of thanksgiving and in the busy activity of sharing out the plunder.

It should be evident that the rhetoric of *Exodus* shows the same fundamentally binary structure of dramatically opposed extremes which is typical of Old English verse generally.[49] While this rhetorical frame is well suited to the strong theological polarities of early Christianity, it is used here to shape a story not to be found in quite this form by the most tireless searcher of scripture or commentary.

Some aspects of the poem are much better understood in terms of heroic tradition than in terms of ecclesiastical thought. The question of heroism itself is one of them. In heroic literature generally, achievement stems from an often ambivalent and subtle co-operation of human will and supernatural aid or sanction. Indeed, whether in the *Iliad* Achilles carries out the will of Olympian Zeus or Zeus accommodates himself to the fierce will of Achilles is notoriously hard to determine.

Obviously in a Christian poem there is far less doubt as to who is in charge. We are told at the beginning of *Exodus* that we ought to listen to Moses, but that is because Moses is above all else the man who listened to God, who was selected, strengthened, honoured by God, and who, face to face with his Maker, was told the potent secrets of Creation and the Divine Name (lines 8-32). There is no trace here of the shy and hesitant Moses of the Bible. We see a man gifted with intelligence and natural qualities of leadership, but his divine inspiration is so overwhelmingly evident that he is virtually without individual character, even in the heroic sense, closer perhaps to one of Homer's gods than to one of his heroes. Doubtless the fact that the typological tradition equates Moses with Christ has something to do with this way of portraying him.

The true heroic protagonist of the poem is not in fact Moses, but a collective hero: the children of Israel. They are not godlike but entirely human, by turns scared, despairing, confident. It is their emotions we are asked to share, as we can see if we look back over the narrative once more from this point of view.

We are first of all interested in them as characters because they have freedom of choice. In their march out of Egypt they have the divine guidance of Moses and the mysterious pillars, but they are free to disobey these guides. The successive aspects of the pillar(s) are of interest from this standpoint. When it first appears, the pillar gives them great confidence and they proceed joyfully. Apparently they feel less secure at night, for the pillar of fire illuminates their camp principally in order to prevent panic of the wilderness from seizing them (107b-19) — which implies that they are susceptible to such panic, as Moses surely is not. When the pillar next assumes a more formidable role (120-4), threatening to destroy by fire those who disobey Moses, the potential of demoralization is even more strongly implied.

After another march, they camp by the Red Sea. Here, in a few lines (130-4), the poet effectively suggests the relaxing of tension: secure, they can now rest and restore their strength with food as they pitch tents on the hills by the sea. So the relieved Danes relaxed in Heorot just before the shattering incursion of Grendel's mother. Here too 'færspell' crashes in upon a peaceful scene, and terror arises (135 ff).

When the Egyptians appear, the Israelites begin to recall the time of slavery and the way the Egyptians broke their compact with Joseph. Here there is a missing leaf, probably containing a passage where the theme of Egyptian perfidy and ingratitude was developed at greater length. Evidently the Israelites, like some of the characters in the episodes concerning feuds in *Beowulf*, had once put faith in human pledges ('wære,' 140, 147) that have now been treacherously violated. These recollections here really express their old fear in the face of Egyptian evil; it is the poet who reminds us in an if-clause (152-3) of the great pledge by God on their behalf.

What they see advancing on them now (154-99) is a nightmare objectification of their own terror. Earlier readers were mistaken in trying to take this passage too literally and realistically. Only pure emotion could produce this fantasy of countless thousands of grim riders, thoroughly organized and strongly motivated by vengeance, accompanied by a lurid retinue of screeching carrion-birds and howling wolves.

It is hard to tell these animals from the dark host of wolfish Egyptians. The climax of the advance is described:

Forþon wæs in wicum   wop up ahafen,
atol æfenleoð;   egesan stodon,
weredum⁵⁰ wælnet,   þa se woma cwom,
flugon frecne spel.   Feond wæs anmod,
werud wæs wigblac,   oðþæt wlance forsceaf
mihtig engel,   se ða menigeo beheold.   (200-5)

Here, as often in Old English verse, the tension reaches its peak with the 'oðþæt'-clause: the tutelary pillar-angel grants them a night's respite by simply pushing the proud Egyptians back and away. Yet this revelation of power seems to escape the Israelites' notice, if not ours; they use their respite only to realize more fully the depth of their plight. They become 'orwenan,' hopeless, huddling all night on the hills until, with the dawn, Moses takes decisive action.

After his speech, Moses urges the Israelites to hurry forward out of the enemy's embrace ('of feonda fæðme,' 294) into what is by implication the great 'fæðm' of God, and he does this in part by transmuting the threatening sea (called a 'hettend' in line 209) into a symbol of security: the great water-walls become a 'wealfæsten' (283) and a 'randgebeorh' (296), 'fægre gestepte' into a 'wrætlicu wægfaru' (297-8). Thus encouraged, as we have seen, the tribes advance in heroic parade. In the light of our present discussion, it is especially unfortunate that there is a break in the manuscript at this point. We must piece out the description of how they march through the sea from two brief references.

The first of these, in the middle of the drowning description, probably but not certainly alludes to the Israelites:

Brim berstende   blodegsan hweop
sæmanna sið,   oðþæt soð Metod
þurh Moyses hand   mod gerymde,
wide wæðde,   wælfæðmum sweop.   (478-81)

It would be logical at least for 'sæmanna' to refer to the Israelites (cf 'sæmen,' 105), and it would be possible to take the two words in 480b as 'modge rymde,' also referring to them: the sea threatened their passage until God, through Moses' hand, cleared them away

(? to the other side?). If these lines do refer to the Israelites, we may conclude that their crossing was a terrifying experience for them.

The second passage comes near the end of the poem, in these exultant hypermetric verses:

... life gefeon   þa hie oðlæded hæfdon
feorh of feonda dome,   þeah ðe hie hit frecne geneðdon,
weras under wætera hrofas.   Gesawon hie þær weallas standan,
ealle him brimu blodige þuhton,   þurh þa heora beadosearo
                                                                wægon.
Hreðdon hildespelle,   siððan hie þam [herge] wiðforon.   (570-4)

This passage stresses the danger and the fear felt by them during the crossing. It rather clearly credits them with heroic behaviour and genuine achievement in the face of such terror. Thus the crossing is not viewed as a retreat or flight, on the one hand, nor do they stroll complacently across in full confidence that they cannot be harmed. The bloody sea-walls tower over them but they keep moving bravely, later to celebrate their own deeds; they have rescued life from the enemy. The phrase 'frecne geneðdon' is a formula for heroic risk and daring. They have been tested, and have passed the test. In his final speech, Moses repeats God's promise to them (554-64), predicting that their triumphant advance will continue indefinitely ('þæt ge feonda gehwone forð ofergangað,' 562). And the song they sing to celebrate their crossing is a marching-song, a 'fyrdleoð.'

Exodus then, it seems to me, offers its message of human salvation largely in heroic terms, terms perhaps quite unfamiliar or uncongenial to Latin exegetes. That salvation is attained through a complex blending or co-operation of divine guidance and individual effort and courage is certainly not an unchristian concept, but what we should note in *Exodus* is the way the traditional heroic imagination seizes this idea and expresses it in its own energetic fashion, with its own strong contrasts and dramatic heightening. By such means the narrative of the escape from Egypt becomes almost entirely self-sufficient, just *there*; it does not have to be pushed impatiently aside so that we can get at its true 'meaning.' Those who would too closely imitate the old exegetes in the way they read the poem do it no service, and perhaps neglect the powerful and valid religious experience the poem offers.

NOTES

1 *The Old English Exodus*, Yale Studies in English 122 (New Haven 1953, repr. Archon Books 1970); hereafter cited as Edition. I wish to thank here my co-editor, Robert Burlin, for suggesting several improvements in this paper.

2 'New Notes on the Old English *Exodus*,' *Anglia* 90 (1972) 289-324; hereafter cited as 'New Notes'

3 *Catalogue of Manuscripts containing Anglo-Saxon* (Oxford 1957), 408; this possible identification is also mentioned by R.M. Wilson, *The Lost Literature of Medieval England* (2d ed., London 1970), 78.

4 *Studies in the History of Old English Literature* (Oxford 1953), 103

5 'The Date and Dialect of *Genesis A* 852-2936 (Part III),' *Anglia* 70 (1952) 285-94; 292

6 'The Relation of the Cædmonian *Exodus* to the Liturgy,' *MLN* 27 (1912) 97-103

7 'A Reading of OE *Exodus*,' *RES* n.s. 20 (1969) 401-17; 417

8 *The Guest-Hall of Eden* (New Haven 1972), 59-60

9 See Geoffrey Shepherd, 'Scriptural Poetry,' in *Continuations and Beginnings*, ed. E.G. Stanley (London 1966), 24; C.L. Wrenn, *A Study of Old English Literature* (London 1967), 103-4; more recently, T.A. Shippey, *Old English Verse* (London 1972), 137.

10 'The Accents and Points of MS. Junius Eleven,' *Transactions of the Philological Society* (1954) 178-205

11 See James W. Earl, 'Christian Tradition in the Old English "Exodus,"' *NM* 71 (1970) 541-70.

12 See, for instance, Farrell, and Neil D. Isaacs, *Structural Principles in Old English Poetry* (Knoxville 1968), 151-9.

13 Isaacs, 157

14 Earl, 547-60

15 Edition, 14-16; Bright's article cited in note 6 above

16 Edition, 15

17 See, for instance, Bernard F. Huppé, *Doctrine and Poetry: Augustine's Influence on Old English Poetry* (Albany 1959), 217-23; the more thoughtful and persuasive article by J.E. Cross and S.I. Tucker, 'Allegorical Tradition and the Old English *Exodus*,' *Neophilologus* 44 (1960) 122-7, which discusses some possible influence from baptismal tradition, though conceding (124) that the poem is 'not symbolically about baptism'; Earl, *passim*; Shepherd, 31.

18 Lee, 43-8

19 Shippey, 136-43 and 153-4

20 'OE *Exodus* and the *Antiphonary of Bangor*,' *NM* 70 (1969) 658-67

21 'Echos d'un rite hiérosolymitain dans un manuscrit du haut Moyen Age anglais,' *Revue de l'histoire des religions* 165 (1964) 13-47. This study should be read with caution, however, since the author seems to attribute the poems to Cæd-mon, dating them extremely early, and regards the late illustrations as having been an integral part of the book from the start.

22 Shepherd, 13

23 I summarize here other possible parallels: Wis. 18:4 and *Exo* 49-53; Wis. 18:12 and *Exo* 40-1; Wis. 18:15-16 and *Exo* 45, 75-6, 485-97a; Wis. 19:7 and *Exo* 71b-72; Wis. 19:7 and *Exo* 283-8, 312.

24 Edition, 19-20

25 Robinson's articles may be found in *Anglia* 80 (1962) 363-78; *NM* 67 (1966) 356-64; *Anglia* 86 (1968) 14-58; *NM* 69 (1968) 161-71.

26 See 'New Notes,' note to 27b-29; and also notes to 58, 59, 377-9, 432-46, 460, 462; and Edition's notes to 184, 389-96, 547 ff (i.e., 580 ff in the MS).

27 See 'New Notes,' notes to 60, 66b, 87-92, 136, 358; and Edition, notes to 72, 81, 353b.

28 'New Notes,' notes to 224-32, 233-46, 266-7a, 415-18, 519-20

29 'New Notes,' notes to 1-7, 15, 71-72, 310 ff, 353b, 519-20

30 'New Notes,' notes to 68, 71-2, 164b, 289, 384-6

31 'New Notes,' notes to 15, 66b, 70, 71-2

32 Found in *Patrologia Latina*, vol 91; see 'New Notes,' notes to 37b, 46, 289, 519-20, 580.

33 See *PL*, vol 68, col 769; and F. Stegmüller, *Reportorium biblicum medii aevi* (Madrid 1951), III, 8, for the attribution.

34 'New Notes,' notes to 81, 91b-2a, 384-6, 432-46, 554-5, 584

35 The instances are collected in 'New Notes,' note to 121.

36 'Untersuchungen zu den altenglischen Gedichten Genesis und Exodus,' *Anglia* 75 (1957) 1-34

37 'On the Dating of the Old English Poems *Genesis* and *Exodus*,' *Anglia* 77 (1959) 1-11

38 'OE "-calla", "ceallian,"' in *Medieval Literature and Civilization: Studies in Memory of G. N. Garmonsway*, ed. D. A. Pearsall and R. A. Waldron (London 1969) 94-9

39 'Some Kinds of Meaning in Old English Poetry,' *Annuale Mediaevale* 11 (1970) 5-21; the quotation is from 17.

40 *The Interpretation of Old English Poems* (London 1972), 133-59

41 Shippey, 134-43; the quotation is from 141.

42 References henceforth to lines after 516 will be to the manuscript order, not the rearrangement in Edition.

43 Earl, 551 ff

44 See the discussion of these lines in 'New Notes.'
45 Earl, 561-3
46 See Edition, note to 280 ff, and Shippey, 138-40.
47 A point made by Isaacs, 158
48 For a similar idea — horror at the dead man's inability to protect himself from outrage — cf the memorable vignette of the hanged man attacked by a raven in *Fortunes of Men* 33-42.
49 See the first chapter of my book, *A Reading of Beowulf* (New Haven 1968).
50 Edition kept the manuscript reading 'weredon wælnet,' translating as a parenthetic 'corselets protected,' but such a statement seems inappropriate as well as awkward (do the Israelites even have their armour on at this point?). Phrases like 'egesan stodon' often take an indirect object in the dative describing the one affected; emending to 'weredum' (or 'werode') would provide one here. Then 'wælnet' 'death-trap(s)' would be in apposition with 'egesan,' and analogous to such compounds as 'inwitnet' (*Beowulf* 2167) and 'searonet' (*Andreas* 64, 943), both of which suggest treacherous entrapment, exactly the situation here.

NORMAN E. ELIASON

On *Wulf and Eadwacer*

Attempts to interpret *Wulf and Eadwacer* have taken two radically different courses, the one necessarily endeavouring to clarify the obscurities in the poem and the other merely trying to justify them. Scholars who have pursued the latter course are not compelled to explain all the obscurities there, for, however inexplicable some of them may be, they are justifiable nonetheless as characteristic of certain genres, most notably riddles or charms. In riddles obscurities are intentional, constituting the very essence of the genre; in charms they provide a suggestion of mystery or magic, the quality which is the most distinctive feature of the genre. But if *Wulf and Eadwacer* is a riddle, as early scholars maintained, it requires a solution, and none of the various solutions which they proposed proved acceptable. For almost a hundred years the riddle interpretation has been abandoned – quite rightly, I believe, for not only is the poem unsolvable as a riddle but there is no good reason for supposing that it is one.

The main reason for this former supposition is the position of the poem in the Exeter Book, where it immediately precedes and is not distinctly set off from the first of two groups of riddles (1-59) included there. The other group (61-95) comes at the end of the manuscript, being separated from the first by some eight folios. The indistinct separation of one poem from another is by no means unique either in the Exeter Book or in other manuscripts. But the separation of poems naturally belonging together – like the two groups of riddles and perhaps also such pairs of poems as *The Wanderer* and *The*

Seafarer, The Wife's Lament and *The Husband's Message*, or *Widsith* and *Deor* — is certainly odd. It clearly indicates that somehow in the manuscript history of the texts recorded in the Exeter Book someone bungled, failing to preserve their original arrangement. The resulting disarrangement is worth keeping in mind, for it affords a clue to what I think *Wulf and Eadwacer* is about.

The latest scholar to pursue the course adopted by those who had attempted to interpret the poem as a riddle is Donald K. Fry,[1] who took a somewhat different tack, however, viewing it instead as a charm. He might have ignored many of the obscurities in the poem, claiming as he legitimately could have that charms are by their nature cryptic. Instead he undertook to demonstrate, by citing parallels in other Old English charms and by reinterpreting several key words in *Wulf and Eadwacer*, that most of the cryptic remarks there are susceptible of reasonable explanation. In all of this he succeeded so well that I was at first convinced by his case. But doubt rose when I noted what he was forced to do with the word 'wen,' which, according to him, is found twice in the poem ('wenum,' 9; 'wena,' 13). In both instances Fry had to assume that there was scribal error, 'wenn-' being mistakenly written as 'wen-.' Such an error, it is true, is not uncommon in Old English manuscripts but here it is unique, for not only does it occur twice within the space of five lines of verse but it occurs only in the one word of crucial significance. This, I can't help feeling, is too unlikely to be credible. And if so, Fry's whole case collapses, for there is no other mention of 'wen' in the poem. Without 'wen,' it is neither a wen charm nor a charm at all.

All other modern scholars[2] have pursued the other course, the one requiring clarification of the obscurities in the poem. Viewing it as the lament of someone caught up in a tragic love-tangle, they are compelled to explain a number of things which in the poem are unclear. The speaker, all assume, is a woman — necessarily so, they reason, since the lament is about separation from a man (Wulf) and includes mention of their child ('uncerne hwelp,' 16). But though thus in full agreement about the identity of the speaker and the kind of tragic situation in which she is involved, scholars disagree about virtually everything else. Still unresolved are such crucial questions as who caused Wulf's separation from her and why, what part Eadwacer played in the affair, who the father of her offspring was, whether Eadwacer or Wulf, why she should refer to this child as a whelp — the only instance in Old English where the term is thus applied to a human offspring —

and why just after referring to it as 'uncerne hwelp' she should mention some poetry in precisely the same way ('uncerne giedd,' 19). For all of these questions except the last — to which we shall turn later — answers have been proposed, but like the earlier riddle-solutions they gain no general acceptance.

Viewed as a dramatic monologue or however else it may be labelled — an elegy, a lyric, or a *Frauenlied* — *Wulf and Eadwacer* remains utterly baffling. The awkward fact that the poem itself does not provide answers to any of the crucial questions which this view poses is got around in two different ways. The first is by maintaining that the underlying story was so well known to the poet's audience that he did not need to fill in the details. Most scholars are now content simply to assume that this was true; some are still futilely attempting to demonstrate its truth by linking up the underlying story with some well-known legend or other. The other way is by maintaining that the obscurity of the poem does not really matter, for, however little we may understand what it is about, it is nonetheless a singularly moving expression of grief.[3] Neither of these ways of dodging the issue settles it.

Another issue which is also dodged, it seems to me, is the one raised by the form of the poem, more particularly its inexplicably irregular versification. The fact that at least twelve of its nineteen lines are irregular in this respect[4] cannot be ignored, as it often is, nor has it ever been satisfactorily explained. Attempts to vindicate these flaws on the ground that they serve a structural function, marking off couplets or stanzas in the poem, are unconvincing. And excusing the flaws as characteristic features of 'popular poetry' merely begs the question.[5]

The careless form of the poem, which surely ought to be admitted rather than glossed over, is evidently the result of haste, not mere ineptitude. Some touches of skill are apparent there, most notably the refrain-like 'ungelic is us,' which has captured everyone's fancy as being felicitous in itself and nicely tantalizing in its repetition. In neither instance, to be sure, is its meaning quite clear, for, explicit though the comparison seems to be, just what it involves is ambiguous. This, I believe, is deliberate, intended to be amusing rather than mystifying, however, or the result of an urge to be clever rather than clear.

If I am right in thinking that the poem was hastily written by someone intent on being amusing rather than clear, the two most striking characteristics of the poem, its careless form and its obscurity — are thus accounted for, and it also suggests what kind of poem it may be.

I am inclined to believe that, instead of a dramatic monologue, addressed to a general audience assumed to know its underlying story
and to be moved by an anonymous woman lamenting her tragic lot
in being separated from her lover, the poem is a private communication addressed to a colleague, ruefully but playfully protesting about
the mishandling of their poetry, which instead of being kept intact —
as it should if it is to be appreciated properly — has been separated,
some of it being copied in one place of a manuscript[6] and the rest in
another, less favourable place. Within the poem, as thus construed,
this separation of their work is the only fact clearly expressed, being
revealed there in the two concluding lines, the meaning of which is
clearer than that of any other pair of lines in the poem — or so it
seems to me and would have seemed also, I should think, to its intended recipient, who without the enlightenment provided there might
have failed to get the point. All the rest of the poem, obscure as it
now seems to us, was presumably not obscure to him, if, as I am assuming, he was aware of the underlying facts and could both grasp
and appreciate the fanciful way they were alluded to. What these
facts were, there is no way of knowing and little point in speculating
about, except for the few possibilities which I shall mention later.
    At this juncture, however, we need the text[7] before us:

<pre>
    Leodum is minum   swylce him mon lac gife;
    willað hy hine aþecgan,   gif he on þreat cymeð.
    Ungelic is us.
    Wulf is on iege,   ic on oþerre.
  5 Fæst is þæt eglond,   fenne biworpen,
    sindon wælreowe   weras þær on ige;
    willað hy hine aþecgan,   gif he on þreat cymeð.
    Ungelic is us.
    Wulfes ic mines widlastum   wenum dogode
 10 þonne hit wæs renig weder   ond ic reotugu sæt;
    þonne mec se beaducafa   bogum bilegde,
    wæs me wyn to þon,   wæs me hwæþre eac lað.
    Wulf, min Wulf,   wena me þine
    seoce gedydon,   þine seldcymas —
 15 murnende mod,   nales meteliste.
    Gehyrest þu, Eadwacer,   uncerne earne hwelp?
    ... bireð Wulf to wuda.
    þæt mon eaþe tosliteð   þætte næfre gesomnad wæs,
    uncer giedd, geador.
</pre>

Instead of a literal, line-by-line translation and complete textual commentary,[8] all that seems necessary to provide here is a brief paraphrase showing what I take to be the sense of the lines and an explanation of why I thus construe them:

1-2   A man is welcome if, instead of alone and empty-handed, he comes bringing gifts; so it is with my people or songs.

3   It is otherwise with Wulf and me.

4-6   We are alone, isolated in two different places, and the place he occupies is especially unfortunate.

7   He would be welcome there, i.e. the position would be tolerable, if he were not alone.

8   That is why it is otherwise with us, unwelcome as we both thus are in our isolation.

9-10   His position sometimes causes me much grief,

11-12   which is mitigated when I consider my own secure position in the manuscript

13-15   but is renewed when I realize that the misplacement of Wulf will never be corrected.

16-17   Are you, Eadwacer — ever alert as you ought to be — aware of our Wulf's plight now that he is thus misplaced?

18-19   (The mistake is an understandable one), for it is easy to separate something which has never been properly combined, such as our joint poetic endeavour.

My interpretation proceeds on the assumption that lines 18-19 are to be construed literally and lines 1-17 figuratively, the reverse of the procedure used in interpreting the poem as a dramatic monologue, for then lines 1-17 are construed literally and 18-19 figuratively, as 'uncer giedd' (19) seems to require. But whether 'giedd,' which means poetry of some sort or other, is emended or given a figurative sense so that it means something else, the result is not very satisfactory, producing an ending just as obscure as all of the rest of the poem is. In a poem as obscure as this one certainly is, it seems reasonable to expect some light somewhere, and even though the light comes only at the end it is surely welcome there. Possibly an inkling of what the poem is about comes earlier, in the opening lines or indeed in the very first word. If so, 'leodum' ('people') — which, however the poem is interpreted, is rather senseless — must be emended to 'leoðum'[9] ('songs'), thus bringing the first and last words of the poem into nice accord.

If the author's real concern as expressed in 18-19 was the separation of some sort of poetry ('giedd'), the joint work ('uncer') of himself and the recipient, the latter was expected to grasp the comparison employed in 1-17, where this separation is likened to the separation of two people, one of whom almost necessarily therefore is given a name (Wulf). Helping the recipient to grasp the comparison is the twice used phrase 'ungelic is us,' which, since explicitly expressed similes such as this are rare in Old English poetry, serves to alert him to the possibility, and which, by being negatively put ('ungelic' rather than 'gelic') serves to warn him that the comparison involves dissimilarities of some sort — as indeed it does.

But the comparison, though fanciful, is not farfetched. What makes it seem so is the way the author develops it, letting his fancy run pretty wild in describing the places where the poetry has been separated (on different islands, in a fortress surrounded by fen and guarded by fierce men), its reception there (less welcome than if it were all together), the ill fate particularly of one portion of the poetry (referred to as Wulf and as their whelp, depicted as having been borne off to the woods, where in his lonely misery he is to be imagined as piteously whimpering) and the author's distress about this (weeping in the rain and becoming sick at the thought that Wulf will never return).[10] Seemingly especially fanciful is the description of the place occupied by the other portion of the poetry, where, as the author puts it, 'some battle-ready man has laid or put me down' (11), which is rendered even more fanciful when 'bogum' is construed as meaning 'in some tree limbs or someone's arms.' I, however, take it to mean 'in folded parchment leaves,'[11] a sense which not only fits the immediate context better but nicely fits the over-all context of the poem as I am interpreting it.

One objection to interpreting it as a private communication is the paucity of information it provides. It reveals virtually none of the things we would like to know nor even the things we might reasonably expect, such as the identity of the author and of the recipient. Neither is named — certainly not the author, nor, I believe, the person he was addressing. To be sure, the latter is called Eadwacer but this is most likely a descriptive epithet rather than a name. Meaning, as it does, 'ever alert or vigilant,'[12] it is evidently a humorously ironic way of gently chiding the recipient for whatever blame he bore in the mishandling of the poetry. If, as I am assuming mainly because it is the simplest among various possibilities, 'Eadwacer' was a scribe, it is interesting rather than puzzling that the author should refer to the poetry as theirs ('uncer giedd') rather than his own. For the same reason I assume that the recipient is this Eadwacer, not some other undesignated person, and therefore I treat lines 16-17 as I do, making the subject of 'bireð' to be someone or something indicated in what I take to be a lacuna filling out line 17. The whelp, to judge by the over-all context, must surely refer to Wulf, a name perhaps inspired by the term or the term inspired by the name.[13] Although Wulf might be regarded as the name of a poet[14] associated with the author in some joint poetic endeavour, it is more likely that the name is intended to designate some poem or poems which the author wrote and was irked to see misplaced. The latter identification best accords with the way the dual form 'uncer' is used, being applied in line 19 to the joint work ('uncer giedd') of the author and his scribe and in line 17 to that portion of their work which has been misplaced (fancifully refer-red to there as 'uncerne hwelp' but previously as 'min Wulf'). What this poetry comprised — either the misplaced portion or the whole work — is impossible to say and idle to guess. Of course if the posi-tion of the poem in the manuscript could safely be regarded as a clue, then the work would seem to be the two groups of riddles which I have mentioned earlier and to which the riddle-like fancy employed in our poem bears some resemblance. But if its position is without significance, the work referred to might be any of the pairs of poems in the Exeter Book which I have also mentioned or any other poetry recorded there, elsewhere, or now lost.

Disappointing as the poem thus proves to be as a source of any worthwhile information, the supposition that it is a private communi-cation cannot be ruled out on this ground alone. Indeed, the suppo-sition gains in credibility thereby, for intimate communications — to judge by those I receive or send — rarely mention facts of any conse-quence or in such way that they make much sense to an outsider.

The other general objection that might be raised is that the inter-pretation I am suggesting succeeds only in downgrading a poem which has won wide acclaim, reducing it to a bit of verse too trivial to merit any acclaim either for its substance or for its execution. In this re-spect, however, it is not anomalous, for among the surviving Old Eng-lish poems found in the Exeter Book and elsewhere there are others which are no better and some that are worse. But trivial as *Wulf and Eadwacer* thus becomes, it is worth notice at least as an instance where an Old English poet, instead of voicing gloomy solemnity, is having a little fun, and where, instead of exercising his fancy to conjure up ominous demons and monsters and dragons of momentous significance, he is doing so here to banter a scribe for his bungling.

This is not the only instance where scribal bungling has provoked a poet to complain and to register his complaint in verse. Chaucer did so too, addressing his communication directly to Adam his scribe and specifying where and how he had bungled. Had Chaucer chosen to chide Adam otherwise, failing to make his meaning perfectly plain or to mention him by name, but instead exercising his fancy as freely as the author of *Wulf and Eadwacer* did, I suspect that the 'Wordes unto Adam'[15] might have caused scholars to struggle for years in a vain effort to untangle its perplexities and perhaps even to make fantastic claims about 'the passionate intensification of grief' expressed there.

NOTES

1 'Wulf and Eadwacer: A Wen Charm,' *Chaucer Review* 5 (1970) 247-63
2 The ones whom I have consulted and taken into account here are: A.C. Bouman, '*Leodum is Minum*: Beadohild's Complaint,' *Neophilologus* 33 (1949) 103-13; John F. Adams, '"Wulf and Eadwacer": An Interpretation,' *MLN* 73 (1958) 1-5; P.J. Frankis, '*Deor* and *Wulf and Eadwacer*: Some Conjectures,' *Medium Ævum* 31 (1962) 161-75; Kemp Malone, 'Two English *Frauenlieder*,' *Comparative Literature* 14 (1962) 106-17; Alain Renoir, '*Wulf and Eadwacer*: A Noninterpretation,' in *Franciplegius: Medieval and Linguistic Studies in Honor of Francis Peabody Magoun, Jr.* (New York 1965), 147-63; Neil D. Isaacs, *Structural Principles in Old English Poetry* (Knoxville, Tenn. 1968), 114-17; Ruth Lehmann, 'The Metrics and Structure of *Wulf and Eadwacer*,' *PQ* 48 (1969) 151-65; Karl Heinz Göller, *Geschichte der altenglischen Literatur* (Berlin 1971), 78-84; and Alvin A. Lee, *The Guest-Hall of Eden: Four Essays on the Design of Old English Poetry* (New Haven 1972), 156-8.
3 Untenable as this critical judgment would seem to be — and to my mind it is simply preposterous — it has gained wide acceptance. The only scholar who is forthright about it, however, is Renoir, who devotes his whole essay to its defence, concluding with the extravagant claim, 'Whether or not the speaker is an exile in a foreign land, whether or not the man who embraces her is her lover, *Wulf and Eadwacer* reaches us through the passionate intensification of grief, which it expresses as few poems have done in any language.'
4 Eight are clearly exceptional in length, four (3, 8, 7, 19) consisting only of half-

lines, each of which is preceded by a line longer than ordinary and somewhat irregular in metre; three (9, 13, 14) are irregular in metre; and one (12) is irregular
in alliteration.

5 Noteworthy is the fact that *The Wife's Lament*, which Malone couples with *Wulf
and Eadwacer*, exhibits none of these features.

6 Not of course by the Exeter Book scribe but by some predecessor. The poem, I
assume, was written in the margin of this earlier work, whence the Exeter Book
scribe mistakenly copied it off.

7 Cited from the Krapp-Dobbie, *The Exeter Book*, (New York 1936), the most
readily available edition. Their text is faithful to that of the manuscript, except
for the alignment, capitalization, and punctuation, which they supply and which
I alter.

8 Which are readily available elsewhere; Malone and Mrs Lehmann provide the most
detailed commentary.

9 The scribal error involved, miswriting 'ð' as 'd,' is a frequent one, the Exeter
Book scribe being guilty of it thirteen verse-lines earlier, where he wrote 'ear-
foða' as 'earfoda' (*Deor* 30).

10 I construe Wulf's 'seldcymas' (14) as litotes, meaning that he will never return,
i.e., that the misplacement is not correctable.

11 That is, by reading the word not as 'bōgum' but as 'bogum.' 'Boga' has various
senses in Old English, all of them referring to something bent, curved, or folded;
hence, though attested by only one citation there, Toller's sense V (in his Supplement to the Bosworth *Anglo-Saxon Dictionary*, Oxford 1921), 'folded parchment,' is wholly acceptable.

12 Much the same meaning Toller assigns the name ('easily roused [?], alert, vigilant') except for the modifier which, in order to be compatible with 'alert' or 'vigilant,' requires the meaning 'keenly' or 'ever' rather than 'easily.' Like Toller, I
am uncertain whether the 'd' of 'Ead-' should be emended to 'ð,' for though the
'd' may be a scribal error for 'ð' (see note 9) it may well represent a phonological
change. Change of 'ð' to 'd,' not uncommon in Old English, is especially likely
in this instance, for when used as combining forms 'eað-' and 'ead-' are often
semantically very similar — a fact which is obscured rather than clarified in several
of the Bosworth-Toller entries.

13 Or, among other possibilities, that the name was suggested by the outcast's place
or by the content or some other feature of the poetry designated thus.

14 If so, 'Wulf' was probably a nickname, his actual name being something like
'Cynewulf' or 'Wulfstan' (see Henry Bosley Woolf, *The Germanic Principles of
Name-Giving* [Baltimóre 1939], 3) — but not, I hasten to add, either of the two
famous Old English writers bearing these names. To identify Wulf as this Wulfstan
would be absurd. Though less absurd, to identify him as Cynewulf would involve

the same sort of desperate conjectures indulged in more than a century ago (see Krapp-Dobbie, lv).

15 The fact that Chaucer's little poem is found in only one manuscript is a clear indication, I believe, that it was a private communication intended solely for Adam's benefit and possible amusement.

J.E. CROSS

Mainly on philology
and the interpretative criticism
of *Maldon*

Philology, as I wish to interpret it, means care for words and precision
about words. It is a necessity to the interpretative critic who listens
receptively and explains with intellectual argument what the poet is
saying and meaning. Philological precision, however, does not imply
rigidity nor, necessarily, definitiveness of interpretation since words
in context are malleable. They are shaped by pressures, of meanings
in other contexts which establish an area of meaning in the language
of the period, of the immediate context of the poetic phrase (viewed,
in Old English poetry, against the corpus of poetic phrases), of the
syntactical context, and, finally, of the context of the poet's intention
as distinguished from emphases *within* the poem, tested against the
attitudes of the age.

I hope not to be misunderstood about what I think poetry is when
I add that a poem to the explicator is the sum and the shaping of the
individual words. The words are the statistics which, in group, are to
be interpreted. All this, I am sure, is truistic and is stated not as a
high philosophy of explicatory criticism but merely as a working procedure — here to test some recent comments on *The Battle of Maldon*.

In a comparatively recent paper George Clark has suggested of *Maldon* that: 'Intuition may identify the poem as heroic, the hero as
Byrhtnoth, and the theme as the praise of heroes and condemnation
of cowards, but orthodox readings of *Maldon* take quite another
course and strand on the shoals of one or more of three recurring
errors which may be described as the lexical, the historical, and the

analogical.'[1] Let us not here consider what intuition is, nor suggest that where Dr Clark's intuition and my attention to words leads is necessarily different, but let us analyse first the 'lexical error' in the 'orthodox readings.'

The crucial 'lexical error' is, apparently, the phrase 'ongunnon lytegian,' for which 'neither the context nor the narrator's tone support Bosworth-Toller's gloss, "to act cunningly", for *lytegian*' (68). 'Lytegian' is a unique word in Old English and Dr Clark proceeds rightly to the dictionary for related words in order to test the lexicographer's interpretation in this instance. But, as it will appear, he goes no further than the dictionaries' citations for the related words. For such a study, however, dictionaries are merely works of reference, always to be tested, since lexicographers establish an area of meaning for a word from its use in individual contexts, and the identification of each example in its own context is, of course, the opinion, although reasoned, of the lexicographer.[2]

The words related to 'lytegian' appear in Old English/Latin glosses, both individual and continuous, and in continuous literary texts. From these Dr Clark chooses two examples from different glossators and one from a continuous rendering of a Latin text in order to dispute the dictionary's interpretation of 'lytegian.'

It is reported, probably apocryphally, that one eminent Anglo-Saxon linguist has said: 'I like glosses, there's nothing literary about them,' but glosses as evidence of precise meaning are of varying value. They need assessment and interpretation as Professor H.D. Meritt has perceptively shown in his life's work. So that when Dr Clark cites BTS[3] which offers 'lytig' (adjective), 'in a good sense, *prudent*,' we should note, most importantly, that all the five examples are found in one Kentish gloss to Proverbs[4] in the tenth-century manuscript Cotton Vespasian D.VI,[5] and, further, that the literary context of the scripture which is glossed may allow a closer definition of what 'lytig' meant to the glossator if he was accurate.[6] 'Lytig' (actually 'letig') glosses 'astutus' at Proverbs 13:16 and at 14:15, 'versutus' at 14:17 and 'callidus' at 22:3. Also 'leti' glosses 'callidus' at Proverbs 12:16 and 'versutus' at 12:23. All the Latin words which are glossed can be used in a good or a bad sense and BTS accurately divides the examples of 'letig,' 'leti' in this text, placing the example of 'letig' at Proverbs 14:17 ('vir versutus odiosus est') 'in a bad sense.' The other examples 'in a good sense' gloss the Latin words, however, in revealing situations. All these present the 'letig' man in opposition to one who helps to define him, at 12:16 against a 'fatuus,' at 12:23 against 'insipientes,' at 13:16 against a 'fatuus,' at 14:15 against an 'innocens,' at 22:3 against an 'innocens.' These individual men of Proverbs are the opposite of fools or innocents. One dissembles about his injuries and does not become angry (12:16), one conceals his knowledge (12:23), one does all things with counsel (13:16), one considers his steps (14:15), one saw the evil and hid himself (22:3). The actual advice to some of the individuals here is clearly not applicable in a specific way to the Vikings at Maldon who certainly do not wish to hide themselves, although they may well have taken counsel and considered their steps, but the sum of the advice suggests a Proverbial ideal of a shrewd man who is no fool. 'Lytig' to the Kentish glossator in the five cases is, I suggest, taken in this limited 'good sense.'

Dr Clark offers another example from a gloss which, for some reason, he does not quote in full from the dictionary, when he says that '*astutia* once corresponds to *of lote* '[7] as evidence that 'lot' (noun) can be used in a good sense as is Latin 'astutia.' Unfortunately the actual gloss both in the dictionary citation and in its context says clearly the opposite. It should be read in full: 'astu, astutia doli, of lote.'[8] 'Astu' is the word glossed in Prudentius's *Psychomachia* 667 which runs: 'nascitur hic inopina Mali lacrimabilis astu / tempestas...' and which the Loeb translator renders: 'and here rises a storm unlooked for through the *cunning* of woeful Evil.'[9] The Latin glosses in this manuscript (Cotton Cleopatra C.VIII) are apparently in a different hand from the vernacular glosses.[10] The Latin glossator thus certainly agrees with the Loeb translator when he adds a modifying genitive 'doli' to 'astutia' since 'dolus' in later classical writings normally means 'guile, cunning, deception.'[11] The Old English glossator could have been influenced by the context in Prudentius (which seems likely since he notes the syntactical function of 'astu' with his '*of* lote') and/or by the Latin gloss so that it is an extreme probability that 'lot' is used in a bad sense here.

Another case is a phrase from the vernacular version of Gregory's *Cura pastoralis* where, in Clark's view,[12] the noun 'lytignes' renders 'astutia' in a good sense in the phrase 'ðære næddran lytignes' as equivalent to 'astutia serpentis.' Here, of course, we are considering the attitude and intention of King Alfred or of one of his helpers. The phrase appears in that section of the *Cura pastoralis* / *Hierdeboc*, entitled in Old English: 'Ðætte on oðre wisan sint to manienne ða bilwitan, on oðre ða ðweoran ond ða lytegan,'[13] and by Gregory: 'Quomodo admonendi simplices et versipelles.'[14] 'Lytegan' here appears to be an extending synonym for 'ðweoran' which is equivalent to 'versipelles,' 'skilled in dissimulation, sly, cunning, crafty, subtle.'[15] Relevantly for the discussion we note that the word 'lytegan' is used in this section to clarify the intention of Gregory, not necessarily as the normal Old English equivalent to the Latin. In Henry Sweet's edition at 237.6 and at 239.3 it is used for 'impuri,' and at 241.14, 15 and at 243.10 it is used together with 'unclænan' for 'impuri.' These 'versipelles,' 'impuri,' 'ðweoran,' 'unclænan,' 'lytegan' are described by their actions, illustrated by the natural analogy of the 'ericius' of Isaiah 34:15 and admonished by scriptural testimonies and in direct speech. Their basic vice is the dishonesty and duplicity of deceit. Obviously there is some pressure from the choice of 'lytig' to describe these people (and from the use of 'lytiglice' (adverb), 'lytelic' (adjective), 'lot' (noun) in a bad sense in this section)[16] on the meaning and use of 'lytignes' in the example cited by Clark where Gregory advises the 'simplices,' 'bilwitan.' Gregory has here quoted Matthew 10:16: 'Estote prudentes sicut serpentes, et simplices sicut columbae' and explains the quotation to indicate that 'prudentia,' 'astutia,' and 'simplicitas' must modify each other. The 'astutia serpentis' should sharpen the simplicity of the dove, but the dove's simplicity should temper the 'astutia' of the serpent: 'quatenus nec seducti per prudentiam calleant, nec ab intellectus studio ex simplicitate torpescant.'[17] But the Anglo-Saxon anticipates the danger inherent in 'prudentia' and/or 'astutia,' which is indicated in Gregory's explanation, even in his version of Gregory's statement describing the good effect of 'astutia' on simplicity. This is the comment which encloses the quotation by the dictionary and Dr Clark:

> Forðæm on ðara acorenra monna heortan sceal ðære nædran lytignes and hire nið ðære culfran biliwitnesse gescirpan, and eft ðære culfran biliwitnesse sceal gemetgian ðære nædran wærscipe and hire nið ...[18]

For Gregory's 'astutia serpentis' the Anglo-Saxon has 'lytignes' and 'nið' in one case, and 'wærscipe' and 'nið' in the other, where, in each case, the second item of the doublet is 'nið,' most certainly a vice or the effect of vice[19] in Old English. We may add that all the references provided by BT and BTS from the OE version of *Cura pastoralis* (and a few more not recorded), for examples of 'lytig,' 'lytelic' (adjective), 'lytelice' (adverb), 'lot' (noun) indicate in their contexts that the words were consistently used 'in a bad sense,' as the dictionaries record.

Dr Clark considers two more OE words, 'belytegian' and 'lutan,' but his handling of these needs only summary discussion. He accepts that 'belytegian' means: 'allure, inveigle, seduce' (BT, s.v.), as it clearly should in the only context in which it occurs, the OE version of *Orosius*, where Philip 'belytegade ealle Crece on his geweald.'[20] Philip had gone 'mid searewan' throughout the Greek nation, the trickery having been his playing-off of the warring city-states against each other. But Clark suggests (68) that 'the meaning of *belytegian* is not conclusive here, compare *belædan*, mislead, and *lædan*, lead.' Once again there is selection from the statement of the dictionary. 'Belædan' (BT, s.v.) is interpreted 'to bring, lead by, mislead, lead,' where 'mislead' as one of four suggestions is obviously the lexicographer's way of 'blanketing the target.'[21] But an analysis of all the examples in BT and BTS will demonstrate to any who wish to test them that in no case *need* a translation 'mislead' be given, and in some examples a translation 'mislead' is erroneous. Where there are Latin equivalents to some examples these include the verbs 'inducere,' 'inferre,' 'inrogare,' 'ingerere,' only one of which can mean 'mislead.'[22] Further, the analysis of the prefix 'be-' in BT[23] is certainly supported by the examples of 'belædan.' This analysis also suggests only two possibilities for the function of 'be-' in 'belytegian,' that it gives 'an intensive signification to a transitive verb' (BT, s.v. 'be' 1) or it does 'not indicate any perceptible variation in the sense' (BT, s.v. 'be' 3). It would appear that 'belytegian' must remain as evidence for the meaning of 'lytegian' as our lexicographers said.

'Lutan' is said to mean: 'to bend, bow, make obeisance' (68) which presumably is the OED interpretation of ME, NE, 'lout,' verb 1, since BT gives for 'lutan': 'to lout, bow, bend forward, stoop, fall down before one.'[24] But, more importantly, no example in OE contexts indicates that the simple physical act of bowing implies 'obsequious' behaviour. This is one of the things which Clark would have the Vikings (not) showing at Maldon. If such a development took place in verbs derived from 'lutan' so as to mean 'to be obsequious,' it had not happened in Old English.

We are now left with one Anglo-Saxon, a tenth-century Kentishman, who used 'lytig' to render Latin words in their contexts both in a good and in a bad sense. But the words related to 'lytegian' are not rare. There are sufficient examples of these words in clear contexts among the examples cited in the dictionaries to indicate an overwhelming probability of such words in unclear contexts having a bad sense. Figures are not necessarily impressive but even non-gamblers who wish to test the dictionaries will appreciate that 'lytegian' 'in a good sense' is an outsider. Leaving aside any case which needs further argument I count, in BT and BTS, eleven examples (plus more unrecorded)[25] for 'lytig,' one for 'lytelic' (adjective), six for 'lytelice' (adverb), ten for 'lot' (noun) all 'in a bad sense' and occurring in texts which include the version of *Boethius*, of *Cura pastoralis*, of *Orosius, The Exeter Gnomes, The Metres of Boethius*, Wulfstan, Ælfric, besides anonymous prose tracts and glosses. The pressure from the other examples seems formidable.

Nevertheless the *Maldon* poet could be the second man in Old English to use 'lytegian' (or a related word) 'in a good sense,' so the explicator should consider other words and phrases within the poem which express the poet's intention. These are evidence for the 'narrator's tone.' One does not wish to retrace old paths but my simple study some time ago[26] of the words which describe the Vikings, although then written to indicate that they were not devils from hell, gives no evidence that this 'hateful' enemy ('laðe gystas,' 86; 'laþ þeod,' 90) would be complimented for astuteness in a good sense in acting 'wisely, sensibly or prudently.' But there is evidence, I suggest, that the Byrhtnoth presented by the poet could fall to the 'lytignes' of the Vikings at this point.

We shall attempt not to fall into Dr Clark's 'historical error' since we regard the poem as imaginative opinion of the actions only based on the real events with which, however, some of the poetic statements certainly have contact. The poet has selected from, elaborated on, and presumably omitted from a knowledge (not necessarily detailed) of the real events to suit his own purpose as distinguished in the poem.

At the quiet opening of the poem as we have it, Byrhtnoth appears as the calm experienced leader preparing a defensive position against the Vikings. He sends away the horses and commands his men to put their minds to battle. His firm intent is reflected in the action of the young man who releases the hawk. Offa's kinsman 'perceived that he (Byrhtnoth) would not suffer "yrhðo,"' and whether this is 'slackness' or 'cowardice,'[27] it reflects favourably on Byrhtnoth's firmness of purpose. Byrhtnoth now places the 'fyrd' telling them 'how they had to stand and defend the position' (19) and leaves them with a last encouragement: 'he ordered them to hold their shields right, firm in their hands, and not be afraid' (20-1).[28] These men play no further part in the poetic battle as a named group and their poetic role here may well be to present a simple revelation of Byrhtnoth's experience in control of men but also as an indication that he was intent on defence.

Now Byrhtnoth dismounts with his beloved 'heorðwerod' and the Viking spokesman makes his contemptuous offer across the water. His harsh speech of threat is important for its effect on Byrhtnoth, although, through it, the poet creates a type Viking in English eyes, and the passage reveals how careful the poet can be about words. The choice put to Byrhtnoth is reiterated by antitheses even within the short verse 'treasure for protection' (31), 'money for peace' (39), but also in balance over the whole line: 'we will confirm a truce for that gold' (35). Lest there be any doubt what the money is, twice it is specifically named as 'tribute' (32), and 'tax' (40), and Byrhtnoth is asked if he wishes to 'ransom' (37) his people. Most contemptuous of all is that no price is named. For the Vikings it is to be 'at their own judgment' (38), a phrase, as we all know, having legal connotation to suggest a meaning similar to our own 'unconditional surrender.'

Despite the statement of *The Anglo-Saxon Chronicle* for 991 AD this year was not the first time that money had been successfully demanded of defending nations by the Vikings. In 865 the Kentishmen had promised 'feoh wiþ þam friðe,' in 872 the Mercians may have bought their enemies off, and perhaps even Alfred had had to do the same in 876.[29] But Byrhtnoth, like his contemporary Archbishop Wulfstan, regarded it as 'shameful extortion.'[30] He is 'yrre and anræd' (44), a phrase which both by denotation and connotation gives an insight into his character as the poet has created him. In translation and dictionary meaning the phrase reads: 'angry and resolute,' but by its use in *Beowulf* (1575) it implies 'as a hero.'[31] Byrhtnoth's first words may carry an implication also. The Viking messenger had begun by addressing the leader in the singular (30); he may then have turned to the people in the plural (31, 32, 34) and finally returned to the leader (36, 37). Byrhtnoth begins his reply: 'Do you hear, seamen, what this people say' (45), when no sound of advice or consultation has been heard from them *in the poem*. Byrhtnoth is confidently and egoistically his own man, as, quite frankly, a tactical commander on the field of such minor battle as this should be, but if, as has been suggested, his 'flaw' is to forget his responsibility to his followers, he may well have left them aside here.

His whole speech is a pointed riposte to the messenger's demands in its echoes and contrasts. The words 'gafol' (46, 61), 'tribute,' and 'sceatt' (56), 'tax,' are taken up, the second word is an echoed line (cf 40, 56). Where the Viking speaks of 'hearde hilde,' ('hard battle' 33), Byrhtnoth comments: 'Nor shall you so softly ('swa softe,' 59) gain treasure.' Where the enemy demand payment 'at their own judgment' (38) the Englishman replies: 'before we give tribute, spear and sword, grim battle, shall *decide the terms* between us' (60, 61) choosing a word 'geseman,' which, in other contexts,[32] is used of judgments to settle disputes satisfactorily or at least acceptably to both parties. It is well chosen here. There are other telling phrases, as we all know; the irony of 'heregeatu' (48), and 'it seems shameful to me for you to go aboard with our tax, without a fight, now that you have come so far here into our country' (55-8), heavy sarcasm carrying the obvious implication: 'Let's make your journey worthwhile.'

The care taken over these opposing speeches is reanalysed here to indicate that Byrhtnoth's speech will bear further detailed observation for his attitude and character. Honour means much to him ('It seems shameful to me,' 55) and, although his mind is still on defence ('here stands a nobleman, undaunted ... who will defend this homeland ...' 51-2), the sarcasm of lines 55-8 implies that he hopes a battle will take place. If it does he is confident in himself ('unforcuð eorl,' 51) and also in enemy slaughter, when he says: 'heathens will fall in the battle,' where, as I have suggested,[33] the phrase 'hæþene æt hilde' (55) is more emphatic against its stylistic background than in Modern English translation.

These are simply words and, seemingly, the high water prevents the armies coming to grips immediately. Yet Byrhtnoth, apparently, has his men near enough to the water for arrows on either side to claim victims. Both armies were restive, as the poet says: 'it seemed to them too long' (66) to wait before they could join battle. The tension is held for a few lines as the two armies are presented 'bestriding' (68) to the River Blackwater 'mid prasse'[34] but all is in readiness.

Now in a dramatically complete short verse: 'The high water ebbed' (72) and the causeway ('bricg,' 74, 78; 'ford,' 81, 88) is clear of water. But Byrhtnoth, true to his intention, offers defence by placing three men in the path of the oncoming Vikings. The Vikings in the poem realize that there is no way to break their resolute resistance. They are no fools in war to whittle away their forces in this way, when they realize that the causeway is held by such 'bitere' defenders.

It is now clear that Byrhtnoth is not to be allowed the defensive battle on the terms which he desired. But he decides to fight forsaking defence, not surprisingly to those who have caught the previous poetic hints about him. A confident man who has prepared himself mentally for battle would need clear-headed patience to refuse. Yet in the poet's implication and statement, this is a foolish and wrong decision, and this opinion is a shock. As Dr Battaglia and I[35] suggested independently in the same year, two points were clear and now remain clear. If the Vikings 'used cunning' ('ongunnon lytegian'), or even by an extremely remote possibility they were 'astute' (on their own behalf, not Byrhtnoth's), Byrhtnoth was deceived and the action is regarded as foolish by the poet. No one may even debate about the second statement. It is the common poetic figure of litotes or understatement.[36] It states the poet's opinion that the leader should not have allowed any leeway to the Vikings at this point of time.[37] The reason for this deluded and wrong action is Byrhtnoth's 'ofermod.'

T.A. Shippey has recently referred to this word in a suggestive statement that: 'in Old English the quality of the hero can even be *verbally* ambiguous.'[38] Such ambiguity or duality of meaning in a word is illustrated by 'wlencu(o)' (*Beowulf* 338-9, 508), but in that poem, of course, to indicate that 'wlencu' is not ambiguous in the individual contexts.[39] A word may have distinct meanings in different contexts or even be ambiguous in one context, but each context needs to be assessed in its own philological terms and in relation to the emphases of the poem. When Mr Shippey generalizes that: 'Old English heroes are not meant to be judged'[40] and refers to Hygelac's fatal raid on the Frisians 'because of *wlenco*,' one cannot ignore its results in the disaster which befell the Geatish nation partly because of this action for this reason. The emphases of the poem limit the semantic possibilities of 'wlencu' in the context, so that either the ethic or the man is judged by the poet with the comment. In *Maldon*, however, it appears that the poetic emphases are against criticism of the heroic ethic, although the continued recall of earlier Germanic and Old English poetic attitudes has been rightly labelled as 'false'[41] to the real conditions of the tenth century. The 'falseness' is, I suggest, deliberate anachronism for idealization of real men from a real battle into noble heroes in a poetic battle. Only a few men, Byrhtnoth and those who fled, are criticized by the poet, cowards because they did not live up to the old ideal, Byrhtnoth not for his part in accepting the ideal and facing the Vikings with boldness, but for giving up a tactical advantage.

The judgment here is on him only among the English loyalists and only for this action. No one doubts that Byrhtnoth behaves heroically and his heroism is not marred by his tactical error. A valid reason for the notice of the mistake by the poet is, of course, that it highlights the heroism of the retainers who speak in the old heroic terms and loyally fight in fulfilment of their stated or presumed vows to their leader.

Against the background of emphases distinguished in the poem and the immediate context of 'ofermod' we now consider the semantic possibilities of the word. Since there has been some slight misrepresentation we recall that 'ofermod' (noun) occurs in three other contexts only, describing Lucifer in *Genesis B* 273, 'se engel ofermodes,' where the genitive of the noun probably functions as an adjective, in the *Instructions for Christians* 130[42] where Paul is said to teach that: 'se ðe hine sylfne to swiðe ahefð / for his ofermode he bið earm for Gode,' and in the continuous gloss to Defensor's *Liber scintillarum* for a quotation of Romans 11:20: 'Noli altum sapere sed time' as: 'nelle þu ofermod witan ac ondræd.'[43] In these contexts 'ofermod' is the sin of pride, although the last case needs a little argument.[44] Although as a noun it is rare, as an adjective it is well exemplified with the meaning 'proud, arrogant,' as are also related nouns 'ofermede,' 'ofermettu' ('pride') in context or against Latin 'superbia,' 'arrogantia,' 'elatio' (as 'self-exaltation').[45] Mr Britton has objected, admittedly in a brief letter to the *Times Literary Supplement* some twenty years ago[46] (but cited and repeated by Dr Clark),[47] that the noun occurs in religious contexts unlike *Maldon*. One sees the point and agrees. But it may be noted that the adjective 'ofermod' is used in a curious text from Cotton Tiberius A.III [48] which offers prognostications from the moon's age. The thirteenth moon is apparently dangerous for starting a project and a child born on that day will be: 'þriste, reaful, ofermod, him sylfum gelicigende.' In terms of usage 'ofermod' meaning 'pride' must be the favourite.

But the possibility remains that a compound may have a meaning in terms of its elements. 'Mod,' as Britton shows from *Beowulf* 1167 and could have noted from *Maldon* itself, 'mod sceal þe mare' (313), has a meaning in context 'courage, spirit.' The element 'ofer' is not, however, in my view, convincingly discussed by Britton, where he directs attention to '*oferhygd* arrogance, pride, *ofernid* extreme need and *oferþrymm* great power,'[49] in order to suggest a 'possible meaning' of 'ofermod' as 'great, high courage.' This 'possibility 'has now become accepted decision in T. A. Shippey's translation 'out of his high heart.'[50] But when two simplices are first compounded, as Britton would have it here, they bring their simplex meanings to the compound. If a compound at a later stage develops a further meaning it may then be no longer parallel with another compound with which it shares one element. In other words, 'ofer' which as a simplex never means 'great' but, in Britton's view, has developed to 'great' in the compound 'oferþrymm' should not now without argument be abstracted from the compound with that new meaning and be applied to 'ofer' in 'ofermod.' Actually, I suggest, he may be wrong even in his basic analysis of 'oferþrymm.' The element 'ofer' in the compounds was the OE preposition and adverb 'ofer'[51] and its meanings as simplex which have relevance to a discussion of these compounds may be represented by the NE words: 'above, over, beyond.' A succession of compounds are created in Old English where these meanings are still clearly seen.[52]

'Oferþrymm' appears only in the Exeter Book poem on *Judgment Day*[53] where the last trumpet at this point announces two things: 'brynehatne leg, / egsan oferþrymm' (52-3), but that 'terror' here has been described a few lines earlier as: 'ne mæg nænig gryre mare / geweorþan æfter woruldre' (43-4). This terror is greater than any in the world and Grein-Köhler[54] rightly render its 'oferþrymm' as 'vis nimia' where 'nimius' means: 'beyond measure, excessive, too great, too much.' It is indeed not simply 'great' but supernatural 'above-power.'

The real extremity of need is also rightly described by 'ofernid,' 'oferneod' (noun) in the two contexts in which this noun appears. In the *Pseudo-Ecgbert Penitential*, the Latin abstracts Augustine of Canterbury's ninth question to Pope Gregory the Great, which is also recorded in Bede's *Ecclesiastical History*. The passage concerns pollutions of the mind which happen during sleep and Gregory decides that both celebrator and receiver of mass are guilty if such pollution arises from gluttony. If he is the masspriest he may celebrate mass: 'quod sacerdos alius in loco deest, ipsa necessitas conpellit' or: 'gif hit oferneod beo and þær oðer sacerd ne beo þæt þa þenunga forð-do.'[55] The force of the Latin, 'necessity compels,' is reflected wholly in the OE noun 'oferneod,' and the situation where no mass would be celebrated if the polluted priest did not act explains that force.

The word 'oferneod' is similarly used in a homiletic piece on care to be taken about baptizing the heathen.[56] As it says, no man has the

right to baptize a heathen, if he has age and sense, until he can learn
what baptism means and what true belief is and when he knows everything it signifies. One manuscript of this text inserts: 'ne beo man
þæs fulluhtes to hræd butan oferneod geweorðe' (nor may a man be
too hasty in baptism except 'oferneod' occur), most likely in a case
of fast-approaching death when the saving of a soul would override
precautions against backsliding.

It seems to me that the force of 'ofer' in these two examples reflects its meaning as simplex and is not happily rendered by NE 'extreme' although there is no other NE alternative.

Britton's third example, 'oferhygd' with its well-attested and normal meaning 'arrogance, pride' which he gives, does not appear to
support his case that 'ofermod' need not mean pride. But we press
doggedly on and note that there are two recorded examples of the
word which might have been cited in his support, both in Alfredian
pieces. One, for which BT suggests 'in a good sense, honourable
pride(?), high spirit'[57] occurs in the OE version of Boethius's *Consolation*:

> 'Gif ðu nu gesawe sumne swiðe wisne man þe hæfde swiðe gooda
> oferhyda and wære þeah swiðe earm and swiðe ungesælig, hwæðer
> ðu wolde cweðan þæt he wære unwyrðe anwealdes and weorð-
> scipes.'[58]

This statement however is based on the Latin:

> 'At si quem sapientia praeditum uideres, num posses eum uel re-
> uerentia uel ea qua est praeditus sapientia non dignum putare?'[59]

Here Boethius is indicating that wisdom is worthy of reverence, and
Alfred reinforces this idea by adding that it is irrespective of a man's
condition. It is difficult to be certain about 'oferhyda' because of the
general Alfredian adaptation of the Latin but one could assume that
here 'oferhygd' might be taken in terms of its original elements as
'overthought,' 'superior thought,' perhaps synonymous with wisdom.
I see no particular reason why even good 'pride' should be brought
in here.

The second example appears in the Alfredian version of Augustine's
Soliloquies in a passage which is based on the Latin:

jubeasque me dum hoc ipsum corpus ago atque porto,
purum, magnanimum, justum, prudentemque esse,[60]

which Alfred modifies:

and geclænsa me ða hwile ðe ic on þisse worulde si,
and gedo me unmodigne (*al.* eadmodne). Sile me ofereda
(*al.* oferhyda) do me gesceawisne (*al.* gescadwisne) and
rihtwisne and foreþancfulne, and fulfremdne.[61]

BTS and Mr Carnicelli call attention to the Latin 'magnanimum' and
BTS suggests a meaning 'magnanimity, high-mindedness,'[62] to which I
have no wish to object.

We may conclude that 'ofermod' and its related words always refer
to the sin of pride in the many clear contexts where they occur (apart
from the case in *Maldon* which is being tested). But in terms of the
elements of the compound it could mean 'over-courage,' which implies excess and presumably a flaw, but not 'great courage.' As a parallel development to one (fairly) certain usage of 'oferhygd' it could
possibly mean 'magnanimity' although there is no evidence that anyone ever used 'ofermod' or related words in this way. Words, as we
suggested, can diverge in development of meaning. And, of course,
'ofermod' must now be placed back in its immediate context of a
'lytegian,' which, with overwhelming probability, is used 'in a bad
sense,' and of the poet's adverse comment on Byrhtnoth's action.
'Pride' or 'over-courage' appear to be the choices for 'ofermod.'

This exercise mainly in semantic analysis has been presented so
that those who still wish to suggest that Byrhtnoth was not deceived,
and that the poet presented him not only as similar to ancient heroes
but as a wholly admirable tactician should realize the grounds both
from the poem and from OE usage on which their case rests.

If a reason is needed why a poet should write in such terms emphasizing the ideal loyalty of the retainers although approving also of the
heroism of the leader, but not his tactical ability, we may offer a
speculation. If the poem, as seems likely,[63] was written during the
reign of Ethelred 'Unræd,' the king who 'could neither give direction
to his people nor hold his greater subjects firmly to their allegiance,'[64]
it could be an indictment by implication of the policy of buying off
the Danes but also against Englishmen who lacked loyalty to their

leaders in those times. This poem could be political propaganda against those whom the cap fitted. If so, our poet would support other and more open critics of the policy of leaders and the action of some followers, notably the anonymous monk of Abingdon and Archbishop Wulfstan.[65]

NOTES

1 George Clark, '*The Battle of Maldon*: A Heroic Poem,' *Speculum* 43 (1968) 52
2 See also valid comments on the lexicographers' difficulties in F.C. Robinson, 'Lexicography and Literary Criticism: A Caveat,' in *Philological Essays in Honour of Herbert Dean Meritt*, ed. J.L. Rosier (The Hague 1970), 99 ff.
3 *An Anglo-Saxon Dictionary, Supplement*, by T.N. Toller (Oxford 1931), s.v. 'lytig' 1. Here and afterwards abbreviated as BTS. *The Dictionary*, by J. Bosworth and T.N. Toller (Oxford 1872), is abbreviated as BT.
4 The glosses were first printed by Zupitza but are now more conveniently available in *Anglo-Saxon and Old English Vocabularies*, ed. T. Wright, second edition ed. and coll. R.P. Wülcker (London 1884), I, col. 57 seq. The section references in Wülcker's text are to the chapters of Proverbs, and my references to Proverbs will identify the examples in Wright-Wülcker.
5 Wülcker, I, col. 55, note 1, dates the manuscript as ninth century but N.R. Ker, *Catalogue of Manuscripts containing Anglo-Saxon* (Oxford 1957), 268, regards it as middle tenth century.
6 Obviously if he was in error no conclusions can be drawn about equivalence of Old English and Latin.
7 Clark, 68
8 BTS, s.v. 'lot.' The gloss is printed in A.S. Napier, *Old English Glosses, chiefly unpublished* (Oxford 1900), 216, among other glosses to Prudentius's *Psychomachia* in MS Cotton Cleopatra C.VIII.
9 Text and translation from *Prudentius*, ed. and trans. H.J. Thomson (London and Cambridge, Mass. 1962), I, 324, 325 resp
10 Ker, 185
11 See the various examples in *A Latin Dictionary*, ed. C.T. Lewis and C. Short (Oxford, 1955 impression), s.v. 'dolus.'
12 Clark, 68
13 *King Alfred's West-Saxon Version of Gregory's Pastoral Care*, ed. H. Sweet, EETS OS 45, 50 (Oxford 1871, 1958 reprint), part I, 237
14 *Regulae Pastoralis Liber*, III, xi (al. xxv), Migne, PL, vol. 76, col. 64
15 Lewis and Short, s.v. 'versipellis' B II

6 'lytiglice,' 241.8, 'mid lytelicum ladungum,' 245.21 and 'lot,' 243.24

7 PL 76, col. 64

8 Sweet, *Pastoral Care*, 237

9 BT and BTS s.v. 'nið'

0 *King Alfred's Orosius*, ed. H. Sweet, EETS OS 79 (Oxford 1883), part I, 112

1 An expression used by the artillery to indicate firing into the area of the target, often when they cannot pinpoint it

2 See Lewis and Short, s.v.; only 'inducere' can mean 'mislead.'

3 BT gives three possibilities for unaccented 'be' as prefix which need testing against 'lædan' and 'lytegian': 1/ giving intensive signification to a transitive verb; 2/ giving a privative sense as in 'beniman,' deprive, 'bereafian,' bereave, 'beheafdian,' behead; 3/ indicating no perceptible variation in sense. It is difficult to see how a privative sense could be applied to the verbs 'to lead, to seduce, trick' except by semantic sophistry.

4 BT s.v. 'lutan'

5 In Sweet's edition of the OE version of *Cura pastoralis*, I, 203, there are five examples of 'lytegan' (adjective, noun) rendering or referring to 'sapientes mundi.' In the *Old English Prudentius Glosses at Boulogne-sur-Mer*, ed. H.D. Meritt (Stanford 1959), 15, 'abered,' 'litig' glosses 'callidus' in Prudentius's *Liber cathemerinon*, lib. III, 1.41 'callidus inlaqueat volucres / aut pedicis dolus aut maculis' (Cunning craft snares birds in gins or meshes).

6 'Oswald and Byrhtnoth, a Christian Saint and Hero Who Is Christian,' *English Studies* 46 (1965) 106-9

7 M.J. Swanton, 'The Battle of Maldon: A Literary Caveat,' *JEGP* 67 (1968) 444, has suggested that 'yrhðo' means 'cowardice' here as it certainly does in some other contexts.

8 It is sometimes assumed that these men are untried warriors. W.A. Samouce, 'General Byrhtnoth,' *JEGP* 62 (1963) 132, says: 'He was aware that some of his freemen had no experience in battle and that some did not even know how to use their shields.' But note that every leader has to dispose his troops, and as to the holding of the shields Byrhtnoth tells them not 'how' but 'that.' I regard this last as an encouragement something like 'and steady, lads.'

9 See *Two of the Saxon Chronicles Parallel*, ed. Charles Plummer and John Earle (Oxford 1889), II, notes, pages 84, 89, 90. The references for 872 and 876 are not in Old English versions of the *Chronicle* but are statements by Latin writers. As Plummer and Earle say (84): 'it is most unjust to make Ethelred II responsible for this system as is very commonly done.'

0 *Sermo Lupi ad Anglos*, ed. D. Whitelock (London 1939, 2nd ed. 1952), 45, 1.109: 'scandlice nydgyld'

1 In 'Oswald and Byrhtnoth,' 103, I suggested that 'all the indications (from the

English speeches) so far presented in the poem emphasise the identification of the English with Germanic heroes' and referred also to the minor details which created a Germanic atmosphere. This attempt at identification is reinforced by the choice of old phrases such as 'yrre and anræd' and 'unforcuð eorl' (51) which by their earlier application can carry the connotation 'as a hero of older times.' See E.B. Irving, 'The Heroic Style in *The Battle of Maldon*,' *Studies in Philology* 58 (1961) 460.

32 BT and BTS, s.v. 'geseman.' It is once used (BTS, s.v. IIa) of a legal settlement meaning apparently 'to make an award in (a suit) as an arbitrator, to give judgment in a suit.' Such an application of the word here would make the word extremely pointed.

33 'Oswald and Byrhtnoth,' 108

34 Swanton, 445, note 18, suggests that where 'prass' occurs elsewhere 'it seems to have been pejorative, meaning something like "pomp, array,"' or 'parade.' There is reason for this statement although only one example of the four cited in BT and BTS is clearly used in a condemnatory context. This is the case from Pseudo-Wulfstan cited in BT. But since the word is rare, at present appears to have no related OE words or cognates in other languages, and occurs elsewhere in homiletic pieces only, one should expect some other indication in the poem of condemnation of the whole body of the English before suggesting that 'prass' is used pejoratively here. Mr Swanton, of course, is concerned to suggest that the old heroic ideal is deflated by the brute reality of conditions in the tenth century. I suggest that the body of the English who are praised for their heroism are idealized towards ancient models of heroism (see below) against that reality.

35 F.J. Battaglia, 'Notes on Maldon: Towards a Definitive *Ofermod*,' *English Language Notes* 2 (1965) 247-9; Cross, 102-3

36 As emphasized by J.R.R. Tolkien, 'The Homecoming of Beorhtnoth, Beorhthelm's Son,' *Essays and Studies* n.s. 6 (1953) 15, note 1. Clark, 70, avoids the implication in the figure when he says that the comment 'does not rebuke the hero ... but rather forewarns the audience of its outcome.' 'Rebuke' may be too strong a word but the comment *is* made on Byrhtnoth's action.

37 As historians concerned with the real event some speculate on Byrhtnoth's action as in *Sweet's Anglo-Saxon Reader* (15th ed., Oxford 1967), 267, that 'had he refused, the Danes would presumably have sailed away and ravaged out of reach of his army' and in O.D. Macrae-Gibson, 'How Historical is *The Battle of Maldon*,' *Medium Ævum* 39 (1970) 100: 'for had they withdrawn and landed elsewhere he might never again have had the chance of setting up a position against them so carefully. He would probably himself have made the suggestion that they should cross if they had not.' Such speculations about the real event do unfortunately appear to affect critical views of the poet's statement about

the event, which is the critics' sole concern. So in order merely to have an opposing view about the real event we may suggest that in a stalemate such as this
when, as appears from the poem, Byrhtnoth has prepared for battle, and the
Vikings actually begin battle by storming the causeway disadvantageously to
them, one side may take a chance to bring about battle. Both armies, after all,
had been restive. If Byrhtnoth had refused the Vikings leeway who is to say that
they would not then have come through the water, as it were, under fire? There
is admittedly a difference between 'not caring about the water,' when unopposed
and when opposed, but it appears that the Vikings did not need to use the causeway when they eventually came across. They could have spread out in this way
even 'under fire,' established a 'bridgehead,' 'consolidated' it and got ashore to
fight. The terminology used here may recall to some readers that battles have
actually been won in such conditions. The poet may thus be indicating that
Byrhtnoth should have waited a little. All of this is speculation about the real
event and I feel no desire to defend mine. If the philological and contextual
evidence, both immediate and in the whole poem, suggest that the poet thought
Byrhtnoth wrong, we critics should merely elucidate his opinion.

38 T.A. Shippey, *Old English Verse* (London 1972), 28
39 It is relevant to note that Shippey makes a choice for 'ofermod' with his translation, 'out of his high heart,' which is not ambiguous. The fact that we readers
may be uncertain about the exact meaning of a word in a given context does not
mean that a writer intended an ambiguity or was using the word with double
meaning.
40 Shippey, ibid
41 Swanton, 442
42 Noted by Swanton, 445, note 19. The text is printed by J.L. Rosier, 'Instructions for Christians,' *Anglia* 82 (1964) 15.
43 *Defensor's Liber Scintillarum, with an interlinear Anglo-Saxon version*, ed. E.W.
Rhodes, EETS OS 93 (Oxford 1889), 82. The reference to the text is inaccurate
in BTS.
44 The preceding quotation (ibid) renders: 'quod hominibus altum est abominatio
est apud deum (Luke 16:15)' as: 'þæt mannum ofermod ys onscunung ys mid
gode' where a Latin glossator has explained 'altum' as 'i superbe.'
45 See 'ofermod' (adjective), 'ofermede,' 'ofermettu' in BT, BTS.
46 *Times Literary Supplement*, 27 February 1953, 137
47 Clark, 69
48 Printed by O. Cockayne, *Leechdoms, Wortcunning and Starcraft of Early England* (London 1866), III, 190
49 Britton, *TLS*, 137
50 Shippey, 28

51 BT and BTS, s.v. 'ofer,' preposition and adverb
52 See the examples of 'ofer' in compounds recorded in BT, BTS.
53 Quoted from *The Exeter Book*, ed. G.P. Krapp and E.V.K. Dobbie (New York 1936), ASPR III, 213
54 *Sprachschatz der Angelsächsischen Dichter* von C.W.M. Grein, neu herausgegeben J.J. Köhler (Heidelberg 1912), s.v. 'oferþrym'
55 Quotations of Latin and Old English from *Die Altenglische version des Halitgar'schen Bussbuches (sog. Poenitentiale Pseudo-Ecgberti)*, ed. J. Raith, Bibl. der Angelsächsischen Prosa 13 (Hamburg 1933), Latin, 43, Old English, 44
56 Printed in *Wulfstan*, ed. A. Napier (Berlin 1883). The quotation is from 123, among the variants at 1.25.
57 BT, s.v. 'oferhygd'
58 King Alfred's *Old English version of Boethius, De Consolatione Philosophiae*, ed. W.J. Sedgefield (Oxford 1899), 62
59 *Anicii Manlii Severini Boethii Philosophiae Consolatio*, ed. L. Bieler, *Corpus Christianorum Series Latina* 94 (Turnholti 1957), lib III, pr. iv, §6, p. 43
60 *Soliloquiorum Libri Duo*, lib I, cap. i, §6, PL 32, col. 872
61 Text from *King Alfred's Version of St Augustine's Soliloquies*, ed. T.A. Carnicelli (Cambridge, Mass. 1969), 56. Variants cited are taken from the extract in MS Cotton Tiberius A.III (Ker, 186 art 9g), printed by W. Logeman, 'Anglo-Saxonica Minora,' *Anglia* 12 (1889) 513. There is a 'c' in the MS over 'o' of 'oferhyda' which is taken as a sign to indicate shortness of the vowel (Logeman, 500, note 38).
62 Carnicelli, 56, note 7; BTS, s.v. 'oferhygd' II
63 Clark, 56, suggests a mid-eleventh-century date for the poem's composition as part of an argument against its historicity. For this he cites evidence from the language of the poem in the transcript which we have. But the language in Elphinston's transcript of the burned and lost item from MS Cotton Otto A.XII tells us about a West-Saxon copy of the poem only. This has a few 'eastern' features which, if anything, suggest that there was a written exemplar for this copy in a non-West-Saxon dialect. Such a deduction negates Clark's comment (55) that: 'in the post-Magoun era it seems dangerous to assume that the story passed in one leap and unaltered from tenth-century Essex to eleventh-century Wessex.' But, more importantly, the West-Saxon copy gives no evidence either way on the date of the original creation of the poem except as a *terminus post quem*.
  The choice of the mid-eleventh century, however, seems curious in terms of the poem's content and the historical situation at that date. The poem has the Danes as an overbearing enemy who demand tribute. But by 1050 Edward the Confessor was king of England following three Danish kings in Cnut and his sons Harold and Harthacnut. During Edward's reign it might appear that if any for-

eigner were to be the enemy to an Englishman it might be the Normans who were among Edward's favourites. Admittedly the only known enemy who raided England was a force of Vikings in 1048 but as F.M. Stenton says (*Anglo-Saxon England* [2nd ed., Oxford 1947], 422) 'the episode ... was of little importance in itself.' One robin does not make the kind of winter for English self-esteem that existed during Ethelred's reign, and Clark's illustrations, 58-9, for the debasement of the English during this period make his point that 'Byrhtnoth's patriotism, leadership and courage stand out brilliantly against this background' (59) more effectively to an audience who knew it from experience than to one which was 'looking back on England's recent and unhappy past' (58).

54 Stenton, 389
55 Stenton, 388

BRUCE MITCHELL

The 'fuglas scyne'
of *The Phoenix*, line 591

583   Swa nu æfter deaðe   þurh dryhtnes miht
       somod siþiaþ   sawla mid lice,
585   fægre gefrætwed,   fugle gelicast,
       in eadwelum   æþelum stencum,
       þær seo soþfæste   sunne lihteð
       wlitig ofer weoredum   in wuldres byrig.
       Ðonne soðfæstum   sawlum scineð
590   heah ofer hrofas   hælende Crist.
       Him folgiað   fuglas scyne,
       beorhte gebredade,   blissum hremige,
       in þam gladan ham,   gæstas gecorene,
       ece to ealdre.   Þær him yfle ne mæg
595   fah feond gemah   facne sceþþan,
       ac þær lifgað a   leohte werede,
       swa se fugel fenix,   in freoþu dryhtnes,
       wlitige in wuldre.   (*Phoenix*)

The words 'fuglas scyne' in line 591b of this passage have long caused
difficulty to interpreters of *The Phoenix*. Ettmüller suggested reading
'fiðrum scyne,' Emerson explained that the phoenix was Christ and
that the 'fuglas scyne,' which he equated to the birds which follow
the phoenix (see 158-67), were 'the throngs of blessed souls which
follow the Lord,' while Dobbie noted that 'the reference here seems
to be to angels, but the poet may simply have become confused by

his Phoenix-symbolism.'[1] Blake accepts Emerson's explanation of lines 591-4a but sees a 'shift in the allegory,' in that in lines 583-90 and again in lines 594b-8 Christ is represented by the sun and the phoenix betokens the blessed who worship him, as the phoenix worships the sun (120-4, 288, and elsewhere). Thus 'the blessed are sometimes compared with the phoenix and sometimes with the birds which follow the phoenix,' and there is 'a certain amount of confusion' and 'a slight harshness.'[2]

Cross, however, in rejecting this explanation along with those of Ettmüller and Dobbie, writes:

> But there may be a simpler explanation that credits the poet with better control. Throughout the anagogical interpretation Christ is clearly the sun and the Phoenix is each good Christian and all good Christians. As the poet says, *þær lifgað a leohte werede, / swa se fugel fenix* 'they [*gæstas gecorene* 'chosen spirits' (593b)] live there [in heaven], always clothed in light, like the Phoenix bird' (596-97a) and, as I have suggested above, the righteous appear to simulate one feature of the Phoenix' beauty in *se beorhta beag* 'the bright ring' (602a), which adorns each of them in heaven. Since the *fuglas scyne* are *beorhte gebredade* 'brightly restored' (592a), a verb used of the Phoenix (372b) to describe its resurrection, *fuglas* must refer to the Phoenix. If the text is not corrupt, it seems to me that the plural *fuglas* may well have been written under the grammatical influence of plural *sawlum* 'souls' within the preceding lines.[3]

I agree with Cross that there is no need to accept a shift in the allegory here. Later on (637b ff) Christ is indeed represented — on the typological or allegorical level — by the phoenix. But it is unnecessary to import this parallel here — on the anagogical level.

It is, however, a nice point whether a poet who makes the grammatical error of writing a plural when he means to write a singular is showing 'better control' than one who confuses his allegory. Moreover, while the last-ditch desperation of a 'corrupt' text or the notion of confusion in allegory does offer some sort of solution, I doubt whether the idea that the poet accidentally wrote a plural for a singular in line 591b solves anything beyond explaining the plural 'folgiað' in line 591a; it merely postpones the problem until we get to 'gæstas gecorene' (593), which is in apposition with 'fuglas scyne'

and would therefore presumably have to be read as singular too, referring to one single spirit following Christ, as the phoenix followed
the sun. Can we really accept this?

I think not, for it runs contrary to the whole logic of the poet's
treatment of the allegory on the anagogical level, which, following
Cross (141-3), I take as running from line 474 to the end of the an-
them to the Father / Son at line 631 and perhaps to line 633 or line
637a.[4] Throughout this section, the blessed in Heaven are always referred to or thought of in the plural, starting with 'him' (474) —
which refers back to the nominative plural 'Meotudes cempan' (471)
— and ending with the verb 'reordiað' (632) or 'singað' (635). Apparent exceptions fall into three groups.

First, there are collective nouns. 'Gæsta gedryht' (615) and 'sib-
gedryht' (618) are both construed first with singular verbs ('hergað'
and 'swinsað') and then with plural verbs ('mærsiað,' 'singað,' and
'bletsiað'). If we include in this section lines 632-7a

> Ðus reordiað ryhtfremmende
> manes amerede in þære mæran byrig,
> cyneþrym cyþað, caseres lof
> singað on swegle, soðfæstra gedryht,
> þam anum is ece weorðmynd
> forð butan ende,

there is also 'soðfæstra gedryht' (635). The use of plural verbs
throughout this passage suggests that the collective is in apposition
with 'ryhtfremmende' (632) and does not directly govern any of the
verbs. Hence I use above Blake's punctuation in preference to that in
Anglo-Saxon Poetic Records, III, which has a semi-colon after 'byrig'
(633) and no comma before 'soðfæstra' (635).

Second, there are the expressions in which the singular of an indefinite pronoun is used with the genitive plural of 'an' or of an adjective. In four of these the reference is to some aspect of mortal man
as an individual in this world, before death or before the Last Judgment: his life in line 487, 'ealdor anra gehwæs'; his fear in lines 503-4,
'Weorþeð anra gehwylc / forht on ferþþe'; the heat he will feel before
the Last Judgment in lines 521-5:

> Hat bið monegum
> egeslic æled, þonne anra gehwylc,

soðfæst ge synnig,   sawel mid lice,
from moldgrafum   seceð meotudes dom,
forhtafæred;

and his work in line 598, 'weorc anra gehwæs.' In the remaining three
the reference is to a reward which each individual will win in Heaven:
a noble and perpetually young body in lines 534-7:

                    Swa bið anra gehwylc
flæsce bifongen   fira cynnes,
ænlic ond edgeong,   se þe his agnum her
willum gewyrceð ...

and a radiant crown, mentioned *twice* in lines 602-7:

Þær se beorhta beag,   brogden wundrum
eorcnanstanum,   eadigra gehwam
hlifað ofer heafde.   Heafelan lixað
þrymme biþeahte.   Ðeodnes cynegold
soðfæstra gehwone   sellic glengeð
leohte in life ...

But even in these the genitive plural emphasizes the fact that the poet
is thinking, not just of one individual who is capable of joining the
blessed, but of all such individuals. This is of course also implicit in
the use of 'gehwa' and 'gehwylc,' to which (as Campbell, *Old English
Grammar*, §719 observes) 'a general inclusive sense is given ... by the
prefix *ġe-*.'
    Third, there are two sentences with a gnomic ring in which the
poet is thinking of the individual in this world, of the human being
who will or can win here the reward of the righteous. Lines 482-5:

Þus eadig eorl   ecan dreames,
heofona hames   mid heahcyning
earnað on elne,   oþþæt ende cymeð
dogorrimes ...

and lines 516-7: 'Wel biþ þam þe mot / in þa geomran tid   gode lic-
ian.'
    The first two of these three groups lend positive support to the

notion that the poet of *The Phoenix* is likely to think of all blessed souls rather than of one individual soul when he turns his mind to Christ in Heaven followed by the company of blessed ones, the soldiers of Christ who have earned their reward. The third group shows that, on the rare occasions when he uses the singular alone (without a genitive plural) in the anagogical section, he is referring (quite naturally) to an individual on earth who must win by his own deeds his share in the collective reward reserved for the souls of all the blessed.

The same distinction obtains in the other allegorical sections. In the typological or allegorical (632 or 637b-77), all the relevant references are in the plural, and all are to the blessed in Heaven. In the moral or tropological (381-473), we have two singular references, both to the individual in this world. The first is lines 381-6, where we are told that 'eadigra gehwylc' will win eternal life as the reward for his deeds. The second is lines 451-65, where we have a catalogue of the deeds by which a 'dryhtnes cempa' on this earth will win the protection of God. But significantly this same expression is used in the plural in lines 470-3 when the transition is being made from the moral to the anagogical level and the poet's interest switches from the temporal world to the heavenly, from the individual on earth to the company of the blessed ones in Heaven:

> Swa nu in þam wicum   willan fremmað
> mode ond mægne   meotudes cempan,
> mærða tilgað;   þæs him meorde wile
> ece ælmihtig   eadge forgildan.

The other relevant references in this section are plural ones, again to the heavenly host.

All this accords with Cross's contention (142-3) that 'throughout the anagogical interpretation Christ is clearly the sun and the Phoenix is each good Christian and all good Christians.' But it also suggests that his postulated singular for 'fuglas scyne' (591) would be out of place in the context of lines 583-98. For, if he were right, we would not only have to take 'gæstas gecorene' (593) as singular (see above); we would also be left without a plural antecedent for 'him' (594) and a plural subject for 'lifgað' (596), and so (as far as I can see in the absence of any explanation from Cross) would be forced to extend the poet's error of singular for plural to these lines. Cross's interpretation would then leave us with the phoenix (= 'fuglas scyne' and the subsequent plurals taken as singulars) being 'swa se fugel fenix' (597). This seems rather pointless and almost as confused as the explanations it attempts to replace.

If, however, we follow the poet's argument in lines 583-98, we find that in lines 583-8 and again in lines 594b-8 he compares the souls of the blessed bright in the protection, the glory, the sunshine, of Christ the Sun to the phoenix, 'þære sunnan þegn' (288). What happens in the intervening lines 589-94a? I suggest that Cross is right in thinking 'that the plural *fuglas* may well have been written under the grammatical influence of the plural *sawlum* "souls" within the preceding lines' (143), but wrong in implying that this was a mistake by the poet. It is my feeling that the plural 'fuglas scyne' is an integral part of the plural sequence 'sawla' (584) ... 'soðfæstum sawlum' (589) ... 'gæstas gecorene' (593) ... 'him' (594) ... 'lifgað' (596) and has the same referent — the blessed souls which follow Christ.

We will, I believe, pay the poet the compliment he deserves if we credit him with saying what he meant rather than if we blame him for an error in his allegory or a slip in his syntax. For in 'fuglas scyne' (591), the *comparison* made in 'fugle gelicast' (585) — which is taken up again in 'swa se fugel fenix' (597) — gives way to a firm albeit momentary *identification* of the souls of the blessed following Christ with so many bright phoenixes following the sun. This identification is the culmination of one of the images which have been in the poet's mind, and it has in it the very essence of poetic kennings like that in *Christ* 858-63:

                        Þa us help bicwom,
    þæt us to hælo   hyþe gelædde,
    godes gæstsunu,   ond us giefe sealde
    þæt we oncnawan magun   ofer ceoles bord
    hwær we sælan sceolon   sundhengestas,
    ealde yðmearas,   ancrum fæste —

unconscious perhaps and incongruous when over-analyzed, but spontaneous and poetically effective when accepted 'with a gladsome mind.'

We can if we wish accept the notion that the poet is 'confused.' If we do, it is the 'confusion' of a poet's imagination, a sort of Old English equivalent of the 'jumping of the points' from one line of imagery to another seen in the switch from 'gun' to 'dog' at the word 'muzzled' in *The Winter's Tale* I.ii.153-7:

> Looking on the lines
> Of my boy's face, methoughts I did recoil
> Twenty-three years and saw myself unbreeched
> In my green velvet coat; my dagger muzzled
> Lest it should bite its master.

POSTSCRIPT, APRIL 1972

I completed the original manuscript of this article in August 1971. In March 1972, I read in A.A. Lee's *The Guest-Hall of Eden* (New Haven and London 1972) the following passage (121): '... *The Phoenix*, where faithful and heroic souls from middle-earth come as perfume-bearing phoenixes to share in the *dreama dream* (658, joy of joys) with "the best of princes" (621).' Although it is not clear that the phrase 'perfume-bearing phoenixes' is a reference to 'fuglas scyne' (591), it would seem possible that Lee has independently reached a conclusion similar to mine about this expression.

NOTES

1 L. Ettmüller, *Engla and Seaxna Scôpas and Bôceras* (Quedlinburg and Leipzig 1850), 276; O.F. Emerson, 'Originality in Old English Poetry,' *RES* 2 (1926) 30; E.V.K. Dobbie, note to *Phoenix* 591 in *Anglo-Saxon Poetic Records* (New York 1936), III, 279

2 N.F. Blake, ed., *The Phoenix* (Manchester 1964), 33 and 85

3 J.E. Cross, 'The Conception of the Old English *Phoenix*,' in *Old English Poetry: Fifteen Essays*, ed. R.P. Creed (Providence, R.I. 1967), 142-3. I acknowledge gratefully my debt to Mr Blake and Professor Cross. Without their work, this note would obviously never have been written.

4 Lines 632-3 (and perhaps 634-7a) seem to be used *apo koinou*, pointing both back to the preceding speech and forward to lines 637b-54, which can be taken as 'represented speech'; see O. Jespersen, *The Philosophy of Grammar* (London 1924), 290-2, though C.W. Kennedy, in both his prose and verse translations, put lines 636-54 in inverted commas. Examples of this sort are relevant to the problem of 'swa cwæð' in *Wanderer* 6 and 111; see Dunning and Bliss, *The Wanderer* (London 1969), 30-6.

DOROTHY WHITELOCK

The list of chapter-headings
in the Old English Bede

There are five manuscripts of the Old English translation of Bede's
Ecclesiastical History of the English Nation:[1] Bodleian Library, MS
Tanner 10, cited as T, of the first half of the tenth century; British
Museum, Cotton MS Otho B.XI, cited as C, written in a mid tenth-
century hand to the end of book V , with Bede's account of his life
and writings added some fifty years later; Corpus Christi College, Oxford, MS 279, part ii, cited as O, of the early eleventh century; Corpus
Christi College, Cambridge, MS 41, cited as B, of the first half of the
eleventh century; and Cambridge University Library, MS Kk. 3.18,
cited as Ca, of the second half of the eleventh century.[2] C was badly
damaged in the Cottonian fire of 1731; some folios survived,[3] and
the editors Whelock[4] and Smith,[5] who saw this manuscript before
the fire, supply some variant readings, which I cite as CW and CS
respectively; there is also a transcript, except for what precedes chapter 1 of book I, made by Laurence Nowell and now British Museum,
Additional MS 43703, which I cite as CN.[6]

   All manuscripts go back on a common archetype which already
had some errors unlikely to have been made by the translator.[7]
Thomas Miller[8] divided the five manuscripts into two groups, one consisting of T and B, the other of C, O, and Ca.[9] He was probably right
in regarding Ca as a copy of O. We can call his first group Y and his
second group Z.

   The most striking difference between these two postulated branches is that each has a completely different treatment of the part ex-

tending from the last few sentences of bk III.16 (beginning 'Quo tempore reuerentissimum antistes Aidan') to the end of bk III.20. In Y, this section is given complete, except for the second part of bk III.17 (from 'Scripsi autem')[10]; but Z omits bk III.19 and 20, and has the rest of this section, including the part of bk III.17 omitted by Y, in a completely different translation.

Miller held that the whole section was missing from the original translation, in all manuscripts, and that the gap was then partly filled in later, independently, in the archetypes of the two branches. This view has been disputed by S. Potter[11] and by J.J. Campbell,[12] both of whom claim that the version in T and B is the work of the original translator, and that only that in the Z branch was made by some other translator, to fill part of the lacuna in its archetype. This view, with which I fully concur, is based on the close agreement in vocabulary and mannerisms between the version in Y and the rest of the translator's work.

Yet there is a difficulty overlooked by these scholars. Both B and Ca have a list of chapter-headings. Cap III.17-20 are omitted not only from the list in Ca, a manuscript of the Z branch, where it was a later translator who filled in part of the missing portion, but also from the list in B, whose version, on the view just outlined, never lacked this section, and hence should have retained the headings for bk III.17-20. This would appear to support Miller's view of a lacuna in all manuscripts, for it would be a strange coincidence if B's list accidentally omitted the headings of precisely the chapters once missing in the Z branch.

We must therefore see if the absence of these headings from B's list can be accounted for without our assuming that the section was once lacking from both branches. If we can, this may have wider implications than allowing us to accept the version of bk III.16-20 in T and B as by the translator of the rest of the work. For we have been slow to realize that, if it is, Miller's main argument for postulating a common archetype for T and B vanishes; their agreement, against the other manuscripts, in their handling of this section need mean no more than that each is independently copying the original work. While Miller was clearly right in seeing that C, O, and Ca form a group, his list of agreements in error between T and B is not impressive,[13] nor can more than a handful of other instances be added to it. Thus one may doubt whether there ever was an archetype Y.

The gap in bk III.16-20, at whatever stage of the transmission it occurred, is likely to be the result of accident, not of deliberate omission, for there seems no conceivable reason why, if the latter, it should begin in the middle of chapter 16, thus leaving the account of a miracle incomplete. The missing section could easily have occupied a gathering which has been lost. The list of chapter-headings may first have been drawn up to fit a manuscript which had lost this section; or an existing list may have been compared with the text of such a manuscript, and brought into agreement with it by the deletion of the headings of the missing chapters. This faulty manuscript would have to be a predecessor of Z, not Z itself, for the three manuscripts, C, O, and Ca, which descend from Z show that this had already inserted into it a new translation of bk III.17 and 18,[14] and yet the list has no headings for these two chapters.

There are two possible explanations why B, with no lacuna in its text, should yet omit cap III.17-20. The B scribe, or a predecessor, may have compared its list with that of a manuscript which omitted these headings, and have deleted them;[15] or B may descend from a manuscript which originally lacked a list, and B or a predecessor have made good this lack by copying, from another manuscript, a list which had been drawn up for a faulty text, or at least had been brought into line with such a text.

The problem is complicated by the fact that both T and O are imperfect at the beginning, and have lost all the preliminary matter. Moreover, when Nowell transcribed C, he omitted everything before bk I.1. None of the preliminary matter in C survived the Cottonian fire. We know, however, that C had a list, for Whelock gave variant readings from it. We may guess that O also once had one, for the list in Ca is in some ways superior to that in C,[16] and Ca is so faithful a copy of O in the rest of the manuscript that this is likely to be its source. But we have no means whatever of knowing whether T ever had a list of chapters.

Whereas in Latin manuscripts of Bede the *capitula* are placed before each of the five books, the Old English version brings them all together, though Ca precedes them with the rubric 'INCIPIUNT CAPITULA LIBRI PRIMI.' Ca numbers them according to the five books, but B numbers them consecutively.[17] This may be because in B there is nothing to distinguish the beginning of a new book. Yet its list does preserve at their proper places rubrics in capitals, for example, 'Her endiat þa capituls [sic] ðaere forman bec. Her onginnat ða capitulas þære oðre bec.' Ca has similar, but briefer rubrics, and Whelock shows that C had at least some of them.[18]

The list is in a more original position in Ca, where it comes after Bede's preface, though separated from it by a West Saxon genealogy and regnal list which is not in Bede.[19] Apart from this insertion, the list of chapters occupies the same position as that to book I in Latin manuscripts. But B has the list right at the beginning, before Bede's preface, and the first heading has been altered to fit the new position; where Ca has: 'I. Be gesetnysse Breotene oððe Hibernia Scotta ealandes,' B begins, without rubric or number, but with a large illuminated initial and a line of very large capitals: 'Ðis is seo gesettnes ðisse Brytene oð Hibernia Scotta ealandes.' One reason for the list preceding the preface could be that a predecessor of B had supplied the list to a text which lacked one, putting it at the beginning of a manuscript which had the preface, in which case the loss of the list was not because all the preliminary matter had been lost, as it now has been in T and O. But the list could have been moved to precede the whole work in order to make it easier to consult it, when one was wanting to find a particular chapter. It is true that in B it is not very helpful for this purpose, for the chapters are unnumbered; yet B is an unfinished manuscript,[20] and it may have been intended that the rubricator should supply numbers to the chapters. Whatever the reason for its position, the fact remains that the list in B agrees with the manuscripts C[21] and Ca, of the Z branch, in omitting the headings for cap III.17-20, though these chapters are in B's text.[22]

B did not copy its list from Ca. This is not possible chronologically, if one accepts the dating of B in the first half of the eleventh century and of Ca in the second. What is more, though Ca very frequently has the better text, since B was given to errors of all kinds and also to deliberate alterations in order to replace archaic or dialect words and archaic syntax, there are several places where its chapter-headings represent those of the Latin list better than those in Ca do.

Before we note some of these, a few words must be said about the type of Latin text used. It was the same as that used for the rest of the translation, one very like that of British Museum, Cotton Tiberius C.II.[23] It included a passage at the end of cap IV.13 which is not in other early Latin manuscripts of Bede. It had cap IV.18 (20), 'Hymnus de illa,' attached to the previous heading, cap IV.17 (19);[24] and it had cap IV.29 (31) and 30 (32) in the reverse order. There are also agreements in detail: in cap V.10 'to drihtne' renders the 'ad dominum' of Tiberius (other manuscripts 'ad Christum') and cap V.11 'se arwurða wer' corresponds to 'uir uenerabilis' of Tiberius (other manuscripts 'uiri uenerabiles'). There are agreements also in the spelling of some proper names.

A few examples will suffice to prove that B is sometimes superior to Ca. In cap I.22 'exteris ... bellis' is 'utgefeohtum' B, 'utgefeohte' Ca; in cap IV.1 'illo ibidem defuncto' is rendered literally, 'him þær forþferendum' in B, but 'hi ðær forðferdon' in Ca; in cap IV.2, B renders 'Theodoro ... peragrante' correctly as 'Þeodoro ðam arcebyscope geondfarendum,' when Ca has 'Þeodorus se arceb' gondferendum'; in cap. I.11, B has 'Constantinus,' where Ca wrongly puts 'Constantius'; and in cap V.20, 'æfter þam bysceope Wilfriðe' B gives the correct sense, when Ca has 'fram' for 'æfter.' In some places Whelock's variants show that better readings in B were also in C: for example, for 'claudo' in cap I.21, B and CW have 'healtan,' Ca 'halgan'; 'intrauerit' in cap I.25 is 'eode' in B and CW, but omitted by Ca; and similarly, 'dederit' in cap III.24 is 'sealde 7 forgeaf' in B and CW, but omitted by Ca. These errors in Ca need not go any further back than the scribe of that manuscript.

It would have been possible, chronologically, for B to have copied its list from C; but it did not, for it avoided C's errors.[25] We may note the following renderings: cap I.21 'emendatis': 'gebetum' B, 'gebettum' Ca, 'gebedum' CW; cap III.22 'Ceddo': 'Cedde' B, Ca, 'Ceadda' CW; cap IV.1 'Brittaniam': 'to Brytene' B, 'to Breotone' Ca, 'to Rome' CW; and cap V.5 'orando': 'gebiddende' B, Ca, 'gelædende' CW.

For our knowledge of C we have to depend on variants cited by Whelock and Smith. Both these editors took Ca as the basis of their text. Since we possess B, we can see that Whelock recorded only a small selection of its variant readings, and we may therefore wonder how far he noted those in C. But the number of differences between B and Ca is so great that he could not have included them in his margins, and would have had to give a large textual apparatus, whereas, if the relation between the lists in C and Ca was similar to that between these manuscripts in the rest of the work, variants in C would be comparatively few, and he may therefore have noted a bigger proportion of them. Smith rarely gives variants to the chapter-headings (which he places at the head of each chapter, not in a list). One cannot safely assume that C agreed with Ca whenever no variant is recorded by these editors.

This must be borne in mind when one examines some evidence

which may suggest that the list in B was free from certain errors which are in both C and Ca, and which must go back to their common source, Z. The instances are:

1   Cap III.10, 'Ut puluis loci illius contra ignem ualuerit,' is translated in B 'þæt on ðære ylcan stowe myl wið fyre wæs fremiende.' Ca is faulty: 'þæt þære ylcan stowe mid fyre wæs freomigende'; Whelock states: 'myl B. *Sed* MSS Cantab. & Cot. *deest.*' Smith puts B's reading in his text, and notes that Ca reads 'mid fyre.' B has the better reading, but it is not impossible that it or some predecessor made sense out of a corrupt heading either by consulting the chapter in the text (though here the word used is 'molde,' common elsewhere in the work, whereas 'myl' is unique in pre-Conquest texts), or by comparing a Latin manuscript.

2   Cap I.19, 'Ut idem causa infirmitatis ibidem detentus ...' is rendered by B 'þæt se ilca bysseop for ðan intingan untrumnesse þær wæs gehæfd.' Instead of 'þær wæs,' Ca has the meaningless 'feria,' while CW has 'færinga,' which makes sense but has no support from the Latin. A misreading of 'þær' as 'fær' seems to lie behind these corruptions. B's reading may well be original, though the expansion of the participial construction by adding 'wæs' could be later.

3   The second part of cap II.16 'et de qualitate regni Eduini' is given in Ca as 'Be þære sibbe 7 stillnysse Eadwines cyninges rices.' Instead of 'stillnesse,' B has 'smiltnysse,' a favourite word for 'serenity' in the Old English Bede, likely to be the original term here. Whelock records this variant in B, leaving one to suppose that C agreed with Ca. Smith gives no variant to 'stillnesse.'

4   In cap III.15, B has correctly 'storm' for 'tempestatem,' when Ca has 'stream.' Whelock records 'storm' for B, without mentioning C; Smith adopts the reading 'storm' in his text, giving the variant 'stream' as Ca. Again, it seems implied that C did not differ from Ca.[26]

Though the evidence is not very strong, it looks as if B took its list from a manuscript free from certain errors in C and Ca, and hence in Z. There is no difficulty in our assuming that B's list comes from a manuscript at an earlier stage than Z, for we saw above that its list agrees with a text in which the lacuna in bk III had not been partly filled by the addition of bk III.17 and 18, as it was in Z.

Before going further, it is necessary to look at a few readings in Ca which at first sight make it appear as if Ca is superior to both C and B, which would imply that these two shared some errors. These readings are:

1 Cap I.14 begins: 'Ut Brettones fame famosa coacti barbaros suis e finibus pepulerint,' which is given in Ca as: 'Ðæt Bryttas mid þy mærran hungre genedde þa elreordian of heora gemærum adrifan,' and in B as: 'Þætte Bryttas mid þi maran hungere genyddon þa elþiodian of hira gemærum adrifon.' In B 'maran' is an error, 'elþiodian' the substitution of a more usual word for 'elreordian,' and 'genyddon' a failure to recognize 'genydde' as a plural past participle. All this could be put down to changes made by B if it were not for Miller's claim that 'nyddon þa elþeodian' is given by Smith as a variant in C. In fact, though Smith does have this variant, he does not assign it to any manuscript, and it is possible that he was slightly misquoting the reading in B. Yet even if C did have this, it is not beyond possibility that two copyists could independently have replaced an unfamiliar by a familiar word, and have mistaken a plural participle for a main verb.

2 The second part of cap III.24, 'et Osuiu pro adepta uictoria possessiones et territoria Deo ad construenda monasteria dederit,' has given much trouble, and both B and Ca make independent errors.[27] The only part of the heading which concerns our present enquiry is when Ca translates 'ad construenda monasteria' as 'mynster on to getimbrianne,' when B has only 'to þam mynstre' and Whelock gives this as the reading of C as well as of B. Ca is closer to the Latin, but the force of this evidence is diminshed when one notes that the previous heading has the phrase 'mynster on to timbrianne,' which Ca may have repeated.

3 In cap IV.19 (21), 'inter Ecfridum et Aedilredum reges' is given in B as 'betweox Ecgferð 7 Æþelred þa twegen ciningas,' and Whelock records 'twegen cyningas' as C's reading. Ca has 'betweox Ec'g'-ferðe 7 Æðelrede þam cyningum.' The dative case after 'betweox' is more common than the accusative in late Old English, and Ca may have omitted 'twegen' as self-evident.

The evidence of the list of headings is therefore inadequate to show C and B sharing errors against Ca.[28]

With no lists for T and O, and so little evidence for C, textual criteria can take us no further. We can see that B did not copy its list from either C or Ca, and that it probably copied a list at an earlier stage than that in Z. This does not let us decide whether B merely deleted the headings, cap III.17-20, by comparing a manuscript of the Z type, or whether it or a predecessor, originally lacking a list, supplied one from such a manuscript.

But there is another line of approach: to see how the list as it has come down to us fits the divisions of the text in the various manuscripts.[29] In general, the divisions correspond to those in the Latin manuscripts, agreeing with Tiberius C.II in three out of the four places where it differs from other early Latin manuscripts;[30] in one place the English version has the arrangement in these.[31] But it sometimes omits to mark the beginning of a chapter, and sometimes it divides a chapter into sections.[32] This latter process seems to have gone further in Z, the archetype of C, O, and Ca, than it had in the manuscripts lying behind T and B.

When one compares the Old English list with the Latin,[33] it becomes clear that the position changes after cap I.23. Up to this point, the Latin is followed closely; headings for bk I.9, 10, 17-22 are retained though the chapters are omitted from the text;[34] so also is cap I.12, though in the text this chapter is attached to its predecessor with no sign of a division; and no new heading is supplied when in bk I.1 all the manuscripts have a division at M.26.27.[35] The Old English list is clearly not being compared with the state of the text.[36] Moreover, in the few places where the Latin heading is not translated literally, there is no sign that the chapter in the English version has been consulted. The addition in cap I.1 of 'Scotta ealandes' represents the translator's practice throughout the work; when, in cap I.5, 'Ut Seuerus receptam Brittaniae partem uallo a cetera distinxerit,' for 'a cetera' one gets 'fram oðrum unatemedon þeodum,' this is translating 'a ceteris indomitis gentibus' in the Latin chapter, which is rendered 'fram oðrum elreordum þeodum' Ca, 'fram elreordigum þeodum' B; the addition of 'to Rome' in the heading and 'on Rome' in the text of bk I.13, in relation to the appeal to Aetius, was a natural assumption. Of greater interest is the alteration of cap I.4, 'Lucius ... Christianum se fieri petierit.' Ca reads: 'bæd hine cristenne beon 7 eac abæd,' and B: 'bæd hine þæt he cristendom lufude 7 eac he hit abæd.' Some corruption lies behind both readings (perhaps one should read 'geworhtne beon' for 'beon' in the form in Ca), but 'bæd 7 eac abæd' seems to be translating the entry of this event in Bede's chronological summary: 'ut Christianus efficeretur, petiit et impetrauit.' If so, since this summary was omitted from the Old English version, the translator of the list appears to have been familiar with the Latin work as a whole.

After cap I.23 the procedure is very different: the list is now brought into line with the state of the Old English text. When this has omitted any chapters, the headings to them are also omitted, except in two places where the absence of the chapter was not obvious.

Bk IV.18 (20) is omitted. It contains Bede's poem on St Æthelthryth, which in several Latin manuscripts is given a separate heading, 'Hymnus de illa,' whereas in Tiberius C.II this is tacked on to cap IV.17 (19). The Old English list ends this heading with '7 be þam hymene þe we be hire geworhton,' taking its wording from Bede's words introducing the poem in the chapter which the Old English version omits: 'hymnum ... in laudem ... eiusdem reginae ... conposuimus' — another indication that the translator of the list was familiar with the Latin text. The change from 'hymnum' to 'be þam hymene' reveals an awareness that the poem itself is not included; but it would only be by reading right through the long chapter, bk IV.17 (19), that anyone would discover that the poem is not even mentioned in it; and so the reference in the heading was allowed to stand.

The second heading which is retained although the chapter is omitted is cap V.15. In the Old English list this is combined with cap V.18 (both text and headings of bk V.16 and 17 being omitted). The Latin headings are:

'XV. Ut plurimae Scottorum ecclesiae instante Adamnano catholicum pascha susceperint, atque idem librum de locis sanctis scripserit.'

'XVIII. Ut Australes Saxones episcopos acceperint Eadberchtum et Eollan, Occidentales Danielum et Aldhelmum; et de scriptis eiusdem Aldhelmi.'

Since there is only one chapter in the Old English text (bk V.15 being omitted), only one heading is given, but it combines the two: 'Ðæt monega cyricean on Hibernia lærendum Athamnano [Ademano B] þa eallgeleaflican Eastran onfengon; 7 be Ealdelmo se ða boc de uirginitate 7 eac oðra manega geworhte; ge eac þæt Suðseaxan agenne biscopas onfengon Eadbyrht 7 Eollan, 7 Weastseaxan onfengon[37] Danielum 7 Aldelmum; 7 be Aldelmes gewritum.' The compiler of this has seen that bk V.18 contains an account of a conversion to the orthodox Easter, not mentioned in its heading; he has assumed that this is what cap V.15 is referring to, failing to notice that bk V.18 is dealing with Aldhelm's conversion of the Britons, not with Adamnan's of the Irish. He then replaces the mention of Adamnan's book by one of Aldhelm's writings, taken from the chapter itself; yet he leaves in the last four words which are now redundant. It is hard to believe that this clumsy combination of headings is the work of the translator of Bede.

Apart from these two special cases, the headings of omitted chapters are not in the list. Another sign that the list was compared with the text is the omission of the headings of chapters which, though they are, in part or in full, in the text, are no longer obvious there because of the way it is set out. Thus cap II.8 is omitted, for the two sentences of the chapter which the text retained are attached to bk II.7 without any sign of division. Cap II.12 is omitted, though the chapter, a long and interesting one on Edwin's vision in East Anglia, is in the text, but there it follows without any break the first sentence of bk II.10, when the rest of this chapter, and all of bk II.11, have been omitted. The list gives cap II.10, though all that this now relates to is the first sentence of the long undivided section in the text. This does not look like the translator's own doing, for he would surely have remembered translating the account of Edwin's vision, and would not have deleted the heading which referred to it. Cap II.17 is omitted, since only the paragraph preceding the letter given in the Latin text has been retained, and attached without division to bk II.16. Bk III.2 is retained in full, but not divided from bk III.1; in this arrangement the Old English text agrees with Tiberius C.II, but this gives the chapter a separate heading, omitted in the Old English list.

Also, after cap I.23, many of the headings have been expanded with material taken from the chapter; for example, cap II.18 adds a reference to the death of Justus and the consecration of Honorius by Paulinus; cap II.20 adds that Edwin was slain by Penda; cap III.22 inserts from the chapter the phrase 'mid geornfulnysse Oswies ðæs cyninges'; and cap III.28 adds that Wilfrid was consecrated by Bishop Æthelbyrht and Ceadda by Bishop Wine. In cap IV.16 (18) 'heahseangere' is translating the 'archicantator' of the chapter, not the 'cantator' of the heading, a word which is rendered 'cyricsangere' and 'sangere' in bk V.20.

New headings are usually supplied where the manuscripts of the Old English version have divisions not in the Latin manuscripts. Bk II.16 is divided in all manuscripts at M.144.21. Cap II.16 has been divided, and the second part, 'et de qualitate regni Eduini,' replaced by 'Be þære sibbe 7 stillnysse [smiltnysse B] Eadwines cyninges rices' to form a new heading. All manuscripts divide bk IV.9 at M.290.5, and a new heading was made for the second section: 'Ðæt Torhtgyð seo Godes þeowen ðreo gear æfter ðære hlæfdian forðfore þa geta on life hæfd wæs.' B, C, and Ca divide bk V.23 at M.476.30 (T and O have ended before this point). In this case a new heading was made for the first part of the chapter, giving a selection of matters dealt with in it: 'Be forðfore Tobias þæs biscopes æt Hrofesceastre 7 Ecgbyrhtes þæs arwurðan biscopes on ðone forman Easterdæg; 7 ðy ylcan geare forðferde Osric Norðanhymbra cyning.' The original heading, 'Qui sit in praesenti status gentis Anglorum uel Brittaniae totius,' rendered 'Hwylc se staðol is on andweardnesse Angelcynnes þeode ge eac ealre Breotone,' is then left to refer to the second section, where, indeed, this topic begins.

A more complicated case occurs in bk IV.12. This is divided in all manuscripts at M.298.12. It is again divided at M.298.27, but only in CN, O, and Ca, there being no break at all in T and B. One new heading is supplied: 'Ðæt se steorra ætywde se is cometa nemned 7 þreo monað wæs wuniende, and symble on uhtatid wæs upyrnende. On þam ylcan geare Ecfrið Norðanhymbra cyning adræfde Wilfirð þone arwyrðan biscop.' This relates only to events mentioned after the second division, which is in CN, O, and Ca only; events in the part preceding this are adequately covered by the original heading of the chapter. It looks as if the supplier of the new heading had before him a text divided as in the Z branch of manuscripts. If so, he did not bother to supply a heading for the section beginning in all manuscripts at M.298.12; it was only a brief paragraph before his manuscript divided again.

There is only one other place where a division occurring in all manuscripts was not given a new heading. This is the final paragraph of bk IV.5, where at M.280.6 all manuscripts begin a new section. But this occurs immediately after the statutes of the synod of Hertford, and each statute has been given a separate paragraph in B, O, and Ca, so that it was necessary to begin a new paragraph after the last statute. It is not surprising, therefore, that no separate heading was felt necessary, especially when this paragraph begins with a back reference to the synod mentioned in the heading to the chapter.

There are two places, however, where the Z group of manuscripts divides a chapter, and yet no heading is supplied for the new section. One is at M.286.9 in bk IV.8. Here B has no sign of division, T begins with 'Eft' in small tinted capitals, yet with nothing like its normal chapter division,[38] but CN, O, and Ca have a full division. It would have been simple to make a heading for the second section by dividing cap IV.8 into two, but this was not done. Similarly, cap V.10 could have been divided, and the second part then used to describe the section of this chapter which begins in CN, O, and Ca at M.414. 15, where T and B have no break. But no heading is supplied for this second section. We must assume either that whoever was bringing the list into line with the text was not always consistent in his practice, or that the manuscript he was using had no clear division in these two places. As we have seen, the failure to supply headings for the two chapters, bk III.17 and 18, which had been added in Z to fill the lacuna, shows that his text was probably a predecessor of Z, and this may not have had these divisions.

Cap I.27-33 have been reserved for separate discussion. This part gave particular trouble, for Bede included many letters which the translator omitted, and the chapters which contained them are represented, if at all, only by the short introductory remarks preceding the letters. The Old English Bede removed the long text of Augustine's *Interrogationes* with Gregory's replies from bk I.27 until after the end of bk III,[39] but the brief paragraph preceding them in bk I.27 was retained at the original place, and cap I.27 is also kept, for it can refer to this. Bk I.28 being omitted, the beginning of bk I.29 is attached to what was kept in bk I.27, without so much as a capital to mark the new chapter, at M.88.28.[40] Nevertheless, the list retains cap I.29. This can be accounted for if the manuscript used was divided as in CN, O, and Ca, which begin a new section at M.90.4, with the last sentence of bk I.29, beginning 'Sende he eac swylce Agustine þæm biscope pallium 7 gewrit'; for it could be thought that cap I.29, 'Þæt se ylca papa Gregorius sende Agustino pallium 7 maran fultum Godes word to læranne,' referred to the part after this division.[41] T and B have no division at this point.

Bk I.30 and 31 are omitted from both the text and the list of chapters. Part of bk I.32 is retained, and is divided from the previous chapter (bk I.29) at M.90.7 in CN, O, and Ca; there is no division here in T or B. All manuscripts start a new chapter with bk I.33. Cap I.32 is retained, but attached to it is most of cap I.33, 'þætte Agustinus Cristes cyrican geedniwode 7 Sče Petres mynster getimbrade,' corresponding to the Latin heading except for the omission of the final words, 'et de primo eius abbate Petro.' Then, surprisingly, follow two further headings referring to bk I.33. The first is: 'Þæt Agustinus Cristes cyrican geedniwode 7 worhte mid þæs cyninges fultume Æðelbyrhtes'; and the second: 'Þætte Agustinus þæt mynster þara apostola Petrus 7 Paulus getimbrade 7 be his þam ærestan abbude Petro.' Thus between them they repeat what has already been given, attached to cap I.32, but with some expansion taken from the text of the chapter, and with the addition of the Abbot Peter. Perhaps, when these two headings for bk I.33 were added, it was intended to delete the now redundant part of the combined heading cap I.32 and 33, and this was forgotten. But this supplying of two headings for bk I.33 becomes comprehensible when one notes that this chapter is divided into two, at M.90.18, at 'Swelce eac mynster getimbrade,' that is, precisely where the account of the founding of the monastery of St Peter and St Paul begins. But this division is only in CN, O, and Ca; there is no break at all in T and B. There can be little doubt that the list of headings fits a text set out like that in CN, O, and Ca better than that in T or B.

We have noted some indications that it was not likely to have been the translator of the work who tried to make the list conform to the state of the text.[42] He can be shown to have been a careful and clear-headed man, who made his selection from Bede's work with remarkable consistency, and remembered to omit Bede's cross references to passages which he had omitted, and to add explanatory expansions made necessary by his omissions.[43] He would surely have made a neater job of fitting the chapter-list to the text.

But this is not to say that he did not himself translate the list of headings. Whoever did, had the same type of Latin manuscript as that used for the rest of the work, one very like Tiberius C.II;[44] but no great weight can be attached to this circumstance, for this type of manuscript was the one most available in pre-Conquest England.[45] Cap I.4, cap I.5, and cap III.18 (20) reveal knowledge of the Latin work, which the translator of Bede certainly knew well. The style of the translation of the list is often over-literal, as is much of the work. The misunderstanding of 'creatus' in cap I.9 and of 'creati' in cap I.11 as 'born' instead of 'made' is found also in bk I.8, where it arises from misconstruing the Latin. 'Hic Constantinum filium ex concubina Helena creatum imperatorem Galliarum relinquit' is translated '7 Constantinus [sic] his sunu þam godan casere, se wæs of Elena þam wife acenned, his rice forlet,' with 'creatum' taken with 'filium' instead of with 'imperatorem.' Similarly, 'Constantinus in Brittania creatus imperator' becomes 'Constantinus se casere wære on Breotone acenned.'

But the main test of authorship is the vocabulary. This agrees closely with that of the rest of the work. The list includes many of the translator's favourite renderings, for example, 'bigenga' ('incola'), 'firenlust' ('luxuria'), 'adl' ('languor'), 'wol' ('pestilentia, pestis'), 'blinnan' ('cesso'), 'intinga' ('causa'), 'wiðerweard' ('adversarius'), 'deofolseoc' ('daemonicus'), 'mægð' ('provincia') and 'geornfulness' ('instantia'). It agrees with the usage in the text in having 'heretoga' for 'dux,' and 'ealdorman' for 'tribunus' and 'primas.' In many cases, the word chosen in the heading is not in the chapter itself. The following renderings are of special interest: 'ge'h'rora' Ca ('gehrero' CW, 'gehroro' B) for 'exterminium' in cap I.14 renders the same Latin word in bk IV.7, but is otherwise unrecorded; 'elreordian' Ca (replaced by 'elþiodian' in B and perhaps in C)[46] for 'barbaros' in cap I.14 is the normal usage of the translator of Bede, whereas other writers use 'elþeodig'; 'trymme[n]dlice' Ca (replaced by 'trumum' in B) for 'exhortatoria' in cap I.23 is a rare word, not in the text of this chapter, but used to translate the same Latin word in bk II.17 (replaced by 'trumlic' B, CW) and in bk V.21; 'lefnysse' Ca, for 'licentia' in cap I.25, is very common in the Old English Bede, but only once recorded elsewhere, in Alfred's laws; B replaces it in this heading and in most other occurrences by 'leafa.' The choice of 'wæs freomigende' Ca ('wæs fremiende' B) for 'ualuerit' in cap III.10 agrees with the translation of the same verb in bk IV.22.[47]

On the other hand, there is a handful of words in the list which are alien to the translator's normal usage. Thus in cap II.4 'obseruando' is translated 'healdnyssa,' and this word occurs also in cap V.21, whereas in the rest of the work words meaning 'observance' are consistently translated 'gehæld' ('gehyld'); in cap I.3 and cap II.9 'imperium' is translated 'cynedome,' but is always (except when it means 'command') 'rice' in the text, as it is in cap I.6; in cap IV.26 'fontem' appears as 'easpring,' but in the text always as 'wyllgespring' or 'wylle'; in cap V.7 'eadem beatorum apostolorum limina' is translated 'ða ylcan þærscwaldas þara eadigra apostola' but in the five occurrences of this phrase in the text, 'limina' is rendered 'stowe,' and 'þærscwald' occurs only for '(mortis) limite' in bk V.6 (M.398.23); in the same heading, B has 'estful' for 'devotus' (and this must lie behind the error 'eft' in Ca), but though this is a common rendering in other works, the translator of Bede always has 'wilsum,' and renders 'devotio' as 'wilsumnes'; in cap V.23 'status' becomes 'staðol,' used only for 'fundamentum' in the text, which uses 'steall' for 'status.' Another word not in the text is 'rihtgeleafful,' used in cap II.2 and cap IV.2 for 'catholica,' and in cap V.22 for 'canonicum.' This is the normal word Werferth uses for 'catholicus,' but the Old English Bede has 'rihtgelyfed' (12 times), 'riht' (10 times), 'eallic' (twice), and 'rihtgesett,' 'ciriclic,' and 'regollic' once each. Finally, we may note that in cap III.13 'a mortis articulo' is over-literally translated 'fram deaðes liðe' Ca ('fram deaþe' B), but in bk III.23 it is 'from þære tide þæs deaþes,' while in bk V.12 (M.432.2) 'in ipso ... mortis articulo' becomes 'in ða seolfan tid heora deaðes.'[48]

The last example need mean no more than that the translator chose to translate more freely as his work advanced. It is not easy to decide how much importance to attach to the other departures from the translator's normal practice. Even for words for which he had a set practice[49] he occasionally has a different rendering, for example, 'þeod' and 'land' instead of 'mægð' for 'provincia,' 'getydnes,' once, instead of 'gelæredness' for 'eruditio,' 'folgað,' once, beside 'þegnung' for 'ministerium,' and so on. It may be possible to get the variation in diction between the list and the rest of the work out of proportion.

Yet if one should feel that some of the diction in the list, such as 'healdnes,' 'estful,' and 'rihtgeleafful,' points to a different person from the translator, may not a few changes have been made by the person who compared the list with a manuscript of the text, who appears not to have been the translator himself?[50] Even if we were to go as far as claiming that the whole list was translated by someone other than the translator, nevertheless the amount of agreement in vocabulary would surely imply that this person had been trained in the same school.

After this, one can only speculate. It would seem likely that the work was provided with a list of chapters at the place of production. The translation of the list may be by the translator of the work. The fact that up to cap I.23 it includes headings for chapters omitted from the work may suggest that he made it, or at least began it, before he had decided what to leave out. He may then have entrusted the task of adding the list to his translation of the rest to a pupil or colleague, who did not at once realize that some chapters had been omitted, and only after cap I.23 began to bring list and text into agreement. The manuscript he used was one which had mislaid a gathering, and hence he omitted the headings of bk III.17-20. This amended list may then have been copied into a manuscript which did not have the lacuna in bk III. This theory would imply that at least two manuscripts were produced at the place of origin, one complete in this respect, as T and B are, the other with the section in bk III missing, as in the text behind C, O, and Ca; into this faulty version two of the missing chapters were inserted later, by a writer whose style and diction were very different from those of the translator, and who was probably working elsewhere.

But this could be an over-simplification. The original centre may have produced more than one manuscript in addition to the faulty one,[51] and, if so, T and B could descend from different manuscripts. The faulty manuscript may have been a copy of the manuscript from which B is descended.[52] I throw out this suggestion because B shares many agreements in error with the manuscripts of the z group, though it avoids a number of their misreadings. I called attention to the shared errors between B and manuscripts of the z group in 1962,[53] but as at that time I accepted the established view of a common archetype for T and B, I could only explain these errors in B, which T avoids, as the result of later contamination. This may be the correct explanation,[54] but it now seems to me that the whole question requires reconsideration. It would, however, swell this paper to inordinate length to attempt to deal with this here.[55]

There may be other possible interpretations of the peculiarities of the chapter-list of the Old English Bede. It seems worth while to draw attention to these peculiarities, for scholars studying the practices of early scriptoria, especially in Anglo-Saxon England,[56] may find it convenient to have the facts set out. They may be able to confirm or refute my tentative interpretation of their implications.

NOTES

1 I am indebted to Miss Janet Bately for reading and making useful comments on this article.

    In this paper, Bede's *Historia ecclesiastica* is referred to by book and chapter, e.g. bk I.15, with the enumeration as in the edition by Charles Plummer, *Venerabilis Baedae opera historica* (Oxford 1896). Chapter-headings are distinguished from the chapters themselves by citing them as, e.g., cap I.15 (with the numbers as in the Latin text). Miller's edition (see below), is cited as M, by page and line. As 'Whitelock,' I refer to my article, 'The Old English Bede,' *Proceedings of the British Academy* 48 (1962) 57-90.

2 There are also three short extracts from bk IV.5, bk I.27, and bk II.3, in British Museum, Cotton MS Domitian IX, f 11, in a hand of about 900. These were printed by J. Zupitza, in *Zeitschrift für deutsches Altertum* 30 (1886) 185.

3 I.e. ff 1-38, some fragmentary; also some folios now bound up in Otho B.X, as ff 55, 58, and 62. On the correct order, see N.R. Ker, *Catalogue of Manuscripts containing Anglo-Saxon* (Oxford 1957), 230.

4 *Historiæ ecclesiasticæ gentis anglorum libri v*, ed. Abraham Whelock (Cambridge 1643 and 1644)

5 *Historiæ ecclesiasticæ gentis anglorum libri quinque*, ed. John Smith (Cambridge 1722)

6 On this see Robin Flower, 'Laurence Nowell and the Discovery of England,' *Proceedings of the British Academy* 21 (1935) 54. I use my own collation of this transcript.

7 See Whitelock, 82, note 30. It is possible that these errors arose when the first fair copy was made from the translator's drafts.

8 On xxiv-xxvi of part i of his edition, *The Old English Version of Bede's Ecclesiastical History of the English People*, part i.I (1890), part i.2 (1891), part ii.1 and part ii.2 (1898) (EETS OS 95, 96, 110, and 111). He prints from T where it is available, from other manuscripts where T has lacunae; in part ii he gives the variants in other manuscripts. Considering its length and complication, the work is remarkably accurate; yet it has a few errors, which I have corrected in my quotations. The other modern edition, *König Alfreds Uebersetzung von Bedas Kirchengeschichte*, ed. J. Schipper, Bibliothek der angelsächsischen Prosa 4, (Leipzig 1899), which gives Ca and B in parallel columns, and variants from other manucripts in footnotes, is far less reliable. The comparative merit of these editions is discussed in an unpublished doctoral dissertation in the University Library, Cambridge, by R.J.S. Grant, 'MS. C.C.C.C. 41, with special regard to the B version of the Old English Bede' (1970), 252-4 and 260. This work includes a detailed description of this manuscript.

9 A stemma of the current view of the manuscript relationships is set out in Whitelock, 81.

10 The omission of this part of bk III.17, consisting of an account of Aidan with a reference to his observing the wrong Easter, is in line with the translator's practice of omitting references to the Easter controversy unless they show the English church reforming the errors of the Celtic church. See Whitelock, 62-3.

11 S. Potter, *On the Relation of the Old English Bede to Werferth's Gregory and to Alfred's Translations*, Mémoires de la Société royale des sciences de Bohème, Classes des lettres (1930), 30-3

12 J.J. Campbell, 'The OE. Bede: Book III, Chapters 16-20,' *Modern Language Notes* 67 (1952) 381-6

13 Miller, xxv. Only shared errors are admissible as evidence. T and B often agree in correct readings against the other manuscripts, but this can be attributed to errors made in the archetype of the Z branch. Several of Miller's examples are of a type that can easily arise by independent error in T and B.

14 One can only speculate why the person who added a new translation of bk III.17 and 18 did not supply one for bk III.19 and 20. The former of these is a long chapter on Fursey's vision. He might have shrunk from so great a task of translation, or have regarded it as an interruption in a historical work, or have poss-

essed it in a separate form; the second is only an account of episcopal succession in East Anglia and Canterbury.

15 It would not be easy to find out from B that these chapters were actually in the text, for B gives no indication where a new book begins, and does not number the chapters. B's exemplar may have shared these defects.

16 Ca avoids the errors in C listed on p. 267.

17 B gives no numbers to cap I.1-4, which are on the first page; it then numbers from V to CXIII, with some errors. The rubricator did not complete his work, so that the last six headings have only a dash beside them, and no number.

18 Whelock gives variants from C for the rubrics at the end of bks I, II, and III. If these were C's only differences from Ca, C was closer to Ca than to B, though it had 'æftere' for 'oðer' after bk II, when B has 'æfteran,' and, like B, had 'þa capitulas' after bk III, which is not in Ca.

19 This is only in Ca, numbered as if it were a third paragraph of Bede's preface. It may once have been in O, but it was never in C; see Whitelock, 60-1.

20 Blank spaces are left frequently for initial letters, and some initials are only sketched in in outline.

21 One can assume that if C had had headings for these chapters, Whelock would have noted it.

22 For further discussion see pp. 277-8.

23 On this manuscript and its relation to others, see Plummer, I, lxxxvi-cxxxii, especially xciii-xcviii; also *Bede's Ecclesiastical History of the English People*, ed. Bertram Colgrave and R.A.B. Mynors (Oxford 1969), xxxix-xlvi. Mynors refers to the two main types as c-type and m-type. On the use by the Old English Bede of a c-type manuscript, see Whitelock, 86, note 123.

24 See Plummer, I, 247, note 1.

25 But C retained a better reading of cap V.10: 'socii eius Heuualdi sint martyrium passi.' CW records 'heawaldas.' Neither Ca nor B has recognized this as a personal name, Ca having: 'his geferan twegen healicne martyrdom wæron þrowiende,' and B: 'his geferan twegen martiras dom wæron þrowiende.'

26 Another example would be 'foresægde' for 'praedixerit' in cap III.15, if Miller were correct in assigning this reading to B in his note, I, 14; but B reads 'sæde,' as correctly given by Miller in II, 7, agreeing with 'sægde' in Ca. Miller gives 'foresægde' as the reading in CS, but though Smith puts this form, in brackets, in his text, he does not assign it to any manuscript, and it may be that 'foresægde' is his own emendation. Whelock puts an asterisk against 'sægde,' but records no variant.

27 Ca, which has, for 'pro adepta uictoria,' 'for ðam sige sealdan him for Gode,' must have taken 'sealdan' (dative singular of the participle) as a finite verb, for it omits 'dederit.' B has 'for ðam sealde him for Godes lufan,' omitting 'sige,' and

The List of Chapter-Headings in the Old English Bede 281

renders 'dederit' as 'sealde 7 forgeaf.' 'Possessiones' was probably rendered 'æhta micle': B has 'ehta micle,' but Ca, taking 'æhta' as if 'eahta' ('eight'), has 'æhta mila'; 'twelf bocland' for 'territoria' comes from the text of the chapter.

28 In the rest of the work, however, there are a number of places where B and CN agree in an erroneous reading, when T, O, and Ca are correct. The implication of this cannot be seen until we know whether O had access to another text, as well as Z; see note 55.

29 A comparison of Nowell's transcript with the surviving parts of C shows that he copied the chapter divisions of his exemplar carefully (even trying to reproduce the decorated initials), and we can therefore accept his evidence for the arrangement of C.

30 Tiberius C.II has no division between bk III.1 and 2; it begins bk IV.2 at what is in other manuscripts the second sentence ('Mox peragrata ...'), attaching the first sentence to the previous chapter; and it omits bk IV.14 and attaches bk IV. 15 to bk IV.13, when the other manuscripts attach it to bk IV.14. No headings for bk IV.14 and 15 are given in the Latin *capitula*, whether of c-type or m-type, or in the Old English list.

31 They begin bk III.13 at 'Nec solum inclyti fama,' when Tiberius C.II does not begin until 'Tempore, inquit, mortalitatis.'

32 It differs also in attaching the first sentence of bk I.25 to the preceding chapter (bk I.23, since it omits bk I.24), and commencing bk I.25 at the second sentence. The first sentence refers to the letter of Gregory in bk I.23.

33 I quote the Old English headings as in Ca, unless B has a variant which affects the argument.

34 They were certainly omitted from B, CN, and Ca. T does not begin until near the end of bk I.15, and O not until near the beginning of bk I.25.

35 Ca begins its chapter-numeration here, with I, having no number at the commencement of the chapter.

36 The discrepancy between the list for bk I and the text gave trouble to the scribe of Ca who supplied numbers to the chapters. When he numbers bk I.8 as XI, Miller (42) says the numbering to the end of bk I is confused. This is unfair on the scribe, who, having more headings than chapters, tried to allot the numbers to the chapters to which the headings referred. Bk I.8 mentions Constantinus, but the heading does not; on the other hand, cap I.11 mentions him, though the part of the chapter in which he occurs is omitted. The scribe therefore assumed that cap I.11 was referring to bk I.8. Bk I.9 and 10 being missing, he numbered bk I.11 as XII, but his text had no division where bk I.12 begins, so he gave XIII to bk I.13. He correctly jumped from XVI to XXIII when his text omits bk I.17-22. He made his chapter numbers agree with the list in bk II, by omitting VI and VII,

since Ca has a lacuna covering most of bk II.6 and 7; he introduced each of the two chapters bk III.17 and 18, supplied in the Z branch, for which his list had no headings, merely by 'Eft oðer cwide,' without any number. Only in bks IV and V does he number his divisions straight through, getting slightly out of line with the list of headings.

37 B repeats 'Eadbyrht' at this point.

38 T normally begins a chapter with a decorated, tinted initial and a whole line of capitals.

39 For a possible reason for this, see Whitelock, 70.

40 This is obscured by all the editors, because they remove the *Interrogationes* back to their position in the Latin text. They therefore begin bk I.29 as if the manuscripts marked it as a new chapter.

41 B has space for about six letters at the end of M.88.30, and begins the next line with 'IN,' and CN also has 'IN,' but in the middle of a line; but there is no division of any kind here in T, O, or Ca.

42 See pp. 271-2.

43 See Whitelock, 61-2.

44 See pp. 266-7.

45 Only for the north of England is there evidence that a Latin text of the m-type was available. As Sir Roger Mynors says he knows no evidence for this (xli, note 2 o the edition cited in note 23 above), it is as well to state that the northern recension of the Anglo-Saxon Chronicle (MSS D, E, and F) used a text of Bede which had the entries in the summary at 697 and 698 which are missing from c-type manuscripts; that the error in the preface to this recension, bringing the Britons 'of Armenia,' seems based on the error of m-type texts, 'armonicano' for 'armoricano'; and that in annal 731 the chronicler dates the death of Archbishop Bryhtwold 'on Id. Iañ.' agreeing with m-type texts, when the c-type reads 'die v iduum Ianuariarum.'

46 See p. 269.

47 'efenbiscop,' in cap II.4 and bk V.19 (M. 460.13), is a word not recorded elsewhere, but it seems so obvious a rendering of 'coepiscopus' that this may be accidental; yet Werferth has 'efenhadan þæs biscopes' for 'coepiscopi.' Another unique word in the Old English Bede is 'gewerian' in the sense 'make a treaty,' which translates 'iuncto ... foedere' in cap I.15 (altered to 'waredon' B) and 'inito ... foedere' in bk I.15.

48 'Arraniae uaesaniae' in cap I.8 becomes 'Arrianiscan gedwolan.' In bk II.5 (M. 110.32), bk III.1 (M. 154.9), and bk IV.17 (M. 312.13) 'wedenheortnes' is used for 'vesania'; but only in the last of these places does it refer to heresy, and 'gedwola' is commonly used by the translator for 'error.'

49 For many words he had no settled rendering: for example, he uses for 'dignus,'

'gedefe(lic),' 'wyrðe,' and 'meodume'; for 'negotium,' 'bigong,' 'scir,' 'intinga,' and 'wise'; for 'solerter,' 'geornlic,' 'geornful,' and 'behygdlic'; for his words for 'catholicus' see p. 276.

50 This person presumably composed the new headings, but as these were taken from the chapters, they naturally show no difference in usage.

51 We know that several contemporary copies of Alfred's *Cura pastoralis* were produced. His verse preface says the work was sent 'south and north' to his scribes, and that the copies were to be brought back for him to circulate to his bishops. British Museum, Cotton MS Tiberius B.XI seems to have been kept at headquarters, and Bodleian MS Hatton 20 has Alfred's prefaces on two leaves added at the beginning, the prose preface in the hand of Tiberius B.XI. See K. Sisam, *Studies in the History of Old English Literature* (Oxford 1953), 140-7. Alfred needed many copies; but there is no evidence that a similar circulation of the Old English Bede was intended.

52 Theoretically, it could have been copied from the manuscript from which T descends, but T does not share a number of errors with the Z group of manuscripts, as B does.

53 See Whitelock, 81, note 22.

54 It is the likely explanation of agreements between B and Ca, when Ca deserts its usual source, O. For these agreements tend to occur when the text is difficult, and a copyist might be led to consult another version. Thus at M. 278.18, T has an over-literal rendering of 'Quod si semel susceptus noluerit inuitatus redire' as 'Gif he æne siða onfongen, haten ham hweorfan, ne wille,' and this, with some spelling differences, is in CN and O; but B expands to 'Gif he æne syþe onfangen sy, hate hine man ham hweorfan, gif he ne wille,' and Ca agrees, except that it omits the first 'he,' has some difference in spelling, and 'nyle' for 'ne wille.' Moreover, the agreements tend to come in patches, as if Ca was intermittently consulting a B-type text. For example, at M. 196.7 the rare word 'eondes' T ('endes,' CN, O) is 'hiwes' B, 'heowes' Ca; at M. 196.19, where T has 'eondes' and B 'hiwæs,' CN, O, and Ca have 'endes,' but Ca has 'hiwæs' written above it; and between these two cases, at M. 196.13, where T, CN, O, and Ca have 'gebætum,' and B has 'gerædum,' Ca has 'rædum' above '-bætum.' Other instances could be added.

55 A prerequisite for such an investigation is a detailed examination of the very numerous alterations made by the scribes in O, to see if they suggest that another text was available for comparison, in addition to the source which O shares with C. For if it were, it would be difficult to be sure, when C and O differ, which of them is representing their common source. Some errors in C could come from that source, but have been corrected in O from another version. One should also note that Nowell's transcript of C proves that this did not have the lacuna in

bk II.5-7 (M. 110.30-118.16), which is in O and Ca. This means that O's exemplar, which had lost this part, cannot have been Z, but some intervening manuscript between Z and O.

56 An examination of the relationship between the chapter-lists and the text in other works of Alfred's reign might repay investigation. Miss Janet Bately will consider the position in the Old English *Orosius* in her forthcoming edition.

It may be of interest to note that the list of headings before the laws of Alfred and Ine was drawn up to fit the division into paragraphs as in the archetype of the surviving manuscripts (the oldest, Corpus Christi College, Cambridge, MS 173, from the mid tenth century), although this division often runs clauses on different topics together in the same paragraph, and occasionally begins a new paragraph in the middle of a subject. As the list of headings gives only one to each paragraph, usually referring only to the first part of it, many of the important clauses in the laws have no headings in the list.

ROWLAND L. COLLINS
PETER CLEMOES

The common origin of Ælfric fragments at New Haven, Oxford, Cambridge, and Bloomington

In recent years, seven fragments of Anglo-Saxon parchment have come to light which, although in four widely separated places today, were probably parts of the same manuscript originally. Dated by their script to the beginning of the eleventh century, they contain portions of homilies and lives of saints by Ælfric, whose quality as a writer of late Old English prose Professor Pope has done so much to elucidate. The kinship of these fragments establishes that the manuscript (or just possibly manuscripts) of which they were a part had important features which no other surviving manuscript of Ælfric's works possesses. The fragments are:

1 THE NEW HAVEN FRAGMENTS
Two strips, *a* and *b*, which represent adjacent portions of the same manuscript leaf and which have been cut vertically from its left-hand side; in the Marie-Louise and James M. Osborn Collection, Yale University Library, New Haven, Connecticut; contain parts of the homily for Palm Sunday in Ælfric's First Series of *Catholic Homilies* (*The Homilies of the Anglo-Saxon Church ... the Sermones Catholici, or Homilies of Ælfric*, ed. Benjamin Thorpe [2 vols, London 1844-6, cited henceforth as Thorpe], I xiv).

2 THE OXFORD FRAGMENT
The upper two-thirds of a strip cut vertically from the left-hand side of a leaf; in the Bodleian Library, Oxford, the shelfmark being MS Eng. th.

c. 74; contains part of the end of the homily for the second Sunday after Easter in Ælfric's First Series of *Catholic Homilies* (Thorpe I xvii) and parts of the beginning of his homily *De fide catholica* for Wednesday in Rogationtide in the same series (Thorpe I xx).

3 THE CAMBRIDGE FRAGMENTS

Two vertical strips, *a* and *b*; *a* has been cut from the middle of one leaf and *b* from the right-hand side of another; in the library of Queens' College, Cambridge, the shelfmark being MS Horne 75; *a* contains part of Ælfric's life of St Apollonaris (*Ælfric's Lives of Saints*, ed. Walter W. Skeat, EETS OS 76, 82, 94, and 114 [2 vols, London 1881-1900, repr. 1966, cited henceforth as Skeat], xxii), and *b* contains part of Ælfric's account of the legendary letter of Christ to Abgarus which formed a supplement to his brief account of the martyrdom of kings Abdon and Sennes (Skeat xxiv) and part of the beginning of Ælfric's summary of Maccabees (Skeat xxv).

4 THE BLOOMINGTON FRAGMENTS

Two strips, *a* and *b*, which represent adjacent portions of the same leaf and which have been cut vertically from its left-hand side; now sewn together in their original contiguity; in the Lilly Library of Indiana University, Bloomington, Indiana, the shelfmark being MS Poole 10; contain part of the end of Ælfric's life of St Apollonaris (Skeat xxii) and part of his account of the martyrdom of kings Abdon and Sennes, just extending into the beginning of his supplementary account of Christ's letter to Abgarus (Skeat xxiv).[1]

THE NEW HAVEN FRAGMENTS (SEE FIGURE 1 AND PLATE 1)

Fragment *a* measures 255 mm vertically and 42 mm across and fragment *b* on average 259 mm vertically (varying from 252 mm to 263 mm) and 43 mm across (tapering somewhat towards the bottom). The height of the margin surviving at the foot of both the recto and the verso of each fragment is about 37 mm. The ragged left-hand edge of *a* seems to be the result not of a cut but of a tear which separated the leaf from its conjugate. The inner lateral margin thus preserved on the recto of *a* is about 20 mm wide.

The surviving text begins at the top of *b* recto, '...st · We wyllað nu fon ...' (Thorpe I, 206, line 21), and continues, with gaps, to '... licað

Ac syððan' (Thorpe I, 212, line 8) at the foot of *a* verso.

Each side of *a* preserves part of each of twenty-seven lines of text and each side of *b* part of each of twenty-eight lines (and descenders from another line above). The amount of text missing between the last line of *b* recto and (ignoring the descenders at the top) the first line of *b* verso indicates that four lines have been lost (apart from the descenders of the fourth) from the top of *b* verso. Thus, the original written space on the verso of the leaf (and, therefore, by normal practice, on the recto, too) consisted of thirty-two lines. Our line numberings refer to these original lines. The rules for the surviving lines are usually 8 mm apart (or slightly more), so that we can assume that the original height of the written space, measured from the tops of letters (but not their ascenders) on line 1 to the rule for line 32, was slightly over 250 mm. The fragments, cut from the left-hand side of their leaf, preserve the beginnings of lines on their recto and the ends of lines on their verso. The amount of text missing from each line indicates that rather less than half of each line of writing has survived. The rulings were made from the verso which is the hair side of the parchment.

A deep stain, 5 or 6 mm wide, runs down the full length of *a* recto, about 5 mm from the right-hand edge (that is, from the cut between *a* and *b*). There is a similar stain running down the lower three-eighths of the verso of *b* at about the same distance from the cut between the strips. Another stain, presumably an offset from leather, appears on the upper left-hand corner of *a* recto. The long vertical stain on *a* recto is marked by a series of holes: the first of these is like an elongated tear and runs from line 7 to line 13; others mar lines 14, 19, and 25, and there is yet another hole in the stain some 11 mm below the rule for line 32. Three holes have also damaged *b*: one occurs between lines 11 and 12, another in the middle of line 21, and another across lines 29 and 30. The lowest (and largest) hole in *b* is in the middle of the vertical stain on the verso. Quite clearly, from the evidence of the stains and the holes, and from the dimensions of the fragments, these strips were used in a bookbinding. The short vertical stain on *b* verso, in combination with the vertical stain on *a* recto, indicates that the two strips were used overlapped for a single joining of board to book: if *a* verso were pressed on to *b* verso, so as to allow the bottom of *a* recto to come between lines 23 and 24 of *b* verso, the stain on *b* verso would continue the long stain on *a* recto and the holes in *b* between lines 11 and 12 and on line 21 would fit the holes in *a* on line 25 and in the lower margin. The strip formed in this way would be between 347 and

350 mm long.

The two fragments were found by Dr James Molloy attached to a binding board in a pile of rubbish in a lumber-room containing part of the old presbytery library at Winchester. Removed from the board, they were sold at the Sotheby sale of 29 July 1965 as lot 576 and were there purchased by Quaritch for the Osborn Collection.

THE OXFORD FRAGMENT (SEE FIGURE 1 AND PLATE 2)

The average measurements of the fragment are 213 mm vertically (varying from 205 mm to 219 mm) and 80 mm across (varying to 66 mm above the horizontal tear at the bottom). The height of the margin surviving at the top of both the recto and the verso is about 18 mm. The ragged left-hand edge of the fragment seems to be the result not of a cut but of a tear separating the leaf from its conjugate. The width of the inner lateral margin thus preserved is about 25 mm on both the recto and (measured from the inner bounding line, see below) the verso.

The text on the first eleven lines of the recto, part of the homily for the second Sunday after Easter in Ælfric's First Series of *Catholic Homilies*, begins 'He oncnæwð his fæder ...' (Thorpe I, 242, line 31) and continues, with gaps, to the end of the homily. Ælfric's homily *De fide catholica*, for Wednesday in Rogationtide and from the same series, begins on the next line; no rubric is preserved, because, presumably, it was on the now lost second half of line 11. The text continues, with gaps, to '... habbað ge gehyred' (Thorpe I, 276, line 34) at the foot of the verso.

Each side preserves part of each of twenty lines of text (with traces of a twenty-first on the recto). The amount of text missing between the traces of line 21 on the recto and the first line on the verso indicates that originally there were five more lines on the recto, that is, twenty-six in all. The rules for the surviving lines are 9 to 11 mm apart, so that we can assume that the original height of the written space, measured from the tops of letters (but not their ascenders) on line 1 to the rule of line 26, was some 250 mm. Cut from the left-hand side of its leaf, the fragment preserves the beginnings of lines on its recto and the ends of lines on its verso. The amount of text missing from each line indicates that about two-fifths of each line of writing have survived. All rulings were made from the recto which is the hair side. Two vertical rules, 9 mm apart, bound the beginnings of lines on the recto and show through to bound the ends of lines on the verso; the horizontal lines touch only the inner of these rules.

The strip of which the surviving fragment was part was used in the binding of a copy of the *Sermones* of Augustine (Paris 1520), which is now Bodleian Library Vet. E1 b.10.[2] While the strip was thus used (with its top towards the bottom of the binding), a paper sheet, which was stuck on to the lower board of the binding,[3] was pressed hard against, and probably lightly pasted to, the left-hand edge of the recto of the strip (that is, the right-hand edge in the upside-down position of the strip in the binding). Over the years the ink on this edge of the recto was attracted to the paper and is still visible in reverse offset on the paper pastedown. The first few letters of each of lines 1 to 20 are clearly visible on the paper; the beginning of line 21, of which only traces survive on the parchment, is clearer on the paper than on the fragment itself; a letter or two of each of lines 22 to 25, now totally missing from the fragment, can easily be read from the paper with a mirror; and smudges on the paper probably indicate where the twenty-sixth line began. All legible readings in the offset are included in the transcript of the text below (p. 307). In addition, the general outlines of the original strip are clearly visible on the paper, both from the stains of paste and moisture and from the impression it has left. As a result we can tell that the length of the strip was originally between 290 mm and 300 mm.

On the verso of the surviving fragment there is a deep stain down its full length, 2 to 7 mm wide, set 4 to 9 mm from the left-hand edge and often completely hiding the writing. Several holes are visible in this stain at irregular intervals, but three can be identified as holes for the threads which tied the binding to the book. Starting with the lowest, these three holes correspond in position to (starting from the top of the spine) the second, third, and fourth bands and, together with the stain, show that the strip was placed between the lower board and the book with its top towards the bottom of the binding and with its verso facing inwards and its recto outwards, and that, at the stain, it was folded along the spine edge, with the larger part of the strip extending out along the board itself. The paper pastedown covered the strip, touching directly the larger part of the recto which faced out from the board. The irregular tear at the bottom of the surviving fragment (at its top, as it was placed in the binding) and the offset on the pastedown indicate that the strip was damaged at some time after it became part of the binding, that part being lost that was on a level with the first band.

The lower board of Vet. E1 b.10 is the only original one to survive; it is preserved separately from the book, with the rest of the original binding and with another leather-covered board of similar age, as Bodleian Library Vet. E1 b.10⚛. The original binding can be precisely identified as the work of a London binder 'K.L.-L.K.' in the second or third decade of the sixteenth century. The decorative motifs stamped on the leather of the lower board, Oldham's classified side-view continuous roll no 6 and Oldham's classified ornament B(1),[4] are associated exclusively with the work of this craftsman.

The Oxford fragment, as a part of the binding of the Augustine's *Sermones*, was in the presbytery library at Winchester. The bulk of this library was sold to the London dealer Weinreb in 1966 and from him this book became part of Hodgson's sale no 4 of 1966-7, 20 January 1967, where, as lot 630, it was purchased by the Bodleian.

THE CAMBRIDGE FRAGMENTS (SEE FIGURE 1 AND PLATE 4)

Each fragment measures 302 mm vertically and 65 to 66 mm across. The height of the margins surviving at the top and bottom of each fragment is, at the top, about 12 mm on *a* recto, 8 mm on *a* verso, 13 mm on *b* recto and 6 mm on *b* verso, and, at the bottom, about 28 mm on *a* and 26 mm on *b*. The ragged right-hand edge of *b* seems not to be the result of a cut but to represent the outer edge of the leaf. The outer lateral margin thus preserved on the verso of *b* is about 25 mm wide.

The text on *a*, part of Ælfric's life of St Apollonaris, begins ' · 7 þam halgan were ...' (Skeat xxii, line 97) and continues, with gaps, to '... þ þu forlæte þine' (Skeat xxii, line 213). The text on the recto and first twenty-six lines of the verso of *b*, part of Ælfric's account of Christ's letter to Abgarus, begins '...rian lande · 7 se ...' (Skeat xxiv, line 83) and continues, with gaps, to '... se soða gele...a on þ...' (Skeat xxiv, line 190). The rest of this item would not have required more space than the missing part of line 26 on the verso. Ælfric's summary of Maccabees begins on the next line. Part of its rubric is preserved on line 27 and the text, which begins on line 28, continues, with gaps, to '... 7 afligde þone cyning' (Skeat xxv, line 8).

Each side of each fragment preserves part of each of the thirty-two lines that made up the original written space. The rules for the lines are 8 mm apart, and the height of the written space, measured from the tops of letters (but not their ascenders) on line 1 to the rule of line

32, is 255 mm. Fragment *a*, cut from the middle of its leaf, preserves the middles of lines. The amount of text missing from each line indicates that about two-fifths of each line of writing have survived. Fragment *b*, cut from the right-hand side of its leaf, preserves the ends of lines on its recto and the beginnings of lines on its verso. The amount of text missing from each line indicates that in this case a quarter, or rather less, of each line of writing has survived. In both instances the rulings were made from the recto, which is the hair side.

Each fragment has a deep stain running down its full length, on *a* at about 9 mm from the right-hand edge of the recto and on *b* at about 10 mm from the left-hand edge of the recto. In each case the stain is more pronounced on the verso, often totally obscuring the writing it covers; on the recto it does not hide any letters. There is·a hole in *a* between lines 22 and 23 and another below line 32; there is a similar hole in *b* between lines 30 and 31. These stains and holes doubtless result from the fragments' use as binding strips: a stain, we can assume, corresponds to a fold next to the spine and a hole corresponds to a thread tying the binding to the book. Further, the upper left corner of *b* has been torn away; the tear, since it extends to the stain, may have been caused by pulling out from an attached thread.

The two fragments were discovered in 1953 by Dr N.R. Ker in the binding of a copy of Hector Boece's *Historia scotorum* (Paris 1527) in the library of Queens' College, Cambridge. They have been removed from this binding and are described as item no 81 in Ker's *Catalogue of Manuscripts containing Anglo-Saxon* (Oxford 1957). As Dr Ker states, 'one strip was pasted at each end [of the book] along the part of the board lying nearest to the spine and beneath the paper pastedown.' He identifies the blind-stamping on the leather binding as Oldham's classified side-view continuous roll no 6 and Oldham's classified ornament B(1).[5] As has already been pointed out (above, p. 290), this particular combination of leather stamps identifies the binding as work of the London binder 'K.L.-L.K.' in the second or third decade of the sixteenth century.

THE BLOOMINGTON FRAGMENTS (SEE FIGURE 1 AND PLATE 3)

The two fragments, *a* and *b*, sewn together in their original relation, measure 282 mm vertically and have a combined average width of 78 mm (varying from 76 mm to 82 mm). The height of the margins surviving at the top and bottom of both the recto and the verso is about 12 mm at the top and about 15 mm at the bottom. The bottom edge seems not to represent the edge of the leaf but to be the result of a cut. The left-hand edge of a is firmly turned under for a width of about 10 mm and there are some fragments of thread in the fold. At first sight, the flap thus formed appears to be part of the conjugate leaf. But its edge, since it is not clean cut, is likely to be the result of a tear separating the conjugates, and the fold and the fragments of thread must be presumed to have had their origin while a was used in a bookbinding or, more probably, when the fragments were preserved after being taken out of the binding. The width of the inner lateral margin thus surviving on the recto of a (from the edge of the flap to the beginning of the written space) is about 23 mm.

The text on the first twenty-two lines of the recto of the combined fragments, part of Ælfric's life of St Apollonaris, begins 'godum geoffrige ...' (Skeat xxii, line 213) and continues, with gaps, to '... mid þam ælmihtigan' (Skeat xxii, line 253). The rest of this item would not have required more space than the now missing part of line 22. Ælfric's account of the martyrdom of kings Abdon and Sennes begins on the next line. Part of its rubric is preserved on line 23 and the text, which begins on line 24, continues, with gaps, to the end of the account (Skeat xxiv, line 80) on line 31 of the verso. Ælfric's supplementary account of Christ's letter to Abgarus begins on the next line, which is the last one on the verso. Any rubric was in the now missing part of this line, and the surviving text consists of only a few words (Skeat xxiv, lines 81-2).

Each side of the fragments preserves part of each of the thirty-two lines that made up the original written space. The rules for the lines are 8 mm apart, and the height of the written space, measured from the tops of letters (but not their ascenders) on line 1 to the rule of line 32, is 252 mm. Cut from the left-hand side of the leaf, the fragments preserve the beginnings of lines on their recto and the ends of lines on their verso. The amount of text missing from each line indicates that rather less than half of each line of writing has survived. The rulings were made from the recto, which is the hair side.

There is a deep stain, varying in intensity, which runs almost the entire vertical length of the verso of each fragment. The stains, which are parallel to each other, are each 10 to 11 mm from the mended cut and presumably were caused by their separate placement along the spine edges in a bookbinding. Other, larger stains along the top of each verso were probably acquired through contact with the paste-down.

The book in which these fragments were used as binding strips is not known, although their history can be traced for over a hundred years. A pencil note in the bottom margin of the recto indicates, rightly, that this half-leaf was part of lot 1111 in the Libri sale on 28 March 1859. Sir Thomas Phillips evidently was the purchaser, for it was subsequently part of lot 22229 in his collection. In 1947, through Messrs Robinson of Pall Mall, Mr George A. Poole, Jr, of Chicago, acquired a number of Phillips manuscripts, including these fragments, which he planned to use in an exhibition illustrating the growth of various styles of printing. In 1958 the Poole Collection was acquired by the Lilly Library and the fragments were first given public notice in 1960.[6]

THE HANDWRITING AND PUNCTUATION

The handwriting on all the fragments is insular minuscule — a small, carefully formed, relatively plain, and regular hand. Dr N.R. Ker assigned the hand of C to the beginning of the eleventh century[7] and described it as 'a rather small but good hand.' The specific characteristics which he noted are that a is square or rounded, that high e ligatures are frequent, and that long s is much more common than low s. He further noted that the title and initial on Cb^V are in metallic red and that the punctuation is by mid-line point only.

Both square and rounded a are present on all four sets of fragments, seemingly without pattern. NH shows square a in the ligature æ ('hæ-ðen,' r11, and 'cwæþ,' r14), medially ('naman,' r30), and terminally ('witega,' r14), and rounded a similarly ('þæs,' r30; 'þam,' r6; and 'þa' and 'beb[o]da,' r31). Both forms appear in the same word: in 'ge-sceafta' (v6) the first a is square; the second, rounded. O likewise has square a in the ligature æ ('þære,' r2), medially ('bugað,' r8), and terminally ('licra,' r17), and rounded a correspondingly ('þære,' r3, and 'fæder,' v18; 'lande,' r6; and 'iudea,' r6). On this fragment, too, both forms can appear in the same word: in 'ealra' (r10) the first a is square; the second, rounded. A single example of a large caroline a should also be noted (r11). The same range of uses of both square and rounded a is to be found on C (square a: 'þærrihte,' a^r19; 'soðan,' b^V19; and 'mund-bora,' a^r2; rounded a: 'wæron,' a^r4; 'þam,' a^r1; and 'sona' and 'swa,' a^r3). Here again both forms appear in the same word: in 'halga' (a^r4) the first a is rounded; the second, square. On B the usage is the same (square a: 'hræd,' r8; 'bearnum,' r2, and 'middaneard,' 'lac,' and 'offrian,' r17; and 'heora,' r27; rounded a: 'betæhte,' r5; 'forþan,' r8; and 'swa,' r11). Both forms appear in the same word: in 'racenteagum' (r30) the first a is rounded; the second, square. A single large caroline a also appears (r8).

Ligature between high e, which is not in the combination æ, and a following letter which does not begin with an ascender is frequent on NH, C, and B, especially when the second letter is a, f, n, r, or low s, but occurs only four times on O (ea twice and er twice). There is no ligature between high e and c, p, or w on any of the fragments and only two (out of many possible examples) between high e and o (B^{V}7 and 10). On all the fragments the ligature is invariable between æ and f, g, n, r (twenty-one examples), low s or t; there is also one example of ligature between æ and w.

All three kinds of s are visible on each set of fragments; namely the two insular forms — the long and the low — and the round form. The long s dominates NH: in the first seventeen lines of the surviving text s occurs twenty-one times; all but two of these are in the long form, the other two being low s's (the second s in 'assa,' r6, and the second s in 'cristes,' r21). Round s can be seen in 'Se' (r25). The low form dominates O: on the recto all examples of s are of this form except the long s's in 'stemne' (5) and the second 'swa' (20) and the round s's at 10, 11, 18, and 21. As Ker states, long s dominates C. In the first fifteen lines of the recto of B all forms of s are long save five: there are three examples of low s (the second s in 'þises,' 9, the second in 'ehtnyssa,' 14, and the second in 'ehtnysse,' 15) and two examples of round s (25). Double s is regularly written as high s followed by low s on NH, C, and B (only three exceptions); of the two examples on O one (r11) consists of two round s's and the other (v12) of high s followed by round s.

The crossing of ð on all the fragments is done by a light curved flourish, ending rather high with an increased heaviness in the line (NH^{V}5, 8, 11, 17, etc; O^{r}1, 3, 4, 5, 6, etc; Ca^{r}1, 2, 5, and 6; and B^{r}3, 4, 5, 6, etc).

The y is regularly dotted on all the fragments. On NH, C, and B the form of y curves gracefully, but decidedly, to the left and up, ending in a thickening of the line. On O, however, this flourish is nowhere shown. All examples of y end with a straight tapering line.

There is no enlarged initial or title on NH, but each of O, C, and B has an initial and, in two cases, a title in metallic red (see O^{r}12; Cb^{V}27-8;

and B^{r}23-4). In the only two cases in which a capital at the beginning of a sentence coincides with the beginning of a line (O^{r}1 and 9) the capital is placed outside the inner vertical ruled line. When n occurs at the end of a line it is regularly written in Roman capital form if some space needs to be filled (NH^{v}9 and 32, B^{v}13 and 16, and Cb^r9). Where Latin occurs in the text (Cb^r12-17) the script is the same as that used for English.

Abbreviations are rare on all the fragments, except for the crossed þ which is regularly used for 'þæt.' The few other abbreviations are apparently without pattern (NH, none; O, 'heofonū,' v3; C, 'þoñ,' a^r7, 'Scriptū,' b^r12, and 'Kls,' b^v27; and B, 'Kls,' r23). The insular ampersand is regularly used on all the fragments, both when 'and' is a separate word and when it is a syllable ('7wyrd,' Ca^r6). The word 'and' is spelled out only once (O^{v}11).

Punctuation is generally by mid-line point on all the fragments. O and C have no other type of punctuation mark, and B has only one deviant: a 'semi-colon' at r31, the 'comma' part of which may very well have been added later. NH at first glance shows a greater variety. The mid-line point is still by far the dominant mark of punctuation, as on the other fragments, but there are four 'semi-colons' (r5, 7, 13, and 14), a 'comma' (v10), and thirteen examples of the punctus elevatus (r7, 8, 9, 11, 13, 21, and 26, and v8, 16, 17, 21, 27, and 29). All the 'commas' in the 'semi-colons,' the one 'comma' on its own, and the upper mark in all the examples of the punctus elevatus can, however, be assumed not to be original, for in each case these marks are crowded, or out of line, or weak, even though their ink sometimes looks no different from that used in the text. The two 'commas' in the 'semi-colons' at r5 and 7 seem graceful and confident, very like the one in the 'semi-colon' at B^{r}31.

Original accents are absent or rare on all the fragments (examples at NH^{v}17 and 31; Ca^r18 and 19, and v17; and B^{r}17, 19, and 32, and v6); there is no original accent on O or Cb. The same kind of stroke is used in the original accents as in the ð (see above).

At NH^{v}24 a substantial error has been corrected by erasing a word (or words) on the line and writing 'lareowa' above, in slightly smaller script. At O^{r}17 there is a similar correction; here the words 'ðinga gesewen' are written above (not across) an erasure, in script slightly smaller than the principal hand, presumably to keep the correction to the length of the erasure. In both cases the correcting hand is identical in style to the main hand. Thus both fragments show textual corrections entered in the same manner (that is, above, not superimposed upon, an erasure).

Although there are variations, the handwriting seems clearly to be the same on all the fragments. With a few exceptions the letter forms are the same throughout — square and rounded a in all positions, high e ligatures (although much less common on O), and all three varieties of s (although long s predominates on all but O, where low s is more frequent). The principal difference is between the form y takes on O and the form it takes on the other fragments: on the former it is much less curved and, thus, less tied to the preceding letter. The punctuation is the same on all fragments, even to similar modifications of mid-line points on NH and B. The patterns of decoration, abbreviation, placement of accents, and corrections are demonstrably similar or without overt conflict in all cases.

The apparent differences in the hand on O all seem to be accounted for by the much wider spacing of the writing. For whatever reason, the scribe does not seem to have had the same interest in conserving space here as he had elsewhere. On the full leaf from which the fragment came, twenty-six lines of text were given the same vertical space as thirty-two on the leaves represented by the other fragments; and similarly the script on O is much more spread out laterally. The peculiarities of the hand fit this general pattern: its dominant low s takes two or three times as much horizontal space as does the long s; its uncurved y is less compact than the curved one; 'and' is spelled out only here; and the high e ligature which is used less frequently on this fragment is a great saver of space.

THE RELATION OF THE FRAGMENTS

In the preceding section it has been argued that the script and original punctuation are the same on all the fragments. There is uniformity, too, it has been shown, in initials, titles, capitals, abbreviations, and original accents; in addition, NH and O have textual corrections entered in the same way and probably by the original scribe, and the original punctuation has been subject to similar modification in NH and B. In the description of the individual fragments it has been shown that the height of the written space was the same on all the leaves which the fragments represent and that all the fragments show ruling from the hair side.

O (containing *Catholic Homilies*) and C (containing *Lives of Saints*) have both been recovered from bookbindings done in London by 'K.L.-L.K.' in the second or third decade of the sixteenth century. This fact seems more significant than the difference between the more generous use of written space in O (26 lines in 250 mm) and the more compact lay-out of NH, C, and B (32 lines in 250-5 mm): surely a single Renaissance London bindery would be more likely to have had one manuscript containing Ælfric's *Catholic Homilies* and *Lives of Saints* than two manuscripts simultaneously, one containing *Catholic Homilies* and *Lives of Saints* (NH, C, and B) and the other containing *Catholic Homilies* (O), and both written by the same scribe and having written space of the same height. It seems safe to infer that O's peculiarities were but brief deviations in what was originally a sizable codex.

C and B, in fact, were once quite intimately related. C*a* was cut from the middle of a leaf (see figure 1). The last line on its verso reads 'nu is se tima · þ þu forlæte þine.' The first words on the recto of B, which was cut from the left-hand side of a leaf (see figure 1), are 'godum geoffrige · Apollonaris him ...' Reference to the Skeat text, based on BM Cotton Julius E.VII, shows that probably only four words are missing in between. The complete sentence would be '... nu is se tima · þ þu forlæte þine ydelnysse and lac ðam godum geoffrige' (Skeat xxii, lines 211-12). The four words concerned are precisely enough to have filled comfortably the bottom line of a strip between C*a* and the spine edge of the leaf from which it was cut. Therefore, in the original manuscript, the leaf from which C*a* came must have directly preceded the one from which B was cut.

C*b* was cut from the right-hand side of a leaf (see figure 1). The text which it preserves follows that with which B ends. The last line of B^v reads 'eac þysne cwyde · gelencgan · 7 be sumum ·' The first line of C*b*^{r} reads '...rian lande · 7 se.' (This line preserves an especially short piece of text, because of a tear on the left-hand side of the strip.) Taking Skeat's text as our guide, we can see that probably eleven words are missing in between. The complete wording would be '... eac þysne cwyde · gelencgan · 7 be sumum · cynincge eow cyðan git · Abgarus wæs geciged · sum gesælig cynincg on syrian lande · ...' (Skeat xxiv, lines 81-3). The eleven words concerned are precisely enough to have filled the first three-quarters of the line of which C*b*^{r}1 is the surviving last quarter. Therefore, in the original manuscript, the leaf from which B was cut must have directly preceded the one from which C*b* came. Thus C and B not only were originally parts of the same manuscript but also were

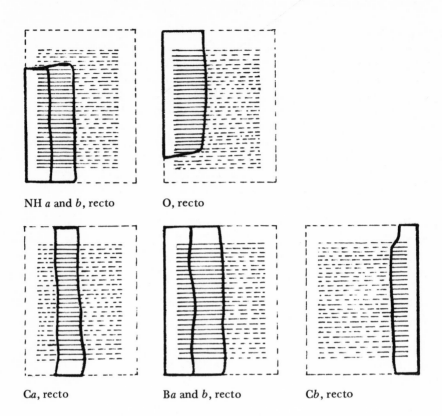

NH *a* and *b*, recto   O, recto

C*a*, recto   B*a* and *b*, recto   C*b*, recto

Figure 1

The Fragments and the leaves from which they were cut

cut from three consecutive leaves: C*a* from the first, B from the second, and C*b* from the third.

It should be remembered that for each of C*a*, B, and C*b* the recto is the hair side. Thus, the three leaves of which these fragments were originally part were in a quire in which the hair sides of the sheets all faced outwards. This is not the 'normal' eleventh-century arrangement outlined by Ker (*Catalogue*, xxiii); in such a 'normal' ordering, the hair side of the outer sheet of the quire faces outward but the flesh side of the next sheet faces out, the hair side of the third, and so on, so that, when one opens a book, a hair side faces another hair side or a flesh side faces flesh. For the three leaves represented by C*a*, B, and C*b*, however, hair sides did not face hair, nor flesh, flesh; a hair side faced a flesh side each time. This arrangement, with all hair sides outwards, is recorded by Ker as an 'old insular custom' (*Catalogue*, xxv). Furthermore, since in each instance the recto is the hair side, these three leaves must have been in the first half of their quire. If this pattern was followed throughout the manuscript, NH, which has its hair side as its verso, was in the second half of its quire, while O, with its hair side as its recto, was another 'first-half' fragment. There is no physical feature, however, to show the order that C*a* + B + C*b*, NH, and O had relative to one another. Since Thorpe I xvii and Thorpe I xx, as consecutive items in O, conform to the sequence of the church year (and since Skeat xxii, xxiv, and xxv in C*a* + B + C*b* do too), it is reasonable to assume that, on the same principle, NH, containing (parts of) Thorpe I xiv, preceded O. As to whether NH and O, containing *Catholic Homilies*, preceded or followed C*a* + B + C*b*, containing *Lives of Saints*, we have no evidence at all. For the purpose of this article NH and O are placed ahead of C*a*, B, and C*b* only because the *Catholic Homilies* are earlier than the *Lives of Saints* in the chronology of Ælfric's works.

Finally, it should be noted that NH and O have been closely connected since the destruction of the manuscript. O was purchased by the Bodleian at Hodgson's in 1967 when it was still part of the binding of a copy of Augustine's *Sermones*. This volume, which possessed only one original board, the lower, came from the dealer Weinreb, who in turn had purchased it from the presbytery library at Winchester in 1966, when that library was disposed of as a whole. The NH fragments were sold at Sotheby's in 1965, and also came from the Winchester presbytery library. Dr James Molloy, who acted as adviser over the sale of the library, found them in a damaged binding from which they were removed and offered for sale ahead of the main collection. O, as part

of the binding of the *Sermones,* was attached to a board and covered
by a paper pastedown which measured 362 mm vertically. If the stains
and holes in the NH fragments are good guides (see above, pp. 287-8),
the two strips were overlapped to form a binding parchment which
was 347 to 350 mm long. The holes in the NH fragments, as overlapped,
would fit fairly well the bands on the copy of the *Sermones* to which
O was attached. It is, then, highly likely that the NH fragments were
attached to the front board of the Augustine, now lost, and that this
front board had for some time been separated from the book when Dr
Molloy removed the fragments for separate sale in 1965. At least it is
certain that NH and O were very near each other in the Winchester
presbytery library before their separation in the mid-sixties.

To sum up, it seems reasonable to conclude that these seven fragments, now separated by thousands of miles, were once parts of a large
codex which contained *Catholic Homilies* and *Lives of Saints* by Ælfric
and which was written in a small script by one scribe very early in the
eleventh century on leaves measuring about 300 mm vertically and with
a space for writing measuring 250 to 255 mm vertically and generally
ruled for thirty-two lines. The tiny fragments that survive today, some
four and a half centuries after this codex was cut up in the London bindery of 'K.L.-L.K.,' may not be a handful from which we know the whole
sack, but at least they form a sample from which we can tell a good deal

THE TEXT

The text of the fragments is transcribed according to the following
principles:

1 All letters which are positively identified from the fragments themselves and which are original are included, even though obscured or
   fragmentary; lost, obscured, or fragmentary letters within the surviving text, whose identity can be confirmed only by reference to
   another manuscript, are indicated by three hiatus dots and discussed
   in the notes; an obscured or fragmentary letter or mark of punctuation at either edge of a strip is ignored unless it is misleading, in
   which case it is discussed in the notes.
2 Marks of punctuation, accents, and capitals are retained if it is reasonably certain that they are original; those that are probably or certainly not original are described in the notes.
3 Abbreviations are not expanded.

4 'Wynn' is transcribed as w; dots over y are omitted; capital ð is transcribed as Ð.
5 A letter unequally divided between adjacent strips is assigned to the strip which preserves the larger part of it; a letter that is equally divided is assigned to the strip which preserves the left half of it.
6 In the cases of NH and B, the cut between adjacent strips is indicated by the space which divides the text from top to bottom.
7 In the case of NH, the lines are numbered according to their position on the original manuscript pages, not according to their position on the extant strips.

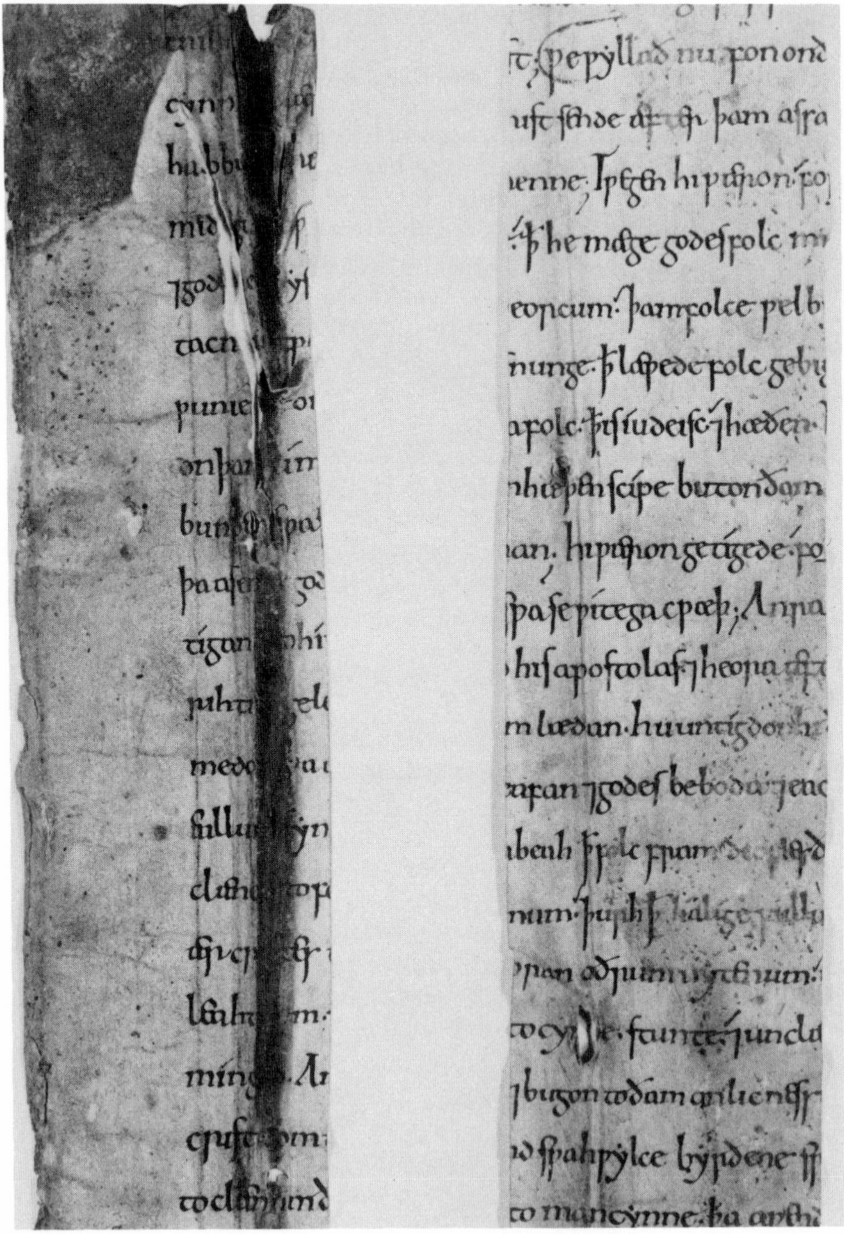

Plate 1 The New Haven Fragments, *a* and *b*, recto, lines 5-26

THE NEW HAVEN FRAGMENTS (NH)

recto (see plate 1)

a			b
...			...
...			...
...			...
...			...
5 ...			st · We wyllað nu fon on ð
cniht[as	þ]e	cr	ist sende æfter þam assa
cynne	[to]	lær	enne · Twegen hi wæron · fo
habba[n	la]re		· þ he mæge godes folc mi
mid god[um]		w	eorcum · þam folce wel b
10 7 godre	[b]ys		nunge · þ læwede folc gebig
tacni[að]		tw	a folc · þ is iudeisc · 7 hæðen ·
wunie[nd]e		o	n hæþenscipe buton ðam
on þa[m	t]im		an · hi wæron getigede · fo
bunden		swa	swa se witega cwæþ · Anra
15 þa asende	god		his apostolas · 7 heora æft
tigan · [7] to hi			m lædan · hu untigdon hi ð
rihtne		gele	afan 7 godes beboda · 7 eac
medon · þa	a		beah þ folc fram deofles ð
eallum		syn	num · þurh þ halige fullu
20 clæne · 7	tof		oran oðrum nytenum ·
ær		cristes	tocy...e · stunte · 7 unclæ
leahtrum		·	7 bugon to ðam anlicness
min god ·	An		d swa hwylce byrðene sw
crist		com	to mancynne · þa awend
25 to clænum	ð		eawum · Se getemeda
þe wæs	gete		med · under þære ealdan
oðres		folc	es þe wæs þa git hæðen ·
fulle þa	ða		crist sende his leorni
ðende ·	far		að geond ealne midd
30 naman	þ		æs fæder · 7 þæs suna ·
þa beb[o]da			þe ic eow tæhte · þæ
his assan	·		Swa eac þa heafodm

4 The descenders survive at the top of *b* recto; comparison with Thorpe I, 206, lines 20-2, indicates that the text to which these descenders belonged was probably '... an ðe manega þæs folces.'   5 A 'comma' added later below the mid-line point after 'st'; similarly after 'lærenne' (7), 'timan' (13), and 'cwæþ' (14).
6 '[as þ] ': all bracketed letters for NH were recovered by John C. Pope.
7 The mid-line point after 'wæron' changed later to a punctus elevatus; similarly after '[la] re' (8), 'weorcum' (9), 'iudeisc' (11), 'getigede' (13), 'stunte' (21), and 'getemed' (26).   11 'iudeisc': an accent added later over first i; similarly 'hæþenscipe' (12), '[t] iman' and 'getigede' (13), 'witega' (14), 'tigan,' 'him,' and 'untigdon' (16), 'min' (23), 'git' (27), and 'midd' (29).   21 'tocy...e': a hole in the parchment has eliminated what must have been m. 'unclæ': the e part of the æ removed by the cut; cf Thorpe's 'unclæne.'   29 'farað': above f is written another f, perhaps for clarity.

verso

	b			*a*
	...			...
	...			...
	...			...
	...			...
5	forðrihte hlaford · forð			...
	alra gesceafta · hi cwædon			· he sent hi eft
	rice · ac we ne synd na gen			ydde · Ðonne
	e beoð forlætene to urum			agenum cyre ·
	es mildheortness · is þ we			untigede sindon ·
10	gifu ge eac ure agen geor			nfulness ·
	orðan ðe ure agen cyr			e næfð nanne
	e ælmihtegan god · Ne h			et crist him
	erædum gefrætewodne			· Ac þone wacan
	tæhte symle eaðmodne			sse 7 þurh
15	niað æt me þ ic eom lið			e · 7 swiðe eaðmod
	tegod be criste · 7 ealle þa			ðing þe he dyde ·
	s án dún · 7 heo is gecwed			en sceawung
	r is seo gelaðung geleaf			fulra manna
	on ðære is symle sibb			e gesyhð butan
20	f we him gelæstaþ · Cris			tes leorning
	san · forþan ðe h... nol			de on nacodum
	weorc · swa swa se witega c			wæð · Drihten

	twisnesse	· Se	nacoda	assa bið mid
	ð mid	wisra	lareowa	mynegungum
25	he ðonne berð	crist	· sw	a swa se apostol
	uldriað forþi	· 7	bera	ð god on eowrum
	n · forðan	ðe we	beoð	tempel 7 fætels
	escyldað · Be	þam	cwæþ	se ylca apostol
	hine fordeþ	· Se [þe]	ne	bið godes templ ·
	þene on his	bæc[e]	We	willað eow
	ne sylfne	to	cyninge	gedón · ac þ folc
	e him	sylfum	licað	Ac syððan

4 The descenders survive at the top of *b* verso; comparison with Thorpe I, 210, lines 1-3, indicates that the text to which these descenders belonged was probably '... að þæra assena · 7 sent.' 6 Second 'hi': an accent added later over i; similarly 'rice' (7), 'mildheortness,' 'untigede,' and 'sindon' (9), 'ælmihtegan' and 'him' (12), 'niað' (15), 'ðing' (16), 'him' and 'leorning' (20), 'witega' (22), 'twisnesse' (23), 'crist' (25), 'uldriað' (26), and 'hine' (29). 8 The mid-line point after 'cyre' changed later to a punctus elevatus; similarly after 'criste' (16), 'dún' (17), 'san' (21), 'n' (27), and 'templ' (29). 9 'mildheortness': t is ill-written and another small t is written above it. 10 A 'comma' added later after the mid-line point following 'geornfulness.' 21 'h...': a hole in the vellum has eliminated what must have been e. 24 'lareowa' written above an erasure for insertion. 28 'ylca': y written above to correct i.

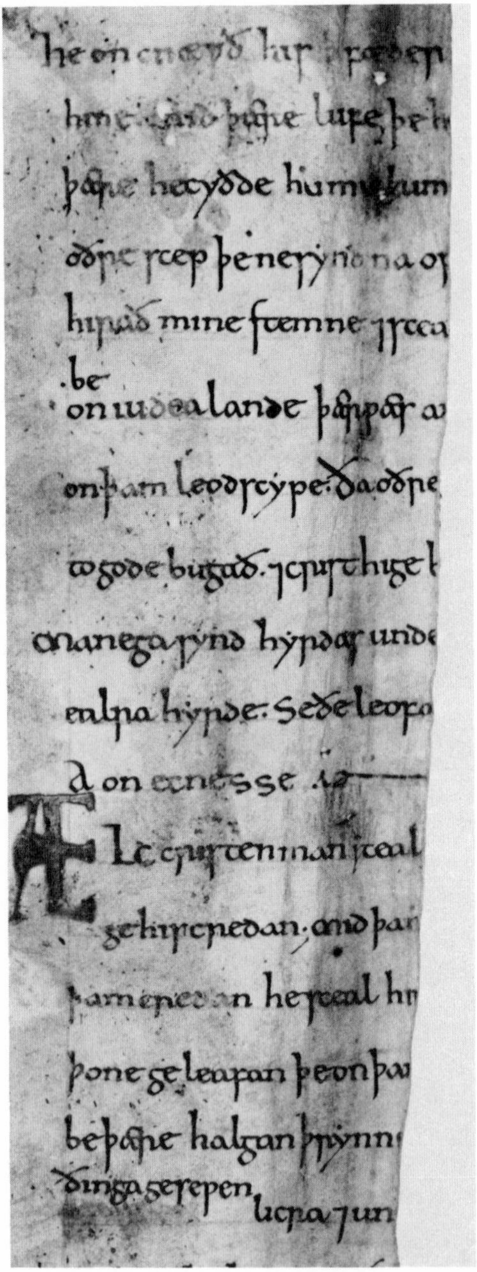

Plate 2

The Oxford Fragment, recto, lines 1-17

THE OXFORD FRAGMENT (O)

recto (see plate 2)

He oncnæwð his fæder
hine · mid þære lufe þe h
þære he cyðde hu miclum
oðre scep þe ne synd na of
5 hirað mine stemne 7 scea
on iudea lande þær wæs a
on þam leodscype · Ða oðre
to gode bugað · 7 crist hi geb
Manega synd hyrdas unde
10 ealra hyrde · Se ðe leofa
A on ecnesse AM
ÆLC cristen man sceal
ge his credan · Mid þam
þam credan he sceal hi
15 þone geleafan þe on þa
be þære halgan þrynn
ðinga gesewenlicra 7 un
forþam þe he is soð god
angynn næfde · ac he s
20 7 ordfruman forgea
Sw[a] s... h
[ða
7 m
but
25 gan]

1 A letter erased between 'his' and 'fæder.'   6 'be' inserted above 'on.'
12 'ÆLC': Æ set out beyond the inner vertical bounding line, extending
from the rule of 11 to the tops of letters on 13, in red metallic ink.   13 'ge'
set in from the inner vertical bounding line to accommodate Æ, above. A 'comma' added later below the mid-line point after 'credan.' 'þam': the last minim of
m removed by the cut; cf Thorpe's 'þam.'   17 'ðinga gesewen' written above
an erasure for insertion.   18 'god': an accent added later over o.
21 'Sw[a]': S set out beyond the inner vertical bounding line; [a] recovered
from offset on the paper.   22-5 Recovered from offset.

verso

  t · He is scyppend se ðe gesceop
  ceaft þ̄ se soða scy...pend ge
  e on heofonū wuniað · 7 syððan þeos
  ð · 7 sæ mid eallum þam þe hyre
5 id anum naman genemnede
  od hi ...esceop þa gesceafta synd
  p se ana is ælmihtig god · he
  him ...ylfum · 7 þurh hine sylfne ·
  on tw... ne mihte he beon æl
10 7 ge...eapen is · næfð nane god
  s þ̄ is g...sceaft · And þ̄ ðe gesceaft
  e un...dæledlic · 7 on annysse
  e f...r · oðer is se sunu · oðer
  þr...a is an godcundnes
15 n... ælmihtig god is se fæder
  h... gast · Ac þeahhwæðere
  ih...g god · þry hi synd on
  þry forþi ðe se fæder bið
  alga gast bið æfre halig gast ·
20 is ... habbað ge gehyred

2 'scy...pend': a wormhole has eliminated what must have been p.
3 'syððan': second ð written above for insertion. 6 '...esceop': the long
vertical stain accounts for the hiatus; similarly on 8-17 and to some extent on
20.

THE CAMBRIDGE FRAGMENTS (C)

a recto

    · 7 þam halgan were · þurh ðone þe hi w
æþen mundbora þe ða burh bewist
na to þam bisceope · 7 sona swa he þid
þe þærinne wæron · 7 se halga wer cwæ
5   mid aðe · gif þin dohtor nu hal bið
st nu his mihte · Rufus him 7wyrd
d leofað · ic herige þoñ godes mihte · 7
þa eode he to þam lice · 7 clypode mid ge
areowe petre · forgeafe his gewiln
10   mæden · of þisum reþan deaðe · fo
ana · Heo aras þa sona · 7 mid hre
ð · 7 nis nan oðer god buton he ana ·
þ mæden wearð gefullod · 7 hire
anna · 7 fela þæra hæþenra fengon
15   es reþnysse · ne dorste geopenian · þ
leaffullan bisceop · 7 mid wistum
ome · 7 þurhwunode mæden · Apoll
ge gelæd · 7 on þam witum geandett
t onwánn awedde þærrihte · 7 his
20   ewerian þone halgan · 7 ofslogon þæ
n þone geleaffullan bisceop in t
forwyrnan · þ he swa ateorode · A
eordode · 7 mid his ræde gehyrte · e
on hwæt ða on ðone feorðan dæg · he
25   dre racenteage feor on wræcsið ·
lice hreoflig · þa axode se bisceop
e halga · Gelyf on þone hælend crist ·
n hælend god · Apollonaris þa hrep
s naman · 7 he wearð hal sona · mid
30   e · Þa awearp se gehæleda his hæþ
leafan wearð gefullod · Hit gela
an gebundon þone bisceop · 7 to

---

2 'æþen': the a part of the æ removed by the cut; cf Skeat's 'hæðen.'

8 'he' written above for insertion.   20 'þæ': the e part of the æ removed by the cut; cf Skeat's 'þæra.'

a verso

    ice · þ... gebæd hine se bisceop be...lic
    a templ toworpen · Þa gesawen ða hæ
    hlyd... be þam geleaffullan were · Be
    synd toworpene þa wuldorfullan go
5   fan ꝥ se is ana soð god · þe swilce wun
    to sl...ge · su... arleasan cweller
    ast...gew...an him to · 7 axode þon
    or...can ...cna · ꝥ swa micel wero
    an oðer miht · buton hælendes crist
10 wu... oðrum spræcum · cwæþ se y
    sun... ðe ge ne seah næfre dæges le
    sona ...elyfað · ꝥ he is soðlice gód · e
    þa cwæþ se bisceop him to · cum
    cwæþ mid geleafan · On ðæs hælen
15 ne · 7 he sona wearð hal · beorhte
    ealle · 7 anmodlice cwædon · ꝥ s
    gelyfdon · þurh þa mihte on gód
    lce gehlyde · to sumum his lan
    la ...ram rauenna · 7 hine sohto
20 n... ealle þa untruman · þe h
    e cyrdon · Þa sendon þa hæþengi
    ꝥ he acwellan hete þone halgan b
    æs... · þurh ðone drihtnes byd
    n gremige · ure godas dyrstiglice
25 e byrig · forþan ðe hit ne bið na ri
    gif hi beoð astyrode · Beoð gesund
    ccan · 7 axode hine sona · hwylcere
    oððe hæþen · Se dema hatte · de
    wer to þam hæþenan deman · Ic e
30 r asende · to þissere gesæligan
    me · Demosten þa andwyrde þa
    nu is se tima · ꝥ þu forlæte þine

1 'þ...': cf Skeat's 'Ða.' A dark stain, varying from 2 mm to 5 mm in width, and running from top to bottom, often completely obscures what was written; here the hidden letter must be a. Portions of the text are further obscured by a gauze which runs the full length of both edges and by a dark stain across the top. 'be...lic': cf Skeat's 'bealdlice.' 3 'hlyd...': cf Skeat's 'gehlyde.' 'geleaf-fullan': second e written above for insertion. 6 'sl...ge · su...': cf Skeat's 'slege · sumum.' 7 'ast...gew...an': cf Skeat's 'ceaster-gewaran.' 8 'or ...can ...cna': cf Skeat's 'wundorlican tacna.' 10 'wu...': cf Skeat's 'be-twux.' 11 'sun...': cf Skeat's 'sunu.' 12 '...elyfað': cf Skeat's 'gely-fað.' 19 '...ram': cf Skeat's 'fram.' 20 'n...': cf Skeat's 'And.' 23 'æs...': cf Skeat's 'adwæscte.'

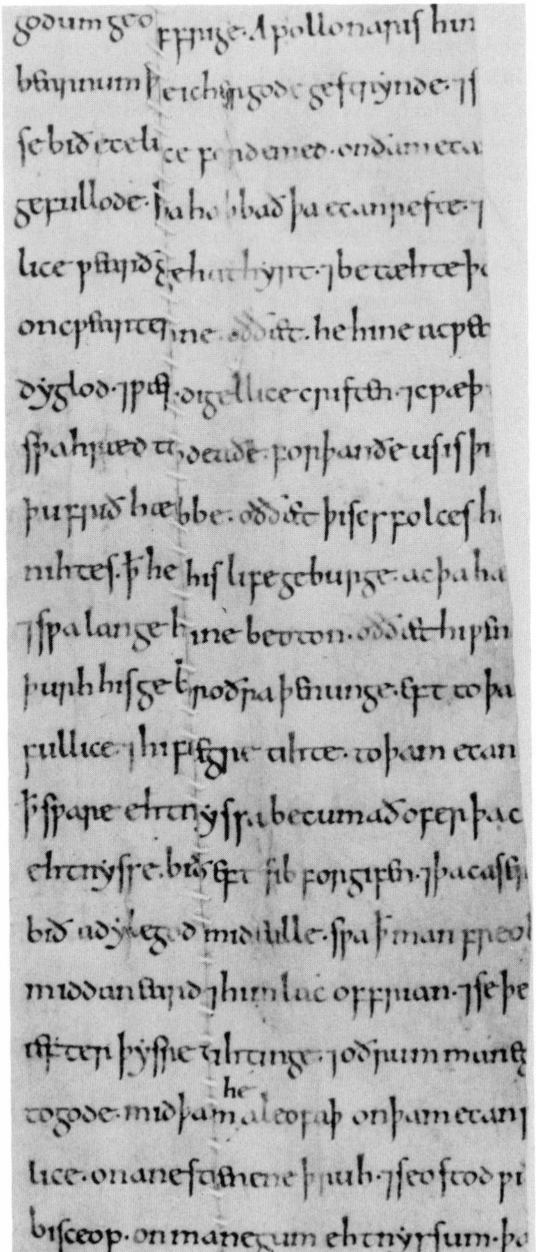

Plate 3

The Bloomington Fragments, *a* and *b*, recto, lines 1-21

THE BLOOMINGTON FRAGMENTS (B)

recto (see plate 3)

	a		*b*
	godum	geo	ffrige · Apollonaris him
	bearnum	þ	e ic hergode gestrynde · 7 s
	se bið	eceli	ce fordemed · on ðam eca
	gefullode ·	þ	a habbað þa ecan reste · 7
5	lice weard	g	ehathyrt 7 betæhte þo
	on	cwearter	ne · oððæt · he hine acwea
	dyglod · 7 wæs		digellice cristen · 7 cwæþ
	swa hræd	to	deaðe · forþan ðe us is þi
	þu frið	hæ	bbe · oððæt þises folces h
10	nihtes ·	þ̄ he	his life geburge · ac þa hæ
	7 swa lange	h	ine beoton · oððæt hi wen
	þurh his	geb	roðra þenunge · eft to þa
	fullice ·	7 hi f	ægre tihte · to þam ecan
	þ̄ sware	ehtn	yssa becumað ofer þa c
15	ehtnysse ·	bið	eft sib forgifen · 7 þa caser
	bið	adylegod	mid ealle · swa þ̄ man freol
	m i d d a n e a r d		7 him lác offrian · 7 se þe
	æfter þysre	t	ihtinge · 7 oðrum maneg
	to gode · mid þa		m hé aleofaþ on þam ecan
20	lice · on ane st		ænene þruh · 7 seo stod wi
	bisceop · on ma		negum ehtnyssum · þa
	endeleas	forþ	i · mid þam ælmihtigan
	· III ·	K+S	AUGUSTI · PASSIO
	ON decies	dag	um · þæs deofellican cas
25	ABDON ·	7 SE	NNES · mid soðum gelea
	casere · þe þa an		a geweold ealles middan
	7 heora rice wun		ode swa swa he ana wol
	7 het hi gebringa		n on bendum to him · wo
	dwyldum 7 to his		deofolgyldum · Hwæt þ
30	racenteagum	to	þam arleasan gebroh
	witum; Decius þ		a het þa halgan cynin
	We offriað ure l		ác þam lyfigendan god

1 'him': the last minim of m removed by the cut; cf Skeat's 'him.'
19 'hé' written above for insertion.   24 'ON': the O surrounds the N; both
in red metallic ink.

verso

b		*a*
	þ decius · se deofles bigg	enga · ðisum is
	nes him · 7wyrdon þus · Hwæ	s bitst þu casere
	don · on urum hælende cr	iste · þe hæfð þa
	alle towurpan · 7 on ecnyss	e fordon · Ða
5	leon · 7 beran · to þam gelea	ffullum cynegum ·
	æhte þa wícan · þam wælhr	eowan · ualeriane ·
	rgað eowrum gebyrdum · 7	bugað to urum
	· gif ge þis ne doþ · eow sceolo	n deor abitan ·
	að us to drihtne gebigedu	m limum · 7 we
10	cnyssum · manna handge	weorc · þe ge habbað
	ydan · 7 lædan swa nacod	e to ðære sunnan
	for god · 7 bebead his cemp	um · þ hi þa criste
	n · mid egeslicum þreatu	m · Ða cwædon
	t · 7 se dema het beswingan	þa halgan hetelice
15	ðan to þam wæferhuse ·	þær ða deor wune
	lætan him to · twa leon · 7	feower beran ·
	ce · grymetigende · to þær	a halgena fotum
	werodon hi swiðor · swa þ	nan man ne
	genealæcan · oððe in t	o þam huse gan ·
20	eora drycræft is gesyn	e swutollice on
	a ware · 7 het þa æt next	an þa hæþenan
	lgan · ða ða þis gedon wæs	· þa het se dema teon
	nan sceoldon sceawian	be him · 7 bysne niman
	wælhreowlice acwealde	Ða æfter þrim
25	haten · 7 he þa halgan li	c · nihtes gelæhte ·
	e leadene þruh · mid m	icelre arwurðnysse ·
	onstantinus se criste	na casere · eft to
	ristes onwrigennysse	· Ge habbað nu ge
	dom forsawon · for cr	istes geleafan · 7
30	w bysne be þam · þ ge n	e bugon fram criste ·
	abbon · buton ælcu	m ende ·
	eac þysne cwyde · gel	encgan · 7 be sumum ·

6 'æhte': the a part of the æ removed by the cut; cf Skeat's 'be-tæhte.'
19 'gan': an accent added later.   28 A 'comma' added later below the mid-line point after 'onwrigennysse.'   31 A 'comma' added later below the mid-line point after 'ende.'

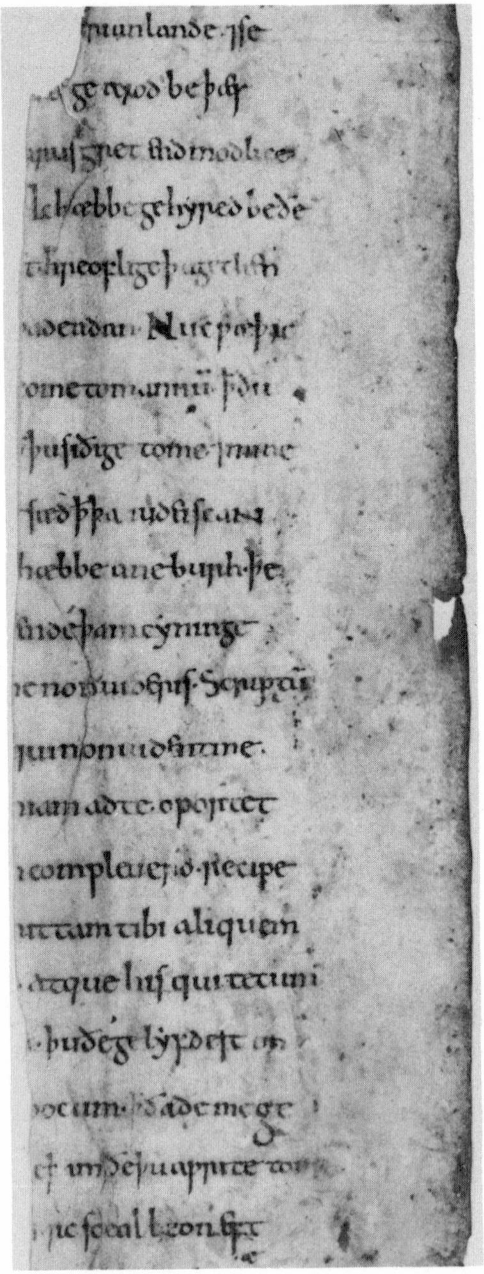

Plate 4

The Cambridge Fragments, *b*, recto, lines 1-21

THE CAMBRIDGE FRAGMENTS (C)

b recto (see plate 4)

```
       rian lande · 7 se
       ge axod be þæs
     arus gret eadmodlice
     Ic hæbbe gehyred be ðe
 5   t · hreoflige þu geclæn
     a deadan · Nu cwæþ ic
     come to mannū · þ ðu
     þu siðige to me · 7 mine
     sæd þ þa iudeiscan
10   hæbbe ane burh · þe
     ende þam cyninge
     e non uideris · Scriptū
     qui non uident me ·
     iam ad te · oportet
15   compleuero · recipe
     ittam tibi aliquem
     atque his qui tecum
     · þu ðe gelyfdest on
     bocum · þ ða ðe me ge
20   e þam ðe þu awrite to
     · 7 ic sceal beon eft
     ic genumen beo ænne
     egearcað · 7 þam ðe ge
     resceawode syþþan
25   æþ ænne of þam hund
     þ he gehælde þone cyning
     e þær untrume · on
     n · Ða gemunde se
     ædan tatheum se wæs
30   a aras se cyning · 7 feoll
     inende beorhtnysse ·
     e soðlice wære cristes
```

22 'ænne': ill-written æ corrected superscript.   25 'æþ': the a part of
the æ removed by the cut; cf Skeat's 'gecwæð.'   29 'ædan': the a part
of the æ removed by the cut; cf Skeat's 'foresædan.'

b verso

    discipulus · him
    cyninge þus · F...r
    to þe · þ þu ges... beo
    gewilnunga · ...n
5   gelyfe on ðone lyfig
    fæstnodon · o...ode
    willan gefyl... · 7 ef
    gelyfe · 7 on hi... halga
    han... on ðæs hælend
10 sona swa he hine hre
    þa wundrode ... he wea
    ær behet þurh his ære
    fotadle · 7 fel... oðre m
    to · On cristes nihte
15 soð be þam hælende · h
    7 cwæþ · Ic eom asend t
    þ ic him eallum cyðe
    cuman his ceasterg
    þone soðan geleaf
20 sylfne syllan to dea
    adames cynne · 7
    ælcum be his dæd
    godne dæl to lace ac
    his mærlican bodu
25 agen · hwi sceolde we o
    se soða gelea...a on þ
      Kl's A U G U
    ÆFter ðam ðe
    hwilcum on hi
30 yfela wide geon
    ealra forcuð... arl
    7 afligde þone cyning

2 'F...r': cf Skeat's 'For-ðan.' A dark stain, varying from 1 mm to 3 mm in width, and running from top to bottom, often completely obscures what was written; all losses of letters from this side of the fragment, unless otherwise noted, were caused by this stain.   3 'ges...': cf Skeat's 'gesund.'   4 '...n': cf Skeat's 'to-eacan.'   6 'o...ode': cf Skeat's 'on rode-hencgene.'   7 'ge-fyl...': cf Skeat's 'gefyllan.'   8 'hi...': cf Skeat's 'his.'   9 'han...': cf Skeat's 'hand'; obscured by a small triangular stain.   11 'wundrode ...': cf Skeat's 'wundrode · þæt.'   13 'fel...': cf Skeat's 'fela.'   14 'nihte': 'mihte' is needed for the sense but the MS is clear.   25 'sceolde': 'sceole' added above as a correction but there is no mark of insertion or correction. 26 'gelea...a': cf Skeat's 'geleafa.'   28 Æ in red metallic ink, extending from the middle of 27 to the rule of 29.   31 'forcuð...': cf Skeat's 'for-cuðost.'

THE SIGNIFICANCE OF THE TEXT

If we assume that the fragments' text of CH I xiv,[8] their text of CH I xvii and their text of CH I xx had a common transmission which took its origin from a single manuscript issued from Ælfric's scriptorium — and we have no reason to think otherwise — this source-manuscript belonged to what may be called the 'middle period' of Ælfric's treatment of the text of CH I. By this is meant the time when he completed CH II, finished his intensive revision of the details of CH I and II[9] and had both series circulating as a twin set;[10] when he composed and issued his *Grammar, Glossary*, and *Colloquy*, wrote his LS and Old Testament pieces and put LS into circulation as a set;[11] and when his substantial lengthening of certain CH items was still to come.[12] Probably we shall not be far out if we think of this phase as occupying up to ten years beginning in 992.[13] The reasons for assigning the source of the fragments' CH I items to this time lie in NH's text of xiv and O's text of xvii. xvii was one of the short CH items which Ælfric substantially augmented: five manuscripts surviving today (Cambridge, University Library, Ii.4.6; BM Cotton Faustina A.IX; CCCC 302; CCCC 188; and Cambridge, Trinity College B.15.34) contain a version of it which has been authentically expanded at the end by an addition almost three times as long as the original homily. Our O fragment does not show this lengthening; it has the original short version, in common with eight other copies, of which four (Oxford, Bodleian Library, Bodley 343;[14] BM Cotton Vitellius C.V; BM Cotton Cleopatra B.XIII; and Cambridge,

University Library, Gg.3.28) belong to the 'middle period' and the
other four belong to two earlier types. In xiv on the other hand NH
has a relatively late reading. At the end of line 30 on the verso it reads
'willað eow,' the next word, originally at the beginning of the next
line, being lost. In so doing it aligns itself with the reading 'willað eow
secgan' in two of the three extant 'middle period' copies, namely CCCC
303 and BM Cotton Vitellius C.V, and in three of the four copies which
belong to two later types, against the reading 'willað secgan eow' in all
the other four copies — two which belong to a pre-'middle period'
type, one of the three which belong to the 'middle period,' namely
Cambridge, University Library, Gg.3.28, and Cambridge, University
Library, Ii.4.6 which is post-'middle period' in type but which, apart
from its authentically augmented and revised version of xvii, drew its
CH I items from a 'middle period' source closely similar to Gg.3.28.
Thus, while a main feature of xvii in O shows that the source of the
CH I texts in our fragments was not later than the 'middle period,' a
particular reading in xiv in NH shows that this source was not earlier
than the 'middle period' either. Furthermore, within the 'middle
period' itself, the reading in xiv shows NH disagreeing with the 'early'
Gg.3.28 and agreeing with the 'late' CCCC 303 and Vitellius C.V.[15] But
too much should not be made of this single distinction, for in fact every
surviving representative of this 'middle period' presents its own individual mix of relatively 'early' and relatively 'late' readings and so makes
it clear that these 'middle period' copies that remain today are a small
fraction of a once much larger number which were derived ultimately
from several exemplars used in Ælfric's scriptorium concurrently for
quite a long time but differing from one another slightly in the amount
of revision each had caught. All that we can conclude with safety is that
the CH I texts in our fragments had their origin in Ælfric's scriptorium
during this period. Equally we can be sure from these CH I texts that
the manuscript to which our fragments belonged was not itself a product of Ælfric's scriptorium. For one thing, the 'middle period' text,
as we have seen, is unlikely to have been current in Ælfric's scriptorium
quite as late as the time to which the fragments' script belongs, and, for
another, the fragments' CH I texts contain a reading which probably
did not arise in Ælfric's scriptorium[16] and several spellings which are
not usual in manuscripts that are close to him.[17] There is no sign, however, of a transmission shared with any other surviving 'middle period'
copy.

Less can be said about the fragments' text of their LS items, since there is not as much comparative material and, so far as we know, Ælfric did not revise LS progressively as he did CH. BM Cotton Julius E.VII[18] is the sole copy of xxii for comparison[19] and the same manuscript and Cambridge, University Library, Ii.1.33 are the only copies of xxiv; several copies are available in the case of xxv, but only a few words of this item survive in our fragments. This rather restricted evidence is, however, enough to show that the fragments' LS texts incorporate at least two unauthorized additions[20] and rather more minor errors than we would expect Ælfric's scriptorium to tolerate.[21] There is no indication that a line of transmission is shared with any other surviving copy. The relatively small amount of corruption results in a text which is at least as good as, and perhaps rather better than, the one in the Julius manuscript, the only surviving copy of the LS set as a whole and, like our fragments, belonging to the first years of the eleventh century. As an aspect of this quality, the system of punctuating by point to mark the ends of the rhythmical phrases, which is present to a greater or less degree in all copies of LS texts and which therefore can be safely attributed to the author, is reproduced more fully in our fragments than in Julius.

The CH I pieces and the LS items in our fragments thus give a similar impression of a text neither produced in Ælfric's scriptorium nor separated from it by a long transmission. It is clear, however, that these two kinds of material do not share an identical transmission, for, whereas the spelling '-ness' is used, as we have seen, eight out of nine times in the CH I items, the normal Ælfrician spelling '-nyss' is invariable in the LS pieces.[22] Since the divergent spellings in the CH I items did not take their origin either from Ælfric's scriptorium or from the scribe who wrote our fragments — for if he were responsible he would have introduced them into his LS texts as well — we must attribute them to a copy of the CH I material intermediate between the one that left Ælfric's scriptorium and the one of which our fragments were part. The particular combination of CH I texts and LS texts to which our fragments witness came about, therefore, outside Ælfric's scriptorium at a point in transmission beyond the required intermediate copy of the CH I pieces and indeed could have occurred for the first time in the copy which partially survives as our fragments.

The significant feature of the selection of CH I items in these fragments is that xvii and xx are consecutive. Thus, the manuscript when complete could not have contained the whole of CH I as an ordered set or even an ordered set of all CH I homilies for the Proper of the Season (for that too would have required xviii and xix). Furthermore, the absence of any other homily by Ælfric which might have intervened between CH I xvii and xx[23] tells against any more widely based sequence. The LS items likewise have their striking feature, namely the occurrence of xxii, xxiv, and xxv as a run unbroken by Skeat xxiii or xxiiib,[24] the two pieces not by Ælfric which come between xxii and xxiv in the Julius copy of the LS set.[25] Evidently, too, CH items were not systematically interposed, for CH II xxxi (and its appendage xxxii), for 25 July, St James the Greater, does not come between LS xxii (on St Apollonaris whose day is 23 July) and xxiv (on St Abdon and St Sennes whose day is 30 July). But this run of three LS items in the order of the church year could have been part of a whole LS set, and indeed there are positive signs that this was probably the case. Every other extant copy containing CH items and LS narratives is later than our fragments and is a mixed selection of one sort or another without the fragments' at least local orderly arrangement both in CH I items for the Proper of the Season, including expositions of pericopes,[26] and in LS narratives. For instance, neither BM Cotton Otho B.X, of the first half of the eleventh century, nor the mid-eleventh-century BM Cotton Vitellius D.XVII, when complete,[27] included any CH expositions of pericopes for the Proper of the Season (nor, indeed, any CH items for the Proper of the Season at all), and Cambridge, University Library, Ii.1.33, of the second half of the twelfth century, includes only CH II xiii.[28] Moreover, although they contain a great deal of LS material, these three manuscripts between them can muster only one run of more than two LS items in consecutive order — and only four two-item runs.[29] Or again, Oxford, Bodleian Library, Bodley 343, a large anthology of homiletic and similar material of the second half of the twelfth century, contains some short runs of CH pericope expositions (for example, I xxiii, xxiv, xxviii, xxxiii, and xxxv) but no runs of LS narratives, while the fragmentary remains of the mid-twelfth-century CCCC 367, so far as they go, are less analogous still. Our fragments, then, are unique in being arranged according to the church year, without any sign of disorder, both in CH I expositions of pericopes for the Proper of the Season and in LS narratives. From this we can infer that the manuscript to which they belonged was probably not a mixed one like the others but kept its CH items and its LS ones apart; and this in turn makes it likely that the three surviving consecutive LS pieces were once part of a whole LS set. The three surviving CH I items on the other hand do not suggest what larger sequence they were in: we have to leave it an open question what other writings by

Ælfric were once present and whether any writings by others were included also. Nor, as has been pointed out already,[30] can we tell whether the CH items preceded or followed the LS ones. But of one thing we can be reasonably sure: the complete contents were substantial. The script of our fragments is economically small, like that of Cambridge, University Library, Gg.3.28, and their format is somewhat larger than that of Gg.3.28. Gg.3.28 runs to 260 leaves (originally more) and contains both series of CH as well as some minor pieces at the end; a full set of LS would have occupied not much beyond a hundred leaves in the manuscript of which our fragments were part.[31] Against this scale we can be confident that this manuscript, if we but had it entire, and especially if it contained a whole set of LS, very early and of good quality, to place beside the one uniquely surviving in Julius E.VII, would be among the major sources of our knowledge of Ælfric's text today.

NOTES

1 We are grateful to the many persons in England and America who have helped us gather information for this essay: to Mr James M. Osborn, surviving donor of the Marie-Louise and James M. Osborn Collection at Yale University, for permission to publish the text of the New Haven fragments; to Professor John C. Pope for significant help with difficult readings on the New Haven fragments and for calling these pieces to our attention when they first became known; to Miss Jean Preston, librarian for the Osborn Collection, who was particularly helpful during R.L.C.'s initial examination of these fragments; to Dr Neil R. Ker who brought the Oxford fragment to our attention as soon as it was acquired by the Bodleian and who has generously shared his knowledge about the fragment and its provenance; to Dr Richard W. Hunt, Keeper of Western Manuscripts at the Bodleian, for generous response to our queries and for permission to publish the text of the Oxford fragment; to the Librarian of Queens' College, Cambridge, for permission to publish the texts of the Cambridge fragments; and to Mr David A. Randall, the Lilly Librarian of Indiana University, for permission to publish the text of the Bloomington fragments and for giving every encouragement in the early stages of this investigation.

2 This fragment was discovered by Dr N.R. Ker in the binding of the *Sermones* when Hodgson's offered the book for sale in January 1967 (see p. 290). He supervised its removal from the decrepit binding.

3 The paper pastedown was originally 368 mm x 247 mm but, presumably at the time of binding, the paper was cut in half across the middle, sliced also at an angle across the major cut, and slightly overlapped before it was pasted down. The final

position is clear from the stains of the paste; the measurements of the paper when pasted to the board must have been 362 mm x 247 mm.

4 J. Basil Oldham, *English Blind-Stamped Bindings* (Cambridge 1952), 57 and plate LV, no 929, and plate LVIII, no 969

5 He also records that the paper pastedown on each board consisted of 'two leaves of an early sixteenth-century edition of Aristotle's Logic in Latin with the commentaries of George of Brussels and Thomas Bricot (ff. lxxiii, lxxvi, and the conjugate leaves: Liber secundus Peryarmenias: 2 cols., 49 lines of text).' He further notes that the pastedowns were printer's waste.

6 Collins, *Times Literary Supplement*, 2 September 1960, 561. Mr Poole's cataloguer, the late Professor Berthold Louis Ullman, had identified the fragment but had not reported its existence. This fragment is now noted in the *Supplement to the Census of Medieval and Renaissance Manuscripts in the United States and Canada*, ed. C.V. Faye and W.H. Bond (New York 1962), 181.

7 NH = the New Haven fragments; O = the Oxford fragment; *Ca* and *b* = the Cambridge fragments; and B = the fragments at Bloomington.

8 In this section CH I and II = the two series of Ælfric's *Catholic Homilies* and LS = his *Lives of Saints*. Lower case Roman numbers refer to individual items in the editions of Thorpe and Skeat, to those in *Homilies of Ælfric: A Supplementary Collection*, EETS 259-60, ed. John C. Pope (1967-8), cited as Pope, and to those in *Angelsächsische Homilien und Heiligenleben*, Bibliothek der angelsächsischen Prosa 3, ed. Bruno Assmann (repr. Darmstadt 1964, with a supplementary introduction by Peter Clemoes), cited as Assmann.

9 For a summary of the first stages of the revision of CH I, see *Ælfric's First Series of Catholic Homilies: British Museum Royal 7 C.xii*, Early English Manuscripts in Facsimile 13, ed. Norman Eliason and Peter Clemoes (Copenhagen 1966), introduction, 28-35.

10 As in Cambridge, University Library, Gg.3.28, of c 1000, the manuscript which gave Thorpe the text for his edition. Each series of CH provides a year's preaching material for a selection of occasions other than saints' days (the Proper of the Season) and for some saints' days (the Proper of the Saints) organized in a single sequence. CH II also provides homilies for the Common of the Saints. Some items in each series are expositions of pericopes (gospel passages appointed to be read in the Mass).

11 Arranged according to the sequence of the church year and consisting mainly of narrative pieces (Skeat ii-xi, xiv, xv, xviii-xxii, xxiv-xxix, xxxi, xxxii, and xxxiv-xxxvi), but also of four homilies for the Proper of the Season written since the completion of CH II (Skeat i, xii, xiii, and xvii), a piece *De memoria sanctorum* (Skeat xvi) probably meant as a general introduction to the set, and three tracts, *Interrogationes Sigewulfi in Genesin*, Pope xxi and *De duodecim abusivis,* appended

at the end. Skeat xxiii, xxiiib, xxx, and xxxiii are not by Ælfric. On the make-up of the LS set as issued by Ælfric, see P.A.M. Clemoes, 'The Chronology of Ælfric's Works,' in *The Anglo-Saxons: Studies in some Aspects of their History and Culture presented to Bruce Dickins*, ed. Peter Clemoes (London 1959), 219-22.

As to the chronology of the issue, it is probably no coincidence that in the comprehensive collection of Ælfric's saints' narratives which is extant in Cambridge, University Library, Ii.1.33 (a manuscript preserving a remarkably pure textual tradition for its late, twelfth-century date), and which draws on CH I, CH II, and a set of LS, the CH I items are 'middle period' in type.

12 As in Cambridge, Corpus Christi College 188, so far as CH I items are concerned; see K. Sisam, *Studies in the History of Old English Literature* (Oxford 1953), 175-8. The passages with which Ælfric augmented CH II homilies have been published as Pope xxiii-xxviii.

13 It was probably in 992 that Ælfric had CH II sufficiently ready for him to send a presentation copy to Sigeric, Archbishop of Canterbury (see Eliason and Clemoes, 35, note 6), and the LS set and at least some of the Old Testament pieces had been composed when Ælfric's early patron, Ealdorman Æthelweard, died in 998 or 1002 (see Clemoes, 'The Chronology of Ælfric's Works,' 243 and note 1).

14 Although the text in this manuscript is an imperfect one which breaks off before it reaches the point at which O's text begins, it clearly reveals the type to which it belongs.

15 These two manuscripts share a common source for this homily.

16 'ælmihtegan god' (NH^{V}12), which involves the unauthorized interpolation of the word 'god.' There is also 'þa asende' (NH^{r}15), against 'þa sende' in all other copies, but probably this is the result of a mere slip which could have occurred in Ælfric's scriptorium.

17 The suffix '-ness' (with or without an inflexion) (NH^{r}22, NH^{V}9, NH^{V}10, NH^{V}14, NH^{V}23, O^{r}11, O^{r}16, and O^{V}14, the only exception being O^{V}12), '(getry)medon' (NH^{r}18), 'git' (NH^{r}27), 'nanne' (NH^{V}11), 'ælmihtegan' (NH^{V}12), 'gesyhð' (NH^{V}19), '(ge)hirað' (O^{r}5), 'leodscype' (O^{r}7), and 'forþam þe' (O^{r}18). The normal Ælfrician spellings are '-nyss,' 'getrymdon,' 'gyt,' 'nænne,' 'ælmihtigan,' 'gesihð,' 'gehyrað,' 'leodscipe,' and 'forþan þe.'

18 The manuscript from which Skeat printed his main text

19 Although more readings can be recovered from the burnt fragments of BM Cotton Vitellius D.XVII than Skeat printed, none of them is relevant to an analysis of the text in our fragments.

20 The words 'buton ælcum ende' (B^{V}31) and 'eac' (B^{V}32). 'ana' (Ca^{r}11; Jul. om.) may be another.

21 'gesawen' (Ca^{V}2; Jul. 'gesawon'), 'ge ne seah' (Ca^{V}11; Jul. 'ne geseah'), 'ge sunde' (Ca^{V}26; Jul. 'ge gesunde'), and 'bitst' (B^{V}2; Jul. and Ii.1.33 'abitst'). 'is ana' (Ca^{V}5;

Jul. 'ana is' is probably another, while 'on þone hælend crist' (Ca^r27; Jul. 'on hælend crist') may be authentic or may result from either scribal inadvertence or unauthorized emendation. 'grymetigende' (B^V17) represents a change from the normal
Ælfrician form 'grymetende' which is in Jul. and Ii.1.33.

22 Nine occurrences (Ca^r15, B^r14, B^r15, B^r21, B^V4, B^V10, B^V26, B^V28, and.Cb^r31).
    Cf also 'ælmihtigan' (B^r22) with 'ælmihtegan' (NH^V12) and 'ænne' (Cb^r22 and 25)
    with 'nanne' (NH^V11).

23 Assmann vi (for the third Sunday after Easter), Pope vii (for the fourth Sunday),
    Pope viii (for the fifth Sunday), Skeat xvii (for Rogationtide), CH II xxi (for Mon-
    day in Rogationtide), CH II xxii-xxiv (for Tuesday in Rogationtide) and (as in the
    arrangement of CH II) CH II xviii (for 1 May, St Philip and St James the Less) and
    CH II xix and xx (3 May, Invention of the Cross and St Alexander, St Eventius,
    and St Theodulus). Ælfric himself would not have been likely to interpose any of
    these items, for his own use of CH I pieces to form part of a comprehensive set for
    the Proper of the Season was certainly not earlier than the augmentation of CH I
    xvii which our fragments lack.

24 The opinion that this was almost certainly so, expressed in 1959 (Clemoes, 'The
    Chronology of Ælfric's Works,' 237; cf 219, note 2) and based on C, was satis-
    factorily confirmed when the existence of B became known in 1960 (see above, p.
    293 and note 6).

25 For evidence that Skeat xxiii and xxiiib were very probably not in the exemplar
    from which the main Julius scribe copied his set of Ælfric's LS, see Clemoes, 'The
    Chronology of Ælfric's Works,' 219, note 2.

26 Two of the fragments' three CH I items — xiv and xvii — are of this kind. It is
    assumed (see above, p. 299) that xiv (NH) preceded xvii (O) in the manuscript
    from which the fragments come.

27 Only charred fragments of each of these manuscripts have survived the fire of 1731;
    we know of their former contents from Wanley's *Catalogus* of 1705.

28 This homily (for the fifth Sunday in Lent) is without a rubric in this copy and is
    likely to have been originally the last item in a group of miscellaneous pieces at the
    end, although it is now placed in second position in the manuscript.

29 vii-x in Vitellius D.XVII; iv-v in Otho B.X and xxii-xxiv (without Skeat xxiii or
    xxiiib between), xxviii-xxix, and xix-xx in Vitellius D.XVII; xv and xvi are con-
    secutive in Ii.1.33, but probably Ælfric gave xvi initial position in his set as a general
    introduction to it (see above, note 11).

30 Above, p. 299

31 About 112

MARIE BORROFF

John Collins Pope: a bibliography

PREFATORY NOTE

In writing a tribute to this Bibliography, one is pleasantly reminded
of the supposed connection of the Latin source of the word 'tribute'
with the number three. For here, sparely spaced like captain jewels in
the carcanet, are the records of three separate but related labours:
three achievements on which a major reputation can rest.

The Rhythm of Beowulf had its origin in a remarkable insight
whereby Old English metre, that odd mythic beast heretofore thought
to have marched with two feet and limped with the other two, was
brought to life and made to go naturally on all fours. For a discovery
of this order, knowledge was essential — an intimate familiarity with
Old English poetry and the work of earlier metrists. And knowledge
was essential, too, for the full application of the basic principle to the
actual configurations of the verses of *Beowulf* which forms the substance of the book. But knowledge alone, without a rare depth of insight, would not have been enough.

The Homilies of Aelfric: A Supplementary Collection represents
another sort of endeavour, one in which every sort of discipline —
historical, textual, philological, critical — is brought to bear on the
letter and spirit of an early text, and the evidence relevant to every
problem is patiently, painstakingly bolted to the bran. The result may
in time be supplemented, but it will never be superseded.

Seven Old English Poems comes from another part of the field: the teaching of Old English in the Graduate School of Yale University. For most of the twenty years during which John Pope presided over that subject, it was a requirement in the doctoral program. Some undertook it with the fully formed intention of specializing in the older language and literature; others had no such intention. Year by year, there were those for whom Old English was a wholly unantici- pated revelation and delight. I hope I may be allowed to speak for them here.

The articles reflect a variety of interests in Old English poetry and prose, and are in their different ways a foretaste of things to come. The latest, as its title indicates, is noteworthy in reflecting a mind that does not fear to think twice: invulnerable, in later life as in earlier, to the deadly darts of pride. Such an example is worth a score of books.

DOCTORAL DISSERTATION

The Manuscripts of Aelfric's Catholic Homilies. Yale University 1931

BOOKS

The Rhythm of Beowulf: An Interpretation of the Normal and Hypermetric Verse Forms in Old English Poetry. New Haven and Oxford: Yale University Press 1942
— 2nd revised edition. New Haven and London: Yale University Press 1966 (hardcover and paperback). 'Preface to the 1966 Edition,' ix-xxxiv
Old English Versification, with Particular Reference to the Normal Verses of 'Beowulf.' New Haven 1957 [mimeograph]

BOOK IN PROGRESS

English Literature before the Norman Conquest (Oxford History of English Literature)

EDITIONS

Seven Old English Poems. Indianapolis and New York: Bobbs-Merrill

Company Inc. 1966 [Typescript edition, Yale University; Department of English, 1964]
The Homilies of Aelfric: A Supplementary Collection. Two volumes. London: Early English Text Society 1967 (Vol I), 1968 (Vol II). EETS nos 259-60

ARTICLES

'Prufrock and Raskolnikov,' *American Literature* 27 (1945) 213-30
'Prufrock and Raskolnikov Again: A Letter from Eliot,' *American Literature* 28 (1947) 319-21
'Three Notes on the Text of *Beowulf,' Modern Language Notes* 67 (1952) 505-12
'*Beowulf* 3150-3151, Queen Hygd and the Word "Geomeowle,"' *Modern Language Notes* 70 (1955) 77-87
'The Emendation "Oreðes ond Attres," *Beowulf* 2523,' *Modern Language Notes* 72 (1957) 321-8
'Preface to the Reproduction,' in Albert S. Cook, ed., *The Christ of Cynewulf.* Photographic reproduction. Hamden, Connecticut: Archon Books 1964 [iii-iv]
'Dramatic Voices in *The Wanderer* and *The Seafarer,*' in *Franciplegius: Medieval and Linguistic Studies in Honor of Francis Peabody Magoun, Jr.* ed. J.B. Bessinger, Jr and R.P. Creed, New York University Press 1965, 164-93. Reprinted in *Essential Articles for the Study of Old English Poetry*, ed. Jess B. Bessinger, Jr, and Stanley J. Kahrl. Hamden, Connecticut: Archon Books 1968, 533-70
'The Lacuna in the Text of Cynewulf's *Ascension (Christ II,* 556b),' *Studies in Language, Literature and Culture of the Middle Ages and Later* [Festschrift for Rudolph Willard], ed. E.B. Atwood and A.A. Hill. Austin: University of Texas Press 1969, 210-19
'Aelfric and the Old English Version of the Ely Privilege,' in *England before the Conquest: Studies in Primary Sources Presented to Dorothy Whitelock*, ed. Peter Clemoes and Kathleen Hughes. Cambridge University Press 1971, 85-113
'Beowulf's Old Age,' in *Philological Essays: Studies in Old and Middle English Language and Literature in Honour of Herbert Dean Meritt*, ed. James L. Rosier. The Hague: Mouton 1971, 55-64

ARTICLE IN PROGRESS

'Further Thoughts on *The Seafarer*,' to be published in *Anglo-Saxon England*, 1975

REVIEWS

Dorothy Whitelock. *The Audience of Beowulf*. Oxford 1951. In *Modern Language Notes* 67 (1952) 353-4
Kemp Malone, ed. *The Thorkelin Transcripts of Beowulf in Facsimile*. Copenhagen 1951. In *Modern Language Notes* 68 (1953) 506-8
Dorothy Bethurum. *The Homilies of Wulfstan*. Oxford 1957. In *Modern Language Notes* 74 (1959) 333-40
Arthur C. Brodeur. *The Art of 'Beowulf,'* Berkeley and Los Angeles, London, 1959. In *Speculum* 37 (1962) 411-17

REVIEW IN PROGRESS

James Hurt. *Aelfric*. New York 1972